ANSI C
A Lexical Guide

ANSI C
A Lexical Guide

 Mark Williams Company

Prentice Hall, Englewood Cliffs, New Jersey 07632

Library of Congress Catalog Card Number: 88-61134

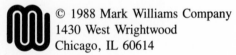
The following trademarks are referenced in the book:
UNIX®, AT&T;
COHERENT™, MWC;
Let's C®, MWC;
Mark Williams C™, MWC;
MS-DOS®, Microsoft;
i8086®, Intel;
PDP-11™, DEC;
and MC68000®, Motorola

The publisher offers discounts on this book when ordered
in bulk quantities. For more information, write:

> Special Sales/College Marketing
> Prentice-Hall, Inc.
> College Technical and Reference Division
> Englewood Cliffs, NJ 07632

Printed in the United States of America

10 9 8 7 6 5 4 3 2 1

ISBN 0-13-037814-3

Prentice-Hall International (UK) Limited, *London*
Prentice-Hall of Australia Pty. Limited, *Sydney*
Prentice-Hall Canada Inc., *Toronto*
Prentice-Hall Hispanoamericana, S.A., *Mexico*
Prentice-Hall of India Private Limited, *New Delhi*
Prentice-Hall of Japan, Inc., *Tokyo*
Simon & Schuster Asia Pte. Ltd., *Singapore*
Editora Prentice-Hall do Brasil, Ltda., *Rio de Janeiro*

Contents

Section 1:
Introduction

ANSI C: A Lexical Guide describes the American National Standards Institute (ANSI) standard for the C programming language. It discusses in clear English every library function, every macro, and every technical term that appears within the Standard. All entries are fully cross-referenced internally to the Standard and to the second edition of *The C Programming Language*; many are illustrated with full C programs.

All material is presented in a lexical format to make it easy for you to find exactly the information you need.

The Mark Williams Company is a software company based in Chicago. Since 1976, we have written operating systems and C compilers for minicomputers and microcomputers.

In this book, Mark Williams Company presents a reading of the ANSI C Standard, based both on our participation on the committee that wrote it, and on our experience as writers of C compilers and operating systems. This book contains *all* the information you need to write strictly conforming C programs that can be compiled and run on *every* computer for which a conforming implementation of C exists.

C and the Standard

The original definition of the C programming language is *The C Programming Language*, by Brian W. Kernighan and Dennis M. Ritchie (Englewood Cliffs, NJ: Prentice-Hall, Inc., 1978). The language was developed at Bell Laboratories; they wanted to implement the UNIX operating system in a high-level language that was easy to maintain, powerful, and portable.

1

From this beginning, C has been widely used as a systems programming language. Compilers, operating systems, and utilities have all been written in C. In time, C began to outgrow its origin as a systems programming language. It attracted programmers who wished to write applications that could be easily ported to many different computer environments in order to broaden their markets.

Constant usage of C revealed areas that had not been considered by its authors, or were ambiguous. To address the limitations of C, each compiler vendor chose to extend C in its own way. The result was the splintering of C into a number of dialects, especially in the way that preprocessor worked and in the suite of library functions available to the programmer. The advent of UNIX system V and Berkeley UNIX version 4.X accelerated this divergence.

By 1983, the C language had matured to the point where many thought that it needed a standard. A standard would resolve ambiguities in the original definition of C, "legalize" commonly used extensions to C, and address issues upon which the original definition was silent.

The X3J11 Committee

ANSI committee X3J11 was formed in 1983 to write the standard for the C language. The Committee consists of representatives from compiler vendors who write for mainframes, minicomputers, microcomputers, and embedded systems, as well as users. In addition, the Committee has observers who participate in the standards process.

At the time of this writing (March 1988), the Committee has submitted two draft review copies of the standard for public comment. Thus, the C community has had an opportunity to review the document, make suggestions, and participate. ANSI requires that the Committee respond in a timely fashion to every comment it receives. It is hoped that the final version of the Standard will be approved by the Committee before the end of 1988.

The Committee used the following principles to guide its work:

- "Existing code is important, existing implementations are not." The Committee attempted to write the Standard in such a way that it broke as little existing code as possible. To break a mass of code simply to preserve an idiosyncrasy of one implementation or another is wrong-headed, and was avoided.

- "C code is portable." The Standard describes the C language in such a way that a program that conforms strictly to its description has a "fighting chance" of being ported to other environments without change. This meant that the Committee had to break a number of programming habits, such as assuming that all users of C programs speak English, or that all computing environments are based upon ASCII or eight-bit bytes.

- "C code can be non-portable." The Standard does not stop a programmer from writing code that is tailored to a particular machine or environment

- "Avoid 'quiet changes'." A change may cause a legal program to behave differently when compiled by an ANSI-compatible compiler than it did when compiled by a pre-ANSI implementation; and a quiet change does so without warning the programmer that something has changed. Given the variety of the implementations of C, some quiet changes were unavoidable. However, they have been noted both in the Rationale and in this manual.

- "A standard is a treaty between implementor and programmer." This means that, among other things, the Standard compromises the needs of the programmer and those of the implementor.

- "Keep the spirit of C." This is the hardest principle to articulate, although the spirit of C was invoked repeatedly during the Committee's debates. The Rationale describes the following principles as embodying the spirit of C:

  "Trust the programmer."
  "Don't prevent the programmer from doing what needs to be done."
  "Keep the language small and simple."
  "Provide only one way to do an operation."
  "Make it fast, even if it is not guaranteed to be portable."

The Committee's original goal was to write one standard that would be acceptable throughout the C community. Soon, however, it became obvious that the entire C community is not homogeneous and that concessions had to be made to sub-communities.

The international community became involved when the International Standards Organization (ISO), which consists of members from various nations, decided in 1985 to write its own standard for C. The ISO's effort used the ANSI standard, as it existed at that time, as a starting point. Both organizations felt that the greatest benefit would be wrought if the two standards synchronized, and in final form, were identical. This goal has been achieved. Some features were introduced to give C a more international scope. These include multibyte characters, locales, and some specialized library functions.

The state of the art in the scientific community has been toward increasing parallelization. To encourage the use of C in scientific endeavors required the adoption of certain idiosyncrasies from FORTRAN, which has long been the principal scientific programming language. To accomodate these users, and give users a chance to port their code from a simple machine to a state-of-the-art supercomputer, a mechanism was developed to specify parameters that do not overlap.

Because C is a language that maps closely to machine code and exploits the architecture of the machine, the Committee made some accomodations to optimization. In particular, it added a new keyword, **noalias**, to solve some longstanding problems in the production of the best possible code from state-of-the-art optimizing compilers.

Differences from Kernighan & Ritchie C

The following summarizes the major differences between ANSI C and the C language described by the first edition of *The C Programming Language*.

Function prototyping
A function prototype is a detailed form of function declaration. It lists the number of arguments the function takes, and the type of each argument. This allows the compiler to compare every function call against the prototype to ensure that the call has the right number and type of arguments. Because some machines allow function calls to be passed quickly if the number of arguments is known, function prototyping allows the compiler to use the faster function-call mechanism because it knows the number of arguments that a call should take.

Keywords
The Standard introduces the keywords **const, enum, noalias, signed, void,** and **volatile**. The old keyword **entry**, which was undefined, was allowed to die.

Library
The Standard describes the C library in some detail. The library includes 127 functions that perform most common programming tasks. Each function has a function prototype that is declared in a standard header file.

Limits
The Standard sets "minimum maxima" for the range of all arithmetic types. These are defined in the headers **float.h** and **limits.h**. It also sets minimal limits on the complexity of programs that can be compiled, e.g., on the number of **case** labels that can be used in a **switch** statement. These must be met by every implemetation that conforms to the Standard.

Locales
The Standard introduces the concept of program locales. A locale may change the way a program executes so that it can conform to local practices. For example, by changing the locale, a program may recognize the comma instead of the period as marking a decimal point, print a different symbol to represent monetary values, and use a locale-specific format for printing the date and time.

long double
The type **long float** is no longer a synonym for **double**, but can be used for a quadruple-precision floating-point number.

New types
The type **size_t** was introduced to hold the object returned by **sizeof**. The type **ptrdiff_t** holds the difference when one pointer is subtracted from another. Both increase the portability of C programs.

Preprocessing
The Standard describes the preprocessor in detail. It introduces the directives **#elif** and **#pragma**. It introduces the preprocessing operators # and ##. The former creates a string literal that names the value that replaces a preprocessing token, and the latter "pastes" two preprocessing tokens into one. The keyword **defined** was introduced for use with the directive **#if**; it allows construction of a more complex version of the directive **#ifdef**.

String literals
ANSI C now concatenates adjacent string literals.

Structure passing
The Standard allows a structure to be passed to a function, to be assigned to another structure, and to be returned by a function.

Trigraph sequences
The Standard creates three-character, or *trigraph*, sequences that can be used to render the characters of the C character set that do not appear in the ISO 646 character set.

Type qualifiers
Types can now be qualified with the keywords **const, noalias**, and **volatile**. These qualifiers direct the compiler in producing efficient code.

Type suffixes
The suffixes **U, L**, and **F** are introduced, to allow more precision in the use of numeric constants.

void
The keyword **void** is now formally incorporated into the language. The type **void *** has been introduced to serve as the generic pointer, and replaces **char *** in that role.

Wide characters
The Standard describes mechanisms to build and manipulate strings of wide characters. These characters are used to print such languages as Japanese, whose character set is too large to be encoded within one byte.

The Standard and This Manual

No description resolves all ambiguity or covers all aspects. That is to say, no standard is ever perfect. The members of X3J11 had the advantage of working with excellent base documents and a well-defined language. On the other hand, they had the disadvantage of trying to standardize a language that grew and changed even as they worked for the heterogeneous group of users who have become accustomed to excellence in the descriptions of "their language".

As we worked with the Standard, we found that the members of X3J11 performed their work very well indeed. However, no language standard makes easy reading. The language must be highly technical and in order to be precise and complete, it must at times seem convoluted. The structure of a standard can also make it difficult for a programmer to find precisely the information that is needed to solve a problem.

ANSI C: A Lexical Guide is a reading of the Standard. This reading is based on our experience in writing C compilers and operating systems and in documenting the C language. It presents the ideas and terms of the Standard in clear English. Descriptions that are spare or difficult in the original have been expanded to make them more easily understood. Topics are illustrated with full C programs, many of which are useful or entertaining.

It is not our intention to replace the ANSI Standard. The Standard is, of course, the final authority concerning the C language. We hope, however, that this manual makes the Standard's description of C accessible to the entire C community. ANSI C is a powerful, graceful language, and the C community stands to benefit from using it.

Section 2:
The Lexicon

This book uses the "lexicon" format that Mark Williams Company designed for its documentation. It consists of 589 articles, each of which discusses one topic in depth. A topic may be a term that the Standard uses, a library function, a macro, or an overview discussion of a number of related topics.

The articles are printed in alphabetical order so that each can be found easily. The index contains several thousand entries and cross-references to help you find exactly the material you need.

The Lexicon as a whole has a logical structure that mimics the structure of the Standard. For an overview of the Lexicon's structure, see Appendix A.

Each article shows its place in the logical structure in two ways: First, the heading for each article includes a "path name" that names its position in the logical structure of the manual as a whole. Second, each article includes cross-references to related topics. It is possible to read from any one article within the Lexicon to any other article, simply by following either the path name or the chain of cross-references. Thus, the Lexicon allows you to find every topic easily, and it makes it easy for you to find related topics and material.

For example, suppose you were interested in reading about standard input and output. You could look up "standard input and output" in the index, which would refer you to the article entitled **STDIO**. This, in turn, will describe all library routines that perform STDIO, and introduce related articles and topics. Or, you could look up a STDIO routine that you already know, such as **printf**, and follow either its path name or its cross-references until you arrive at the article that has exactly the information you need. Or, most easily, you could just look for the topic that interests you by name; the chances are good that you will find it right there.

Example — Definition
  (Standard/path/name)
  Give an example of the Lexicon format
  #include < sample.h >
  sample *Example(sample *variable*, **sample** *anothervariable);*

This page gives an example of a Lexicon entry. The first line of each entry gives its name and the category of the entry, e.g., **Definition** or **C keyword**. The second line of each entry gives the entry's *path name*. The path name is the entry's position in the logical structure of the Lexicon as a whole. Appendix A gives the full logical structure of the Lexicon. If the entry describes a library function, the path name is followed by the function prototype. The body is followed in many instances by a full C program that demonstrates the subject being discussed.

The example is followed by cross-references to the Standard, to second edition of *The C Programming Language*, and to related articles within the Lexicon.

Example
This gives an example of an example program.

```
#include <stdio.h>
#include <stdlib.h>
main()
{
      printf("Many entries have complete C programs\n");
      printf("as examples.\n");
      return(EXIT_SUCCESS);
}
```

Cross-references
A reference to the Standard
A reference to *The C Programming Language*

See Also
all related articles in the Lexicon

Notes
Into this section go warnings, information of historical interest, and all other information that does not relate directly to the topic under discussion.

! to ~

! — Operator
(Language/expressions/unary operators)
Logical negation operator
!operand

The operator **!** is the logical negation operator. Its operand must be an expression with scalar type. **!** then inverts the logical result of its operand. This result has type **int**.

If *operand* is nonzero, *!operand* yields zero; if *operand* is zero, then *!operand* yields one.

The expression *!operand* is equivalent to **(0==*operand*)**.

Cross-references
Standard, §3.3.3.3
The C Programming Language, ed. 2, p. 204

See Also
!=, ~, unary operators

!= — Operator
(Language/expressions/equality operators)
Inequality operator
operand1 **!=** *operand2*

The operator **!=** compares *operand1* with *operand2*. The result of this operation is one if the operands are *not* equal, and zero if they are.

The operands must be one of the following:

- Arithmetic types.
- Pointers to compatible types (ignoring qualifiers on these types).
- A pointer to an object or incomplete type, and a pointer to **void**.
- A pointer and NULL.

If both operands have arithmetic type, they undergo usual arithmetic conversion before being compared. If one operand is a pointer to an object and the other is a pointer to **void**, the pointer to an object is converted to a pointer to **void** for purposes of the comparison.

Example
For an example of using this operator in a program, see **bitwise operators**.

Cross-references
Standard, §3.3.9
The C Programming Language, ed. 2, pp. 41, 207

See Also
!, = =, equality operators

" — Punctuator
(Language/lexical elements/string literal)
String literal character

The quotation mark '"' marks the beginning and end of a string literal. To embed a quotation mark within a string literal, use the escape sequence '\ "'.

Cross-references
Standard, §3.1.2.5
The C Programming Language, ed. 2, p. 194

See Also
string literal

— Operator
(Language/preprocessing/macro replacement)
String-ize operator

The operator # is read and translated by the preprocessor. It must be followed by one of the formal parameters of a function-like macro. The token sequence that would have replaced the formal parameter in the absence of the # is instead converted to a string literal, and the string literal replaces the both the # and the formal parameter. This process is called *string-izing*.

For example, the consider the macro:

```
#define display(x) show((long)(x), #x)
```

When the preprocessor reads the following line

```
display(abs(-5));
```

it replaces it with the following:

```
show((long)(abs(-5)), "abs(-5)");
```

The preprocessor replaced **#x** with a string literal that names the sequence of token that replaces **x**.

The following rules apply to interpreting the # operator:

1. If a sequence of white-space characters occurs within the preprocessing tokens that replace the argument, it is replaced with one space character.

2. All white-space characters that occur before the first preprocessing token and after the last preprocessing token is deleted.

3. The original spelling of the token that is stringized is retained in the string produced. This means that as the string is formed, the translator appropriately escapes any backslashes or quotation marks in the tokens.

Example

The following uses the operator # to display the result of several mathematics routines.

```
#include <errno.h>
#include <math.h>
#include <stddef.h>
#include <stdio.h>

void show(double value, char *name)
{
    if (errno)
        perror(name);
    else
        printf("%10g %s\n", value, name);
    errno = 0;
}

#define display(x) show((double)(x), #x)

main(void)
{
    extern char *gets();
    double x;
    char string[64];

    for(;;) {
        printf("Enter a number: ");
        fflush(stdout);
        if(gets(string) == NULL)
            break;
```

```
        x = atof(string);
        display(x);
        display(cos(x));
        display(sin(x));
        display(tan(x));
        display(acos(cos(x)));
    }
}
```

Cross-references
Standard, §3.8.3.2
The C Programming Language, ed. 2, pp. 90, 230

See Also
##, #define, macro replacement

— Operator
(Language/preprocessing/macro replacement)
Token-pasting operator

The operator ## is is used by the preprocessor. It can be used in both object-like and function-like macros. When used immediately before or immediately after an element in the macro's replacement list, it joins the corresponding preprocessor token with its neighbor. This is sometimes called "token pasting".

As an example of token pasting, consider the macro:

```
#define printvar(number) printf("%s\n", variable ## number)
```

When the preprocessor reads the following line

```
printvar(5);
```

it substitutes the following code for it:

```
printf("%s\n", variable5);
```

The preprocessor throws away all white space both before and after the ## operator.

The ## operator must not be used as the first or last entry in a replacement list.

All instances of the ## operator are resolved before further macro replacement is performed.

Cross-references
Standard, §3.8.3.3
The C Programming Language, ed. 2, pp. 90, 230

See Also
#, #define, macro replacement

Notes
Some pre-ANSI translators supported token pasting by replacing a comment in a macro replacement list with no space. ANSI translators always replace a comment with one space, no matter where that comment appears.

The order of evaluation of multiple **##** operators is unspecified.

#define — Preprocessing directive
(Language/preprocessing/macro replacement)
Define an identifier as a macro
#define *identifier replacement-list*
#define *identifier* (*parameter-list*$_{opt}$) *replacement-list*

The preprocessing directive **#define** tells the preprocessor to regard *identifier* as a macro.

#define can define two kinds of macros: *object-like*, and *function-like*.

Object-like Macros
An object-like macro has the syntax

```
#define identifier replacement-list
```

This type of macro is also called a *manifest constant*.

The preprocessor searches for *identifier* throughout the text of the translation unit, excluding comments, string literals, and character constants, and replaces it with the elements of *replacement-list*, which is then rescanned for further macro substitutions.

For example, consider the directive:

```
#define BUFFERSIZE 75
```

When the preprocessor reads the line

```
malloc(BUFFERSIZE);
```

it replaces it with:

```
malloc(75);
```

Function-like Macros

A function-like macro is more complex. The preprocessor looks for *identifier*(*argument-list*) throughout the text of the translation unit, excluding comments, string literals, and character constants. The number of comma-separated arguments in *argument-list* must match the number of comma-separated parameters in the *parameter-list* of the macro's definition. The list is optional in the sense that some function-like macros do not have any parameters.

In the following description, *argument* means the sequence of tokens in *argument-list* that occupies the same relative position as the parameter under discussion occupies in *parameter-list*. The preprocessor replaces *identifier*(*argument-list*) with the *replacement-list* specified in the definition after it performs the following substitutions: If a parameter is followed or preceded by the operator ##, then the parameter is replaced by the argument. If a parameter is preceded by #, then the # and the parameter are replaced by a string literal that contains the argument. All other instances of parameters are replaced by the argument after the argument has first been exhaustively scanned for further preprocessor macro expansions. All instances of ## are converted to token-paste operations.

For example, the consider the macro:

```
#define display(x) show((long)(x), #x)
```

When the preprocessor reads the following line

```
display(abs(-5));
```

it replaces it with the following:

```
show((long)(abs(-5)), "abs(-5)");
```

When an argument to a function-like macro contains no preprocessing tokens, or when an argument to a function-like macro contains a preprocessing token that is identical to a preprocessing directive, the behavior is undefined.

Macro Rescanning

As noted above, the preprocessor searches for macro identifiers throughout the text of the translation unit, excluding comments, string literals, and character constants. The text of replaced macros is also scanned for macro replacements, but it is not part of the text of the translation unit (i.e., source file), so it does not follow the same rules.

After it replaces the identifier of an object-like macro or the *identifier*(*argument-list*) of a function-like macro with the appropriate *replacement-list*, the preprocessor continues to scan for further macro invocations, starting with the *replacement-list*.

While the preprocessor scans the *replacement-list*, it suppresses the definition of the macro that produced the list. If the preprocessor recognizes a second macro invocation and replaces it before it processes the tokens that replace the first invocation, then it suppresses the definitions of both the first and the second macros while it processes the *replacement-list* of the second macro.

The preprocessor suppresses a definition as long as any of the tokens that remain to be processed are derived directly from the original macro replacement or from further macro replacements that use parts of the original macro replacement. Thus, when the object-like macro definition

```
#define RECURSE      RE ## CURSE
```

is invoked by the token **RECURSE**, it is replaced by the token **RECURSE** formed by pasting **RE** and **CURSE** together, but the scanning of the replacement list would not invoke the macro RECURSE a second time. Likewise, the function-like macro definition

```
#define RECURSE(a, b)    a ## b(a, b)
```

when invoked with the sequence **RECURSE(RE, CURSE)** would be replaced by the token sequence **RECURSE(RE, CURSE)**, but the scanning of the replaced token sequence would not invoke the macro **RECURSE()** again.

Be warned that you should not test a PC-based compiler for compliance with these macro definitions unless you are prepared to turn off your machine. If the compiler fails to detect the recursion, it may become locked in an infinite loop, and there may be no other way to terminate the substitution.

Example
For an example of using a function-like macro in a program, see **#**.

Cross-references
Standard, §3.8.3
The C Programming Language, ed. 2, pp. 229*ff*

See Also
#, ##, #undef, macro replacement

Notes
A macro expansion always occupies exactly one line, no matter how many lines are spanned by the definition or the actual parameters.

A macro definition can extend over more than one line, provided that a backslash '\' appears before the newline character that breaks the lines. The size of a **#define** directive is therefore limited by the maximum size of a logical source line, which can be up to at least 509 characters long.

A macro may be redefined only if the new definition matches the old definition in all respects except the spelling of white space.

#elif — Preprocessing directive
(Language/preprocessing/conditional inclusion)
Include code conditionally
#elif *constant-expression* *<newline>* *group*$_{opt}$

The preprocessing directive **#elif** conditionally includes code within a program. It can be used after any of the instructions **#if**, **#ifdef**, or **#ifndef**, and before **#endif** that ends the chain of conditional-inclusion directives.

If the conditional expression of the preceding **#if**, **#ifdef**, or **#ifndef** directive is false and the *constant-expression* that follows **#elif** is non-zero, then *group* is included within the program up to the next **#elif**, **#else**, or **#endif** directive. An **#if**, **#ifdef**, or **#ifndef** directive may be followed by any number of **#elif** directives.

The *constant-expression* must be an integral expression, and it cannot include a **sizeof** operator, a cast, or an enumeration constant. All macro substitutions are performed upon the *constant-expression* before it is evaluated. All integer constants are treated as long objects, and are then evaluated. If *constant-expression* includes character constants, all escape sequences are converted into characters before evaluation. The implementation defines whether the result of evaluating a character constant in *constant-expression* matches the result of evaluating the same character constant in a C expression. For example, it is up to the implementation whether

```
#elif 'z' - 'a' == 25
```

yields the same value as:

```
else if ('z' - 'a' == 25)
```

Cross-references
Standard, §3.8.1
The C Programming Language, ed. 2, p. 91

See Also
#else, #endif, #if, #ifdef, #ifndef, conditional inclusion

#else — Preprocessing directive
(Language/preprocessing/conditional inclusion)
Include code conditionally
#else *newline* *group*$_{opt}$

The preprocessing directive **#else** conditionally includes code within a program. It is preceded by one of the directives **#if**, **#ifdef**, or **#ifndef**, and may also be preceded by any number of **#elif** directives. If all preceding directives evaluate to false, then the code introduced by **#else** is included within the program up to the **#endif** directive that concludes the chain of conditional-inclusion directives.

A **#if**, **#ifdef**, or **#ifndef** directive can be followed by only one **#else** directive.

Example
For an example of using this directive in a program, see **assert**.

Cross-references
Standard, §3.8.1
The C Programming Language, ed. 2, p. 91

See Also
#elif, #endif, #if, #ifdef, #ifndef, conditional inclusion

#endif — Preprocessing directive
(Language/preprocessing/conditional inclusion)
End conditional inclusion of code
#endif

The preprocessing directive **#endif** must follow any **#if**, **#ifdef**, or **#ifndef** directive. It may also be preceded by any number of **#elif** directives and an **#else** directive. It marks the end of a sequence of source-file statements that are included conditionally by the preprocessor.

Example
For an example of using this directive in a program, see **assert**.

Cross-references
Standard, §3.8.1
The C Programming Language, ed. 2, p. 91

See Also
#elif, #else, #if, #ifdef, #ifndef, conditional inclusion

#error — Preprocessing directive
(Language/preprocessing)
Error directive
#error *message newline*

The preprocessing directive **#error** prints *message* when an error occurs.

Cross-references
Standard, §3.8.5
The C Programming Language, ed. 2, p. 233

See Also
preprocessing

Notes
The intent of this directive is to have translation cease immediately. However, this is not required.

#if — Preprocessing directive
(Language/preprocessing/conditional inclusion)

Include code conditionally
#if *constant-expression newline group*$_{opt}$

The preprocessing directive **#if** tells the preprocessor that if *constant-expression* is true, then include the following lines of code within the program until it reads the next **#elif**, **#else**, or **#endif** directive.

The *constant-expression* must be an integral expression, and it cannot include a **sizeof** operator, a cast, or an enumeration constant. All macro substitutions are performed upon the *constant-expression* before it is evaluated. All integer constants are treated as long objects, and are then evaluated. If *constant-expression* includes character constants, all escape sequences are converted into characters before evaluation.

It is up to the implementation whether the result of evaluating a character constant in *constant-expression* matches the result of evaluating the same character constant in a C expression. For example, it is up to the implementation whether

```
#if 'z' - 'a' == 25
```

yields the same value as:

```
if ('z' - 'a' == 25)
```

Cross-references
Standard, §3.8.1
The C Programming Language, ed. 2, p. 91

See Also
#elif, #else, #endif, #ifdef, #ifndef, conditional inclusion

Notes
The keyword **defined** determines whether a symbol is defined to **#if**. For example,

```
#if defined(SYMBOL)
```

or

```
#if defined SYMBOL
```

is equivalent to

```
#ifdef SYMBOL
```

except that it can be used in more complex expressions, such as

```
#if defined FOO && defined BAR && FOO==10
```

#ifdef — Preprocessing directive
(Language/preprocessing/conditional inclusion)
Include code conditionally
#ifdef *identifier newline group*$_{opt}$

The preprocessing directive **#ifdef** checks whether *identifier* has been defined as a macro name. If *identifier* has been defined as a macro, then the preprocessor includes *group* within the program, up to the next **#elif**, **#else**, or **#endif** directive. If *identifier* has not been defined, however, then *group* is skipped.

An **#ifdef** directive can be followed by any number of **#elif** directives, by one **#else** directive, and must be followed by an **#endif** directive.

Example
For an example of using this directive in a program, see **assert**.

Cross-references
Standard, §3.8.1
The C Programming Language, ed. 2, p. 91

See Also
#elif, #else, #endif, #if, #ifndef, conditional inclusion, defined

Notes
This is the same as:

```
#if defined IDENTIFIER
```

#ifndef — Preprocessing directive
(Language/preprocessing/conditional inclusion)
Include code conditionally
#ifndef *identifier newline group*$_{opt}$

The preprocessing directive **#ifndef** checks whether *identifier* has been defined as a macro name. If *identifier* has *not* been defined as a macro, then the preprocessor includes *group* within the program up to the next **#elif**, **#else**, or **#endif** directive. If *identifier* has been defined, however, then *group* is skipped.

An **#ifndef** directive can be followed by any number of **#elif** directives, by one **#else** directive, and by one **#elif** directive.

Cross-references
Standard, §3.8.1
The C Programming Language, ed. 2, p. 91

See Also
#elif, #else, #endif, #if, #ifndef, conditional inclusion, defined

Notes
This is the same as:

```
#if !defined IDENTIFIER
```

#include — Preprocessing directive
(Language/preprocessing)
Read another file and include it
#include *<file>*
#include *"file"*

The preprocessing directive **#include** tells the preprocessor to replace the directive with the contents of *file*.

The directive can take one of two forms: either the name of the file is enclosed within angle brackets (*<file>*), or it is enclosed within quotation marks (*"file"*).

Most often, the file being included is a *header*, which is a file that contains function prototypes, macro definitions, and other useful material. As its name implies, it most often appears at the head of a program. The header is sought in an implementation-defined manner. The header name must be a string of characters, possibly followed by a period '.' and a single letter, usually (but not always) 'h'. The implementation must provide a unique mapping from each header to the environment. It must be able to read the period, plus at least six character to its left and one character to its right. This mapping is not required to be case sensitive.

The Standard refrains from describing further on the grounds that it is impossible to describe a portable file system.

#include directives may be nested up to at least eight deep. That is to say, a file included by an **#include** directive may use an **#include** directive to include a third file. That third file may also use a **#include** directive to include a fourth file, and so on, up to at least eight files.

A subordinate header file is sought relative to the original source file, rather than relative to the header that calls it directly. For example, suppose that under the UNIX operating system, a file **example.c** resides in directory **/v/fred/src**. If **example.c** contains the directive **#include < header1.h >**. The operating system will look for **header1.h** in the standard directory, **/usr/include**. If **header1.h** includes the directive **#include <../header2.h >** then the implementation should look for **header2.h** not in directory **/usr**, but in directory **/v/fred/src**.

Some file systems allow characters to be used in file names that are used as delimiters in other file systems. Therefore, if any of the characters "*", "\', or ',' are part of a file name, behavior is undefined. If "" is part of a file name between angle-bracket delimiters, behavior is also undefined.

A **#include** directive may also take the form **#include** *string*, where *string* is a macro that expands into either of the two forms described above.

Cross-references
Standard, §2.2.4.1, §3.8.2
The C Programming Language, ed. 2, p. 88

See Also
header, header names, Language, preprocessing

Notes
If the header's name is enclosed within quotation marks, note that the name is *not* a string literal, although it looks exactly like one. Thus, a backslash '\' does not introduce an escape character.

Trigraphs that occur within a **#include** directive are substituted, because they are processed by an earlier phase of translation than are **#include** directives.

#line — Preprocessing directive
(Language/preprocessing)
Reset line number
#line *number newline*
#line *number filename newline*
#line *macros newline*

#line is a preprocessing directive that resets the line number within a file. The Standard defines the line number as being the number of newline characters read, plus one.

#line can take any of three forms. The first, **#line** *number*, resets the current line number in the source file to *number*. The second, **#line** *number filename*, resets the line number to *number* and changes the name of the file referred to by to *filename*. The third, **#line** *macros*, contains macros that have been defined by earlier preprocessing directives. When the macros have been expanded by the preprocessor, the **#line** instruction will then resemble one of the first two forms and be interpreted appropriately.

number specifies the number of the next source line in the file, not the number of the **#line** directive's source line.

Cross-references
Standard, §3.8.4
The C Programming Language, ed. 2, p. 233

See Also
preprocessing

Notes
Most often, **#line** is used to ensure that error messages point to the correct line in the program's source code. A program generator may use this directive to associate errors in generated C code with the original sources. For example, the program generator **yacc** uses **#line** instructions to link the C code it generates with the **yacc** code written by the programmer.

#pragma — Preprocessing directive (Language/preprocessing)
Perform implementation-defined task
#pragma *preprocessing-tokens*$_{opt}$ *newline*

The preprocessing directive **#pragma** causes the implementation to behave in an implementation-defined manner. A **#pragma** might be used to give a "hint" to the translator about the best way to generate code, optimize, or diagnose errors. It may also pass information to the translator about the environment, or add debugging information. The design of **#pragma** is left up to the implementation.

Cross-references
Standard, §3.8.6
The C Programming Language, ed. 2, p. 233

See Also
preprocessing

Notes
An unrecognized pragma is ignored. Because of this subtlety, one should be careful when porting code that contains pragmas to other implementations.

#undef — Preprocessing directive
(Language/preprocessing/macro replacement)
Undefine a macro
#undef *identifier*

The preprocessing directive **#undef** tells the C preprocessor to disregard *identifier* as a macro. It undoes the effect of the **#define** directive.

#undef does not give an error if *identifier* is not defined. It can also undefine macros that are predefined by the implementation, other than those specified by the Standard to be unreadable.

Cross-references
Standard, §3.8.3.5
The C Programming Language, ed. 2, p. 230

See Also
#define, macro replacement

Notes
If an implementation has defined a function both as a macro and as a library function, then the directive

```
#undef function
```

undefines the macro version, and forces the implementation to use the library version.

Some previous implementations allowed a user to "stack" macro definitions and "unstack" them by **#undef**ing them one level at a time. The Standard, however, states that one **#undef** directive undefines all previous definitions.

% — Operator
(Language/expressions/multiplicative operators)
Remainder operator
operand1 % operand2

The operator % divides *operand1* by *operand2* and yields the remainder.

Both *operand1* and *operand2* must have integral type. Both undergo the usual arithmetic conversions before they are divided, and the type of the result is that to which the operands were converted. If *operand2* is zero, the behavior is undefined. If either operand is negative, the sign of the result is implementation-defined.

The remainder operation normally throws away the quotient. The division operator / returns the quotient of a division operation, and throws away the remainder. If you wish to obtain both quotient and remainder, use the functions **div** or **ldiv**. To obtain the remainder from floating-point division, use the function **fmod**.

Cross-references
Standard, §3.3.5
The C Programming Language, ed. 2, p. 205

See Also
/, div, fmod, ldiv, multiplicative operators

% = — Operator
(Language/expressions/assignment operators)
Remainder assignment operator
operand1 % = *operand2*

The operator % = divides *operand1* by *operand2* and assigns the remainder to *operand1*. It is equivalent to the expression:

```
operand1 = operand1 % operand2
```

Each operand must have an integral type. If the value of *operand2* is zero, the result is undefined.

Cross-references
Standard, §3.3.16.2
The C Programming Language, ed. 2, pp. 50, 208

See Also
%, assignment operators

& — Operator
(Language/expressions/unary operators)
&operand
operand1 **&** *operand2*

The operator **&** has two meanings, depending upon whether it has one operand or two. In the former instance, it yields the address of its operand. In the latter instance, it performs a bitwise AND operation upon its operands.

Address-of Operator

When used with one operand, **&** yields the value of the address of its operand in the form of a pointer to the type of its operand. The operand must be an lvalue or function designator, with the following restrictions: the operand may not be a bit-field, and it may not be declared with the storage-class specifier **register**. The resulting pointer has the type "pointer to *type*", where *type* is the type of the operand.

ANSI C allows you to take the address of a function or array.

Bitwise AND Operator

When used with two operands, **&** performs a bitwise AND operation. Its syntax is as follows:

> *AND-expression:*
>   *equality-expression*
>   *AND-expression* & *equality-expression*

Each operand must have integral type. Each undergoes the normal arithmetic conversions before the operation. **&** yields a result whose type is the same as the promoted operands.

A bitwise AND operation compares the operands bit by bit. It sets a bit in the object it creates only if the corresponding bits in both operands are set.

For example, consider an environment that uses extended ASCII. Here, the character ')' has the bit pattern:

```
0010 1001
```

and the character 'L' has the bit pattern:

```
0100 1100
```

The operation ')'&'L' yields an object with the following bit pattern:

```
0000 1000
```

Only one bit was set in the result because in only one instance were both corresponding bits set in the operands.

The **&** operation is sometimes called the "intersection" of two bit sets.

Example
For an example of using this operator in a program, see **bitwise operators**.

Cross-references
Standard, §3.3.3.2, §3.3.10
The C Programming Language, ed. 2, pp. 48, 93

See Also
bitwise operators, unary operators

&& — Operator
(Language/expressions/logical operators)
Logical AND operator
operand1 **&&** *operand2*

The operator **&&** performs a logical AND operation. Both *operand1* and *operand2* must have scalar type. Its syntax is as follows:

> *logical-AND-expression:*
> > *inclusive-OR-expression*
> > *logical-AND-expression* && *inclusive-OR-expression*

The result of this operation has type **int**. The result has a value of one if both operands are true (i.e., nonzero). If either operand is false (zero), then the result has a value of zero.

The operands are evaluated from left to right; if *operand1* is false, then *operand2* is not evaluated. If *operand2* is an expression that yields a side-effect, the results of the **&&** operation may not be what you expect. If *operand1* is false, *operand2* is not evaluated and its side-effect not generated.

Cross-references
Standard, §3.3.13
The C Programming Language, ed. 2, p. 207

See Also
||, logical operators

&= — Operator
(Language/expressions/assignment operators)
Bitwise-AND assignment operator
operand1 **&=** *operand2*

The operator **&=** performs a bitwise AND operation on *operand1* and *operand2* and assigns the result to *operand1*. It is equivalent to the expression

```
operand1 = operand1 & operand2
```

Both operands must have integral type.

Cross-references
Standard, §3.3.16.2
The C Programming Language, ed. 2, pp. 50, 208

See Also
&, assignment operators

() — Punctuator
(Language/lexical elements/punctuators)

functionname **(** *arguments* **)**
(*newtype* **)** *identifier*
(*primary expression* **)**

The characters () have two uses in the C world: as punctuators and as operators. Parentheses must be used in pairs.

When the parentheses follow an identifier, they indicate that it names a function. When used with a function declaration, a function prototype, or a function definition, the parentheses may enclose a list of parameters for the function and the type of each parameter. When used with a function call, they enclose a list of arguments to be passed to the function.

When parentheses precede an identifier and enclose a typename alone, then they function as the cast operator. Here, the type of the identifier is changed, or *cast*, to the type enclosed within parentheses.

Finally, when parentheses enclose an expression, that expression is by definition considered to be a primary expression. This means that the expression is resolved before any outer expression is evaluated.

To see the variety of uses for (), consider the following expression:

```
if ((fileptr = (void *)fopen("filename", "r")) == NULL)
```

The outermost pair of parentheses enclose the arguments to **if**. The next innermost pair of parentheses enclose the expression

```
fileptr = (void *)fopen("filename", "r")
```

which must be resolved before it is compared with NULL. The pair of parentheses that enclose the type **void *** casts the object returned by **fopen** to type **void ***. Finally, the parentheses that follow **fopen** mark that identifier as a function and enclose the arguments that are passed to it, in this case the string literals **filename** and **r**.

Cross-reference
Standard, §3.1.6, §3.3.2.2, §3.3.4

See Also
cast operators, function calls, function definition, function prototype, operators, punctuators

Notes
Under ANSI C, parentheses affect the grouping of expressions. This is a quiet change from the definition in the first edition of *The C Programming Language*, which allowed translators to rearrange expressions in the presence of parentheses on expressions that involved commutative and associative operators (binary **+** and *****). The *as if* rule still applies in this case: if the translator can produce the same results, it is free to rearrange expressions in the face of parentheses.

* — Operator
(Language/expressions/multiplicative operators)

*pointer
typename ***** *type-qualifier-list*$_{opt}$ *identifier*
operand1 ***** *operand2*

The character ***** is used both as an operator and as a punctuator.

Multiplication Operator
When the ***** appears between two operands with arithmetic type, it is the multiplicative operator. It multiplies its operands and yields the product. Both operands undergo normal arithmetic conversion. The type of the result is the one to which both operands were converted.

Indirection Operator
When ***** is used before one operand that is of a pointer type, it *dereferences* the pointer. That is, it yields the value of the object to which the pointer points. If the pointer points to a function, then the result is a function designator. If the pointer points to an object, the resulting lvalue has the type of the object to which the pointer points.

If indirection is performed on any pointer to an incomplete type, the behavior is undefined. This means that no pointer with type **void *** can be dereferenced.

Pointer Punctuator
When the ***** is used in a declaration, it indicates that the variable being declared is a pointer. For example, consider the following:

```
int example1;
int *example2;
```

Here, **example1** has type **int**, and **example2** has type "pointer to **int**".

Cross-references
Standard, §3.1.6, .3.3.2, §3.3.5, §3.5.4.1
The C Programming Language, ed. 2, pp. 94, 205

See Also
multiplicative operators, pointer, punctuators, unary operators

*/ — Comment Delimiter
(Language/lexical elements/comment)

The characters ***/** together mark the end of a comment.

Cross-references
Standard, §3.1.9
The C Programming Language, ed. 2, p. 192

See Also
/*, comment

*= — Operator
(Language/expressions/assignment operators)
Multiplication assignment operator
operand1 ***=** *operand2*

The operator ***=** multiplies *operand1* by *operand2* and assigns the product to *operand1*. It is equivalent to the expression:

```
operand1 = operand1 * operand2
```

Each operand must have an arithmetic type.

Cross-references
Standard, §3.3.16.2
The C Programming Language, ed. 2, pp. 50, 208

See Also
*, assignment operators

+ — Operator
(Language/expressions/additive operators)

+operand
operand1 + operand2

The operator + has two uses, depending upon whether it is used with two operands or one. In the former instance, it indicates that the given operand should be computed without any associative or commutative regrouping that the translator might normally apply to expressions. In the latter, it adds the two operands together.

The Unary + Operator

The unary operator + takes an operand that has a scalar type and yields its value. If the operand has a negative value, then a negative value is returned. The operand undergoes integral promotion, and the type returned is that to which the operand is promoted.

The Addition Operator

The addition operator + adds two operands. Both operands may have arithmetic types, or one of the operands may be a pointer and the other an integral type.

If both operands have arithmetic types, then each undergoes integral conversion before addition is performed; the type of the result is the type to which both are converted.

When an integral type is added to a pointer, the value of the integral operand is first multiplied by the size of the object to which the pointer points, in bytes, and then addition is performed. The result of the addition operation returns a pointer that is appropriately offset from the pointer operand.

Pointer addition is often used for pointers that point to arrays. Note the following rules for incrementing a pointer to an array:

- If a pointer points to an array, then the result of addition will point to another member of the same array — assuming that the array is large enough.

- If a pointer to an array is incremented and the resulting pointer does *not* point to a member of the array or one past the last member, then behavior is undefined.

- Behavior is also undefined if the pointer operand and the result of the addition operation do not point to the same array object *and* the result of the addition operation is then redirected with the unary * operator. In other words, it is legal for a translator to test array bounds.

Cross-references
Standard, §3.3.3.3, §3.3.6
The C Programming Language, ed. 2, pp. 203, 205

See Also
++, -, additive operators, unary operators

++ — Operator
(Language/expressions/unary operators)
Increment operator
operand++
++operand

The operator ++ increments its operand. When it appears before its operand, it is called the *pre-increment operator*; when it appears after its operand, it is called the *post-increment operator*. In both cases, it is equivalent to *operand* = *operand*+1. *operand* must be a modifiable lvalue.

These operators differ as follows: with the prefix operator, the value of the operand is used *after* it is incremented; whereas with the postfix operator, the value of the operand is used *before* it is incremented.

The following example illustrates the difference between the preincrement and postincrement operators.

```
#define MAX   10
int x = 0, count = 0;

/* loop 1 */
while (++x < MAX)
     count++;

/* loop 2 */
while (x++ < MAX)
     count++;
```

The first loop will iterate nine times, the second will iterate ten times. The first loop preincrements the loop variable **x** before using it within the conditional expression. The second loop, which uses the postincrement operator, first uses the current value of **x** in the conditional, then increments its value.

Cross-references
Standard, §3.3.2.4, §3.3.3.1
The C Programming Language, ed. 2, p. 46

See Also
--, unary operators

+ = — Operator
(Language/expressions/assignment operators)
Addition assignment operator
operand1 **+ =** *operand2*

The operator **+ =** adds the value of *operand1* with that of *operand2* and stores the sum within *operand1*. It is equivalent to the expression:

```
operand1 = operand1 + operand2
```

Both operands have arithmetic types, or *operand1* has a pointer type and *operand2* has integral type.

Example
For an example of using this operator in a program, see **character testing**.

Cross-references
Standard, §3.3.16.2
The C Programming Language, ed. 2, pp. 50, 208

See Also
-=, assignment operators

Notes
The lvalue *operand1* is evaluated only once.

, — Operator
(Language/expressions)
identifier1 **,** *identifier2*
expression1 **,** *expression2*

The character ',' can be used as punctuator or an operator.

The Comma Punctuator
When it is used as a punctuator, the comma separates the parameters in a function declaration, the parameters to a function-like macro, the arguments to a function call, or the items in a list of identifiers. For example, in the expression

```
int foo, bar, baz;
```

the comma separates the identifiers being declared, all of which are of type **int**.

The Comma Operator

When used outside of a declaration or parameter list, the comma acts as an operator. The comma operator evaluates its left argument first, then its right argument. The value and type of the comma expression is that of the right operand.

For example, the following shows how the comma operator is used in a loop:

```
int i, j;
    . . .
for (i=j=0; i<10 && j<25; i++, j++);
```

This loop uses the comma operator to help increment two variables upon each iteration.

Cross-references

Standard, §3.3.17
The C Programming Language, ed. 2, p. 62

See Also

expressions

Notes

A comma expression cannot be an lvalue.

- — Operator

(Language/expressions/unary operators)

-operand
operand1 - operand2

The operator - has two uses, depending upon whether it is used with two operands or one. In the former situation, it subtracts the operand to its right from the operand to its left. In the latter, it returns the negated value of its operand.

Subtraction Operator

The operator - can subtract the following operands from each other:

- Two arithmetic types.

- Two pointers to objects that have compatible types and compatible qualification.

- Two pointers that point to objects that have compatible types, but not necessarily compatible qualification.

- An integral type from a pointer.

When both operands have arithmetic type, each undergoes integral promotion. The type of the result is that to which the operands were promoted. Its value is the difference when the right operand is subtracted from the left.

When one pointer is subtracted from another, the result is of type **ptrdiff_t**. This type is defined in the header **stddef.h**. If two pointers that do not point to the same array are subtracted from each other, behavior is undefined. The only exception is the expression

```
(X+1) - X
```

where, if **X** points to the last member of the array, the result is one by definition.

If two pointers that point to the same array are subtracted from each other, the result is automatically divided by the size of an array member. This yields a value that is the same as would result if the two appropriate array subscripts had been subtracted from each other. If the result of pointer subtraction points past the end of an array, the behavior is undefined. The sole exception, again, is the expression given above.

When subtracting a scalar from a pointer, the result is as if the scalar were multiplied by the size of the object pointed to by the pointer, and then subtracted.

Negation Operator

The unary operator - takes an operand with arithmetic type. The operand first undergoes normal integral promotion. The type of the resulting expression is the one to which the operand was promoted; and the value of the resulting expression is the negated value of the operand.

Cross-references

Standard, §3.3.3.3, §3.3.6
The C Programming Language, ed. 2, pp. 203, 205

See Also

+, --, arithmetic operators, unary operators

-- — Operator

(Language/expressions/unary operators)
Decrement operator
operand--
--operand

The operator -- decrements its operand. When it appears before its operand, it is called the *pre-decrement operator*; when it appears after its operand, it is called the *post-decrement operator*. In both cases, it is equivalent to *operand = operand - 1*.

These operators differ as follows: with the prefix operator, the value of the operand is used *after* it is decremented; whereas with the postfix operator, the value of the operand is used *before* it is decremented.

Cross-references
Standard, §3.3.2.4, §3.3.3.1
The C Programming Language, ed. 2, p. 46

See Also
++, unary operators

-= — Operator
(Language/expressions/assignment operators)
Subtraction assignment operator
operand1 -= *operand2*

The operator -= subtracts the value of *operand2* from that of *operand1* and stores the difference within *operand1*. It is equivalent to the expression:

```
operand1 = operand1 - operand2
```

Both operands have arithmetic types, or *operand1* has pointer type and *operand2* has integral type.

Cross-references
Standard, §3.3.16.2
The C Programming Language, ed. 2, pp. 50, 208

See Also
+=, assignment operators

-> — Operator
(Language/expressions/postfix operators)
Select a member
objectpointer -> *membername*

The operator -> selects a member of a structure or a **union** through a pointer.

objectpointer must point to a structure or **union**. *membername* must name a member of the structure or **union** to which *objectpointer* points. For example, consider the following:

```
struct example {
      int member1;
      long member2;
      example *member3;
};
```

```
struct example structure;
struct example *pointer = &structure;
```

To select **member1** within **structure** via **pointer**, use the expression:

```
pointer->member1
```

Behavior is implementation-defined if one member of a **union** is accessed after another member has been stored within the **union**.

Cross-references
Standard, §3.3.2.3
The C Programming Language, ed. 2, p. 131

See Also
., member, postfix operators

. — Operator
(Language/expressions/postfix operators)
Member selection
objectname . membername

The operator **.** is used to select a member of a structure or a **union**.

objectname must name a structure or **union**. *membername* must be a member of the structure or **union** that *objectname* names. For example, consider the following:

```
struct example {
        int member1;
        long member2;
        example *member3;
};
struct example object;
```

To read **member1** within **object**, use the expression:

```
object.member1
```

Cross-references
Standard, §3.3.2.3
The C Programming Language, ed. 2, p. 128

See Also
->, member, postfix operators

/ — Operator
(Language/expressions/multiplicative operators)
Division operator
operand1 / operand2

The operator **/** divides *operand2* by *operand1* and yields the quotient. Each operand must have arithmetic type and undergoes the usual arithmetic promotion before the operation is performed. The result of the operation has the type to which the operands are promoted. If the result of **X/Y** can be represented, then **(X/Y)*Y+(X%Y)** must equal **X**.

If *operand2* is zero, the result is undefined. If either operand is negative, the result is either the largest integer that is less than the algebraic quotient, or the smallest integer that is greater than the algebraic quotient, whichever the implementation prefers. For example, in the expression

```
7 / -2
```

the algebraic quotient is **-3.5**. The implementation determines whether the result is **-4** (the largest integer less than the algebraic quotient) or **-3** (the smallest integer greater than the algebraic quotient).

The division operation normally throws away the remainder. The remainder operator **%** returns the remainder of a division operation and throws away the quotient. If you wish to obtain both quotient and remainder, use the functions **div** or **ldiv**.

Cross-references
Standard, §3.3.5
The C Programming Language, ed. 2, p. 205

See Also
%, div, ldiv, multiplicative operators

/* — Comment Delimiter
(Language/lexical elements/comment)

The characters **/*** together mark the beginning of a comment.

Cross-references
Standard, §3.1.9
The C Programming Language, ed. 2, p. 192

See Also
***/,** comment*

/= — Operator
(Language/expressions/assignment operators)
Division assignment operator
operand1 /= operand2

The operator *$/=$* divides *operand1* by *operand2*, and assigns the quotient to *operand1*. It is equivalent to the expression:

```
operand1 = operand1 / operand2
```

Each operand must have arithmetic type.

If the value of *operand2* is zero, behavior is undefined.

Cross-references
Standard, §3.3.16.2
The C Programming Language, ed. 2, pp. 50, 208

See Also
/, assignment operators

: — Punctuator
(Language/lexical elements/punctuators)

When punctuator **:** follows an identifier, it marks the identifier as being a label. When it precedes an integer constant in the declaration of a structure or **union**, it marks the constant as giving the size of a bit-field.

Cross-reference
Standard, §3.1.6
The C Programming Language, ed. 2, p. 66

See Also
?:, bit-fields, goto, label, punctuators

; — Punctuator
(Language/lexical elements/punctuators)

The punctuator **;** marks the end of a statement.

Cross-reference
Standard, §3.1.6

See Also
punctuators, statements

< — Operator
(Language/expressions/relational operators)
Less-than operator
operand1 < *operand2*

The operator < compares two operands. It yields one if *operand1* is less than *operand2*, and zero if *operand1* is greater than or equal to *operand2*.

See **relational operators** for more information on the types of operands that can be compared.

Cross-references
Standard, §3.3.8
The C Programming Language, ed. 2, pp. 41, 206

See Also
< =, >, relational operators

<< — Operator
(Language/expressions/bitwise operators)
Bitwise left-shift operator
operand1 << *operand2*

The operator << shifts the bits in *operand1* to the left by *operand2* places. This is called the *bitwise left shift* operation.

Both operands must have integral types. Both undergo the usual arithmetic conversions, and the result has the type to which the left operand was promoted.

A bitwise left-shift operation moves the bits of an object to the left, and fills the vacated bits with zeroes. For example, consider an environment that uses extended ASCII. Here, the character constant '?' has the bit pattern:

```
0011 1111
```

In this environment, the expression

```
'?' << 4
```

yields the following pattern of bits:

```
0000 0011 1111 0000
```

The "nybbles" to the left result from the promotion of the **char** to type **int**. All bits are shifted four places to the left, and the four vacated bits to the right are filled with zeroes.

The left-shift operation is sometimes called the "logical" shift operation, which will fill vacated bits with zeroes.

If *operand2* is negative or is larger than the number of bits in *operand1*, behavior is undefined.

Example
For a practical example of the operator < <, see **rand()**.

Cross-references
Standard, §3.3.7
The C Programming Language, ed. 2, pp. 48, 207

See Also
< < =, > >, **bitwise operators**

< < = — Operator
(Language/expressions/assignment operators)
Bitwise left-shift assignment operator
operand1 < < = *operand2*

The operator < < = shifts the bits in *operand1* to the left by *operand2* places, and assigns the result to *operand1*. It is equivalent to the expression:

```
operand1 = operand1 << operand2
```

Both operands must have integral type.

If *operand2* is negative or has a value greater than the number of bits in *operand1*, behavior is undefined.

Example
For an example of using this operator in a program, see **bitwise operators**.

Cross-references
Standard, §3.3.16.2
The C Programming Language, ed. 2, pp. 50, 208

See Also
< <, assignment operators

< = — Operator
(Language/expressions/relational operators)
Less-than or equal-to operator
operand1 < = *operand2*

The operator < = compares two operands. It returns one if *operand1* is less than or equal to *operand2*, and it returns zero if *operand1* is greater than *operand2*.

See **relational operators** for more information on the types of operands that can be compared.

Example
For an example of using this operator in a program, see **bitwise operators**.

Cross-references
Standard, §3.3.8
The C Programming Language, ed. 2, pp. 41, 206

See Also
<, > =, relational operators

= — Operator
(Language/expressions/assignment operators)
Assignment operator
operand1 = *operand2*

The operator = copies the value of *operand2* into *operand1*. The value of *operand2* is converted to the type of *operand1* before they are copied.

The following types of operands are allowed:

- Both have an arithmetic type. *operand1* may be qualified.

- Both are compatible structures or **unions**. *operand1* may be qualified.

- Both are pointers to compatible types. *operand1* may be a pointer to a qualified type. *operand2* may be NULL. Either may be of type **void ***, assuming the other points to an object or an incomplete type.

operand1 must be a modifiable lvalue.

Cross-references
Standard, §3.3.16.1
The C Programming Language, ed. 2, pp. 50, 208

See Also
= =, assignment operators

= = — Operator
(Language/expressions/equality operators)
Equality operator
operand1 = = *operand2*

The operator = = compares *operand1* with *operand2*. The result is one if the operands are equal, and zero if they are not.

The operands must be one of the following:

- Arithmetic types.

- Pointers to compatible types (ignoring qualifiers on these types).

- A pointer to an object or incomplete type and a pointer to **void**.

- A pointer and NULL.

If both operands have arithmetic type, they undergo usual arithmetic conversion before being compared. If one operand is a pointer to an object and the other is a pointer to **void**, the pointer to an object is converted to a pointer to **void** for purposes of the comparison.

If two pointers to functions compare equal, then they point to the same function; likewise, if two pointers to data objects compare equal, then they point to the same object. However, on machines that provide separate spaces for instructions and data, a pointer to a function may compare equal to a pointer to a data object. Therefore, you should not depend on being able to distinguish function pointers from data object pointers by value. Further, on machines that allow many pointer values to refer to the same object (e.g., i8086 LARGE model), two pointers that do not compare equal may nonetheless point to the same object.

Cross-references
Standard, §3.3.9
The C Programming Language, ed. 2, pp. 41, 207

See Also
!=, equality operators

Notes

Perhaps the commonest mistake made by C programmers is to use the assignment operator '=' in place of the equality operator '= =' where a conditional expression is expected. For example:

```
if (variable1 = variable2)    /* WRONG */
      dosomething();
```

Here, the value of **variable2** is copied into **variable1**; whether the expression succeeds or not depends upon the value of **variable2** rather than the equality of the two variables. Hence, the condition will be true as long as this operand has a value other than zero. This code will translate, often without generating a warning message, but probably will not run correctly.

Type conversion will affect comparison, particularly if a **char** is being compared with an integral type with a negative value. For example, consider the comparison:

```
char variable;
    . . .
if (variable == -1)
      dosomething();
```

Here, **variable** is promoted to an **int** before it is compared with -**1**. However, if **char** is unsigned by default, when it is expanded, it can never compare equal to a negative number. For maximum portability, when using **chars** that may take negative values, declare them as type **int** or type **signed char**.

Comparing **float**s and **double**s for equality is usually a mistake, especially as a control expression in a loop. Implementations of floating-point arithmetic are often inexact.

> — Operator

(Language/expressions/relational operators)

Greater-than operator
operand1 > *operand2*

The operator > compares two operands. It returns one if *operand1* is greater than *operand2*; and it returns zero if *operand1* is less than, or equal to, *operand2*.

See **relational operators** for more information on the types of operands that can be compared.

Cross-references

Standard, §3.3.8
The C Programming Language, ed. 2, pp. 41, 206

> = — Operator
(Language/expressions/relational operators)

Greater-than or equal-to operator
operand1 > = *operand2*

The operator > = compares two operands. It returns one if *operand1* is greater than, or equal to, *operand2*; it returns zero if *operand1* is less than *operand2*.

See **relational operators** for more information on the types of operands that can be compared.

Cross-references

Standard, §3.3.8
The C Programming Language, ed. 2, pp. 41, 206

See Also

< =, >, relational operators

> > — Operator
(Language/expressions/bitwise operators)

Bitwise right-shift operator
operand1 > > *operand2*

The operator > > shifts the bits in *operand1* to the right by *operand2* places. This is called the *bitwise right shift* operation.

Both operands must have integral type. Both undergo the usual arithmetic conversions, and the result has the type to which the left operand was promoted.

A bitwise right-shift operation moves the bits of an object to the right. The vacated bits are filled with zeroes, unless *operand1* is signed and has a negative value. In that case, the vacated bits will propagate the sign bit (i.e., be filled with ones).

For example, consider an environment that uses extended ASCII. Here, the character constant '?' has the bit pattern:

```
0011 1111
```

In this environment, the expression

```
'?' >> 4
```

yields the following pattern of bits:

```
0000 0000 0000 0011
```

The two "nybbles" to the right result from the promotion of the **char** to type **int**. All bits are shifted four places to the right, and the four vacated bits to the left are filled with zeroes. The nybble **1111** disappears.

The right-shift operation is sometimes called the "arithmetic" shift operation.

If *operand2* is negative or is larger than the number of bits in *operand1*, behavior is undefined.

Example

For an example of using this operator in a program, see **srand**.

Cross-references
Standard, §3.3.7
The C Programming Language, ed. 2, pp. 48, 207

See Also
< <, > > =, bitwise operators

> > = — Operator
(Language/expressions/assignment operators)
Bitwise right-shift assignment operator
operand1 > > = *operand2*

The operator > > = shifts the bits in *operand1* to the right by *operand2* places, and assigns the result to *operand1*. It is equivalent to the expression:

```
operand1 = operand1 >> operand2
```

Both operands must have integral type.

If *operand2* is negative or has a value larger than the number of bits in *operand1*, behavior is undefined.

Example
For an example of using this operator in a program, see **bitwise operators**.

Cross-references
Standard, §3.3.16.2
The C Programming Language, ed. 2, pp. 50, 208

See Also
> >, assignment operators

?: — Operator
(Language/expressions)
Conditional operator
conditional ? expression1 : expression2

The conditional operator **?:** causes one or the other of two expressions to be executed. Its syntax is as follows:

> *conditional-expression:*
> > *logical-OR-expression*
> > *logical-OR-expression ? expression*
> > > *: conditional-expression*

If the *logical-OR-expression* evaluates to true (nonzero), then *expression* is evaluated; otherwise, *conditional-expression* is evaluated. The operator as a whole yields the result of whichever expression is executed.

The *logical-OR-expression* must have a scalar type. The conditional operator may take the following types:

- Both are arithmetic types. Each undergoes normal arithmetic conversion, and the result has the type to which they are converted.

- Both have compatible structure or **union** types. They are converted to a common type, and the result has that type.

- Both are **void** types. The result is of type **void**.

- Both are pointers to compatible types, whether qualified or unqualified. The result is a pointer that is qualified by all the qualifiers of both operands.

- One is a pointer and the other NULL. The result is of the pointer's type.

- One points to an object or incomplete type, and the other is type **void ***. Both operands are converted to type **void *** before evaluation, and the result also has that type.

The logical expression can also be a scalar identifier, constant, or function.

Example
For an example of using this operator in a program, see **character-case mapping**.

Cross-references
Standard, §3.3.15
The C Programming Language, ed. 2, p. 51

See Also
expressions

Notes
The conditional operator does not yield an lvalue. For example:

```
int x, a, b;
(x ? a : b) = 5;    /* WRONG */
```

is incorrect, but

```
int x;
int *ptr1, *ptr2;
*(x ? ptr1 : ptr2) = 5; /* RIGHT */
```

is correct.

[] — Operator
(Language/expressions/postfix operators)
Array subscript operator
arrayname[*size*]

The array-subscript operator [] is used in different contexts. It is used to declare an array, with or without the array size. It is used as a subscript operator, and it can also be used when passing an array as an argument. *arrayname* is the name of the array to be accessed; *size* is the number of objects in the array.

The Standard states that one of the items, *arrayname* and *size*, must be a pointer, and the other an integer. To calculate the address of an element within an array, the integer is multiplied by the size of an element of the array, and the product added to value of the pointer. In most C programs, *arrayname* gives the pointer and *size* the integer offset.

The operator [] can also be used to select an object within an array; the objects are numbered from zero through *size*-1. For example, if *arrayname* points to an array of **ints**, and if *size* is equal to six, then the expression

```
arrayname[4]
```

is equivalent to:

```
*(arrayname+4)
```

This expressions yields not an address, but the contents of the array at the requested point.

An array can be followed by more than one pair of brackets. Such arrays are called *multidimensional*. To see how such an array works, consider the following multidimensional array:

```
#define DIMENSION1 5
#define DIMENSION2 10
int arrayname[DIMENSION1][DIMENSION2];
```

Here, **dimension1** holds five objects, each of which is the size set by **dimension2**: in this instance, ten **int**s. Thus, the expression

```
arrayname[3][5];
```

is equivalent to writing:

```
*(arrayname+(3*DIMENSION2)+5)
```

An expression of the form

```
arrayname[3];
```

indicates an entire row of the array. This is sometimes called a "slice".

Cross-references

Standard, §3.3.2.1
The C Programming Language, ed. 2, pp. 97*ff*

See Also

array, postfix operators

Notes

Given the Standard's description of how an array is accessed, the elements of an array access may be reversed. For example, given the following code,

```
int arrayname[5];
int counter = 3;
```

the expressions

```
arrayname[counter]
```

and

```
counter[arrayname]
```

should yield the same result. Using these expressions interchangeably will result in programs that are very hard to read and maintain.

^ — Operator

(Language/expressions/bitwise operators)

Bitwise exclusive OR operator
operand1 ^ *operand2*

The operator ^ performs an bitwise exclusive OR operation.

Each operand must have integral type, and each undergoes the usual arithmetic conversions. The result has integral type.

A bitwise exclusive OR operation compares the bit patterns of the operands, then sets each bit in its result if either, but not both, of the corresponding bits in the operands is set.

For example, consider an environment which uses extended ASCII. In this environment, the character **9** is represented by the bit pattern

```
0011 1001
```

and the character **w** by the bit pattern:

```
0111 0111
```

Thus, the operation:

```
'9' ^ 'w';
```

yields the following bit pattern:

```
0000 0000 0100 1110
```

The extra "nybbles" to the left are created by the promotion of the character constants to type **int**. If the corresponding bits in the operands were both set to one, the bit in the result was set to zero.

Example

For an example of using this operator in a program, see **srand**.

Cross-references

Standard, §3.3.11
The C Programming Language, ed. 2, pp. 48, 207

See Also

^=, |, **bitwise operators**

^ = — Operator
(Language/expressions/assignment operators)
Bitwise exclusive-OR assignment operator
operand1 ^= *operand2*

The operator ^= performs a bitwise exclusive-OR operation on *operand1* and *operand2*, and assigns the result to *operand1*. It is equivalent to the expression

```
operand1 = operand1 ^ operand2;
```

Both operands must have integral type.

Cross-references
Standard, §3.3.16.2
The C Programming Language, ed. 2, pp. 50, 208

See Also
^, assignment operators

_ _DATE_ _ — Macro
(Language/preprocessing)
Date of translation

_ _DATE_ _ is a macro that is defined by the implementation. It represents the date that the source file was translated. It is a string literal of the form

```
"Mmm dd yyyy"
```

where **Mmm** is the same three-letter abbreviation for the month as is used by **asctime**; **dd** is the day of the month, with the first **d** being a space if translation occurs on the first through the ninth day of the month; and **yyyy** is the current year. If the date of translation is not available, then a valid, implementation-defined date must be supplied.

The value of this macro remains constant throughout the processing of the translation unit. This macro may not be the subject of a **#define** or **#undef** preprocessing directive.

Cross-references
Standard, §3.8.8
The C Programming Language, ed. 2, p. 233

See Also
_ _FILE_ _, _ _LINE_ _, _ _STDC_ _, _ _TIME_ _, preprocessing

_ _FILE_ _ — Macro
(Language/preprocessing)
Source file name

_ _FILE_ _ is a macro that is defined by the implementation. It represents, as a string constant, the name of the current source file being translated.

This macro may not be the subject of a **#define** or **#undef** preprocessing directive, but it may be altered with the **#line** preprocessing directive.

Cross-references
Standard, §3.8.8
The C Programming Language, ed. 2, p. 233

See Also
#line, _ _DATE_ _, _ _LINE_ _, _ _STDC_ _, _ _TIME_ _, preprocessing

_ _LINE_ _ — Macro
(Language/preprocessing)
Current line within a source file

_ _LINE_ _ is a macro that is defined by the implementation. It represents the current line within the source file. The Standard defines the current line as being the number of newline characters read, plus one.

This macro may not be the subject of a **#define** or **#undef** preprocessing directive.

Cross-references
Standard, §3.8.8
The C Programming Language, ed. 2, p. 233

See Also
_ _DATE_ _, _ _FILE_ _, _ _STDC_ _, _ _TIME_ _, preprocessing

_ _STDC_ _ — Macro
(Language/preprocessing)
Mark a conforming translator

_ _STDC_ _ is a macro that is defined by the implementation. If it is defined to be equal to one, then it indicates that the translator conforms to the Standard.

The value of this macro remains constant throughout the entire program, no matter how many source files it comprises. This macro may not be the subject of a **#define** or **#undef** preprocessing directive.

Example
For an example of using this macro in a program, see **assert**.

Cross-references
Standard, §3.8.8
The C Programming Language, ed. 2, p. 233

See Also
_ _DATE_ _, _ _FILE_ _, _ _LINE_ _, _ _TIME_ _, **preprocessing**

Notes
If an implementation is not fully compatible with the Standard, then it should not define this macro. A value greater than one may indicate compliance with a later version of the Standard.

_ _TIME_ _ – Macro
(Language/preprocessing)
Time source file is translated

_ _TIME_ _ is a macro that is defined by the implementation. It represents the time that a source file is translated. It is a string literal of the form:

    "hh:mm:ss"

This is the same format used by the function **asctime**. If the time of translation is not available, then a valid, implementation-defined string must be supplied.

The value of this macro remains constant throughout the processing of the translation unit. This macro may not be the subject of a **#define** or **#undef** preprocessing directive.

Cross-references
Standard, §3.8.8
The C Programming Language, ed. 2, p. 233

See Also
_ _DATE_ _, _ _FILE_ _, _ _LINE_ _, _ _STDC_ _, **preprocessing**

_IOFBF – Macro
(Library/STDIO)
Indicate stream is to be fully buffered
#include <stdio.h>

_IOFBF is a macro that is defined in the header **stdio.h**. When used with the function **setvbuf**, it indicates that the stream being manipulated is to be fully buffered.

Cross-references
Standard, §4.9.1, §4.9.9.6
The C Programming Language, ed. 2, p. 243

See Also
buffer, _IOLBF, _IONBF, setbuf, setvbuf, STDIO, stdio.h

_IOLBF — Macro
(Library/STDIO)
Indicate stream is to be line-buffered
#include < stdio.h >

_IOLBF is a macro defined in the header **stdio.h**. When used with the function **setvbuf**, it indicates that the stream being manipulated is to be line-buffered.

Cross-references
Standard, §4.9.1, §4.9.9.6
The C Programming Language, ed. 2, p. 243

See Also
buffer, _IOFBF, _IONBF, setbuf, setvbuf, STDIO, stdio.h

_IONBF — Macro
(Library/STDIO)
Indicate stream is to be unbuffered
#include < stdio.h >

_IONBF is a macro defined in the header **stdio.h**. When used with the function **setvbuf**, it indicates that the stream being manipulated is to be unbuffered.

Cross-references
Standard, §4.9.1, §4.9.9.6
The C Programming Language, ed. 2, p. 243

See Also
buffer, _IOFBF, _IOLBF, setbuf, setvbuf, STDIO, stdio.h

{} — Punctuator
(Language/lexical elements/punctuators)

The punctuators {}, or "braces", are used to delimit a block, and to group initializers. Braces must be used in pairs.

Cross-reference
Standard, §3.1.6

See Also
block, initialization, punctuators

| — Operator
(Language/expressions/bitwise operators)
Bitwise inclusive OR operator
operand1 | operand2

The operator | performs an bitwise inclusive OR operation. It has the following syntax:

> *exclusive-OR-operation:*
>> *exclusive-OR-expression*
>> *inclusive-OR-expression | exclusive-OR-expression*

Each operand must have integral type; each undergoes the usual arithmetic conversions. The result has integral type.

A bitwise inclusive OR operation compares the bit patterns of the operands. It then sets each bit in the result if either, or both, of the corresponding bits in each of the operands is set.

For example, consider an environment which uses extended ASCII. Here, the character **9** is represented by the bit pattern

```
0011 1001
```

and the character **w** by the bit pattern:

```
0111 0111
```

Thus, the operation:

```
'9' | 'w'
```

yields the following bit pattern:

```
0000 0000 0111 1111
```

The extra "nybbles" to the left are created by the promotion of the character constants to type **int**.

The bitwise inclusive OR operation is also called the "union" of two bitsets.

Example
For an example of using this operator in a program, see **bitwise operators**.

Cross-references
Standard, §3.3.12
The C Programming Language, ed. 2, pp. 48, 207

|= — Operator
(Language/expressions/)
Bitwise inclusive-OR assignment operator
operand1 |= *operand2*

The operator |= performs a bitwise inclusive OR operation on *operand1* and *operand2*, and assigns the result to *operand1*. It is equivalent to the expression

```
operand1 = operand1 | operand2
```

Both operands must have integral type.

Cross-references
Standard, §3.3.16.2
The C Programming Language, ed. 2, pp. 50, 208

See Also
|, **assignment operators**

|| — Operator
(Language/expressions/logical operators)
Logical OR operator
operand1 || *operand2*

The operator || performs a logical OR operation. Both *operand1* and *operand2* must have scalar type. Its syntax is as follows:

logical-OR-expression:
    logical-AND-expression
    logical-OR-expression | | *logical-AND-expression*

The result of the || operation has type **int**. The value of the result is one if either operand is true (nonzero); if both operands are false (equal to zero), the result has a value of zero.

The operands are evaluated from left to right. If *operand1* is true, then *operand2* is not evaluated. If *operand2* is an expression that yields a side-effect, the results of the || operation may not be what you expect: if *operand1* is true, *operand2* is not evaluated and its side-effect not generated.

Cross-references
Standard, §3.3.14
The C Programming Language, ed. 2, p. 208

See Also
&&, logical operators

~ — Operator
(Language/expressions/unary operators)
Bitwise complement operator
~operand

The operator ~ is the bitwise complement operator. Its operand has an integral type, which undergoes integral promotion. The result is an object whose type is that of the promoted operand and whose bit pattern inverts that of the operand. This is also called a "one's complement operation".

For example, consider the object:

```
char example = 'a';
```

In an environment that uses extended ASCII, **example** will have the following bit pattern:

```
0110 0001
```

Thus, the expression ~**example** promotes **example** to an **int**, and then generates an object with the following bit pattern:

```
1111 1111 1001 1110
```

As can be seen, the lower eight bits have been flipped. The eight bits on the left were added when the object was promoted to **int**. These new bits were initially set to zeroes when the character was promoted to an **int**, then the complement operation flipped the zeroes to ones. In this case, the sign bit is said to *propagate*.

Example
For an example of using this operator in a program, see **bitwise operators**.

Cross-references
Standard, §3.3.3.3
The C Programming Language, ed. 2, p. 204

See Also
!, bitwise operators, integral promotion, unary operators

A

abort() — Library function
(Library/general utilities/environment communication)
End program immediately
void abort(void)

abort terminates a program's execution immediately. It is used to "bail out" of a program when a severe, unrecoverable problem occurs. It does not return.

The implementation defines whether **abort** cleans up a program by flushing buffers or closing streams.

abort may call the signal handler established for the signal **SIGABRT**, if present, as if the call

```
raise(SIGABRT);
```

had been invoked. This handler will indicate to the environment that the program has terminated unsuccessfully.

Example
This example simply aborts itself. For an example that uses **abort** in a more realistic manner, see **signal**.

```
#include <stdlib.h>
#include <stdio.h>

main(void)
{
    puts("...Dave ... I can feel my memory going ...");
    abort();
}
```

Cross-references
Standard, §4.10.4.1
The C Programming Language, ed. 2, p. 252

See Also
atexit, environment communication, exit, getenv, program termination, system

Notes
Some implementations of **abort**, specifically the one included with UNIX system V, permit it to return. The Standard forbids **abort** to return.

abs() — Library function
(Library/general utilities/integer arithmetic)
Compute the absolute value of an integer
#include < stdlib.h >
int abs(int *n*);

abs returns the absolute value of integer *n*. The *absolute value* of a number is its distance from zero. This is *n* if *n* > = **0**, and -*n* otherwise.

Example
This example checks whether **abs** is defined for all values on your implementation.

```
#include <limits.h>
#include <stdio.h>
#include <stdlib.h>

main(void)
{
    if(INT_MAX != abs(INT_MIN))
        printf("abs of %d is undefined\n", INT_MIN);
    return(EXIT_SUCCESS);
}
```

Cross-reference
Standard, §4.10.6.1
The C Programming Language, ed. 2, p. 253

See Also
div, integer arithmetic, labs, ldiv

Notes
On two's complement machines, the absolute value of the most negative number may not be representable.

In some implementations, **abs** is declared in the header **math.h**. The Standard moved this function to **stdlib.h** on the grounds that it does not return **double**. This change may require that some existing code be altered.

acos() — Library function
(Library/mathematics/trigonometric functions)
Calculate inverse cosine
#include < math.h >
double acos(double *arg*);

acos calculates the inverse cosine of *arg*, which should be in the range of from -1.0 to 1.0. Any other argument will trigger a domain error.

acos returns the result, which is in the range of from zero to π radians.

Cross-references
Standard, §4.5.2.1
The C Programming Language, ed. 2, p. 251

See Also
asin, atan, atan2, cos, sin, tan, trigonometric functions

additive operators — Overview
(Language/expressions)

C has two additive operators: + and -. The former adds two operands together; the latter subtracts its right operand from its left operand.

Cross-references
Standard, §3.3.6
The C Programming Language, ed. 2, p. 205

See Also
+, -, expressions

address — Definition
(Definitions)

An *address* designates a location in memory.

Example
The following prints the address and contents of a given byte of memory.

```
#include <stdio.h>
main()
{
    char byte = 'a';
    printf("Address==%p  Contents==\"%c\"\n",
        &byte, byte);
}
```

Cross-reference
The C Programming Language, ed. 2, p. 94

See Also
&, Definitions, pointer

aggregate types — Definition
(Language/lexical elements/identifiers/types)

The term *aggregate type* refers to arrays and structure types, which are aggregates of individual members.

Cross-reference
Standard, §3.1.2.5

See Also
array types, struct, types

alias — Definition
(Definitions)

An *alias* for an object is alternative way to access that object.

Because C uses pointers, it can be impossible for the translator to keep track of all possible aliases for an object. Often, the translator must use "worst-case aliasing assumptions" when memory is read; these assumption are explained below.

The Standard refers to aliasing in two places. The first is in the introduction to the section on expressions (3.3). Here, the translator is allowed to assume that the only way to reference a given object is by an object of the same type, a pointer to an object of that type, or by a character pointer. Type qualifiers and sign do not count in this situation. The reason a character pointer is assumed to point to any type of object is one of historical practice.

By making use of this information concerning types, a translator is said to make more favorable aliasing assumptions, and produce better code. For example, consider the following code fragment:

```
fn(int *ip, float *fp)
{
    int i;
    float f;
```

```
ip = &i;   /* line 1 */
*fp = f;   /* line 2 */
}
```

Normally in an assignment to a dereferenced pointer (line 2), the translator must assume that such a statement can overwrite the values of all global variables and the values of all local variables that have had their addresses taken.

Because **fp** is a pointer to **float**, the assignment to ***fp** need not invalidate the value of **i**. The translator must assume only that the current values of other **float**s may have been changed.

Any attempt to trick the translator, such as with a statement of the form

```
*fp = (float) i;
```

generates undefined behavior.

The second place in which the Standard refers to aliasing is with regard to the keyword **noalias**. Declaring an object to be **noalias** is a hint to the translator that this object has no aliases, not even of the same type. **noalias** also implies that this parameter does not overlap with any other parameters. See the article on **noalias** for more information.

See Also
Definitions, noalias, type qualifier

alignment — Definition
(Definitions)

The term *alignment* refers to the fact that some environments require the addresses of certain data types to be evenly divisible by a certain integer. Different processors have different alignment requirements. For example, the Motorola 68000 requires that every **int** have an address that is even (i.e., that is evenly divisible by two). The translator must ensure that data objects are aligned properly so that fetches to memory will be performed efficiently and on the correct data types.

The environment may require that empty bytes of "padding" be inserted into structures to ensure that every type is aligned properly. For example, on the M68000 the following structure

```
struct example {
    char member1;
    int member2;
};
```

will actually consist of four bytes: one byte to hold the **char**, two bytes to hold the **int**, and between them, one byte of padding to ensure that the **int** is aligned properly. Often, the alignment of a **struct** member will be the maximum alignment required to align any of its members' data types.

Because different environments require different forms of alignment, a program that is intended to be portable should not assume that the members of a structure abut each other.

An object of type **char *** has the least strict alignment.

Cross-references
Standard, §1.6
The C Programming Language, ed. 2, p. 185

See Also
char, Definitions, struct

argc — Definition
(Environment/execution environment/hosted environment)

argc is the conventional name for the first argument to the function **main**. It is of type **int**. It gives the number of strings in the array pointed to by **argv**, which is the second argument to **main**.

By definition, the value of **argc** is never negative.

Cross-references
Standard, §2.1.2.2
The C Programming Language, ed. 2, p. 114

See Also
argv, execution environment, hosted environment, main

Notes
In most UNIX implementations, **argc** will be at least one.

argument — Definition
(Definitions)

An *argument* is an expression that appears between the parentheses of a function call or invocation of a function-like macro. Multiple arguments are separated by commas. For example, the following function call

```
example(arg1, arg2, arg3);
```
has three arguments.

Cross-references
Standard, §1.6
The C Programming Language, ed. 2, p. 201

See Also
conversions, Definitions, parameter

Notes
The Standard uses the term "argument" when it refers to the actual arguments of a function call or macro invocation. It uses the term "parameter" to refer to the formal parameters given in the definition of the function or macro.

argv — Definition
(Environment/execution environment/hosted environment)
char *argv[];

argv is the conventional name for the second argument to the function **main**. It points to an array of pointers to type **char**. The strings to which **argv** points are passed by the host environment. Each may change the behavior of the program, and each may be modified by the program. Thus, the strings are called *program parameters*.

The number of pointers in the **argv** array is given by **argc**, which is the first argument to **main**. By definition, **argv[0]** always points to the name of the program; if the name is not available from the environment, then ***argv[0]** must be a null character. **argv[1]** through **argv[argc-1]** point to the set of program parameters; **argv[argc]** must be a null pointer.

Cross-references
Standard, §2.1.2.2
The C Programming Language, ed. 2, p. 114

See Also
argc, execution environment, hosted environment, main

Notes
The pointers in the **argv** array are usually passed on the command-line that invokes the program. Environments in which programs are represented by visual icons selected by a mouse may have other mechanisms for passing "command-line" parameters.

arithmetic types — Definition
(Language/lexical elements/identifiers/types)

The set of *arithmetic types* includes all integral and floating types. The former consists of all integer types, **char**, and enumerated types; the latter consists of the types **float**, **double**, and **long double**. The arithmetic types can be used with arithmetic operators to form arithmetic expressions.

Cross-references
Standard, §3.1.2.5
The C Programming Language, ed. 2, p. 196

See Also
types

array declarators — Definition
(Language/declarations/declarators)

An *array declarator* declares an array. It can also establish the size of the array and cause storage to be allocated for it. Its syntax is as follows; *opt* indicates *optional.*

> *array-declarator* [*constant-expression*$_{opt}$]

For example, consider the declaration:

```
int example[10];
```

The brackets '[ ]' establish that **example** is an array; the constant **10** establishes that **example** has ten elements. Thus, **example** is established to be an array of ten **ints**; memory is reserved for the ten members.

The constant expression that sets the size of an array must be an integral constant greater than zero. It must be known by translation phase 7 so the appropriate amount of storage can be allocated.

An array declarator may be empty; for example:

```
int example[];
```

In this case, **example** is an incomplete type. It will be completed when it is initialized.

Cross-references
Standard, §3.5.4.2
The C Programming Language, ed. 2, p. 216

See Also

[], declarators, initialization

Notes

For two array types to be compatible, the type of element in each, the number of dimensions in each, and the size of each corresponding dimension (except the first) must be identical.

array types — Definition
(Language/lexical elements/identifiers/types)

An *array type* is a set of objects, all of which have the same type and which are stored contiguously within memory. The type of the elements is called the *element type*.

For example, **int array[32]** it is an array with an element type of **int** and 32 elements. The array is called an "array of **int**".

An incomplete array type is an array whose size is not yet known.

An array with more than one dimension is called a *multidimensional array*. Such an array is stored in row-major order, unlike an array in FORTRAN, which stores multidimensional arrays in column-major order.

Cross-reference

Standard, §3.1.2.5

See Also

[], array declarators, types

ASCII — Definition
(Definitions)

ASCII is an acronym for the American Standard Code for Information Interchange. It is a table of seven-bit binary numbers that encode the letters of the alphabet, numerals, punctuation, and the most commonly used control sequences for printers and terminals.

The extended ASCII character set defines eight-bit encodings. The lower 127 characters are those of standard ASCII, and the higher 127 characters are also defined.

The Standard has purposely *not* specified the character encoding required by an implementation. Though other language standards have been described purely in terms of ASCII, C has been implemented in enough non-ASCII environments that it would have been overly constraining to describe C in ASCII.

Though the standard ASCII character set is used commonly throughout the United States, other countries use the ISO 646 character set, which is an invariant subset of standard ASCII. See the entry on **trigraphs** for a discussion of the representing C characters in environments in which not all of the 127 ASCII characters are available.

The following table gives the lower 127 ASCII characters in octal, decimal, and hexadecimal numbers.

000	0	0x00	NUL	< **ctrl-@** >	Null character
001	1	0x01	SOH	< **ctrl-A** >	Start of header
002	2	0x02	STX	< **ctrl-B** >	Start of text
003	3	0x03	ETX	< **ctrl-C** >	End of text
004	4	0x04	EOT	< **ctrl-D** >	End of transmission
005	5	0x05	ENQ	< **ctrl-E** >	Enquiry
006	6	0x06	ACK	< **ctrl-F** >	Positive acknowledgement
007	7	0x07	BEL	< **ctrl-G** >	Alert
010	8	0x08	BS	< **ctrl-H** >	Backspace
011	9	0x09	HT	< **ctrl-I** >	Horizontal tab
012	10	0x0A	LF	< **ctrl-J** >	Line feed
013	11	0x0B	VT	< **ctrl-K** >	Vertical tab
014	12	0x0C	FF	< **ctrl-L** >	Form feed
015	13	0x0D	CR	< **ctrl-M** >	Carriage return
016	14	0x0E	SO	< **ctrl-N** >	Shift out
017	15	0x0F	SI	< **ctrl-O** >	Shift in
020	16	0x10	DLE	< **ctrl-P** >	Data link escape
021	17	0x11	DC1	< **ctrl-Q** >	Device control 1 (XON)
022	18	0x12	DC2	< **ctrl-R** >	Device control 2 (tape on)
023	19	0x13	DC3	< **ctrl-S** >	Device control 3 (XOFF)
024	20	0x14	DC4	< **ctrl-T** >	Device control 4 (tape off)
025	21	0x15	NAK	< **ctrl-U** >	Negative acknowledgement
026	22	0x16	SYN	< **ctrl-V** >	Synchronize
027	23	0x17	ETB	< **ctrl-W** >	End of transmission block
030	24	0x18	CAN	< **ctrl-X** >	Cancel
031	25	0x19	EM	< **ctrl-Y** >	End of medium
032	26	0x1A	SUB	< **ctrl-Z** >	Substitute
033	27	0x1B	ESC	< **ctrl-[** >	Escape
034	28	0x1C	FS	< **ctrl-** >	Form separator
035	29	0x1D	GS	< **ctrl-]** >	Group separator
036	30	0x1E	RS	< **ctrl-^** >	Record separator
037	31	0x1F	US	< **ctrl-_** >	Unit separator
040	32	0x20	SP		Space
041	33	0x21	!		Exclamation point
042	34	0x22	"		Quotation mark
043	35	0x23	#		Pound sign (sharp)

044	36	0x24	$	Dollar sign
045	37	0x25	%	Percent sign
046	38	0x26	&	Ampersand
047	39	0x27	'	Apostrophe
050	40	0x28	(	Left parenthesis
051	41	0x29	)	Right parenthesis
052	42	0x2A	*	Asterisk
053	43	0x2B	+	Plus sign
054	44	0x2C	,	Comma
055	45	0x2D	-	Hyphen (minus sign)
056	46	0x2E	.	Period
057	47	0x2F	/	Virgule (slash)
060	48	0x30	0	
061	49	0x31	1	
062	50	0x32	2	
063	51	0x33	3	
064	52	0x34	4	
065	53	0x35	5	
066	54	0x36	6	
067	55	0x37	7	
070	56	0x38	8	
071	57	0x39	9	
072	58	0x3A	:	Colon
073	59	0x3B	;	Semicolon
074	60	0x3C	<	Less-than symbol (left angle bracket)
075	61	0x3D	=	Equal sign
076	62	0x3E	>	Greater-than symbol (right angle bracket)
077	63	0x3F	?	Question mark
0100	64	0x40	@	At sign
0101	65	0x41	A	
0102	66	0x42	B	
0103	67	0x43	C	
0104	68	0x44	D	
0105	69	0x45	E	
0106	70	0x46	F	
0107	71	0x47	G	
0110	72	0x48	H	
0111	73	0x49	I	
0112	74	0x4A	J	
0113	75	0x4B	K	
0114	76	0x4C	L	
0115	77	0x4D	M	
0116	78	0x4E	N	
0117	79	0x4F	O	
0120	80	0x50	P	
0121	81	0x51	Q	

0122	82	0x52	R	
0123	83	0x53	S	
0124	84	0x54	T	
0125	85	0x55	U	
0126	86	0x56	V	
0127	87	0x57	W	
0130	88	0x58	X	
0131	89	0x59	Y	
0132	90	0x5A	Z	
0133	91	0x5B	[	Left bracket (left square bracket)
0134	92	0x5C	\	Backslash
0135	93	0x5D	]	Right bracket (right square bracket)
0136	94	0x5E	^	Circumflex
0137	95	0x5F	_	Underscore (underbar)
0140	96	0x60	'	Grave
0141	97	0x61	a	
0142	98	0x62	b	
0143	99	0x63	c	
0144	100	0x64	d	
0145	101	0x65	e	
0146	102	0x66	f	
0147	103	0x67	g	
0150	104	0x68	h	
0151	105	0x69	i	
0152	106	0x6A	j	
0153	107	0x6B	k	
0154	108	0x6C	l	
0155	109	0x6D	m	
0156	110	0x6E	n	
0157	111	0x6F	o	
0160	112	0x70	p	
0161	113	0x71	q	
0162	114	0x72	r	
0163	115	0x73	s	
0164	116	0x74	t	
0165	117	0x75	u	
0166	118	0x76	v	
0167	119	0x77	w	
0170	120	0x78	x	
0171	121	0x79	y	
0172	122	0x7A	z	
0173	123	0x7B	{	Left brace (left curly bracket)
0174	124	0x7C	|	Vertical bar
0175	125	0x7D	}	Right brace (right curly bracket)
0176	126	0x7E	~	Tilde
0177	127	0x7F	DEL	Delete

See Also
Definitions, trigraph sequences

asctime() — Library function
(Library/date and time/time conversion)
Convert broken-down time to text
#include < time.h >
char *asctime(const struct tm **timestruct***);**

The function **asctime** converts the data pointed to by *timestruct* into a text string of the form:

```
Wed Dec 10 13:57:33 1987\n\0
```

The structure pointed to by *timestruct* must first be initialized by either the function **gmtime** or the function **localtime** before it can be used by **asctime**. See the entry for **tm** for further information on this structure.

asctime returns a pointer to the string it creates.

Example
This example uses **asctime** to display Universal Coordinated Time.

```
#include <time.h>
#include <stdio.h>
#include <stdlib.h>

main(void)
{
    printf(asctime(gmtime(NULL)));
    return(EXIT_SUCCESS);
}
```

Cross-references
Standard, §4.12.3.1
The C Programming Language, ed. 2, p. 256

See Also
ctime, gmtime, localtime, strftime, time conversion, time_t, tm

Notes
asctime writes its string into a static buffer that will be written by another call to either **asctime** or **ctime**.

The name "asctime" is short for "ASCII time"; its use, however, is not limited to implementations on ASCII systems.

The Standard describes the following algorithm with which **asctime** can generate its string:

```
char *
asctime(const struct tm *timeptr)
{
    static const char wday_name[7][3] = {
        "Sun", "Mon", "Tue", "Wed", "Thu", "Fri", "Sat"
    };
    static const char mon_name[12][3] = {
        "Jan", "Feb", "Mar", "Apr", "May", "Jun",
        "Jul", "Aug", "Sep", "Oct", "Nov", "Dec"
    };
    static char result[26];

    sprintf(result, "%.3s %.3s%3d %.2d:%.2d:%.2d %d\n",
        wday_name[timeptr->tm_wday],
        mon_name[timeptr->tm_mon],
        timeptr->tm_mday, timeptr->tm_hour,
        timeptr->tm_min, timeptr->tm_sec,
        1900 + timeptr->tm_year);

    return result;
}
```

as if rule — Definition
(Rationale)

The Standard's *as if rule* defines how implementors should treat some models and examples within the Standard. The Standard does *not* command implementors to implement all of its models and standards. Rather, implementors should write their implementations to bring about the same result, *as if* the model had been implemented directly.

For example, consider the following expression:

```
char c1, c2, c3;
c2 = c1 + c3;
```

The Standard states that such an expression must be performed *as if* **c1** and **c3** had been promoted to **int**s before performing the arithmetic. An implementation may do precisely that — promote the **char**s to **int**s before performing the arithmetic. An implementor, however, may choose not to promote the operands to **int**s if the same result is obtained. It is *as if* the operands were promoted and integer arithmetic performed, when in fact, the program was optimized by performing character arithmetic.

Cross-reference
Rationale, §2.1

See Also
Rationale

asin() — Library function
(Library/mathematics/trigonometric functions)
Calculate inverse sine
#include < math.h >
double asin(double *arg***);**

asin calculates the inverse sine of *arg*, which must be in the range of from -1.0 to 1.0; any other value will trigger a domain error.

asin returns the result, which is in the range $\pi/2$ to π.

Cross-references
Standard, §4.5.2.2
The C Programming Language, ed. 2, p. 251

See Also
acos, atan, atan2, cos, sin, tan, trigonometric functions

assert() — Macro
(Library/diagnostics)
Check assertion at run time
#include < assert.h >
void assert(int *expression***);**

assert checks the value of the given *expression*. If the *expression* is false (zero), **assert** prints a message into the standard error stream and calls **abort**. It is useful for verifying that a necessary condition is true.

The error message includes the text of the assertion that failed, the name of the source file, and the line within the source file that holds the expression in question. These last two elements consist, respectively, of the values of the preprocessor macros _ _FILE_ _ and _ _LINE_ _.

Because **assert** calls **abort**, it never returns.

To turn off **assert**, define the macro **NDEBUG** prior to including the header **assert.h**. This forces **assert** to be redefined as

```
#define assert(ignore)
```

Example

This program generates an error if your implementation does not conform to the Standard.

```
#include <assert.h>
#include <stdio.h>
#include <stdlib.h>

main(void)
{
#ifdef STDC
    assert(STDC);
#else
    fprintf(stderr, "Not ANSI C\n");
#endif
    return(EXIT_SUCCESS);
}
```

Cross-references

Standard, §4.2.1.1
The C Programming Language, ed. 2, p. 253

See Also

abort, assert.h, diagnostics, NDEBUG

Notes

The Standard requires that **assert** be implemented as a macro, not a library function. If a program suppresses the macro definition in favor of a function call, its behavior is undefined.

The Standard requires that **assert** handle integer expressions correctly. Some implementations may also evaluate scalar expressions, but this is not required.

Finally, note that turning off **assert** with the macro **NDEBUG** will affect the behavior of a program if the expression being evaluated normally generates side effects.

assert is useful for debugging, and for testing boundary conditions for which more graceful error recovery has not yet been implemented.

assert.h — Header
(Library/diagnostics)
Header for assertions
#include <assert.h>

assert.h is the header file that defines the macro **assert**.

Cross-references
Standard, §4.2
The C Programming Language, ed. 2, pp

See Also
assert, diagnostics, header, NDEBUG

assignment operators — Overview
(Language/expressions)

The C language comes equipped with the following assignment operators:

=	simple assignment
+ =	add and assign
- =	subtract and assign
* =	multiply and assign
/ =	divide and assign
% =	modulus and assign
& =	bitwise AND and assign
< < =	bitwise left shift and assign
> > =	bitwise right shift and assign
| =	bitwise inclusive OR and assign
^ =	bitwise exclusive OR and assign

They have the following syntax:

assignment-expression:
 conditional-expression
 unary-expression assignment-operator assignment-expression

assignment-operator: one of
 = += -= *= /= %= &= <<= >>= |= ^=

The assignment operator = simply copies the value of its right operand into its left operand. The other assignment operators perform an arithmetic or bitwise operation that involves both operands, and then assigns the result to the left operand. For this reason, they are called *compound assignment operators*. For example,

```
   a += b
```

is equivalent to:

```
   a = a+b
```

The left operand must be a modifiable lvalue. The types of the operands vary from operator to operator. See the entry for each for more information. The resultant type is the unqualified type of the left operand.

The other operators work in similar fashion with their respective operations.

Cross-references

Standard, §3.3.16
The C Programming Language, ed. 2, p. 50, 208

See Also

expressions, operators

Notes

The Standard states that the order of evaluation of operands is unspecified. Although it may seem logical that the right operand would be evaluated first and the result then stored into the left operand, this is not necessarily the case.

Obsolete assignment operators of the form = + are no longer recognized.

Each assignment operator is now described as one token. This means that the characters of an assignment operator can no longer be separated by white space.

atan() — Library function
(Library/mathematics/trigonometric functions)

Calculate inverse tangent
#include < math.h >
double atan(double *arg*);

atan calculates the inverse tangent of *arg*, which may be any real number.

atan returns the result, which is in the range of from $-\pi/2$ to $\pi/2$ radians.

Cross-references

Standard, §4.5.2.3
The C Programming Language, ed. 2, p. 251

See Also

acos, asin, atan2, cos, sin, tan, trigonometric functions

atan2() — Library function
(Library/mathematics/trigonometric functions)
Calculate inverse tangent
#include < math.h >
double atan2(double *num*, **double** *den*);

atan2 calculates the inverse tangent of the quotient of its arguments *num* and *den*. These may be any real number except zero.

atan2 returns the result, which is in the range of from -π to π. The sign of the return value is drawn from the signs of both arguments.

Cross-references
Standard, §4.5.2.4
The C Programming Language, ed. 2, p. 251

See Also
acos, asin, atan, cos, sin, tan, trigonometric functions

Notes
atan2 is provided in addition to **atan**, to compute arc tangents for numbers that yield very large results.

atexit() — Library function
(Library/general utilities/environment communication)
Register a function to be performed at exit
#include < stdlib.h >
int atexit(void (**function***)(void));**

atexit registers a function to be executed when the program exits. *function* points to the function to be executed. The registered function returns nothing. **atexit** provides a way to perform additional clean-up operations before a program terminates.

The functions that **atexit** registers are executed when the program exits normally, i.e., when the function **exit** is called or when **main** returns. The functions registered by **atexit** can perform clean-up is needed, beyond what is ordinarily performed when a program exits.

atexit returns zero if *function* could be registered, and nonzero if it could not.

Example

This example sets one function that displays messages when a program exits, and another that waits for the user to press a key before terminating.

```
#include <stdlib.h>
#include <stdio.h>

void
lastgasp(void)
{
    perror("Type return to continue");
}

void
get1(void)
{
    getchar();
}

main(void)
{
    /* set up get1() as last exit routine */
    atexit(get1);
    /* set up lastgasp() as exit routine */
    atexit(lastgasp);

    /* exit, which invokes exit routines */
    exit(EXIT_SUCCESS);
}
```

Cross-references

Standard, §4.10.4.2
The C Programming Language, ed. 2, p. 253

See Also

environment communication, exit

Notes

atexit must be able to register at least 32 functions.

Functions registered by **atexit** are executed when **exit** is called. They are executed in *reverse* order of registration.

atof() — Library function
(Library/general utility/string conversion)
Convert string to floating-point number
#include <stdlib.h>
double atof(const char *_string_);

atof converts the string pointed to by _string_ into a double-precision floating point number, and returns the number it has built. It is equivalent to the call

```
strtod(string, (char **)NULL);
```

string must point to the text representation of a floating-point number. It can contain a leading sign, any number of decimal digits, and a decimal point. It can be terminated with an exponent, which consists of the letters 'e' or 'E' followed by an optional leading sign and any number of decimal digits. For example,

```
1.23
123e-2
123E-2
```

are strings that can be converted by **atof**.

atof ignores leading blanks and tabs; it stops scanning when it encounters any unrecognized character.

Cross-references
Standard, §4.10.1.1
The C Programming Language, ed. 2, p. 251

See Also
atoi, atol, string conversion, strtod, strtol, strtoul

Notes
The character that **atof** recognizes as representing the decimal point depends upon the program's locale, as set by the function **setlocale**. See **localization** for more information.

The functionality of **atof** has largely been subsumed by the function **strtod**, but the Standard includes it because it is used so widely in existing code.

atoi() — Library function
(Library/general utilities/string conversion)
Convert string to integer
#include <stdlib.h>
int atoi(const char *_string_);

78 atol()

atoi converts the string pointed to by *string* into an integer. It is equivalent to the call

```
(int)strtol(string, (char **)NULL, 10);
```

The string pointed to by *string* may contain a leading sign and any number of numerals. **atoi** ignores all leading white space. It stops scanning when it encounters any non-numeral other than the leading sign character and returns the **int** it has built.

Cross-references
Standard, §4.10.1.2
The C Programming Language, ed. 2, p. 251

See Also
atof, atol, string conversion, strtod, strtol, strtoul

Notes
The functionality of **atoi** has largely been subsumed by the function **strtol**, but the Standard includes it because it is used so widely in existing code.

atol() — Library function
(Library/general utility/string conversion)
Convert string to long integer
#include <stdlib.h>
long atol(const char **string***);**

atol converts the string pointed to by *string* to a **long**. It is equivalent to the call

```
strtol(string, (char **)NULL, 10);
```

The string pointed to by *string* may contain a leading sign and any number of numerals. **atol** ignores all leading white space. It stops scanning when it encounters any non-numeral other than the leading sign and returns the **long** it has built.

Cross-references
Standard, §4.10.1.3
The C Programming Language, ed. 2, p. 251

See Also
atof, atol, string conversion, strtod, strtol, strtoul

Notes

The functionality of **atol** has largely been subsumed by the function **strtol**, but the Standard includes it because it is used so widely in existing code.

auto — C keyword
(Language/declarations/storage-class specifiers)
Automatic storage duration
auto *type identifier*

The storage-class specifier **auto** declares that *identifier* has automatic storage duration.

Cross-references

Standard, §3.5.1
The C Programming Language, ed. 2, p. 210

See Also

storage-class specifiers, storage duration

B

basic types — Definition
(Language/lexical elements/identifiers/types)

The *basic types* are the integer and floating types. These are the types that C defines, and they are all scalar rather than aggregate. All other types are constructed from the basic types.

Cross-references
Standard, §3.1.2.5
The C Programming Language, ed. 2, p. 195

See Also
floating types, integer types, types

behavior — Definition
(Definitions)

The term *behavior* refers to the way an implementation reacts to a given construct. When a construct conforms to the descriptions within the Standard, then its behavior should be predictable from the Standard's descriptions alone. When a construct does not conform to the descriptions within the Standard, then one of the following four types of abnormal behavior results:

Unspecified behavior
This is behavior produced by a correct construct for which the Standard supplies no description. An example is the order in which a program evaluates the arguments to a function.

Undefined behavior
This is behavior produced by an erroneous construct for which the Standard supplies no description. An example of a construct that generates undefined behavior is attempting to divide by zero.

The Standard does not mandate how a conforming implementation reacts when it detects a construct that will produce undefined behavior: it may pass over it in silence, with unpredictable (and usually unwelcome) results; generate a diagnostic message and continue to translate or execute; or stop translation or execution and produce a diagnostic message.

A portable program, however, should not depend upon undefined behavior performing in any predictable way. Undefined behavior is precisely that: undefined. Whatever happens, happens — from printing an error message to reformatting your hard disk.

Implementation-defined behavior
> This is behavior produced by a correct construct that is specific to a given implementation. An example is the number of **register** objects that can actually be loaded into machine registers. The Standard requires that the implementation document all such behaviors.

Locale-specific behavior
> This is behavior that depends upon the program's locale. An example is the character that the function **atof** recognizes as marking a decimal point. The Standard requires that an implementation document all such behaviors.

Cross-reference
Standard, §1.6

See Also
compliance, Definitions

Notes
For a program to be maximally portable, it should not rely on any of the above deviants of behavior.

bit — Definition
(Definitions)

The term *bit* is an abbreviation for *binary digit*. It is the element of storage that can hold either of exactly two values. A contiguous sequence of bits forms a byte; a byte consists of at least eight bits. The macro **CHAR_BIT** specifies the number of bits that constitute a byte for the execution environment.

On most machines a bit cannot be addressed directly; a byte is the smallest unit of storage that can be addressed.

Cross-reference
Standard, §1.6

See Also
Definitions, bit-field, bitwise operations, byte

bit-fields — Definition
(Language/declarations)

A *bit-field* is a member of a structure or **union** that is defined to be a cluster of bits. It provides a way to represent data compactly. For example, in the following structure

```
struct example {
     int member1;
     long member2;
     unsigned int member3 :5;
}
```

member3 is declared to be a bit-field that consists of five bits. A colon ':' precedes the integral constant that indicates the *width*, or the number of bits in the bit-field. Also, the bit-field declarator must include a type, which must be one of **int**, **signed int**, or **unsigned int**. If a bit-field is declared to be in type **int**, the implementation defines whether the highest bit is used to hold the bit-field's sign.

The Standard states, "An implementation may allocate any addressable storage unit large enough to hold a bit-field." This suggests that if a bit-field is defined as holding more bits than are normally held by an **int**, then the implementation may place the bit-field into a larger data object, such as a **long**.

If two bit-fields are declared side-by-side and together are small enough to fit into an **int**, then they must be packed together. However, if together they are too large to fit into an **int**, then the implementation determines whether they are in separate objects or if the second bit-field is partly within the object that holds the first and partly within a second object.

The implementation also defines where the bit-field resides within its object — whether it is built from the low-order bit up, or from the high-order bit down. For example, consider an implementation in which an **int** has 16 bits. If a five-bit bit-field is declared to be part of an **int**, and that bit-field is initialized to all ones, then the **int** may appear like this under one implementation:

```
0000 0000 0001 1111/* low-order bits set */
```

and like this under another:

```
1111 1000 0000 0000/* high-order bits set */
```

A bit-field that is not given a name may not be accessed. Such an object is useful as "padding" within an object so that it conforms to a template designed elsewhere.

A bit-field that is unnamed and has a length of zero can be used to force adjacent bit-fields into separate objects. For example, in the following structure

```
struct example {
     int member1;
     int member2 :5;
     int :0;
     int member3 :5;
};
```

the zero-length bit-field forces **member2** and **member3** to be written into separate objects, regardless of the default behavior of the implementation.

Finally, it is not allowed to take the address of a bit-field.

Cross-references
Standard, §3.5.2.1
The C Programming Language, ed. 2, pp

See Also
declarations, structure, union

Notes
Because bit-fields have many implementation-specific properties, they are not considered to be highly portable. In addition, bit-fields use minimal amounts of storage, but the amount of computation needed to manipulate and access them may negate this benefit. Bit-fields must be kept in integral-sized objects because many machines cannot access a quantity of storage smaller than a "word" (a word is generally used to store an **int**).

bitwise operators — Overview
(Language/expressions)

The C language describes five operators that perform bitwise operations; these are operations that manipulate the bits of operands. The operators are as follows:

&	Bitwise AND operation
<<	Bitwise left shift operation
>>	Bitwise right shift operation
|	Bitwise inclusive OR operation
^	Bitwise exclusive OR operation

The syntax for these operators is as follows:

AND-expression:
    equality-expression
    AND-expression & *equality-expression*

shift-expression:
    additive-expression
    shift-expression << *additive expression*
    shift-expression >> *additive expression*

inclusive-OR-expression:
    exclusive-OR-expression
    inclusive-OR-expression | *exclusive-OR-expression*

exclusive-OR-expression:
    AND-expression
    exclusive-OR-expression ^ *AND-expression*

All operands must have integral type, and each undergoes the usual arithmetic conversion before the operation is performed. In the case of the **&**, **|**, and ^ operators, the result has integral type; in the case of the **< <** and **> >** operators, the result has the type to which the left operand was promoted.

Example

The following example translates an integer into a string of zeroes and ones to display its bit pattern. It demonstrates most of the bitwise operators.

```
#include <limits.h>
#include <stdio.h>
#include <stdlib.h>

/* Turn an int into a string of zeroes and ones */
void
printbit(unsigned int number)
{
    unsigned int i;

    /* no. of bits in int for execution environment */
    unsigned int bits = sizeof(int)*CHAR_BIT;

    /* set rightmost bit in this variable */
    unsigned int checker = 1;

    /*
     * move bit all the way to left; do it this
     * way for portability
     */
    checker <<= bits-1;

    /* check if corresponding bit is set */
    for (i = 1; i <= bits; i++) {
        putchar((number & checker) ? '1' : '0');

        /* insert spaces between "nybbles" */
        if (i%4 == 0)
            putchar(' ');
        /* shift bit to right */
        checker >>= 1;
    }
```

```
      /* flush output buffer */
      putchar('\n');
}
main(int argc, char *argv[])
{
      int n1, n2;

      if (argc != 3) {
          fprintf(stderr, "Usage: example int1 int2\n");
          exit(EXIT_FAILURE);
      }

      n1 = atoi(argv[1]);
      n2 = atoi(argv[2]);

      printf("bit patterns for %d and %d:\n", n1, n2);
      printbit(n1);
      printbit(n2);

      printf("~%d:\n", n1);
      printbit(~n1);

      printf("~%d:\n", n2);
      printbit(~n2);

      printf("%d & %d:\n", n1, n2);
      printbit(n1 & n2);

      printf("%d | %d:\n", n1, n2);
      printbit(n1 | n2);

      printf("%d ^ %d:\n", n1, n2);
      printbit(n1 ^ n2);

      return(EXIT_SUCCESS);
}
```

Cross-references
Standard, §3.3.7
The C Programming Language, ed. 2, pp. 48, 205

See Also
&, < <, > >, |, ^, expressions

block — Definition
(Definitions)

A *block* is a set of statements that forms one syntactic unit. It can have its own declarations and initializations.

In C terminology, a block is marked off by braces '{ }'. Block-scoped variables are visible only in the block in which they are declared.

Cross-references
Standard, §3.6.2
The C Programming Language, ed. 2, p. 55

See Also
auto, compound statement, Definitions, scope

Notes
Another term for "block" is *compound statement*.

break — C keyword
(Language/statements/jump statements)
Exit unconditionally from loop or switch
break;

break is a statement that causes the program to exit immediately from the smallest enclosing **switch, while, for,** or **do** statement.

Example
For an example of this statement, see **printf**.

Cross-references
Standard, §3.6.6.3
The C Programming Language, ed. 2, p. 64

See Also
C keywords, continue, goto, jump statements, return

broken-down time — Definition
(Library/date and time)

The term *broken-down time* refers to time broken down into individual elements, such as seconds, minutes, hours, and day of the year. Broken-down time is stored in the structure **tm**.

The functions **localtime** and **gmtime** convert calendar time into broken-down time, and store what they create in **tm**.

The functions **strftime** and **ctime** convert calendar time into a string that can be printed and read by humans. **ctime** produces a standard UNIX-style string. **strftime**, however, generates a string using the conventions for the program's locale, as set by the function **setlocale**.

Finally, the function **mktime** converts broken-down time to calendar time.

Cross-references
Standard, §4.12
The C Programming Language, ed. 2, p. 255

See Also
calendar time, date and time, daylight savings time, local time, tm, universal coordinated time

bsearch() — Library function
(Library/general utilities/searching-sorting)
Search an array
#include <stdlib.h>
void *bsearch(const void *item, const void *array, size_t number,
    size_t size, int (*comparison)(const void *arg1, const char *arg2));

bsearch searches a sorted array for a given item.

item points to the object sought. *array* points to the base of the array; it has *number* elements, each of which is *size* bytes long. Its elements must be sorted into ascending order before it is searched by **bsearch**.

comparison points to the function that compares *item* with an element of *array*. *comparison* must return zero if its arguments match, a number greater than zero if the element pointed to by *arg1* is numerically greater than the element pointed to by *arg2*, and a number less than zero if the element pointed to by *arg1* is numerically less than the element pointed to by *arg2*.

bsearch returns a pointer to the array element that matches *item*. If no element matches *item*, then **bsearch** returns NULL. If more than one element within *array* matches *item*, which element is matched is unspecified.

Example
This example uses **bsearch** to translate English into "bureaucrat-ese".

```
#include <stdio.h>
#include <stdlib.h>
#include <string.h>
struct syntab {
     char *english, *bureaucratic;
} cdtab[] = {
/* The left column is in alphabetical order */

     "affect",      "impact",
     "after",       "subsequent to",
     "building",    "physical facility",
     "call",        "refer to as",
     "do",          "implement",

     "false",       "inoperative",
     "finish",      "finalize",
     "first",       "initial",
     "full",        "in-depth",
     "help",        "facilitate",

     "lie",         "inoperative statement",
     "order",       "prioritize",
     "talk",        "interpersonal communication",
     "then",        "at that point in time",
     "use",         "utilize"
};

int
comparator(key, item)
char *key;
struct syntab *item;
{
     return(strcmp(key, item->english));
}

main(void)
{
     struct syntab *ans;
     char buf[80];

     for(;;) {
          printf("Enter an English word: ");
          fflush(stdout);

          if(gets(buf) || !strcmp(buf, "quit") == NULL)
               break;
```

```
        if((ans = bsearch(buf, (void *)cdtab,
                sizeof(cdtab)/ sizeof(struct syntab),
                sizeof(struct syntab),
                comparator)) == NULL)
            printf("%s not found\n");
        else
            printf("Don't say \"%s\"; say \"%s\"!\n",
                ans->english, ans->bureaucratic);
    }

    return(EXIT_SUCCESS);
}
```

Cross-references

Standard, §4.10.5.1
The C Programming Language, ed. 2, p. 253

See Also

qsort, searching-sorting

Notes

The name **bsearch** implies that this function performs a binary search. A binary search looks at the midpoint of the array, and compares it with the element being sought. If that element matches, then the work is done. If it does not, then **bsearch** checks the midpoint of either the upper half of the array or of the lower half, depending upon whether the midpoint of the array is larger or smaller than the item being sought. **bsearch** bisects smaller and smaller regions of the array until it either finds a match or can bisect no further.

It is important that the data be sorted, or **bsearch** will return an indeterminate result.

buffer — Definition
(Library/STDIO)

A *buffer* is a region of memory that is associated with a stream. It holds data after they are read from the stream, or before they are written into it.

The term *buffering* refers to the way that a stream's buffer works. The Standard describes three types of buffering:

Full buffering
> Data are read from and written into the stream in buffer-sized chunks. Data are transferred either when needed or when the stream is explicitly flushed.

Line buffering
> Data are read from the stream when the buffer is empty. Data are written into the stream when the buffer becomes full, when a newline character is written, or when the buffer is explicitly flushed.

Unbuffered
> Data are transferred to or from the stream in the units that the program uses to read from or write into the stream.

The functions **fopen** and **freopen** establish a buffer for every stream they open. The default type of buffering is full buffering. The default size of the buffer is **BUFSIZ** characters. **BUFSIZ** is a macro that is defined in the header **stdio.h**, and is equal to at least 256.

The functions **setbuf** and **setvbuf** let you change the type of buffering used with a stream, change the size of a buffer, or redirect buffering into a buffer of your own creation.

Example
For an example of altering a buffer, see **setvbuf**.

Cross-references
Standard, §4.9.3, §4.9.5, §4.9.6

See Also
BUFSIZ, file, setbuf, setvbuf, STDIO, stdio.h, stream

BUFSIZ — Macro
(Library/STDIO)
Default size of buffer
#include < stdio.h >

BUFSIZ is a macro defined in the header **stdio.h**. It is used by the functions **fopen**, **freopen**, and **setbuf** to establish the default size of a stream's buffer. Whenever a stream is opened, a buffer of **BUFSIZ** bytes is automatically associated with it.

BUFSIZ cannot be less than 256.

Cross-references
Standard, §4.9.2, §4.9.5.3, §4.9.5.4, §4.9.5.5
The C Programming Language, ed. 2, p. 243

See Also
buffer, STDIO, stdio.h, stream

byte — Definition
(Definitions)

A *byte* is a contiguous set of at least eight bits. It is the unit of storage that is large enough to hold each character within the basic C character set. It is also the smallest unit of storage that a C program can address.

The least significant bit is called the *low-order bit*, and the most significant bit is the *high-order bit*.

In terms of C programming, a byte is synonymous with the data type **char**: a **char** is defined to be equal to one byte's worth of storage. The macro **CHAR_BIT** gives the number of bits in a byte for the execution environment.

Cross-reference
Standard, §1.6

See Also
bit, char, Definitions

C

calendar time — Definition
(Library/date and time)

The term *calendar time* refers to the time returned by function **time**. It represents the current time and date, as organized by the Gregorian calendar.

Calendar time is encoded in the data type **time_t**, which is returned by the function **time**. The Standard states only that **time_t** is an arithmetic type capable of representing time under the local environment. How calendar time is represented depends upon the environment or the implementation.

Calendar time can be converted by the functions **gmtime** or **localtime** into "broken-down time." This breaks out the individual elements of time, such as the year, month, day, hour, and minute.

The functions **strftime** and **ctime** convert calendar time into a string that can be printed and read by humans. **ctime** produces a standard UNIX-style string. **strftime**, however, generates a string using the conventions for the program's locale, as set by the function **setlocale**.

Finally, the function **mktime** converts broken-down time into calendar time.

Cross-reference
Standard, §4.12

See Also
broken-down time, date and time, local time, daylight savings time, time_t, universal coordinated time

calloc() — Library function
(Library/general utilities/memory management)
Allocate and clear dynamic memory
#include < stdlib.h >
void *calloc(size_t *count*, **size_t** *size*);

calloc allocates a portion of memory large enough to hold *count* items, each of which is *size* bytes long. It then initializes every byte within the portion to zero.

calloc returns a pointer to the portion allocated. The pointer is aligned for any type of object. If it cannot allocate the amount of memory requested, it returns NULL.

Example

For an example of this function, see **stdarg**.

Cross-references

Standard, §4.10.3.1
The C Programming Language, ed. 2, p. 167

See Also

alignment, free, malloc, memory management, realloc

Notes

If *count* or *size* is equal to zero, then the behavior of **calloc** is implementation defined: **calloc** returns either NULL or a unique pointer. This is a quiet change that may silently break some existing code.

case — C keyword
   (Language/statements/labelled statements)
   Mark entry in switch table
   case *expression*:

case is a label that introduces an entry within the body of a **switch** statement. The value of the **switch** statement's conditional expression is compared with the value of every **case** label's expression. When the two match, then the program jumps to the point marked by that **case** label and execution continues from there. Execution continues until a **break** statement is encountered.

Each **case** label must mark an expression whose value differs from those of every other **case** label for that **switch** statement. See **switch** for more information.

Example

For an example, see **printf**.

Cross-references

Standard, §3.6.1
The C Programming Language, ed. 2, p. 58

See Also

break, C keywords, default, labelled statements, switch

Notes

Every conforming implementation must be able to accept at least 257 **case** labels within a **switch** statement.

cast operators — Definition
(Language/expressions)
Convert the type of an expression
(*newtype*) *identifier* ;

A *cast operator* temporarily gives an operand a new type. *newtype* may have scalar type or type **void**; *identifier* must have scalar type.

The syntax of a cast operation is as follows:

> *cast-expression:*
>   *unary-expression*
>   (*type-name*) *cast-expression*

To indicate a cast operation, the name of the new type must be enclosed by the cast operator ().

An integral type can be cast to another integral type. For the rules that govern the behavior of such a cast, see **conversions**.

A pointer can also be cast to another type. The following rules govern the cast of a pointer:

- A pointer may be cast to an integral type. The size of the integer required to hold a pointer depends upon the implementation (and implicitly, upon the environment). If the pointer is not large enough to hold the value of the pointer, the behavior is undefined. Likewise, an integer may be cast to a pointer; this behavior, however, is implementation-defined.

- Assignment of a qualified pointer to an unqualified pointer results in undefined behavior.

- A pointer that points to an object or an incomplete type may be cast to a pointer to another object or incomplete type. Whether the cast pointer works correctly depends upon the alignment of the object to which it points: casting to an object with a stricter alignment may not work. **char** has the least strict alignment of all types. If a pointer is cast to point to an object with equal or less strict alignment, and then is re-cast to its original type, the re-cast pointer will compare equal to the original pointer.

- A pointer to a function of one type may be cast to a pointer to a function of another type. If it is re-cast to its original type, then the re-cast pointer will compare equal to the original pointer. However, if the pointer is cast to type other than the actual type of the function, and then is used to access the function, the behavior is undefined.

Cross-references
Standard, §3.3.4
The C Programming Language, ed. 2, pp. 45, 205

See Also
conversions, expressions, pointer

Notes
A cast expression is not an lvalue.

A cast expression may cause the translator to generate code to convert the given operand to the type specified in the cast.

With the Standard's introduction of **void *** as the "generic" pointer (which has strictest alignment of any type), pointers may be cast without harm from type **void *** to any other pointer type and back again.

ceil() — Library function
(Library/mathematics/integer-value-remainder)
Integral ceiling
#include < math.h >
double ceil(double z);

The function **ceil** returns the "ceiling" of a function, or the smallest integer less than z. For example, the ceiling of 23.2 is 23, and the ceiling of -23.2 is -23.

ceil returns the value expressed as a **double**.

Cross-references
Standard, §4.5.6.1
The C Programming Language, ed. 2, p. 251

See Also
fabs, floor, fmod, integer-value-remainder

char — C keyword
(Language/lexical elements/identifiers/types)

The data type **char** is the smallest addressable unit of data. It consists of one byte of storage, and it can encode all of the characters that can be used to write a C program. **sizeof(char)** returns one by definition, with all other data types defined as multiples thereof.

A **char** may be either signed or unsigned; this is up to the implementation. If a **char** holds any of the characters that make up the C character set, then it is positive. ANSI C allows the corresponding types **signed char** and **unsigned char**.

Programmers can create signed and unsigned versions of **char** where needed.

The range of values that can be encoded within a **char** are set by the macros **CHAR_MIN** and **CHAR_MAX**. These are defined in the header **limits.h**. The minimum values of these macros depend upon whether the implementation sign-extends a **char** when it is used in an expression. If the implementation does sign extend, then **CHAR_MIN** is equal to **SCHAR_MIN** (at least -127) and **CHAR_MAX** is equal to **SCHAR_MAX** (at least +127). If it does not sign extend, however, **CHAR_MIN** is equal to zero and **CHAR_MAX** is equal to **UCHAR_MAX** (at least +255).

Cross-references
Standard, §3.1.2.5
The C Programming Language, ed. 2, p. 211

See Also
signed char, types, unsigned char

CHAR_BIT — Macro
(Environment/environmental considerations/limits/numerical)

CHAR_BIT is a macro that is defined in the header **limits.h**. It gives the number of bits in the smallest possible data object (which is, by definition, a **char**). It must be at least eight.

Example
For an example of using this macro in a program, see **rand**.

Cross-references
Standard, §2.2.4.2
The C Programming Language, ed. 2, p. 257

See Also
limits.h, numerical limits

CHAR_MAX — Macro
(Environment/environmental considerations/limits/numerical)

CHAR_MAX is a macro that is defined in the header **limits.h**. It gives the largest value that can be held in an object of type **char**. If the implementation defines **char** as being signed by default, then **CHAR_MAX** is equal to **SCHAR_MAX**; otherwise, it is defined to be equal to **UCHAR_MAX**.

Cross-references
Standard, §2.2.4.2
The C Programming Language, ed. 2, p. 257

See Also
limits.h, numerical limits

CHAR_MIN — Macro
(Environment/environmental considerations/limits/numerical)

CHAR_MIN is a macro that is defined in the header **limits.h**. It gives the smallest value that can be held by an object of type **char**. If the implementation defines **char** as being signed by default, then **CHAR_MIN** is equal to **SCHAR_MIN**; otherwise, it defined to be zero.

Cross-references
Standard, §2.2.4.2
The C Programming Language, ed. 2, p. 257

See Also
limits.h, numerical limits

character-case mapping — Overview
(Library/character handling)
#include <ctype.h>

The Standard's list of character-handling functions includes two that change the case of alphabetic characters, as follows:

tolower   Convert character to lower case
toupper   Convert character to upper case

The Standard defines upper-case characters as being those for which the function **isupper** returns true. Likewise, lower-case characters are those for which the function **islower** returns true. The action of these functions is affected by the program's locale, for a locale may force a program to use a non-ASCII character set, or even force it to use a character set that does not distinguish between upper and lower case. For more information about setting a locale, see **localization**.

Example
This example demonstrates **tolower** and **toupper** by reading a file and reversing the case of all of its characters.

```
#include <stddef.h>
#include <stdio.h>
#include <stdlib.h>
#include <string.h>

void
fatal(const char *message)
{
    fprintf(stderr, "%s\n", message);
    exit(EXIT_FAILURE);
}

main(int argc, char *argv[])
{
    FILE *fp;
    int ch;

    /* check number of arguments */
    if (argc != 2)
        fatal("usage: example filename");

    /* open file */
    if((fp = fopen(argv[1], "r")) == NULL)
        fatal("cannot open text file");

    /* read file, convert characters, print them */
    while ((ch = fgetc(fp)) != EOF)
        putchar(isupper(ch) ? tolower(ch) : toupper(ch));
    return(EXIT_SUCCESS);
}
```

Cross-references
Standard, §4.3.2
The C Programming Language, ed. 2, p. 249

See Also
character handling, character testing

character constant — Definition
(Language/lexical elements/constants)

A *character constant* is a constant that encodes a character or escape sequence. Its syntax is as follows:

character-constant:
   'c-char-sequence'
   'char-sequence'

c-char-sequence:
   c-char
   c-char-sequence c-char

c-char:
      any character in the source character set except the
          apostrophe, the backslash, or the newline
      escape-sequence

escape-sequence:
   simple-escape-sequence
   octal-escape-sequence
   hexadecimal-escape-sequence

simple-escape-sequence: one of
   \' \" \? \\
   \a \b \f \n \r \t \v

octal-escape-sequence:
   \ *octal-digit*
   \ *octal-digit octal-digit*
   \ *octal-digit octal-digit octal-digit*

hexadecimal-escape-sequence:
   \x *hexadecimal-digit*
   hexadecimal-escape-sequence hexadecimal-digit

A character constant consists of one or more characters or escape sequences that are enclosed within apostrophes ''. To include a literal apostrophe within a character constant, use the escape sequence \'.

A character is regarded as having type **char** as it is read, and it yields an object with type **int**. If a character constant contains one character or escape sequence, then the numeric value of that character is written into an **int**-length object. For example, under an implementation that uses ASCII, the character constant **'a'** yields an **int**-length object with the value of 0x61. If a character constant contains more than one character or escape sequence, the result is implementation-defined.

Because the constant being read is regarded as having type **char**, the value of a character constant can change from implementation to implementation, depending upon whether the implementation uses a signed or unsigned **char** by default. For example, in an environment in which a **char** has eight bits and uses two's-complement arithmetic, the character constant **'\xFF'** will yield an **int** with a value of either -1 or +255, depending upon whether a **char** is, respectively, signed or unsigned by default.

A *wide-character constant* is a character constant that is formed of a wide character instead of an ordinary, one-byte character. It is marked by the prefix 'L'. For example, in the following

    L'm' ;

stores the numeric value of 'm' in the form of a wide character.

Example
For an example of using character constants in a program, see **putchar**.

Cross-references
Standard, §3.1.3.4
The C Programming Language, ed. 2, p. 193

See Also
constants, escape sequences

Notes
Although octal escape sequences are limited to three octal digits, hexadecimal escape sequences can be arbitrary length. However, when the value of a hexadecimal escape sequence exceeds that which can be represented in an **int**, behavior is defined by the implementation.

character display semantics — Definition
(Environment/environmental considerations)

The Standard describes the semantics by which characters are displayed on an output device. The *active position* is where the output device will print the next character produced by the function **fputc**. On a video terminal, it usually is marked by a cursor. The locale defines the direction of printing, whether from left to right, from right to left, or from top to bottom.

The following escape sequences can be embedded within a string literal or character constant to affect the behavior of an output device:

\a   Generate an alert signal. The alert may take the form of ringing a bell or printing a visual signal on a screen.

\b   Backspace: move the active position back one position. If the active position is already at the beginning of the line, the behavior is undefined.

\f   Form feed: move the active position to the beginning of the next page. On a hard-copy printer, it feeds a fresh sheet of paper. On a video terminal, it may take the form of clearing the screen and moving the cursor to the "home" position.

\n Newline: move the active position to the beginning of the next line.

\r Return: move the active position to the beginning of the current line.

\t Horizontal tab: move the active position to the beginning of the next horizontal tabulation field. If the active position is already at or past the last horizontal tabulation field on the current line, the behavior is undefined.

\v Vertical tab: move the active position to the beginning of the next vertical tabulation field. If the active position is already at or past the last vertical tabulation field, the behavior is undefined.

Every implementation must define each of these escape sequences as being a unique value that can be stored in one **char** object.

Cross-reference
Standard, §2.2.2

See Also
character sets, environmental considerations, escape sequence, trigraph sequences

character handling — Overview
(Library)
#include <ctype.h>

The Standard's repertoire of library functions includes 13 that test or alter individual characters, as follows:

Character testing

isalnum	Check if a character is a numeral or letter
isalpha	Check if a character is a letter
iscntrl	Check if a character is a control character
isdigit	Check if a character is a numeral
isgraph	Check if a character is printable
islower	Check if a character is a lower-case letter
isprint	Check if a character is printable
ispunct	Check if a character is a punctuation mark
isspace	Check if a character is white space
isupper	Check if a character is a upper-case letter
isxdigit	Check if a character is a hexadecimal numeral

Case mapping

tolower	Convert character to lower case
toupper	Convert character to upper case

All are declared in the header **ctype.h**.

The Standard's descriptions of these functions are designed to remove any dependency upon ASCII. This allows these functions to be used in non-ASCII environments, e.g., on machines that use EBCDIC.

The operation of all character-handling functions (with the exception of **isdigit** and **isxdigit**) is modified by the program's locale, as set by the function **setlocale**. This allows these function to test and modify characters using a locale-specific character set. The calls

```
setlocale(LC_CTYPE, locale);
```

or

```
setlocale(LC_ALL, locale);
```

force these functions to use the locale-specific character set. See **localization** for more information.

Cross-references

Standard, §4.3
The C Programming Language, ed. 2, p. 248

See Also

character, testing, character-case mapping, Library

Notes

Although these functions are described as "character handling," they are defined as taking an argument of type **int** to allow them to accept the special value of **EOF** and locale-specific character sets.

character sets — Definition
(Environment/environmental considerations)

A C program uses two character sets: one for its translation and the other for execution. The Standard severs any dependency of C upon the ASCII character set. Therefore, a program should not depend upon characters being arranged in any special order.

The translation character set is the set of characters from which a C program may be written. It includes the following characters:

```
A    B    C    D    E    F    G    H    I
J    K    L    M    N    O    P    Q    R
S    T    U    V    W    X    Y    Z
```

a	b	c	d	e	f	g	h	i
j	k	l	m	n	o	p	q	r
s	t	u	v	w	x	y	z	

!	"	#	%	&	'	(	)	*
+	,	-	/	:	;	<	=	>
?	[	\	]	^	_	{	|	}
~								

In addition, the space character and characters for vertical tab, horizontal tab, newline, and form feed must be included. Any one of these special characters can be embedded within a character constant or a string literal by encoding it with an *escape sequence*. Each escape sequence begins with a backslash '\'; see **escape sequences** for a list of the available sequences.

Some of the C characters may be encoded using a *trigraph*. This allows a C program to be written on a host that uses the ISO 646 character set, which does not contain the full set of C characters.

Finally, characters that are outside the C character set may be embedded within string literals and character constants by using multibyte characters. See **multibyte characters** for more information.

The execution character set includes all characters that may be used during the execution of a program. This character set is defined by the implementation, and is set by the locale under which the program is executed. See **localization** for more information.

Cross-references
Standard, §2.2.1
The C Programming Language, ed. 2, p. 229

See Also
environmental considerations, escape sequences, localization, multibyte characters, trigraph sequences

character testing — Library function
(Library/character handling)
#include < ctype.h >

The Standard describes the following 11 functions that test characters:

isalnum	Check if a character is a numeral or letter
isalpha	Check if a character is a letter
iscntrl	Check if a character is a control character
isdigit	Check if a character is a numeral
isgraph	Check if a character is printable, except space

islower	Check if a character is a lower-case letter
isprint	Check if a character is printable, including space
ispunct	Check if a character is a punctuation mark
isspace	Check if a character is white space
isupper	Check if a character is a upper-case letter
isxdigit	Check if a character is a hexadecimal numeral

The actions of all of the above functions, with the exception of **isdigit** and **isxdigit**, are affected by the program's locale, as set by the function **setlocale**, because a given locale may use a non-ASCII character set. For more information on setting a locale, see **localization**.

Example

This example counts the types of characters in a text file.

```
#include <ctype.h>
#include <stddef.h>
#include <stdio.h>
#include <stdlib.h>

static long count[11];

main(int argc, char *argv[])
{
    register FILE *ifp;
    register c;

    if(argc != 2) {
        printf("usage: ctype filename");
        exit(EXIT_FAILURE);
    }

    if((ifp = fopen(argv[1], "rb")) == NULL) {
        printf("Can't open %s\n", argv[1]);
        exit(EXIT_FAILURE);
    }
```

```
while(EOF != (c = fgetc(ifp))) {
     count[0]  += isalnum(c);
     count[1]  += isalpha(c);
     count[2]  += iscntrl(c);
     count[3]  += isdigit(c);
     count[4]  += isgraph(c);
     count[5]  += islower(c);
     count[6]  += isprint(c);
     count[7]  += ispunct(c);
     count[8]  += isspace(c);
     count[9]  += isupper(c);
     count[10] += isxdigit(c);
}

printf("%ld are alpha or digit\n", count[0]);
printf("%ld are alpha\n", count[1]);
printf("%ld are control characters\n", count[2]);
printf("%ld are decimal digits\n", count[3]);
printf("%ld are printable, except space\n", count[4]);
printf("%ld are lower case letters\n", count[5]);
printf("%ld are printable, including space\n", count[6]);
printf("%ld are punctuation chars\n", count[7]);
printf("%ld are white space chars\n", count[8]);
printf("%ld are upper case letters\n", count[9]);
printf("%ld are hexadecimal digits\n", count[10]);

return(EXIT_SUCCESS);
}
```

Cross-references
Standard, §4.3.1
The C Programming Language, ed. 2, p. 249

See Also
character handling, case mapping

clearerr() — Library function
(Library/STDIO/error handling)
Clear a stream's error indicator
#include <stdio.h>
void clearerr(FILE *fp);

When a file is manipulated, a condition may occur that would cause trouble should the program continue to manipulate that file. This could be an error (e.g., a read error), or the program may have read to the end of the file. Most environments use two indicators to signal that such a condition has occurred: the *error indicator* and the *end-of-file* indicator.

When an error occurs, the error indicator is set to a value that indicates what error occurred. The end-of-file indicator is set when the end of a file is read. By checking these indicators, a program can see if all is going well. Under some implementations, a file may not be manipulated further until both indicators have been reset to their normal values.

clearerr resets to normal the error indicator and the end-of-file indicator for the stream pointed to by *fp* to permit further manipulation of the file.

Cross-references
Standard, §4.9.10.1
The C Programming Language, ed. 2, p. 248

See Also
error handling, feof, ferror, perror

Notes
These indicators are cleared when a file is opened or when the file-position indicator is reset by the function **rewind**. Successful calls to **fseek, fsetpos**, or **ungetc** clear the end-of-file indicator.

CLK_TCK — Macro
(Library/date and time)
#include < time.h >

CLK_TCK is a macro that is defined in the header **time.h**. It represents the number of "ticks" in a second. A "tick" is the unit of time measured by the function **clock**.

clock returns the type **clock_t**. To determine how many seconds a program required to run to the given point, divide the value returned by **clock** by the value of **CLK_TCK**.

Example
For an example of using this macro in a program, see **clock**.

Cross-references
Standard, §4.12.1
The C Programming Language, ed. 2, p. 255

See Also
clock, clock_t, date and time

clock() — Library function
(Library/date and time/time manipulation)
Get processor time used
#include <time.h>
clock_t clock(void);

clock calculates and returns the amount of processor time a program has taken to execute to the current point. Execution time is calculated from the time the program was invoked. This, in turn, is set as a point from the beginning of an era that is defined by the implementation. For example, under the COHERENT operating system, time is recorded as the number of milliseconds since January 1, 1970, 0h00m00s UTC.

The value **clock** returns is of type **clock_t**. This type is defined in the header **time.h**. The Standard defines it merely as being an arithmetic type capable of representing time. If **clock** cannot determine execution time, it returns -1 cast to **clock_t**.

To calculate the execution time in seconds, divide the value returned by **clock** by the value of the macro **CLK_TCK**, which is defined in the header **time.h**.

Example
This example measures the number of times a **for** loop can run in one second on your system. This is approximate because **CLK_TCK** can be a real number, and because the program probably will not start at an exact tick boundary.

```
#include <stdio.h>
#include <stdlib.h>
#include <time.h>

main(void)
{
    clock_t finish;
    long i;

    /* finish = about 1 second from now */
    finish = clock() + CLK_TCK;
    for(i = 0; finish > clock(); i++)
        ;

    printf("The for() loop ran %ld times in one second.\n", i);
    return(EXIT_SUCCESS);
}
```

Cross-references
Standard, §4.12.2.1
The C Programming Language, ed. 2, p. 255

See Also
CLK_TCK, clock_t, difftime, mktime, time, time manipulation

clock_t — Type
(Library/date and time)
System time
#include <time.h>

clock_t is a data type that is defined in the header **time.h**. It is an arithmetic type, and is the type returned by the function **clock**.

The unit that **clock_t** holds is implementation-defined. The macro **CLK_TCK** expands to a number that expresses how of many of these units constitute one second of real time.

Example
For an example of using this type in a program, see **clock**.

Cross-references
Standard, §4.12.1
The C Programming Language, ed. 2, p. 255

See Also
CLK_TCK, clock, date and time, time_t

close — Definition
(Library/STDIO)

To *close* a file means to dissociate it from the stream that controls it. Any buffers associated with the stream are flushed, to ensure that the file receives all data intended for it. When a file is closed, it can no longer be accessed by your C program. To regain access, you must open it again.

To close a file, use the function **fclose**.

Cross-references
Standard, §4.9.3
The C Programming Language, ed. 2, p. 241

See Also
buffer, fclose, file, freopen, open, STDIO, stdio.h, stream

command processor — Definition
(Library/general utilities)

The *command processor* is the part of an environment that interprets and executes user commands.

The function **system** provides a means to detect if an environment has a command processor and can send commands to the processor from within a C program.

Cross-reference
Standard, §4.10.4.5

See Also
environment communication, system

comment — Definition
(Language/lexical elements)

A *comment* is text that is embedded with a program but is ignored by the translator. It is intended to guide the reader of the code.

A comment is introduced by the characters /*. The only exceptions are when these characters appear within a string literal or a character constant. In these instances, the characters /* have no special significance. When /* is read, all text is ignored until the characters */ are read. Once a comment is opened, the translator does nothing with the text except scan it for multi-byte characters and for the characters */ that close the comment.

The translator replaces a comment with a single white-space character; this is done during phase 3 of translation.

Cross-references
Standard, §3.1.9
The C Programming Language, ed. 2, p. 192

See Also
/, /, lexical elements, translation phases

Notes
The Standard's definition of a comment does not allow comments to "nest." That is, you cannot have a comment within a comment. This may require that some code be revised. If you wish to exclude some code from translation temporarily, a

sounder practice is to use the preprocessing directives **#ifdef** and **#endif**. For example,

```
#ifdef DEBUG
    . . .
#endif
```

will include code only if **DEBUG** has been defined as being a macro.

It is possible to open a comment inadvertently. For example, the code

```
int *intptr, int1, int2;
    . . .
int2 = int1/*intptr;
```

inadvertently creates a comment symbol out of the division operator '/' and the pointer-dereference operator '*'. *Caveat utilitor.*

compatible types — Definition
(Language/declarations/type definitions)

To judge whether two types are compatible, several factors must be considered.

Scalar types

First, the base types must be identical. Second, all specifiers must match, except for signedness (i.e., it does not matter whether either or both are signed or unsigned). Third, all type qualifiers must match. There are special semantics to determine whether qualified objects are compatible to ensure that qualified types are not "hidden". See the entry **type qualifiers** for more information.

Structures

For two structures to be compatible, they must have the same "tagged type". For example, the structures

```
FILE struct1;
FILE struct2;
```

are compatible, because the tagged type of each is **FILE**. On the other hand, in the following code

```
struct s1 { int s1_i } s1;
struct s2 { int s2_i } s2;
```

the structures **s1** and **s2** are not compatible.

Pointers

For two pointers to be compatible, they must point to the same type of object. Other pointers may be compatible if they are suitably cast.

Cross-reference
Standard, §3.1.2.6, §3.5.2-4

See Also
type definitions, types

compile — Definition
(Definitions)

To *compile* a program means to translate it with a compiler. A compiler is a translator that takes a set of high-level source instructions (i.e., C code) and produces a set of machine instructions that implement the behavior that the source instructions describe.

See Also
Definitions, interpret, link

compliance — Definition
(Definitions)

Compliance refers to the degree to which a program and an implementation conform to the Standard's descriptions of the C language.

A *strictly conforming program* is one that uses only the features of the language and the library routines that are described within the Standard. It does not produce any behavior that is implementation defined, unspecified, or undefined. It does not exceed any minimum maximum set by the Standard. A strictly conforming program should be maximally portable to any environment for which a conforming implementation exists.

A *conforming program* is any program that can be translated by a conforming implementation. It may use library functions other than those described in the Standard, it may evoke non-Standard behavior, and it may use extensions to the language that are recognized by the implementation.

There are two varieties of *conforming implementation*: *conforming hosted implementation* and *conforming freestanding implementation*. A conforming hosted implementation is one that can translate any strictly conforming program. A conforming freestanding implementation is one that can translate any strictly conforming program whose use of macros and functions is restricted to those defined in the headers **float.h**, **limits.h**, **stdarg.h**, and **stddef.h**.

Every implementation must be accompanied by a document that describes all implementation-defined behavior, locale-specific behavior, and extensions to the language.

Cross-reference
Standard, §1.7

See Also
behavior, Definitions, limits

composite types — Definition
(Language/lexical elements/identifiers/types)

A *composite type* is any type that is constructed from two or more declarations. Each subsequent declaration of a composite type adds more information to it.

Composite types are constructed in only a few instances. One is when an incomplete array type is declared, followed by a later declaration that allocates storage for the array:

```
int array[];
      . . .
int array[] = { 3, 6, 9 };
```

Here, the composite type is an array type with three elements.

Another instance is when an old-style function declarator is followed by a prototype-style function declaration:

```
long newfunction();
long newfunction(int, long, char *);
```

The resulting composite type is the function declaration plus the list of prototype parameters. Hence, all calls to **newfunction** that are within the scope of this prototype declaration will be checked against this prototype.

Cross-reference
Standard, §3.1.2.5

See Also
types

compound statement — Definition
(Language/statements)

A *compound statement* is a cluster of statements that are handled as one syntactic unit. It may have its own declarations and initializations.

The syntax of a compound statement is as follows:

compound statement:
      { *declaration-list*$_{opt}$ *statement-list*$_{opt}$ }

declaration-list:
      declaration
      declaration-list declaration

statement-list:
      statement
      statement-list statement

Variables declared and initialized within a compound statement have automatic duration: that is, they disappear when the final '}' of the statement is read. These variables are evaluated and their values stored in the order in which they appear within the compound statement.

Cross-references
Standard, §3.6.2
The C Programming Language, ed. 2, p. 222

See Also
block, statements

Notes
Another name for a compound statement is *block.*

conditional inclusion — Overview
(Language/preprocessing)

The preprocessor can conditionally select lines of code from a source file. If you wish, you can construct a chain of directives to include and exclude exactly the material you want.

Conditional inclusion is introduced by one of the following three preprocessing directives: **#if**, **#ifdef**, or **#ifndef**. If the directive evaluates to true, then all lines of code that follow the directive are included within the program, up to the first succeeding **#elif**, **#else**, or **#endif** directive.

The expression that follows an **#if** or **#elif** directive is a *constant-expression*. It must be an integral expression, and it cannot include a **sizeof** operator, a cast, or an enumeration constant. All macro substitutions are performed upon the expression before it is evaluated. All integer constants are treated as long objects, and are then evaluated. If *constant-expression* includes character constants, all escape sequences are converted into characters before evaluation. It is up to the implementation whether the result of evaluating a character constant in *constant expression* matches the result of evaluating the same character constant in a C expression. For example, it is up to the implementation whether

```
#if 'z' - 'a' == 25
```

yields the same result as:

```
if ('z' - 'a' == 25)
```

The directives **#ifdef** and **#ifndef** are each followed by an *identifier*. Each directive checks to see if *identifier* has been defined as a macro. If it has been, then **#ifdef** includes the code that follows it, and **#ifndef** excludes it; whereas if *identifier* has *not* been defined as a macro, then **#ifdef** excludes the following code and **#ifndef** includes it.

The keyword **defined** can be used with the directive **#if** to mimic the function of **#ifdef**. For example, the directive

```
#if defined EXAMPLE
```

is identical to:

```
#ifdef EXAMPLE
```

#if, **#ifdef**, or **#ifndef** may be followed by one or more **#elif** directives. **#elif**, like **#if**, is governed by a *constant-expression*. The only difference is that an **#elif** directive is not evaluated unless the preceding **#if**, **#ifdef**, or **#ifndef** directive and all preceding **#elif** directives have evaluated as false.

The directive **#else** follows the **#if**, **#ifdef**, or **#ifndef** directive that introduces the conditional inclusion, as well as all succeeding **#elif** directives. It does not evaluate an expression. If all of the preceding directives evaluate as false, then the code that follows the **#else** directive is included, up to the **#endif** directive. If any of the preceding directives evaluate as true, however, then the **#else** directive's code is skipped. A chain of conditional directives can have only one **#else** directive.

Finally, the directive **#endif** marks the end of a chain of conditional-inclusion directives.

The preprocessor includes only the code from the first directive whose condition is true.

Cross-references
Standard, §3.8.1
The C Programming Language, ed. 2, p. 91

See Also
#elif, #else, #endif, #if, #ifdef, #ifndef, defined, preprocessing

const — C keyword
(Language/declarations/type qualifier)
Qualify an identifier as not modifiable

The type qualifier **const** marks an object as being unmodifiable. An object declared as being **const** cannot be used on the left side of an assignment, or have its value modified in any way. Because of these restrictions, an implementation may place objects declared to be **const** into a read-only region of storage.

Judicious use of **const** allows the translator to optimize more thoroughly, for it does not have to include code to check whether the object has been modified.

Most of the prototypes for library functions use **const** to mark identifiers that are not modified by the function.

Cross-references
Standard, §3.5.3
The C Programming Language, ed. 2, p. 40

See Also
noalias, type qualifier, volatile

constant expressions — Definition
(Language)

A *constant expression* is one that represents a constant. Constant expressions are required in a variety of situations: when the value of an enumeration constant is set; when the size of an array is declared; as a constant to be used in a **case** statement; or as the size of a bit-field declaration. Its syntax is as follows:

> *constant-expression:*
> *conditional-expression*

Every constant expression must return a value that is within the range representable by its type. No constant expression can contain assignment operators, increment or decrement operators, function calls, or the comma operator. The only exception is when it used as the operand to the operator **sizeof**.

The Standard describes the following varieties of constant expressions:

Address constant expression
> This type of constant is an expression that points to an object or a function. The operators [], *, &, ., and -> may be used to create an address constant, as may a pointer cast.

Arithmetic constant expression
> This type of constant has an arithmetic type, and is one the following:

- character constant

- enumeration constant

- floating constant

- integer constant

- **sizeof** expression

An arithmetic constant expression can be cast only to another arithmetic type, except when it is an operand to **sizeof**.

Integral constant expression
> This type of constant has integral type, and is one of the following:

- character constant

- enumeration constant

- a floating constant that is the immediate operand of a cast.

- integer constant

- **sizeof** constant

When a constant expression is used to initialize a static variable, it must resolve, when translated, into one of the following:

- An address constant.

- An address constant for an object type, plus or minus an integral constant expression.

- An arithmetic constant expression.

Initializers on local variables that are not declared **static** are not so restrictive.

Cross-references
Standard, §3.4
The C Programming Language, ed. 2, p. 38

See Also
constants, expressions, initializers, Language, void expression

Notes
Constant expressions can be combined when translated. The precision and accuracy of such translation-time evaluation must be at least those of the execution environment. This requirement was designed with cross-compilers in mind, where the execution environment might differ from translation environment.

A constant expression may be resolved into a constant by the translator. Therefore, it can be used in any circumstance that calls for a constant. For this reason, the Standard forbids the use in an **#if** statement in a constant expression that queries the run-time environment. A program that does include a **#if** statement that queries the environment will not run the same when translated by an ANSI-compatible translator.

constants — Overview
(Language/lexical elements)

A *constant* is a lexical element that represents a set numerical value. The four categories of constants are as follows:

character constants	a character constant or wide-character constant
enumeration constants	a constant used in an **enum**
floating constants	a floating-point number
integer constants	an integer

Each type is determined by the form of the token. For example,

    5L

defines a constant of type **long**, and

    5.03

is a floating-point constant.

Cross-references
Standard, §3.1.3
The C Programming Language, ed. 2, pp. 192*ff*

See Also
constant expressions, lexical elements

constraints — Definition
(Definitions)

A *constraint* is a restriction that the syntax and semantics of the language set upon the interpretation of the elements of the language. If a program violates a constraint, the translator must issue a diagnostic message.

Cross-reference
Standard, §1.6

See Also
Definitions, diagnostic message

continue — C keyword
(Language/statements/jump statements)
Force next iteration of a loop
continue;

continue forces the next iteration of a **for, while,** or **do** loop. It works only upon the smallest enclosing loop.

continue forces a loop to iterate by jumping to the end of the loop, which is where iteration evaluation is made. For example, the code

```
while(statement) {
        .  .  .
    if (statement)
        continue;
        .  .  .
}
```

is equivalent to:

```
while(statement) {
        .  .  .
    if (statement)
        goto end;
        .  .  .
    end: ;
}
```

Example
For an example of this statement, see **mktime.**

Cross-references
Standard, §3.6.6.2
The C Programming Language, ed. 2, p. 64

See Also
break, C keywords, goto, jump statements, return

control character — Definition
(Library/character handling)

A *control character* is any character in a locale-defined character set that is not a printing character.

Cross-references
Standard, §4.3
The C Programming Language, ed. 2, p. 249

See Also
character handling, printing character

conversions — Definition
(Language)

The term *conversion* means to change the type of an object, function, or constant, either explicitly or implicitly. Explicit conversion occurs when an object or function is cast to another type by a cast operator. Implicit conversion occurs when the type of the object or function is changed by an operator without a cast operator being used.

When an object or function is converted into a compatible type, its value does not change.

The following paragraphs summarize conversion for different types of objects.

Enumeration constants
These constants are always converted implicitly to **int**s.

Floating types
When a floating type is converted to an integral type, the fractional portion is thrown away. If the value of the integral part cannot be represented by the new type, behavior is undefined.

When a **float** is promoted to **double** or **long double**, its value is unchanged. Likewise, when a **double** is promoted to a **long double**, its value is unchanged.

A floating type may be converted to a smaller floating type. If its value cannot be represented by the new type, behavior is undefined. If its value lies within the range of values that can be represented by the smaller type but cannot be represented precisely, then its value is rounded to the next highest or next lowest value, depending upon the implementation.

Integral types
A **char**, a **short int**, an enumerated type, or a bit-field, whether signed or unsigned, may be used in any situation that calls for an **int**. The type to be promoted is converted to an **int** if an **int** can hold all of its possible values. If an **int** cannot hold all of its possible values, then it is converted to an **unsigned int**. This rule is called *integral promotion*. This conversion retains

the value of the type to be promoted, including its sign. Thus, it is called a *value-preserving* promotion.

Some current implementations of C use a scheme for promotion that is called *unsigned preserving*. Under this scheme, an **unsigned char** or **unsigned short** is always promoted to **unsigned int**. Under certain circumstances, a program that depends upon unsigned-preserving promotion will behave differently when subjected to value-preserving promotion, and probably without warning. This is a quiet change that may break some existing code.

An integral type may be converted to a floating type. If its value lies within the range of values that can be represented by the floating type, but it cannot be represented precisely, then its value is rounded to the next highest or next lowest value, depending upon the implementation.

Signed and unsigned integers

The following rules apply when a signed or an unsigned integer is converted to another integral type:

- When a positive, signed integer is promoted to an unsigned integer of the same or larger type, its value is unchanged.

- When a negative integer is promoted to an unsigned integer of the same or larger type, it is first promoted to the signed equivalent of the unsigned type. It is then converted to unsigned by incrementing its value by one plus the maximum value that can be held by the unsigned type. On two's complement machines, the bit pattern of the promoted object does not changed. The only exception is that the sign bit is copied to fill any extra bits of new type, should it be larger than the old type.

- When a signed or unsigned integer is demoted to a smaller, unsigned type, its value is the non-negative remainder that occurs when the value of the original type is divided by one plus the maximum value that can be held by the smaller type.

- When a signed or unsigned integer is demoted to a smaller, signed type, if its value cannot be represented by the new type, the result is implementation-defined.

- When an unsigned integer is converted to a signed type of the same size, if its value cannot be represented by the new type, the result is implementation-defined.

Usual arithmetic conversions

Many binary operators convert their operands and yield a result of a type common to both. The rules that govern such conversions are called the *usual arithmetic conversions*. The following lists the usual arithmetic conversions. If two conflict, the rule *higher* in the list applies:

- If either operand has type **long double**, the other operand is converted to **long double**.

- If either operand has type **double**, the other operand is converted to **double**.

- If either operand has type **float**, the other operand is converted to **float**.

- If either operand has type **unsigned long int**, then the other operand is converted to **unsigned long int**.

- If one operand has the type **long int** and the other operand has type **unsigned int**, the other operand is converted to **long int** if that type can hold all of the values of an **unsigned int**. Otherwise, both operands are promoted to **unsigned long int**.

- If either operand has type **long int**, the other operand is converted to **long int**.

- If either operand has type **unsigned int**, the other operand is converted to **unsigned int**.

- If none of the above rules apply, then both operands have type **int**.

Cross-references

Standard, §3.2
The C Programming Language, ed. 2, pp. 197*ff*

See Also

explicit conversion, function designator, implicit conversion, integral promotions, Language, lvalue, null pointer constant, value preserving, void expression

Notes

The "as if" rule gives implementors some leeway in applying the rules for usual arithmetic conversions. For example, the conversion rules specify that operands of type **char** must first be widened to type **int** before the operation is performed; however, if the same result would be produced by performing the operation on **char** operands, then the operands need not be widened.

Because the Standard now allows single-precision floating-point arithmetic on **float** operands, some round-off error could occur. Casts will force the operands in question to be promoted, and the operation to be carried out with the wider type.

cos() — Library function
(Library/mathematics/trigonometric functions)
Calculate cosine
#include < math.h >
double cos(double *radian***);**

cos calculates and returns the cosine of its argument *radian*, which must be expressed in radians.

Example
For an example of this function, see **sin**.

Cross-references
Standard, §4.5.2.5
The C Programming Language, ed. 2, p. 251

See Also
acos, asin, atan, atan2, sin, tan, trigonometric functions

cosh() — Library function
(Library/mathematics/hyperbolic functions)
Calculate hyperbolic cosine
#include < math.h >
double cosh(double *value***);**

cosh calculates and returns the hyperbolic cosine of *value*. A range error will occur if the argument is too large.

Cross-references
Standard, §4.5.3.1
The C Programming Language, ed. 2, p. 251

See Also
hyperbolic functions, sinh, tanh

create — Definition
(Library/STDIO)

To *create* a file means that the environment creates the appropriate control structures so that data can be written onto a storage device and retrieved from it. When a file is created, it is given a unique name. In some environments, opening a file that does not exist will create that file; in others, a file must be opened and data written before that file is created.

When a file is created and given the name of an existing file, the data that had been associated with that file name are discarded.

To create a file, use the functions **fopen** or **freopen**.

Cross-reference
Standard, §4.9.3

See Also
close, file, open, STDIO, stdio.h, stream

ctime() — Library function
(Library/date and time/time conversion)
Convert calendar time to text
#include < time.h >
char *ctime(const time_t * *timeptr*);

The function **ctime** reads the calendar time pointed to by *timeptr*, and converts it into a string of the form

```
Tue Dec 10 14:14:55 1987\n\0
```

ctime is equivalent to:

```
asctime(localtime(timeptr));
```

timeptr points to type **time_t**, which is defined in the header **time.h**.

Example
This example displays the current time.

```
#include <stdio.h>
#include <stdlib.h>
#include <time.h>

main(void)
{
     time_t t;
     time(&t);

     printf(ctime(&t));
     return(EXIT_SUCCESS);
}
```

Cross-references
Standard, §4.12.3.2
The C Programming Language, ed. 2, p. 256

See Also
asctime, gmtime, localtime, strftime, time conversion, time_t

ctype.h — Header
(Library/character handling)
Header for character-handling functions
#include <ctype.h>

ctype.h is the header file that declares the functions used to handle characters. These are as follows:

isalnum	Check if a character is a numeral or letter
isalpha	Check if a character is a letter
iscntrl	Check if a character is a control character
isdigit	Check if a character is a numeral
isgraph	Check if a character is printable
islower	Check if a character is a lower-case letter
isprint	Check if a character is printable
ispunct	Check if a character is a punctuation mark
isspace	Check if a character is white space
isupper	Check if a character is a upper-case letter
isxdigit	Check if a character is a hexadecimal numeral
tolower	Convert character to lower case
toupper	Convert character to upper case

Cross-references
Standard, §4.3
The C Programming Language, ed. 2, p. 248

See Also
character handling, character-case mapping

D

date and time — Overview
(Library)
#include < time.h >

The Standard describes nine functions that can be used to represent date and time, as follows:

Time conversion

asctime	Convert broken-down time to text
ctime	Convert calendar time to text
gmtime	Convert calendar time to Universal Coordinated Time
localtime	Convert calendar time to local time
strftime	Format locale-specific time

Time manipulation

clock	Get processor time used by the program
difftime	Calculate difference between two times
mktime	Convert broken-down time into calendar time
time	Get current calendar time

These functions use the following structures:

clock_t	System time
time_t	Calendar time
tm	Broken-down time

Finally, the macro **CLK_TCK** is used to convert the value returned by the function **clock** into seconds of real time.

Cross-references
Standard, §4.12
The C Programming Language, ed. 2, pp. 255*ff*

See Also
broken-down time, calendar time, daylight saving time, local time, Library, universal coordinated time

daylight saving time — Definition
(Library/date and time)

Daylight saving time refers to the practice of shifting clock settings during the summer months in order to move a portion of daylight time from the morning to the evening.

In the United States, daylight saving time is invoked by shifting all clocks forward by one hour on the first Sunday in April; clocks are shifted back by one hour on the last Sunday in October to return to standard time. Not all countries use daylight saving time, and each has its own practices of how much to shift time and when to do it. Practices may vary greatly within a country.

The structure **tm** contains a field, **tm_isdst**, which notes whether daylight saving time is in effect: it is set to a positive number if daylight saving time is in effect, to zero if it is not, and to a negative number if information about daylight saving time is not available. The Standard does not include a mechanism to describe daylight saving time for a locale, although an implementation may include such a mechanism as an extension to the library.

Cross-references
Standard, §4.12
The C Programming Language, ed. 2, p. 255

See Also
calendar time, broken-down time, date and time, local time, tm, universal coordinated time

DBL_DIG — Macro
(Environment/environmental considerations/limits/numerical)
#include < float.h >

DBL_DIG is a macro that is defined in the header **float.h**. It is an expression that defines the number of decimal digits of precision representable in an object of type **double**. It must be at least ten.

Cross-references
Standard, §2.2.4.2
The C Programming Language, ed. 2, p. 258

See Also
float.h, numerical limits

DBL_EPSILON — Macro
(Environment/environmental considerations/limits/numerical)
#include < float.h >

DBL_EPSILON is a macro that is defined in the header **float.h**. It is an expression that yields the smallest positive floating-point number representable in a **double**, such that 1.0 plus it does not test equal to 1.0. It must yield a value that is at most 1E-9.

Example
For an example of using this macro in a program, see **sin**.

Cross-references
Standard, §2.2.4.2
The C Programming Language, ed. 2, p. 258

See Also
float.h, numerical limits

DBL_MANT_DIG — Macro
(Environment/environmental considerations/limits/numerical)
#include <float.h>

DBL_MANT_DIG is a macro that is defined in the header **float.h**. It is an expression that represents the number of digits in the mantissa of an object of type **double** in the numeric base set by the macro **FLT_RADIX**.

Cross-references
Standard, §2.2.4.2
The C Programming Language, ed. 2, p. 258

See Also
float.h, numerical limits

DBL_MAX — Macro
(Environment/environmental considerations/limits/numerical)
#include <float.h>

DBL_MAX is a macro that is defined in the header **float.h**. It is an expression that yields the largest number that can be represented in an object of type **double**. It must yield a value of at least 1E+37.

Cross-references
Standard, §2.2.4.2
The C Programming Language, ed. 2, p. 257

See Also
float.h, numerical limits

DBL_MAX_10_EXP — Macro
(Environment/environmental considerations/limits/numerical)
#include <float.h>

DBL_MAX_10_EXP is a macro that is defined in the header **float.h**. It is an expression that yields the largest power, such that ten raised to it remains a floating-point number that can be encoded by type **double**. This value this expression yields must be at least 37.

Cross-references
Standard, §2.2.4.2
The C Programming Language, ed. 2, p. 258

See Also
float.h, numerical limits

DBL_MAX_EXP — Macro
(Environment/environmental considerations/limits/numerical)
#include <float.h>

DBL_MAX_EXP is a macro that is defined in the header **float.h**. It is an expression that yields the largest power such that **FLT_RADIX** raised to it minus one remains a floating-point number that can be held by an object of type **double**.

Cross-references
Standard, §2.2.4.2
The C Programming Language, ed. 2, p. 258

See Also
float.h, numerical limits

DBL_MIN — Macro
(Environment/environmental considerations/limits/numerical)
#include <float.h>

DBL_MIN is a macro that is defined in the header **float.h**. It is an expression that yields the smallest number that can be represented by type **double**. It must yield a value of at most 1E-37.

Cross-references
Standard, §2.2.4.2
The C Programming Language, ed. 2, p. 258

See Also
float.h, numerical limits

DBL_MIN_10_EXP — Macro
(Environment/environmental considerations/limits/numerical)
#include < float.h >

DBL_MIN_10_EXP is a macro that is defined in the header **float.h**. It is an expression that yields the smallest power, such that ten raised to it remains a floating-point number that can be encoded in type **double**. It must be at most -37.

Cross-references
Standard, §2.2.4.2
The C Programming Language, ed. 2, p. 258

See Also
float.h, numerical limits

DBL_MIN_EXP — Macro
(Environment/environmental considerations/limits/numerical)
#include < float.h >

DBL_MIN_EXP is a macro that is defined in the header **float.h**. It is an expression that yields the smallest power such that **FLT_RADIX** raised to it minus one remains a floating-point number that can be held by an object of type **double**.

Cross-references
Standard, §2.2.4.2
The C Programming Language, ed. 2, p. 258

See Also
float.h, numerical limits

decimal-point character — Definition
(Library)

The Standard defines the *decimal-point character* as being the character that marks the beginning of the fraction in a floating-point number. How this character is represented depends upon the program's locale. The locale specifier

LC_NUMERIC describes how a particular locale represents the decimal-point character. In the **C** locale, it is the period '.'.

This character is used by the functions that convert a floating-point number to a string, or read a string and convert it to a floating-point number, i.e., **atof, fprintf, fscanf, printf, scanf, sprintf, sscanf, strtod, vfprintf, vprintf,** and **vsprintf.** This character is *not* used within C source; for example,

```
sqrt(1,2);
```

passes two integer constants to **sqrt**, even if ',' is the decimal-point character for the current locale. Therefore, to print a C source file use the **C** locale, even if the program establishes another locale.

Cross-reference
Standard, §4.1.1

See Also
Library, localization

declarations — Overview
(Language)

A *declaration* gives the type, storage class, linkage, and scope of a given identifier. Its syntax is as follows; note that *opt* indicates *optional*:

> *declaration:*
>> *declaration-specifiers init-declarator-list$_{opt}$:*
>
> *declaration-specifiers:*
>> *storage-class-specifier declaration-specifiers$_{opt}$*
>> *type-specifier declaration-specifiers$_{opt}$*
>> *type-qualifier declaration-specifiers$_{opt}$*
>
> *init-declarator-list:*
>> *init-declarator*
>> *init-declarator-list , init-declarator*
>
> *init-declarator:*
>> *declarator*
>> *declarator = initializer*

If a declaration also causes storage to be allocated for the object declared, then it is called a *definition.*

Declarators may be within a list, separated by commas. Each declarator has the type given at the beginning of the list, although a declarator may also have additional type information. For example,

```
int example1, *example2;
```

declares two variables: **example1** has type **int**, whereas **example2** has type "pointer to **int**."

Objects may be initialized when they are declared. See **initialization** for more information.

Cross-references
Standard, §3.5
The C Programming Language, ed. 2, pp. 210*ff*

See Also
bit-fields, declarators, definition, initialization, Language, linkage, scope, storage-class specifiers, type qualifiers, type specifiers

declarators — Overview
(Language/declarations)

A *declarator* consists of an object being declared plus its array, pointer, and function modifiers. The syntax is as follows; *opt* indicates *optional*:

declarator:
    pointer$_{opt}$ direct-declarator

direct-declarator:
    identifier
    (*declarator*)
    direct-declarator [*constant-expression$_{opt}$*]
    direct-declarator (*parameter-type-list*)
    direct-declarator (*identifier-list$_{opt}$*)

pointer:
    * *type-qualifier-list$_{opt}$*
    * *type-qualifier-list$_{opt}$ pointer*

type-qualifier-list:
    type-qualifier
    type-qualifier-list type-qualifier

parameter-type-list:
    parameter-list
    parameter list , . . .

parameter-list:
    parameter-declaration
    parameter-list , parameter-declaration

parameter-declaration:
        declaration-specifiers declarator
        declaration-specifiers abstract-declarator$_{opt}$

identifier-list
        identifier
        identifier-list , identifier

For example,

```
int arrayname[10];
```

declares an array.

```
int functionname( int arg1, int arg2, char *arg3 );
```

declares a function.

```
int *pointername;
```

declares a pointer.

An implementation must be able to support at least 12 levels of declarators. Most implementations had given a lower limit.

Cross-references
Standard, §3.5.4
The C Programming Language, ed. 2, pp. 215*ff*

See Also
array declarators, declarations, function declarators, pointer declarators

Notes
To clarify some terminology that may be confusing:

A *declaration* encompasses the object declared, plus its specifiers, qualifiers, and levels of declarators.

A *declarator* consists of the object declared, plus its levels of specifiers (which set array dimensions, functions, or pointers).

A *definition* is a declaration that allocates storage.

default — C keyword
(Language/statements/labelled statements)
Default entry in switch table

default is a label that marks the default entry in the body of a **switch** statement. If none of the **case** labels match the value of the **switch** statement's conditional expression, then the **switch** statement jumps to the point marked by the **default**

label, and begins execution from there.

Example
For an example of this label, see **printf**.

Cross-references
Standard, §3.6.1
The C Programming Language, ed. 2, p. 58

See Also
C keywords, case, labelled statements, switch

Notes
A **switch** statement is not required to include a **default** label, but it is good programming practice to include one.

defined — C keyword
(Language/preprocessing/macro replacement)
Check if identifier is defined /
defined(*identifier* **)**
defined *identifier*

The Standard describes a new C keyword, **defined**. This keyword is used to check if *identifier* has been defined as macro. The preprocessing directives

```
#if defined(identifier)
```

and

```
#if defined identifier
```

have exactly the same effect as the directive:

```
#ifdef identifier
```

The **defined** operator is permitted only within **#if** and **#elif** expressions. It may not be used in any other context.

defined is not a reserved word. It can be used in more complex conditional statements, i.e.:

```
#if LEVEL==3 && defined FOO
```

Cross-references
Standard, §3.8.1
The C Programming Language, ed. 2, p. 91

See Also
#if, #ifdef, keywords, macro replacement

definition — Definition
(Language/declarations)

A *definition* is a declaration that also allocates storage for the item declared. For example,

```
int example[];
```

declares that **example** names an array of **int**s. Because the declaration does not say how large of an array **example** is, no memory is reserved; thus, this is a declaration but not a definition.

However, the declaration

```
int example[10];
```

declares that **example** names an array of ten **int**s. Because the declaration states how large **example** is, an appropriately sized portion of memory is reserved for it. Thus, this declaration is also a definition.

declaration and *definition* are easily confused, because the words are used in ways that are somewhat contrary to their normal English meanings.

A function definition is a special kind of definition that operates by its own rules. See **function definition** for more details.

Cross-references
Standard, §3.5
The C Programming Language, ed. 2, pp. 201, 210

See Also
declarations, function definition

Definitions — Overview
(Standard)

These definitions apply to topics throughout this Lexicon:

> address
> alignment
> argument
> ASCII
> behavior
> bit
> block

> byte
> compile
> compliance
> constraints
> diagnostic message
> false
> function
> implementation
> interpret
> link
> manifest constant
> null character
> object
> obsolescent
> parameter
> portability
> rvalue
> translation
> true

Cross-references
Standard, §1.6

See Also
Standard

derived types — Definition
(Language/lexical elements/identifiers/types)

The term *derived type* refers to any type that is derived from a basic, enumerated, or incomplete type. The set of derived types includes the following types:

> array types
> function types
> pointer types
> structure types
> union types

Cross-references
Standard, §3.1.2.5
The C Programming Language, ed. 2, p. 196

See Also
array types, enumerated types, function types, incomplete types, pointer, struct, types, union

diagnostic message — Definition
(Definitions)

A *diagnostic message* is a message produced by an implementation, that warns the user of a particular condition within the program. The conditions that produce such messages and their wording are defined by the implementation. Certain program constructs require that the translator issue a diagnostic message.

Cross-reference
Standard, §1.6

See Also
constraints, Definitions, diagnostics

diagnostics — Overview
(Library)

The term *diagnostics* has two meanings in the ANSI Standard. The first is a set of macros that are used to test an expression at run time. The second refers to the way a translator warns a user that a program contains an error.

Run-Time Diagnostics

The Standard describes a mechanism whereby an expression can be tested at run time. The macro **assert** tests the value of a given expression as the program runs. If the expression is false, **assert** prints a message into the standard error stream and then calls **abort**.

assert is defined in the header **assert.h**. This header also defines the macro **NDEBUG**. If you define this macro before including **assert.h**, **assert** is redefined as follows:

```
#define assert(ignore)
```

This turns off **assert**. If an expression evaluated by **assert** has any side effects, using **NDEBUG** will change the program's behavior.

Diagnostic Warnings

Every conforming implementation of C must produce at least one diagnostic for every translation unit that contains one or more errors of syntax rules or syntax constraints. A diagnostic can be either a fatal error, which prints a message and aborts translation, or simply a warning that prints a message and allows translation to proceed. The wording of the messages and how they are produced is defined by the implementation.

A conforming implementation may generate a diagnostic message if it detects a condition that produces undefined behavior. However, it is *not* required to do so.

Cross-reference
Standard, §2.1.1.3

See Also
diagnostic message, translation environment, translation unit

difftime() — Library function
(Library/date and time/time manipulation)
Calculate difference between two times
#include <time.h>
double difftime(time_t *newtime*, **time_t** *oldtime*);

difftime subtracts *oldtime* from *newtime*, and returns the difference in seconds.

Both arguments are of type **time_t**, which is defined in the header file **time.h**. It is an arithmetic type capable of representing time.

Example
This example uses **difftime** to show an arbitrary time difference.

```
#include <stdio.h>
#include <stdlib.h>
#include <time.h>

main(void)
{
    time_t    t1, t2;

    time(&t1);
    printf("Press enter when you feel like it.\n");
    getchar();
    time(&t2);

    printf("You waited %f seconds\n", difftime(t2, t1));
    return(EXIT_SUCCESS);
}
```

Cross-references
Standard, §4.12.2.2
The C Programming Language, ed. 2, p. 256

See Also
clock, mktime, time, time manipulation, time_t

digit — Definition
(Language/lexical elements/identifiers)

A *digit* is any of the following characters:

> 0   1   2   3   4   5   6   7   8   9

Cross-reference
Standard, §3.1.2

See Also
identifiers, nondigit

div() — Library function
(Library/general utilities/integer arithmetic)
Perform integer division
#include <stdlib.h>
div_t div(int *numerator*, **int** *denominator***);**

div divides *numerator* by *denominator*. It returns a structure of the type **div_t**. This structure consists of two **int** members, one named **quot** and the other **rem**. **div** writes the quotient into **quot** and the remainder into **rem**.

The sign of the quotient is positive if the signs of the arguments are the same; the sign of the quotient is negative if the signs of the arguments differ. The sign of the remainder is the same as the sign of the numerator.

If the remainder is non-zero, the magnitude of the quotient is the largest integer less than the magnitude of the algebraic quotient. This is not guaranteed by the operators **/** and **%**, which merely do what the machine implements for divide.

Example
For an example of this function, see **memchr**.

Cross-references
Standard, §4.10.6.2
The C Programming Language, ed. 2, p. 253

See Also
/, div_t, integer arithmetic, ldiv

Notes

The Standard includes this function to permit a useful feature found in most versions of FORTRAN, where the sign of the remainder will be the same as the sign of the numerator. Also, on most machines, division produces a remainder. This allows a quotient and remainder to be returned from one machine-divide operation.

If the result of division cannot be represented (e.g., because *denominator* is set to zero), the behavior of **div** is undefined.

div_t — Type

(Library/general utilities)
Type returned by **div()**
#include <stdlib.h>

div_t is a typedef that is declared in the header **stdlib.h**. It is the type returned by the function **div**.

div_t is a structure that consists of two **int** members, one named **quot** and the other **rem**. The Standard does not specify their order within **div_t**. **div** writes its quotient into **quot** and its remainder into **rem**.

Example

For an example of using this type in a program, see **memchr**.

Cross-references

Standard, §4.10.6.2
The C Programming Language, ed. 2, p. 253

See Also

div, general utilities, integer arithmetic, stdlib.h

do — C keyword

(Language/statements/iteration statements)
Loop construct
do { *statement* } **while(***condition***);**

do establishes conditional loop. Unlike the loops established by **for** and **while**, the condition in a **do** loop is evaluated *after* the operation is performed. This guarantees that at least one iteration of the loop will be executed.

do always works in tandem with **while**. For example

```
do {
    puts("Next entry? ");
    fflush(stdout);
} while(getchar() != EOF);
```

prints a prompt on the screen and waits for the user to reply. The **do** loop is convenient in this instance because the prompt must appear at least once on the screen before the user replies.

Cross-references
Standard, §3.6.5.2
The C Programming Language, ed. 2, p. 63

See Also
break, C keywords, continue, for, iteration statements, while

domain error — Definition
(Library/mathematics)

The *domain* of a function is that set of values over which the function is defined. It is thought of as the set of input values for the function. An attempt to evaluate the function for a value not in this set will trigger the function to set a domain error by setting **errno** to the value of the macro **EDOM**. The function will return an implementation-defined value.

Cross-reference
Standard, §4.5.1

See Also
EDOM, errno, math.h, mathematics

double — C keyword
(Language/lexical elements/identifiers/types)

A **double** is a data type that represents a double-precision floating-point number. It is defined as being at least as large as a **float** and no larger than a **long double**.

Like all floating-point numbers, a **double** consists of one sign bit, which indicates whether the number is positive or negative; bits that encode the number's *exponent*; and bits that encode the number's *mantissa*, or the number upon which the exponent works. The exponent often uses a *bias*. This is a value that is subtracted from the exponent to yield the power of two by which the fraction will be increased. The format of a **double** and the range of values that it can encode are set in the following macros, all of which are defined in the header **limits.h**:

DBL_DIG
> This holds the number of decimal digits of precision. This must be at least ten.

DBL_EPSILON
> Where b indicates the base of the exponent (default, two) and p indicates the precision (or number of base b digits in the mantissa), this macro holds the minimum positive floating-point number x such that $1.0 + x$ does not equal 1.0, b^1-p. This must be at least 1E-9.

DBL_MAX
> This holds the maximum representable floating-point number. It must be at least 1E+37.

DBL_MAX_EXP
> This is the maximum integer such that the base raised to its power minus one is a representable floating-point number.

DBL_MAX_10_EXP
> This holds the maximum integer such that ten raised to its power is within the range of representable finite floating-point numbers. It must be at least +37.

DBL_MANT_DIG
> This gives the number of digits in the mantissa.

DBL_MIN
> This gives the minimum value encodable within a **double**. This must be at least 1E-37.

DBL_MIN_EXP
> This gives the minimum negative integer such that when the base is raised to that power minus one is a normalized floating-point number.

DBL_MIN_10_EXP
> This gives the minimum negative integer such that ten raised to that power is within the range of normalized floating-point numbers. It must be at least -37.

Cross-references

Standard, §2.2.4.2, §3.1.2.4, §3.1.3.1, §3.5.2
The C Programming Language, ed. 2, p. 211

See Also

float, long double, types

E

EDOM — Macro
(Library/mathematics)
Domain error
#include < math.h >

EDOM is a macro that is defined in the header **math.h**. It is a non-zero integral constant that is used to indicate a domain error. This error occurs when a mathematics function attempt to compute a value for a number that lies outside of its legal domain. For example, a domain error occurs if you attempt to use the function **asin** to compute the arc sine of a number that either is greater than one or less than -1.

When a domain error occurs, the global variable **errno** is set to **EDOM**.

Cross-references
Standard, §4.5.1
The C Programming Language, ed. 2, p. 250

See Also
domain error, ERANGE, errno, mathematics, math.h

else — C keyword
(Language/statements/selection statements)
Conditionally execute a statement
else *statement*;

else is the flip side of **if**: if the condition described in the **if** statement equals zero, then the statement introduced by **else** is executed. If, however, the condition described in the **if** statement is nonzero, then the statement it introduces is executed and the statement introduced by **else** is ignored.

An **else** statement is associated with the first preceding **else**-less **if** statement that is within the same block, but not within an enclosed block. For example,

```
if(conditional1) {
        if(conditional2)
                statement1
} else
        statement2
```

the **else** is associated with the **if** statement that uses *conditional1*, not the one that uses *conditional2*. On the other hand, in the code

```
if(conditional1)
        if(conditional2)
                statement1
else
        statement2
```

which does not use braces, the **else** is associated with the **if** statement that uses *conditional2*, not the one that uses *conditional1*.

Example

For an example of this statement, see **exit**.

Cross-references

Standard, §4.6.4.1
The C Programming Language, ed. 2, pp. 55*ff*

See Also

if, selection statements, switch

enum — C keyword
(Language/declarations/type definitions)
Enumerated data type
enum *identifier* **{** *enumerations* **}**

An **enum** is a data type whose possible values are limited to a set of constants. Its syntax is as follows; *opt* indicates *optional*:

> *enum-specifier:*
>   enum *identifier*$_{opt}$ **{** *enumerator-list* **}**
>   enum *identifier*

> *enumerator-list:*
>   *enumerator*
>   *enumeratorlist* , *enumerator*

> *enumerator:*
>   *enumeration-constant*
>   *enumeration-constant* = *constant-expression*

For example,

```
enum opinion { yes, no, maybe };
```

declares type **opinion** to have one of three constant values; these are identified by the members **yes**, **no**, and **maybe**.

The translator assigns values to the identifiers from left to right, beginning with zero and increasing by one for each successive term. In the above example, the values of **yes, no,** and **maybe** are set, respectively, to zero, one, and two. Thus, the following example

```
enum opinion guess;
    . . .
guess = no;
```

sets the value of **guess** to one.

All enumerated identifiers must be distinct from all other identifiers in the program. The identifiers act as constants and are used wherever constants are appropriate.

If a member of an enumeration is followed by an equal sign and an integer, the identifier is assigned the given value and subsequent values increase by one from that value. For example,

```
enum opinion {yes, no=50, maybe};
```

sets the values of the members **yes, no,** and **maybe** to 0, 50, and 51, respectively. More than one enumerator can have the same value; for example:

```
enum opinion {yes, no=50, nah=50, nope=50, maybe};
```

assigns duplicate values to the members **no, nah,** and **nope.**

An enumeration constant always has type **int.**

Cross-references
Standard, §3.5.2.2
The C Programming Language, ed. 2, p. 39

See Also
type definitions

Notes
Prior to the introduction of enumerated data types in C, programmers would create lists of manifest constants whose values took the values that enumerated constants now take.

Unlike more strongly typed languages, in which enumerated constants are checked to ensure that they are part of the specified set of values, **enum**s in C are only required to be of type **int.** No additional checking is performed on enumeration constants.

enumerated types – Definition
(Language/lexical elements/identifiers/types)

An *enumerated type* is the type of an enumeration, which is a set of named integer constant values.

Cross-references
Standard, §3.1.2.5
The C Programming Language, ed. 2, p. 196

See Also
enum, types

enumeration constant – Definition
(Language/lexical elements/constants)

An *enumeration constant* is a member of an enumeration. Its syntax is as follows:

```
enumeration-constant:
     identifier
```

This constant has type **int**.

For example, in the enumeration

```
enum example { blue, green, yellow };
```

blue is an enumeration constant.

Cross-references
Standard, §3.1.3.3
The C Programming Language, ed. 2, pp. 39, 194

See Also
constants, enum

Environment – Overview
(Standard)

The *environment* is the computing context within which a program is translated and executed.

Chapter 2 of the Standard describes two environments: the *translation environment* and the *execution environment*. This separation is necessary because C programs are often translated on one machine and executed on another, or *cross-compiled*.

The details of each environment are dictated in large part by the hardware.

In the translation environment, the environment is controlled by the implementation of C used to translate the program.

An execution environment, on the other hand, has two varieties: *freestanding* and *hosted*. In essence, a freestanding environment is one in which the program is *not* run under an operating system. One example of a freestanding environment is a microprocessor used as a washing-machine controller. Under a freestanding environment, the environment is custom-built, and may operate in many different ways. A hosted environment is one in which the program is run under a general-purpose operating system. In a hosted environment, the environment is controlled largely by the operating system.

The environment sets the size of each data type and the complexity of C program that can be translated; respectively, these are called *numerical limits* and *translation limits*.

The translation limits are exclusively the concern of the translation environment, and thus of the implementation. For example, the number of **case** labels that can follow a single **switch** statement is a translation limit. The Standard describes a set of minimal environmental limits that must be met or exceeded by every conforming implementation of C. The Standard also describes in the detail the order in which the tasks of program translation must be performed.

The numerical limits may vary between the translation environment and the execution environment. The numerical limits of the translation environment may not be less than those of the execution environment. The Standard describes a set of minimal numerical limits, or *minimum maxima*, that must be met or exceeded by every conforming implementation of C. Further, every numerical limit must be described in a macro. The macros that describe the numerical limits for integral types are kept in the header **limits.h**, and the macros that describe the numerical limits for floating types are kept in the header **float.h**. The Standard also describes how a program must be executed under a hosted environment.

The set of characters recognized by the translation environment may differ from that recognized by the execution environment. The set recognized by the execution environment may be changed by resetting the program's locale. The Standard descibes *escape sequences* that affect the behavior of an output device. It also describes *trigraph sequences* that permit a programmer to use characters in the C character set that lie outside the ISO 646 standard invariant character set.

Cross-reference
Standard, §2.0

See Also

environmental considerations, environment communication, execution environment, Standard, translation environment

environmental considerations — Overview
(Environment)

The Standard describes a number of elements of the environment that must be set by a conforming implementation. These include the character sets for both the translation and the execution environments, the semantics of how characters are displayed on an output device, the way signals are processed, and environmental limits for both integral and floating types.

Cross-reference
Standard, §2.2

See Also

character display semantics, character sets, Environment, limits, signals/interrupts, trigraph sequences

environment communication — Overview
(Library/general utilities)
#include < stdlib.h >

The Standard describes five functions that allow a program to communicate with the execution environment. They are as follows:

abort	End a program immediately
atexit	Register a function to be performed at exit
exit	Terminate a program gracefully
getenv	Read environmental variable
system	Suspend a program and execute another

abort raises the signal **SIGABRT** within the environment and exits. What occurs when a program aborts depends entirely upon the behavior of the abort signal handler. **exit**, on the other hand, terminates a program gracefully. All buffers are flushed, all open files are closed, and a status code is returned to the environment.

atexit registers with the environment a function to be executed when the program exits. An implementation must be able to register at least 32 functions, and execute them when the program exits.

getenv reads an environmental variable. This form of variable defines an aspect of the environment that may affect how a program runs.

Finally, **system** suspends the operation of a program and invokes a secondary program to be executed. When the secondary program exits, the environment returns control to program that invoked it.

Cross-reference
Standard, §4.10.5

See Also
argc, argv, execution environment, general utilities

environment list — Definition
(Library/general utilities)

An *environment list* is a group of strings, each of which defines an aspect of the environment that may affect how a program runs. Each member of the environment list is an *environment variable*.

Not every environment maintains an environment list. A program can read an environment variable by using the function **getenv**.

Cross-reference
Standard, §4.10.4.4

See Also
environment communication, getenv

EOF — Macro
(Library/STDIO)
Indicate end of a file
#include <stdio.h>

EOF is an indicator that is returned by several STDIO functions to indicate that the current file position is the end of the file. Its value is defined by the implementation, but a common value is -1 on many systems, which is also a common error return.

The actual bytes used to delineate the end of a file may vary between implementations.

Many STDIO functions, when they read **EOF**, set the end-of-file indicator that is associated with the stream being read. Before more data can be read from the stream, its end-of-file indicator must be cleared. Resetting the file-position indicator with the functions **fseek, fsetpos**, or **ftell** will clear the indicator, as will returning a character to the stream with the function **ungetc**.

Example
For an example of this macro in a program, see **tmpfile**.

Cross-references
Standard, §4.3, §4.9.1; Rationale, §4.3
The C Programming Language, ed. 2, p. 151

See Also
file, stream, STDIO, stdio.h

equality operators — Overview
(Language/expressions)

The C language has two equality operators: = = and !=. Their syntax is as follows:

equality-expression:
    relational-expression
    equality-expression == *relational-expression*
    equality-expression != *relational-expression*

The result from each operator has type **int**.

The operator = = compares its operands for equality. The result of an equality expression is one if the operands are equal, and zero if they are not.

The operator !=, on the other hand, compares for inequality. The result of an inequality expression one if the operands are not equal, and zero if they are.

The operands must be one of the following:

• Arithmetic types.

• Pointers to compatible types (ignoring qualifiers on these types).

• A pointer to an object or incomplete type and a pointer to **void**.

• A pointer and NULL.

If both operands have arithmetic type, they undergo usual arithmetic conversion before being compared.

Pointers
If two pointers to functions compare equal, then they point to the same function. Likewise, if two pointers to data objects compare equal, then they point to the same object. In general, however, a pointer to a function may compare equal to a pointer to a data object on machine architectures that provide separate instruction and data spaces. Programmers should not depend on being able to distinguish function pointers from data object pointers by value. Further, two pointers that do not compare equal may nonetheless point to the same thing on machine architectures that

allow many pointer values to refer to the same object (e.g., i8086 LARGE-model addressing).

Cross-references
Standard, §3.3.9
The C Programming Language, ed. 2, pp. 41, 207

See Also
expressions

Notes
Structures cannot be compared for equality. This is because structure members may have "padding" between them, which means that a byte-by-byte comparison is not reliable. Also, comparison of structures is not an operation that can be performed efficiently on all machines.

One method to compare two structures for equality is to compare their members. If structures are cleared with the functions **calloc** or **memset** before their members are set, they can be compared with the function **memcmp**.

See **struct** for more information on structures.

ERANGE — Macro
(Library/mathematics)
Range error
#include <math.h>

ERANGE is a macro that is defined in the header **math.h**. It is a non-zero integral constant that is used to indicate a range error. This error occurs when a mathematics function attempts to calculate a value that is too large to be encoded by a **double**.

When a range error occurs, the global variable **errno** is set to **ERANGE**.

Cross-references
Standard, §4.5.1
The C Programming Language, ed. 2, p. 250

See Also
EDOM, errno, mathematics, math.h, range error

errno — Macro
(Library/errors)
External integer that holds error status
#include < errno.h >

errno is a macro that is defined in the header **errno.h**. It expands to a global integer of type **volatile int**.

When a program begins to execute, **errno** is initialized to zero. Thereafter, whenever a mathematics function or other library function wishes to return information about any error that occurs during its operation, it writes the appropriate error number into **errno**, where it can be read either by the environment or by another function. The significance of each value stored in **errno** is determined by the environment or the implementation.

The Standard describes two macros whose values can be stored in **errno**: **ERANGE** and **EDOM**. The former indicates that a range error has occurred, and the latter that a domain error has occurred. Both are defined in the header **math.h**. The Standard allows an implementation to define other error macros. Each must begin with a capital 'E' plus at least one other capital letter.

The functions **perror** and **strerror** can be used to translate the contents of **errno** into a text message.

Example
For an example of using this macro in a program, see **vfprintf**.

Cross-references
Standard, §4.1.3
The C Programming Language, ed. 2, p. 248

See Also
EDOM, ERANGE, errno.h, errors, mathematics

Notes
Only certain library functions set **errno**, and then only if certain error conditions occur. Remember that it is your responsibility to clear **errno** before the function in question is called. Other functions may also set **errno**.

Although it is widely believed that a program that checks the value of **errno** after each function is more portable than one that does not, this is not necessarily true. Some implementations use in-line expansion of library function to speed execution, and so forego the use of **errno**. The cautious programmer is best advised to check the value of input arguments before calling a library function and, of course, to check its return value before checking **errno**.

errno.h — Header
    (Library/errors)
    Define errno and error codes
    #include <errno.h>

errno.h is a header that holds information relating to the reporting of error conditions. It defines the macro **errno**, which expands to global variable of type **volatile int**. If an error condition occurs, a function can write a value into **errno**, to report just what type of error occurred.

errno.h can also include macros that expand to define specific error conditions. The Standard mandates that each such macro begin with a capital 'E' and include at least one other capital letter. The Standard describes two such macros, **ERANGE** and **EDOM**, which indicate, respectively, a range error and a domain error. These are defined in the header **math.h**.

Cross-references
Standard, §4.1.3
The C Programming Language, ed. 2, p. 248

See Also
EDOM, ERANGE, errno, errors

error handling — Overview
    (Library/STDIO)

The Standard describes four STDIO routines that are used to handle error conditions, as follows:

clearerr	Clear a stream's error indicator
feof	Examine a stream's end-of-file indicator
ferror	Examine a stream's error indicator
perror	Write error message into standard error stream

Cross-references
Standard, §4.9.10
The C Programming Language, ed. 2, pp. 164, 248

See Also
file access, file operations, file positioning, input-output, STDIO

errors — Overview
(Library)

The Standard describes the following mechanism by which certain designated library functions can report errors. The header **errno.h** defines a global variable called **errno**. When a program begins, this variable is set to zero. Thereafter, whenever a function encounters an error condition, it sets **errno** to a value that indicates just what went wrong.

The Standard describes two macros that indicate error conditions: **ERANGE** and **EDOM**. Both are defined in the header **math.h**, and they indicate, respectively, range error and domain error. An implementation may define its own set of additional error macros; each must begin with a capital 'E' plus at least one other capital letter.

The function **perror** reads the value stored in **errno** and translates it into a text that it writes into the standard error stream. The function **strerror** takes an error number as an argument and returns a pointer to the same message that would be produced by **perror**. The actual error numbers and the messages they produce are defined by the implementation.

Cross-references
Standard, §4.1.3
The C Programming Language, ed. 2, p. 248

See Also
errno.h, Library

escape sequences — Definition
(Language/lexical elements/constants/character constant)

An *escape sequence* is a set of characters that, together, represent one character that may have a special significance. The Standard recognizes the following escape sequences:

\'	The literal apostrophe
\"	The literal quotation mark
\?	The literal question mark
\\	The literal backslash
\a	Alert; ring the bell or print visual alert

\b	Horizontal backspace
\f	Form feed; force output device to begin a new page
\n	Newline; move to next line
\r	Carriage return; move to beginning of line
\t	Horizontal tabulation; move to next tabulation mark
\v	Vertical tabulation; move to next tabulation mark
NNN	Octal number
\x*NN*	Hexadecimal number

An escape sequence may be embedded within a character constant or a string literal. In a string literal, the apostrophe may be represented either by itself or by its escape sequence, whereas in a character constant the quotation mark may be represented by itself or by its escape sequence.

Two question marks together may introduce a trigraph, which is interpreted even within a string literal. If you want to print two literal question marks, use the escape sequence \?\?. For more information, see **trigraph sequences**.

The escape sequences \a through \v let you use characters that control the output device.

A backslash followed by one, two, or three octal digits encodes an octal number. For example, in ASCII implementations of C, the escape sequence '\141' encodes the octal value 141 into an **int**-length object. When interpreted under an environment that uses ASCII, this prints the letter 'a'. Likewise, the escape sequence \x followed by an arbitrary number of hexadecimal digits encodes a hexadecimal number.

Example

The following example demonstrates the use of the escape sequence \b, which prints a backspace character. It prints a message, backspaces over it, and then prints a message of a more benign nature.

```
#include <stdio.h>
main()
{
    printf("ACID FLASH!\b\b\b\b\b\b\b\b\b\b\bhello, world\n");
}
```

Cross-references

Standard, §2.2.2, §3.1.3.4
The C Programming Language, ed. 2, p. 193

See Also
character constant, constants, string literal, trigraph sequences

Notes
Some implementations of C have defined the escape sequences **\a** and **\x** differently. Programs written with such implementations will behave differently when compiled under a conforming implementation, and probably without warning. This is a quiet change that may break some existing code.

Some implementations of C permit the digit '8' to be used with an octal number. For example, the character constant **'\078'** is regarded by these implementations as being equivalent to octal 100. Under ANSI C, **'\078'** will be interpreted as representing octal 7 plus the character constant **'8'**. This, too, is a quiet change that may break some existing code.

The escape sequence '\0' is used by many existing implementations to represent the null character.

exception — Definition
(Language/expressions)

An *exception* is said to occur when an expression generates a result that cannot be represented by the hardware or defined mathematically, e.g., division by zero. When an exception occurs, behavior is undefined.

Cross-references
Standard, §3.3
The C Programming Language, ed. 2, p. 255

See Also
expressions

execution environment — Overview
(Environment)

An *execution environment* is the environment under which a program is executed. This does not have to be the same environment under which the the program is translated, although it may be.

The Standard describes two varieties of execution environment: a *freestanding environment* and a *hosted environment*. Basically, the difference is that the former environment does not have an operating system and the latter does. The Standard describes minimal rules for a freestanding environment on the grounds that such an environment is often custom-designed. The execution of a program under a hosted environment, however, is carefully described, with rules given for program startup, program execution, and program termination.

Cross-reference
Standard, §2.1.2

See Also
Environment, freestanding environment, hosted environment, initialized, program execution, program startup, program termination, translation environment

exit() — Library function
(Library/general utilities/environment communication)

Terminate a program gracefully
#include <stdlib.h>
void exit(int *status***);**

exit terminates a program gracefully. Unlike the function **abort**, **exit** performs all processing that is necessary to ensure that buffers are flushed, files are closed, and allocated memory is returned to the environment.

When it is called, **exit** does the following:

1. It executes all functions registered by the function **atexit**, in reverse order of registration. These functions must execute as if **main** had returned. If any function accesses an **auto**, its behavior is undefined.

2. It flushes all buffers associated with output streams, closes the streams, and removes all files created by the function **tmpfile**.

3. It returns control to the host environment. If *status* is zero or **EXIT_SUCCESS**, then the program indicates to the environment that the program terminated with success. How it does so is defined by the implementation. If *status* is set to **EXIT_FAILURE**, then the program indicates that the program terminated with failure. Again, how this is done is defined by the implementation. If *status* is set to any other value, the status returned to the environment is defined by the implementation.

exit does not return to its caller.

Example
This program exits, and returns the first argument on the command line to the operating system as an exit code.

```
#include <math.h>
#include <stddef.h>
#include <stdio.h>
#include <stdlib.h>
```

```
main(int argc, char *argv[])
{
     if(argc == 1)
          exit(EXIT_SUCCESS);
     else
          exit(atoi(argv[1]));
}
```

Cross-references
Standard, §4.10.4.3
The C Programming Language, ed. 2, p. 252

See Also
**abort, atexit, environment communication, getenv, program termination,
system**

EXIT_FAILURE — Macro
(Library/general utilities)
Value to indicate that a program failed to execute successfully
#include <stdlib.h>

EXIT_FAILURE is a macro that is defined in the header **stdlib.h**. It is used as an
argument to the function **exit** to indicate that the program failed to execute successfully.

Example
For an example of using this macro in a program, see **memchr**.

Cross-references
Standard, §4.10.4.3
The C Programming Language, ed. 2, p. 252

See Also
environment communication, exit, general utilities, stdlib.h

EXIT_SUCCESS — Macro
(Library/general utilities)
Value to indicate that program executed successfully
#include <stdlib.h>

EXIT_SUCCESS is a macro that is defined in the header **stdlib.h**. It is used as an
argument to the function **exit**, to indicate that the program executed successfully.

Example

For an example of using this macro in a program, see **memchr**.

Cross-references

Standard, §4.10.4.3
The C Programming Language, ed. 2, p. 252

See Also

environment communication, exit, general utilities, stdlib.h

exp() — Library functions
(Library/mathematics/exponent-log functions)

Compute exponential function
#include < math.h >
double exp(double *z***);**

exp returns the exponential function of *z*, or *e* to the *z* power, where *e* is the base of the natural logarithms. It is the inverse of the function **log**.

Cross-references

Standard, §4.5.4.1
The C Programming Language, ed. 2, p. 251

See Also

exponent-log functions, frexp, log, log10, modf

explicit conversion — Definition
(Language/conversions)

The term *explicit conversion* refers to the deliberate changing of an object's type by means of a cast operation.

For example, one type of pointer can be cast to another, as follows:

```
char *charptr;
int  *intptr;
    . . .
intptr = (int *)charptr;
```

A cast can be used to defeat optimizations performed by the translator. For instance, if an implementation performs single-precision arithmetic on operands of type **float**, an explicit cast will force the operation to be performed in the wider type **double**:

```
float f1, f2, f3;
    . . .
f3 = (double) f1 * f2;
```

Cross-references
Standard, §3.2
The C Programming Language, ed. 2, p. 45

See Also
(), cast operators, conversions, implicit conversion

Notes
A cast is not an lvalue. This renders constructs such as

```
(int *)pointer++;   /* WRONG */
```

invalid under ANSI C.

exponent-log functions — Overview
(Library/mathematics)

The Standard describes six functions that manipulate exponents and calculate logarithms. They are as follows:

exp	Compute exponential
frexp	Fracture floating-point number
ldexp	Multiply floating-point number
log	Compute natural logarithm
log10	Compute common logarithm
modf	Separate exponent and fraction

Cross-reference
Standard, §4.5.4

See Also
hyperbolic functions, integer-value-remainder, mathematics, power functions, trigonometric functions

expressions — Overview
(Language)

An *expression* consists either of an operand alone, or a combination of operators and operands. It computes a value, calls a function, generates a side effect, or does any combination of these tasks.

All expressions fall into one of the following categories, depending upon the operator that governs it:

Additive operators
   +
   -

Assignment operators
   =
   + =
   - =
   * =
   / =
   % =

   & =
   < < =
   > > =
   | =
   ^ =

Bitwise operators
   &
   < <
   > >
   |
   ^

Cast operators
   ()

Equality operators
   = =
   ! =

Function calls
   ()

Function prototypes
   ()

Logical operators
   &&
   ||

Multiplicative operators
   *
   /
   %

Postfix operators
> []
> ()
> .
> ->
> ++
> --

Primary expressions
Relative operators
> <
> <=
> >
> >=

Unary operators
> &
> ~
> *
> +
> -

> !
> ++
> --
> **sizeof**

Each of the above has its own entry; refer to it for more information about a given operator or class of operators.

All expressions resolve eventually to a primary expression, which has a distinct value or no value at all. When several expressions are joined into one larger expression, the order in which sub-expressions are evaluated is set by the precedence of the operators. See **operators** for a table that gives the precedence of operators.

Cross-references
Standard, §3.3
The C Programming Language, ed. 2, pp. 199*ff*

See Also
alias, Language

expression statement — Definition
(Language/statements)

An *expression statement* is a statement whose expression is evaluated without returning a result. Its syntax is as follows; *opt* stands for *optional*.

> *expression-statement:*
>> *expression*~*opt*~ ;

This indicates that an empty expression (one that consists only of a semicolon ';') is legal. An expression statement is used simply to generate the expression's side effects. The side effects may include assignments and calls to functions.

Cross-references
Standard, §3.6.3
The C Programming Language, ed. 2, p. 222

See Also
null statement, statements, void expression

extern — C keyword
(Language/declarations/storage-class specifiers)
External linkage
extern *type identifier*

The storage-class specifier **extern** declares that *identifier* has external linkage.

Cross-references
Standard, §3.5.1
The C Programming Language, ed. 2, pp. 210, 211

See Also
linkage, storage-class specifiers

external definitions — Overview
(Language)

A *definition* is a declaration that reserves storage for the thing declared. An *external definition* is a definition whose identifier is defined outside of any function. This makes the object available throughout the file or the program, depending upon whether it has, respectively, internal or external linkage.

The syntax of an external definition is as follows:

translation-unit:
    external-declaration
    translation-unit external-declaration

external-declaration:
    function-definition
    declaration

If an identifier has external linkage and is used in an expression (except as an operand to the **sizeof** operator), then an external definition must exist for that identifier somewhere in the program.

There are two varieties of external definition: **function definitions** and **object definitions**. See the appropriate entries for more information.

Cross-references
Standard, §3.7
The C Programming Language, ed. 2, p. 226

See Also
declaration, definition, function definition, linkage, object definition

external name — Definition
(Language/lexical elements/identifiers)

An *external name* is an identifier that has external linkage. The number and range of characters that may form an external name depends upon the implementation. The minimum maximum for the length of an external name is six characters, and an implementation is not obliged to recognize both upper-case and lower-case characters. An implementation may exceed these limits.

Cross-references
Standard, §3.1.2
The C Programming Language, ed. 2, p. 35

See Also
identifiers, internal name, linkage

F

fabs() — Library function
(Library/mathematics/integer-value-remainder)

Compute absolute value
#include < math.h >
double fabs(double z**);**

fabs calculates and returns the absolute value for a double-precision floating-point number. It returns z if z is zero or positive, and it returns -z if z is negative.

Example

For an example of this function, see **sin**.

Cross-references

Standard, §4.5.6.2
The C Programming Language, ed. 2, p. 251

See Also

abs, ceil, floor, fmod, integer-value-remainder

false — Definition
(Definitions)

In the context of a C program, an expression is *false* if it is zero.

See Also

Definitions, true

fclose() — Library function
(Library/STDIO/file access)

Close a stream
#include < stdio.h >
int fclose(FILE *fp**);**

fclose closes the stream pointed to by fp.

fclose flushes all of fp's output buffers. Unwritten buffered data are handed to the host environment for writing into fp, and unread, buffered data are thrown away. It then dissociates the stream pointed to by fp from the file (i.e., "closes" the file). If the buffer associated with fp was allocated, it is then de-allocated.

The function **exit** calls **fclose** for open streams.

fclose returns zero if it closed *fp* correctly, and **EOF** if it did not.

Example
For an example of this function, see **fopen**.

Cross-references
Standard, §4.9.5.1
The C Programming Language, ed. 2, p. 162

See Also
fclose, fflush, file access, fopen, freopen, setbuf, setvbuf

Notes
The function **exit** closes open stream, which flushes their buffers.

feof() — Library function
(Library/STDIO/error handling)
Examine a stream's end-of-file indicator
#include <stdio.h>
int feof(FILE *_fp_);

feof examines the end-of-file indicator for the stream pointed to by *fp*. It returns zero if the indicator shows that the end of file has *not* been reached, and returns a number other than zero if the indicator shows that it has.

Examples
This example checks whether a file can be read directly to the end.

```
#include <stdio.h>
#include <stdlib.h>
#include <stddef.h>

main(int argc, char *argv[])
{
    long size;
    FILE *ifp;

    if(argc != 2) {
        printf("usage: example inputfile\n");
        exit(EXIT_FAILURE);
    }
```

```
    if((ifp = fopen(argv[1], "rb")) == NULL) {
        printf("Cannot open %s\n", argv[1]);
        exit(EXIT_FAILURE);
    }

    for(size = 0; EOF != fgetc(ifp); size++)
        ;

    if(feof(ifp))
        printf("EOF at character %ld\n", size);

    if(ferror(ifp)) {
        printf("Error at character %ld\n", size);
        perror(NULL);
    }
    return(EXIT_SUCCESS);
}
```

Cross-references
Standard, §4.9.10.2
The C Programming Language, ed. 2, p. 176

See Also
clearerr, error handling, ferror, perror

ferror() — Library function
(Library/STDIO/error handling)
Examine a stream's error indicator
#include <stdio.h>
int ferror(FILE *fp);

ferror examines the error indicator for the stream pointed to by *fp*. It returns zero if an error has occurred on *fp*, and a number other than zero if one has not.

Cross-references
Standard, §4.9.10.3
The C Programming Language, ed. 2, p. 164

See Also
clearerr, error handling, feof, perror

Notes
Any error condition noted by **ferror** will persist either until the stream is closed, until **clearerr** is used to clear it, or until the file-position indicator is reset with **rewind**.

ferror does not return the error status on all implementations. Some other mechanism must be used to determine what error has occurred.

fflush() — Library function
(Library/STDIO/file access)
Flush output stream's buffer
#include <stdio.h>
int fflush(FILE *fp);

fflush flushes the buffer associated with the file stream pointed to by *fp*. If *fp* points to an output stream, then **fflush** hands all unwritten data to the host environment for writing into *fp*. If, however, *fp* points to an input stream, behavior is undefined.

In many environments, **stdout** is buffered. There, **fflush** can be used to write a prompt that is not terminated by a newline.

fflush returns zero if all goes well, and returns **EOF** if a write error occurs.

The function **exit** calls **fclose** to flush all output buffers before the program exits.

Example
This example asks for a string and returns it in reply.

```
#include <stdio.h>
#include <stddef.h>
#include <stdlib.h>
#include <string.h>
static char reply[80];
char *
askstr(char *msg)
{
    printf("Enter %s ", msg);
    /* required by the absence of a \n */
    fflush(stdout);
    if(gets(reply) == NULL)
        exit(EXIT_SUCCESS);
    return(reply);
}
```

```
main(void)
{
    for(;;)
        if(!strcmp(askstr("a string"), "quit"))
            break;
    return(EXIT_SUCCESS);
}
```

Cross-references
Standard, §4.9.5.2
The C Programming Language, ed. 2, p. 242

See Also
fclose, file access, fopen, freopen, setbuf, setvbuf

fgetc() — Library function
     (Library/STDIO/input-output)
     Read a character from a stream
     #include < stdio.h >
     int fgetc(FILE *fp);

fgetc reads a character from the stream pointed to by *fp*. Each character is read in-itially as an **unsigned char**, then converted to an **int** before it is passed to the calling function. **fgetc** then advances the file-position indicator for *fp*.

fputc returns the character read from *fp*. If the file-position indicator is beyond the end of the file to which *fp* points, **fputc** returns **EOF** and sets the end-of-file in-dicator. If a read error occurs, **fgetc** returns **EOF** and the stream's error indicator is set.

Example
For an example of this function, see **tmpfile**.

Cross-references
Standard, §4.9.7.1
The C Programming Language, ed. 2, p. 246

See Also
fgets, fputc, fputs, getc, getchar, gets, input-output, putc, putchar, puts, ungetc

fgetpos() — Library function
(Library/STDIO/file positioning)
Get value of file-position indicator
#include <stdio.h>
int fgetpos(FILE **fp***, fpos_t ****position***);**

fgetpos copies the value of the file-position indicator for file stream *fp* into the area pointed to by *position*. *position* is of type **fpos_t**, which is defined in the header **stdio.h**. The information written into *position* can be used by the function **fsetpos** to return the file-position indicator to where it was when **fgetpos** was called.

fgetpos returns zero if all went well. If an error occurred, **fgetpos** returns non-zero and sets the integer expression **errno** to the appropriate value. See **errno** for more information on its use.

Example

This example seeks to a random line in a very large file.

```
#include <math.h>
#include <stdarg.h>
#include <stddef.h>
#include <stdio.h>
#include <stdlib.h>
#include <time.h>

void
fatal(char *format, ...)
{
    va_list argptr;

    if(errno)
        perror(NULL);
    if(format != NULL) {
        va_start(argptr, format);
        vfprintf(stderr, format, argptr);
        va_end(argptr);
    }
    exit(EXIT_FAILURE);
}
```

```
main(int argc, char *argv[])
{
    int c;
    long count;
    FILE *ifp, *tmp;
    fpos_t loc;

    if(argc != 2)
        fatal("usage: fscanf inputfile\n");
    if((ifp = fopen(argv[1], "r")) == NULL)
        fatal("Cannot open %s\n", argv[1]);
    if((tmp = tmpfile()) == NULL)
        fatal("Cannot build index file");

    /* seed random-number generator */
    srand((unsigned int)time(NULL));

    for(count = 1;!feof(ifp); count++) {
        /* for monster files */
        if(fgetpos(ifp, &loc))
            fatal("fgetpos error");

        if(fwrite(&loc, sizeof(loc), 1, tmp) != 1)
            fatal("Write fail on index");
        rand();
        while('\n' != (c = fgetc(ifp)) && EOF != c)
            ;
    }

    count = rand() % count;
    fseek(tmp, count * sizeof(loc), SEEK_SET);

    if(fread(&loc, sizeof(loc), 1, tmp) != 1)
        fatal("Read fail on index");

    fsetpos(ifp, &loc);
    while((c = fgetc(ifp)) != EOF) {
        if('@' == c)
            putchar('\n');
        else
            putchar(c);

        if('\n' == c)
            break;
    }
    return(EXIT_SUCCESS);
}
```

Cross-references
Standard, §4.9.9.1
The C Programming Language, ed. 2, p. 248

See Also
file positioning, fseek, fsetpos, ftell, rewind

Notes
The Committee introduced **fgetpos** and **fsetpos** to manipulate a file whose file-position indicator cannot be stored within a **long**.

fgets() — Library function
(Library/STDIO/input-output)
Read a line from a stream
#include <stdio.h>
char *fgets(char **string***, int** *n***, FILE ****fp***);**

fgets reads characters from the stream pointed to by *fp* into the area pointed to by *string* until either *n*-1 characters have been read, a newline character is read, or the end of file is encountered. It retains the newline, if any, and appends a null character to the end of of the string.

fgets returns the pointer *string* if its read was performed successfully. It returns NULL if it encounters the end of file or if a read error occurred. When a read error occurs, the contents of *string* are indeterminate.

Example
This example displays a text file. It breaks up lines that are longer than 78 characters.

```
#include <stdarg.h>
#include <stddef.h>
#include <stdio.h>
#include <stdlib.h>
#include <string.h>

void
fatal(char *format, ...)
{
    va_list argptr;
```

```
          if(errno)
              perror(NULL);
          if(format!=NULL) {
              va_start(argptr, format);
              vfprintf(stderr, format, argptr);
              va_end(argptr);
          }
          exit(EXIT_FAILURE);
     }
main(int argc, char *argv[])
{
     char buf[79];
     FILE  *ifp;

     if(argc != 2)
          fatal("usage: fgets inputfile\n");
     if(NULL == (ifp = fopen(argv[1], "r")))
          fatal("Cannot open %s\n", argv[1]);

     while(fgets(buf, sizeof(buf), ifp) != NULL) {
          printf("%s", buf);
          if(strchr(buf, '\n') == NULL)
              printf("\\\n");
     }
     return(EXIT_SUCCESS);
}
```

Cross-references
Standard, §4.9.7.2
The C Programming Language, ed. 2, p. 247

See Also
fgetc, fputc, fputs, getc, getchar, gets, input-output, putc, putchar, puts, ungetc

file — Definition
(Library/STDIO)

A *file* is a mass of bits that has been named and stored on a mass-storage device.

Opening a File
To read a file, alter its contents, or add data to it, a C program must use a *stream*. The term *opening a file* means to establish a stream through which the program can access the file. The stream governs the way data are accessed. The information the stream needs to access the file are encoded within a **FILE** object. Because

environments vary greatly in the information they need to access a file, the Standard does not describe the internals of the **FILE** object. If a file does not exist when a program attempts to open it, then it is *created*. Because some environments distinguish the format for a text file from that for a binary file, the Standard distinguishes between opening a stream into text mode and opening it into binary mode.

To open a file, use the functions **fopen** or **freopen**. The former simply opens a file and assigns a stream to it. The latter reopens a file; that is, it takes the stream being used to access one file, assigns it to another file, and closes the original file. **freopen** can also be used to change the mode in which a file is accessed.

Buffering

When a file is opened, it is assigned a *buffer*. Access to the file are made through the buffer. Data written or, in some instances, read from the file are kept in the buffer temporarily, then transmitted as a block. This increases the efficiency with which programs communicate with the environment. To change the type of buffering performed, the size of the buffer used, or to redirect buffering to a buffer of your own creation, use the functions **setbuf** or **setvbuf**. See the entry for **buffer** for more information on the types of buffers used with files.

File-position Indicator

A file has a *file-position indicator* associated with it; this indicates the point within the file where it is being written to or read. Use of this indicator allows a program to walk smoothly through a file without having to use internal counters or other means to ensure that data are received sequentially. It also allows a program to access any point within a file "randomly" — that is, to access any given point in the file without having to walk through the entire file to reach it.

The manipulation of the file-position indicator can vary sharply between binary and text files. In general, the file-position indicator for a binary file is simply incremented as a character is read or written. For a text file, however, manipulation of the file-position indicator is defined by the implementation. This is due to the fact that different implementations represent end-of-line characters differently. To read the file-position indicator, use the functions **fgetpos** or **ftell**; to set it directly, use the functions **fseek** or **fsetpos**.

Error Conditions

When a file is being manipulated, a condition may occur that could cause trouble should the program continue to read or write that file. This could be an error, such as a read error, or the program may have read to the end of the file.

To help prevent such a condition from creating trouble, most environments use two indicators to signal when one has occurred: the *error indicator* and the *end-of-file* indicator. When an error occurs, the error indicator is set to a value that encodes the type of error that occurred; and when the end of the file is read, then the end-of-file indicator is set. By reading these indicators, a program may discover if all is going well. Under some implementations, however, a file may not be manipulated further unless both indicators are reset to their normal values.

To discover the setting of the end-of-file indicator, use the function **feof**. To discover the setting of the error indicator, use **ferror**. To reset the indicators to their normal values, use the function **clearerr**.

Closing a File

When you have finished manipulating a file, you should close it. To close a file means to dissociate it from the stream with which you had been manipulating it. When a file is closed, the buffer associated with its stream is flushed to ensure that all data intended for the file are written into it. To close a file, use the function **fclose**.

Cross-reference
Standard, §4.9.3

See Also
buffer, close, create, open, STDIO, stdio.h, stream

Notes

When data are written into a binary file, the file is not truncated by the write. This allows writes to binary files to be performed at random positions throughout the file without truncating the file at the position written. Whether a text file may be truncated when data are written into it depends upon the implementation. This is due to the fact that text files in some environments use record structuring.

FILE — Type
(Library/STDIO)
Descriptor for a stream
#include < stdio.h >

The type **FILE** is defined in the header **stdio.h**. It describes a *stream*, which can access either a file on a mass-storage device or a peripheral device.

When the function **fopen** opens a file, it creates a **FILE** and returns a pointer to it. That pointer is used by other STDIO routines to access the stream that the **FILE** describes. For more information about what it means to open a file, see **file**.

Cross-references
Standard, §4.9.3
The C Programming Language, ed. 2, p. 160

See Also
buffer, file, STDIO, stream

Notes
The form of the **FILE** object is left up to the implementation. The intent is to have it be an implementation-defined "black box". It is not wise to manipulate it or dissect it directly; a program that does is not portable.

file access — Overview
(Library/STDIO)
#include <stdio.h>

The Standard describes six functions with which you can gain access to a stream, or control the manner in which it is accessed. They are as follows:

fclose	Close a stream
fflush	Flush an output stream's buffer
fopen	Open a stream
freopen	Close and reopen a stream
setbuf	Set an alternate buffer for a stream
setvbuf	Set an alternate buffer for a stream

Cross-references
Standard, §4.9.5
The C Programming Language, ed. 2, pp. 160*ff*

See Also
error handling, file operations, file positioning, input-output, STDIO

FILENAME_MAX — Macro
(Library/STDIO)
Maximum length of file name
#include <stdio.h>

FILENAME_MAX is a macro that is defined in the header **stdio.h**. It gives the maximum length of a file name that the implementation can open.

Cross-references
Standard, §4.9.1
The C Programming Language, ed. 2, p. 242

See Also
fopen, stdio.h

file operations — Overview
(Library/STDIO)
#include <stdio.h>

The Standard describes four library functions that let you manipulate files directly. They are as follows:

remove	Remove a file
rename	Rename a file
tmpfile	Create a temporary file
tmpnam	Generate a name for a temporary file

Cross-reference
Standard, §4.9.4

See Also
error handling, file access, file positioning, input-output, STDIO

file-position indicator — Definition
(Library/STDIO)

The *file-position indicator* marks the point at which a file is being written or read.

Under some environments, the file-position indicator for a text file has a format very different from that of the indicator for a binary file. Therefore, the Standard distinguishes the way a STDIO function manipulates a text file's indicator from the way it manipulates a binary file's indicator. For a binary file, the file-position indicator is simply incremented as a character is read or written; for a text file, however, the implementation defines the way the the file-position indicator is changed.

To read the file-position indicator, use the functions **fgetpos** or **ftell**; to set it directly, use the functions **fseek** or **fsetpos**. These functions differ chiefly in that **fseek** and **ftell** return the file-position indicator in the form of a **long**. **fgetpos** and **fsetpos**, on the other hand, return an object of the type **fpos_t**, and are designed to be used with a file whose file-position indicator is too large to fit into a **long**.

Cross-reference
Standard, §4.9.3

See Also
file, SEEK_CUR, SEEK_END, SEEK_SET, STDIO, stdio.h, stream

file positioning — Overview
(Library/STDIO)

Manipulate file-position indicator
#include < stdio.h >

The Standard describes five functions that manipulate the file-position indicator, as follows:

fgetpos	Get the value of the file-position indicator (**fpos_t**)
fseek	Set the file-position indicator
fsetpos	Set the file-position indicator (**fpos_t**)
ftell	Get the value of the file-position indicator
rewind	Reset the file-position indicator

fgetpos and **fsetpos** differ from **fseek** and **ftell** mainly in that they return a value of type **fpos_t** instead of a **long**. **fpos_t** is defined in the header **stdio.h**. It was created so that **fgetpos** and **fsetpos** can be used to manipulate a file whose file-position indicator is too large to fit into a **long**. This may be an extremely large file, or a file in an environment whose file-position indicator is a non-scalar value, such as a track/sector/offset or node/extent/offset.

Cross-references

Standard, §4.9.9
The C Programming Language, ed. 2, p. 248

See Also

error handling, file access, file operations, file-position indicator, input-output, STDIO

float — C keyword
(Language/lexical elements/identifiers/types)

A **float** is a data type that represents a single-precision floating-point number. It is defined as being no larger than a **double**.

Like all floating-point numbers, a **float** consists of one sign bit, which indicates whether the number is positive or negative; bits that encode the number's *exponent*; and bits that encode the number's *mantissa*, or the number upon which the exponent works. The exponent often uses a *bias*. This is a value that is subtracted from the exponent to yield the power of two by which the mantissa will be increased. The format of a **float** and the range of values that it can encode are set in the following macros, all of which are defined in the header **limits.h**:

FLT_DIG
> This holds the number of decimal digits of precision. This must be at least ten.

FLT_EPSILON
> Where b indicates the base of the exponent (default, two) and p indicates the precision (or number of base b digits in the mantissa), this macro holds the minimum positive floating-point number x such that $1.0 + x$ does not equal 1.0, b^{1-p}. This must be at least 1E-5.

FLT_MAX
> This holds the maximum representable floating-point number. It must be at least 1E+37.

FLT_MAX_EXP
> This is the maximum integer such that the value of **FLT_RADIX** raised to its power minus one is a representable finite floating-point number.

FLT_MAX_10_EXP
> This holds the maximum integer such that ten raised to its power is within the range of representable finite floating-point numbers. It must be at least +37.

FLT_MANT_DIG
> This gives the number of digits in the mantissa.

FLT_MIN
> This gives the minimum value encodable within a **float**. This must be at least 1E-37.

FLT_MIN_EXP
> This gives the minimum negative integer such that when the value of **FLT_RADIX** is raised to that power minus one is a normalized floating-point number.

FLT_MIN_10_EXP
> This gives the minimum negative integer such that ten raised to that power is within the range of normalized floating-point numbers.

A **float** constant is represented by the suffix **f** or **F** on a floating-point constant.

Example
For an example of a program that uses **float**, see **sin**.

Cross-references
Standard, §2.2.4.2, §3.1.2.4, §3.1.3.1, §3.5.2
The C Programming Language, ed. 2, p. 211

See Also
double, float.h, long double, types

float.h — Header
(Environment/environmental considerations)

The header **float.h** defines a set of macros that return the limits for computation of floating-point numbers.

The following formula defines a floating-point number:

$$x = s \times b^e \times \sum_{k=1}^{p} f_k \times b^{-k}, \ e_{min} \le e \le e_{max}$$

where s indicates the sign (+1 or -1), b indicates the base in which the exponent is represented (any integer greater than one), e indicates the exponent (any integer between the minimum value e_{min} and the maximum value e_{max}), p indicates the precision (that is, the number of digits in the mantissa, using base b), and, finally, f_k the mantissa digits.

The following lists the macros defined in **float.h**. With the exception of **FLT_ROUNDS**, each macro is an expression; each value given is the minimum maximum that each expression must yield. The prefixes **DBL**, **FLT**, and **LDBL** refer, respective, to **double**, **float**, and **long double**.

DBL_DIG
Number of decimal digits of precision. Must yield at least ten.

DBL_EPSILON
Smallest possible floating-point number x, such that 1.0 plus x does not test equal to 1.0. Must be at most 1E-9.

DBL_MANT_DIG
Number of digits in the floating-point mantissa for base **FLT_RADIX**.

DBL_MAX
Largest number that can be held by type **double**. Must yield at least 1E+37.

DBL_MAX_EXP
Largest integer such that the value of **FLT_RADIX** raised to its power minus one is less than or equal to **DBL_MAX**.

DBL_MAX_10_EXP
Largest integer such that ten raised to its power is less than or equal to **DBL_MAX**.

DBL_MIN
> Smallest number that can be held by type **double**.

DBL_MIN_EXP
> Smallest integer such that the value of **FLT_RADIX** raised to its power minus one is greater than or equal to **DBL_MIN**.

DBL_MIN_10_EXP
> Smallest integer such that ten raised to its power is greater than or equal to **DBL_MAX**.

FLT_DIG
> Number of decimal digits of precision. Must yield at least six.

FLT_EPSILON
> Smallest floating-point number x, such that 1.0 plus x does not test equal to 1.0. Must be at most 1E-5.

FLT_MANT_DIG
> Number of digits in the floating-point mantissa for base **FLT_RADIX**.

FLT_MAX
> Largest number that can be held by type **float**. Must yield at least 1E + 37.

FLT_MAX_EXP
> Largest integer such that the value of **FLT_RADIX** raised to its power minus one is less than or equal to **FLT_MAX**.

FLT_MAX_10_EXP
> Largest integer such that ten raised to its power is less than or equal to **FLT_MAX**.

FLT_MIN
> Smallest number that can be held by type **float**.

FLT_MIN_EXP
> Smallest integer such that the value of **FLT_RADIX** raised to its power minus one is greater than or equal to **FLT_MIN**.

FLT_MIN_10_EXP
> Smallest integer such that ten raised to its power is greater than or equal to **FLT_MIN**.

FLT_RADIX
> Base in which the exponents of all floating-point numbers are represented.

FLT_ROUNDS
> Manner of rounding used by the implementation, as follows:
>
> -1   Indeterminable, i.e., no strict rules apply
> 0   Toward zero, i.e., truncation
> 1   To nearest, i.e., rounds to nearest representable value

2 Toward positive infinity, i.e., always rounds up
3 Toward negative infinity, i.e., always rounds down

Any other value indicates that the manner of rounding is defined by the implementation.

LDBL_DIG
Number of decimal digits of precision. Must yield at least ten.

LDBL_EPSILON
Smallest floating-point number x, such that 1.0 plus x does not test equal to 1.0. Must be at most 1E-9.

LDBL_MANT_DIG
Number of digits in the floating-point mantissa for base **FLT_RADIX**.

LDBL_MAX
Largest number that can be held by type **long double**. Must yield at least 1E+37.

LDBL_MAX_EXP
Largest integer such that the value of **FLT_RADIX** raised to its power minus one is less than or equal to **LDBL_MAX**.

LDBL_MAX_10_EXP
Largest integer such that ten raised to its power is less than or equal to **LDBL_MAX**.

LDBL_MIN
Smallest number that can be held by type **long double**. Must be no greater than 1E-37.

LDBL_MIN_EXP
Smallest integer such that the value of **FLT_RADIX** raised to its power minus one is greater than or equal to **LDBL_MIN**.

LDBL_MIN_10_EXP
Smallest integer such that ten raised to its power is greater than or equal to **LDBL_MIN**.

Cross-references
Standard, §2.2.4.2
The C Programming Language, ed. 2, p. 257

See Also
environmental considerations, header, numerical limits

floating constant — Definition
(Language/lexical elements/constants)

A *floating constant* is a constant that represents a floating-point number. Its syntax is as follows; *opt* indicates *optional*:

floating-constant:
    fractional-constant exponent-part$_{opt}$ floating-suffix$_{opt}$
    digit-sequence exponent-part floating-suffix$_{opt}$

fractional-constant:
    digit-sequence$_{opt}$. digit-sequence$_{opt}$
    digit-sequence .

exponent-part:
    e *sign$_{opt}$ digit-sequence*
    E *sign$_{opt}$ digit-sequence*

sign: one of
    +   -

digit-sequence:
    digit
    digit-sequence digit

floating-suffix: one of
    f   l   F   L

A floating constant has three parts: the *value*, an *exponent*, and a *suffix*. Both the exponent and the suffix are optional.

The value section gives the value of the floating-point number. It also has three parts: a sequence of decimal digits, a period, and another set of digits. The first set of digits gives the whole-number part of the number, the period indicates the end of the whole-number part and the beginning of the fractional part, and the second sequence of digits encodes the fractional part. The period (which is sometimes called the "radix point") is always the character that marks the end of the whole-number sequence, regardless of the character recognized by the program's locale. In other words, the format of the C language floating constant is not locale-sensitive.

The exponent is used when the floating constant uses exponential notation. Here, the exponent gives the power of ten by which the base value is multiplied. For example,

```
1.05e10
```

represents the number

    1.05*10^10

or

    10,500,000,000

stored as a **double**. The exponent is introduced by the characters **e** or **E** followed by either **+** or **-**, which indicates the sign of the exponent. There follows the exponent itself, which consists of a sequence of decimal digits.

Finally, a floating constant may be followed by the suffixes **f**, **F**, **l**, or **L**. The first two indicate that the constant is of type **float**; the latter two, that the constant is of type **long double**. If a floating constant has no suffix, the translator assumes that it is of type **double**.

Cross-references
Standard, §3.1.3.1
The C Programming Language, ed. 2, p. 194

See Also
constants, float

floating types — Definition
(Language/lexical elements/identifiers/types)

The term *floating types* refers to any of the types **float, double**, or **long double**. The representation of floating types is unspecified.

Cross-references
Standard, §3.1.2.5
The C Programming Language, ed. 2, p. 196

See Also
arithmetic types, types

Notes
The name *floating types* refers to floating-point representation. However, these may be represented in any way the implementation dictates. They are used to represent real numeric values.

floor() — Library function
      (Library/mathematics/integer-value-remainder)
Numeric floor
#include < math.h>
double floor(double z);

floor returns the "floor" of a number, or the largest integer not greater than z. For example, the floor of 23.2 is 23, and the floor of -23.2 is -24.

floor returns the value expressed as a **double**.

Cross-references
Standard, §4.5.6.3
The C Programming Language, ed. 2, p. 251

See Also
ceil, fabs, fmod, integer-value-remainder

FLT_DIG — Macro
      (Environment/environmental considerations/limits/numerical)
#include < float.h>

FLT_DIG is a macro that is defined in the header **float.h**. It is an expression that defines the number of decimal digits of precision for type **float**. It must evaluate to at least six.

Cross-references
Standard, §2.2.4.2
The C Programming Language, ed. 2, p. 257

See Also
float.h, numerical limits

FLT_EPSILON — Macro
      (Environment/environmental considerations/limits/numerical)
#include < float.h>

FLT_EPSILON is a macro that is defined in the header **float.h**. It is an expression that yields the smallest positive floating-point number representable as type **float**, such that 1.0 plus it does not test equal to 1.0. It must yield a value of at most 1E-5.

Cross-references
Standard, §2.2.4.2
The C Programming Language, ed. 2, p. 257

See Also
float.h, numerical limits

FLT_MANT_DIG — Macro
(Environment/environmental considerations/limits/numerical)
#include < float.h >

FLT_MANT_DIG is a macro that is defined in the header **float.h**. It is an expression that represents the number of digits in the mantissa of type **float**, in the numeric base set by the macro **FLT_RADIX**.

Cross-references
Standard, §2.2.4.2
The C Programming Language, ed. 2, p. 257

See Also
float.h, numerical limits

FLT_MAX — Macro
(Environment/environmental considerations/limits/numerical)
#include < float.h >

FLT_MAX is a macro that is defined in the header **float.h**. It is an expression that yields the largest number that can be represented by type **float**. It must yield a value of at least 1E+37.

Cross-references
Standard, §2.2.4.2
The C Programming Language, ed. 2, p. 257

See Also
float.h, numerical limits

FLT_MAX_10_EXP — Macro
(Environment/environmental considerations/limits/numerical)
#include < float.h >

FLT_MAX_10_EXP is a macro that is defined in the header **float.h**. It is an expression that yields the *largest* power, such that ten raised to it remains a floating-point number that can be encoded by type **float**. The value this expression yields must be at least 37.

Cross-references
Standard, §2.2.4.2
The C Programming Language, ed. 2, p. 257

See Also
float.h, numerical limits

FLT_MAX_EXP — Macro
(Environment/environmental considerations/limits/numerical)
#include < float.h >

FLT_MAX_EXP is a macro that is defined in the header **float.h**. It is an expression that yields the *largest* power such that **FLT_RADIX** raised to it minus one remains a floating-point number that can be held by type **float**.

Cross-references
Standard, §2.2.4.2
The C Programming Language, ed. 2, p. 257

See Also
float.h, numerical limits

FLT_MIN — Macro
(Environment/environmental considerations/limits/numerical)
#include < float.h >

FLT_MIN is a macro that is defined in the header **float.h**. It is an expression that yields the smallest number that can be represented by type **float**. It must yield a value of at most 1E-37.

Cross-references
Standard, §2.2.4.2
The C Programming Language, ed. 2, p. 257

See Also
float.h, numerical limits

FLT_MIN_10_EXP — Macro
(Environment/environmental considerations/limits/numerical)
#include <float.h>

FLT_MIN_10_EXP is a macro that is defined in the header **float.h**. It is an expression that yields the smallest power, such that ten raised to it remains a floating-point number that can be encoded by type **float**. It must be at most -37.

Cross-references
Standard, §2.2.4.2
The C Programming Language, ed. 2, p. 257

See Also
float.h, numerical limits

FLT_MIN_EXP — Macro
(Environment/environmental considerations/limits/numerical)
#include <float.h>

FLT_MIN_EXP is a macro that is defined in the header **float.h**. It is an expression that yields the smallest power such that **FLT_RADIX** raised to it minus one remains a floating-point number that can be held by type **float**.

Cross-references
Standard, §2.2.4.2
The C Programming Language, ed. 2, p. 257

See Also
float.h, numerical limits

FLT_RADIX — Macro
(Environment/environmental considerations/limits/numerical)
#include <float.h>

FLT_RADIX is a macro that is defined in the header **float.h**. It is an expression that represents the radix of exponent representation for a floating-point number. That is, it gives the numeric base for the exponent for a floating-point number. It must be at least two.

Cross-references
Standard, §2.2.4.2
The C Programming Language, ed. 2, p. 257

See Also
float.h, numerical limits

FLT_ROUNDS – Macro
(Environment/environmental considerations/limits/numerical)
#include < float.h >

FLT_ROUNDS is a macro that is declared in the header **float.h**. It indicates the rounding mode for floating-point addition, as follows:

-1	Indeterminable, i.e., no strict rules apply
0	Toward zero, i.e., truncation
1	To nearest, i.e., rounds to nearest representable value
2	Toward positive infinity, i.e., always rounds up
3	Toward negative infinity, i.e., always rounds down

Any other value indicates an implementation-specific form of rounding.

Cross-references
Standard, §2.2.4.2
The C Programming Language, ed. 2, p. 257

See Also
float.h, numerical limits

fmod – Library function
(Library/mathematics/integer-value-remainder)
Calculate modulus for floating-point number
#include < math.h >
double fmod(double *number***, double** *divisor***);**

fmod divides *number* by *divisor* and returns the remainder. If *divisor* is nonzero, the return value will have the same sign as *divisor*. If divisor is zero, however, it will either return zero or set a domain error.

Cross-references
Standard, §4.5.6.4
The C Programming Language, ed. 2, p. 251

See Also
ceil, fabs, floor, integer-value-remainder

fopen() — Library function
(Library/STDIO/file access)
Open a stream for standard I/O
#include < stdio.h >
FILE *fopen (const char *file, const char *mode);

fopen opens *file*, and allocates and initializes the data stream associated with it. This makes the file available for STDIO operations. Under some execution environments, *file* may name either a file on a mass-storage device or a peripheral device. *file* can be no more than **FILENAME_MAX** characters long.

mode points to a string that consists of one or more of the characters "rwab+"; this indicates the mode into which the file is to be opened. The following set of mode strings are recognized:

a	Append, text mode
ab	Append, binary mode
a+	Append, text mode
ab+	Append, binary mode
a+b	Append, binary mode
r	Read, text mode
rb	Read, binary mode
r+	Update, text mode
rb+	Update, binary mode
r+b	Update, binary mode
w	Write, text mode
wb	Write, binary mode
w+	Update, text mode
wb+	Update, binary mode
w+b	Update, binary mode

Note the following:

- Opening *file* into any of the 'a' (append) modes means that data can be written only onto the end of the file. These modes set the file-position indicator to point to the end of the file. All other modes set it to point to the beginning of the file.

- To open *file* into any of the 'r' (read) modes, it must already exist and contain data. If *file* does not exist or cannot be opened, then **fopen** returns NULL.

- When a file is opened into any of the 'w' (write) modes, it is truncated to zero bytes if it already exists, or created if it does not.

- Opening *file* into any of the '+' (update) modes allows you to write data into it or read data from it. When used with 'r' or 'w', data may be read from *file* or written into it at any point. When used with 'a', data may be written into it only at its end. To switch from reading a file to writing into it, either the stream's input buffer must be flushed with **fflush** or the file-position indicator repositioned with **fseek, fsetpos**, or **rewind**.

fopen returns a pointer to the **FILE** object that controls the stream. It returns NULL if the file cannot be opened, for whatever reason.

fopen can open up to **FOPEN_MAX** files at once. This value must be at least eight, including **stdin, stdout**, and **stderr**.

Example
This example opens a test file and reports what happens.

```
#include <stdio.h>
#include <stdlib.h>
#include <stddef.h>

main(int argc, char *argv[])
{
    FILE *fp;

    if(argc != 3) {
        fprintf(stderr, "usage: fopen filename mode\n");
        exit(EXIT_FAILURE);
    }

    if((fp = fopen(argv[1], argv[2])) == NULL) {
        perror("Fopen failure");
        exit(EXIT_FAILURE);
    }

    fclose(fp);
    return(EXIT_SUCCESS);
}
```

Cross-references
Standard, §4.9.5.3
The C Programming Language, ed. 2, p. 160

See Also
fclose, fflush, file access, freopen, setbuf, setvbuf

Notes

To update an existing file, use the mode **r+**

fopen associates a fully buffered stream with *file* only if *file* does not access an interactive device.

A conforming implementation must support all of the modes described above. It may also offer other modes in which to open a file.

FOPEN_MAX — Macro
(Library/STDIO)
Maximum number of open files
#include < stdio.h >

FOPEN_MAX is a macro that is defined in the header **stdio.h**. It gives the maximum number of streams that a program can have open at any one time. This cannot be set to less than eight, including **stdin**, **stdout**, and **stderr**. Hence, there are at least five additional streams for use by a program. For maximum portability, a program that requires more than five streams should check the value of this macro.

Cross-references

Standard, §4.9.1
The C Programming Language, ed. 2, p. 242

See Also

fopen, stdio.h, stream

for — C keyword
(Language/statements/iteration statements)
Loop construct
for(*initialization*; *condition*; *modification*) *statement*

for introduces a conditional loop. It takes three expressions as arguments; these are separated by semicolons ';'. *initialization* is executed before the loop begins. *condition* describes the condition that must be true for the loop to execute. *modification* is the statement that modifies *variable* to control the number of iterations of the loop. For example,

```
for (i=0; i<10; i++)
```

first sets the variable **i** to zero; then declares that the loop will continue as long as **i** remains less than ten; and finally, increments **i** by one after every iteration of the loop. This ensures that the loop will iterate exactly ten times (from **i= =0** through **i= =9**). The statement

```
for(;;)
```

will loop until its execution is interrupted by a **break, goto,** or **return** statement.

The **for** statement is equivalent to:

> *initialization* ;
> while(*condition*) {
>   *statement*
>   *modification* ;
> }

Example

For an example of this statement, see **putc**.

Cross-references

Standard, §3.6.5.3
The C Programming Language, ed. 2, pp. 60*ff*

See Also

break, C keywords, continue, do, iteration statements, while

fpos_t — Type
(Library/STDIO)

Encode current position in a file

The type **fpos_t** is defined in the header **stdio.h**. It is used by the functions **fgetpos** and **fsetpos** to encode the current position within a file (the *file-position indicator*). Its type may vary from implementation to implementation.

fpos_t and its functions are designed to manipulate files whose file-position indicator cannot be encoded within a **long**. For small files (i.e., less than four gigabytes) you can use the related functions **fseek** and **ftell**.

Cross-references

Standard, §4.9.1, §4.9.9.1, §4.9.9.3
The C Programming Language, ed. 2, p. 248

See Also

fgetpos, file, FILE, file-position indicator, fsetpos, stdio, stdio.h

Notes

The actual type of **fpos_t** is left to the implementation. The intent is to define a data type that can be obtained by a call to **fgetpos** and used on later calls to **fsetpos**. It is not wise to try to manipulate this type directly or to dissect it. Code that depends on specific properties of this type may not be portable.

fprintf() – Library function
(Library/STDIO/input-output)
Print formatted text into a stream
#include <stdio.h>
int fprintf(FILE *‍*fp*, const char *‍*format*, ...);

fprintf constructs a formatted string and writes it into the stream pointed to by *fp*. It can translate integers, floating-point numbers, and strings in a variety of text formats.

format points to a string that can contain text, character constants, and one or more *conversion specifications*. A conversion specification describes how a particular data type is to be converted into text. Each conversion specification is introduced with the percent sign '%'. (To print a literal percent sign, use the escape sequence "%%".) See **printf** for further discussion of the conversion specification, and for a table of the type specifiers that can be used with **fprintf**.

After *format* can come one or more arguments. There should be one argument for each conversion specification in *format*, and the argument should be of the type appropriate to the conversion specification. For example, if *format* contains conversion specifications for an **int**, a **long**, and a string, then *format* should be followed by three arguments, being, respectively, an **int**, a **long**, and a **char ***.

If there are fewer arguments than conversion specifications, then **fprintf**'s behavior is undefined. If there are more, then every argument without a corresponding conversion specification is evaluated and then ignored. If an argument is not of the same type as its corresponding conversion specifier, then the behavior of **fprintf** is undefined. Thus, presenting an **int** where **fprintf** expects a **char *** may generate unwelcome results.

If it could write the formatted string, **fprintf** returns the number of characters written; otherwise, it returns a negative number.

Example
This example prints two messages: one into **stderr** and the other into **stdout**.

```
#include <stdio.h>
#include <stdlib.h>

main(void)
{
    fprintf(stderr, "A message to stderr.\n");
    printf("A message to stdout.\n");
    return(EXIT_SUCCESS);
}
```

Cross-references
Standard, §4.9.6.1
The C Programming Language, ed. 2, p. 243

See Also
fscanf, input-output, printf, scanf, sprintf, sscanf, vfprintf, vprintf, vsprintf

Notes
The Standard mandates that **fprintf** be able to construct and output a string of up to at least 509 characters.

The Standard does not include the conversion specifier 'r', which is used by many implementations to pass an array of arguments to **fprintf**. The function **vfprintf** provides much of the functionality provided by the 'r' specifier.

The character that **fprintf** uses to represent the decimal point is affected by the program's locale, as set by the function **setlocale**. For more information, see **localization**.

fputc() — Library function
(Standard/STDIO/input-output)
Write a character into a stream
#include < stdio.h >
int fputc(int *character*, **FILE** **fp*);

fputc converts *character* to an **unsigned char**, writes it into the stream pointed to by *fp*, and advances the file-position indicator for *fp*.

fputc returns *character* if it was written successfully; otherwise, it sets the error indicator for *fp* and returns **EOF**.

Example
The following example uses **fputc** to copy the contents of one file into another.

```
#include <stdarg.h>
#include <stdio.h>
#include <stdlib.h>

void
fatal(char *format, ...)
{
    va_list argptr;
```

```
            if(errno)
                  perror(NULL);
            if(format != NULL) {
                  va_start(argptr, format);
                  vfprintf(stderr, format, argptr);
                  va_end(argptr);
            }
            exit(EXIT_FAILURE);
      }

      main(int argc; char *argv[];)
      {
            FILE *ifp, *ofp;
            int ch;

            if(argc != 3)
                  fatal("usage: fputc oldfile newfile\n");

            if((ifp = fopen(argv[1], "r")) == NULL)
                  fatal("Cannot open %s\n", argv[1]);
            if((ofp = fopen(argv[2], "w")) == NULL)
                  fatal("Cannot open %s\n", argv[2]);

            while ((ch = fgetc(ifp)) != EOF)
                  if (fputc(ch, ofp) == EOF)
                        fatal("Write error for %s\n", argv[2]);
            return(EXIT_SUCCESS);
      }
```

Cross-references
Standard, §4.9.7.3
The C Programming Language, ed. 2, p. 247

See Also
fgetc, fgets, fputs, input-output, putc, putchar, puts, ungetc

fputs() — Library function
(Library/STDIO/input-output)
Write a string into a stream
#include <stdio.h>
int fputs(char **string***; FILE ****fp***);**

fputs writes the string pointed to by *string* into the stream pointed to by *fp*. The
terminating null character is not written. Unlike the related function **puts**, it does
not append a newline character to the end of *string*.

fputs returns a non-negative number if it could write *string* correctly; if it could not, it returns **EOF**.

Cross-references
Standard, §4.9.7.4
The C Programming Language, ed. 2, p. 247

See Also
fgetc, fgets, fputc, getc, getchar, gets, input-output, putc, putchar, puts, ungetc

fread() — Library function
(Library/STDIO/input-output)
Read data from a stream
#include <stdio.h>
size_t fread(void *buffer, **size_t** *size*, **size_t** *n*, **FILE ****fp***);**

fread reads up to *n* items, each being *size* bytes long, from the stream pointed to by *fp* and copies them into the area pointed to by *buffer*. It advances the file-position indicator by the amount appropriate to the number of bytes read.

fread returns the number of items read. If the value returned by **fread** is not equal to *n*, use the functions **ferror** and **feof** to find, respectively, if an error has occurred or if the end of file has been encountered.

Example
This example reads data structures into an array of structures. It is more to be read than used.

```
#include <stddef.h>
#include <stdio.h>
#include <stdlib.h>
#define COUNT 10

struct aStruct {
      double d;
      float  f;
      int    i;
} arrayStruct[COUNT];

main(void)
{
      int i;
      FILE *ifp;
```

```
if((ifp = fopen("a.s", "rb")) == NULL) {
    perror("Cannot open a.s");
    exit(EXIT_FAILURE);
}
/*          buffer      blocksize           count FILE */
i=fread(arrayStruct,sizeof(struct aStruct),COUNT,ifp);
if(i != COUNT) {
    fprintf(stderr, "Only read %d blocks\n", i);
    return(EXIT_FAILURE);
}
return(EXIT_SUCCESS);
}
```

Cross-references

Standard, §4.9.8.1
The C Programming Language, ed. 2, p. 247

See Also

fwrite, input-output

Notes

If an error occurs while data are being read, then the value of the file-position indicator is indeterminate. If either *size* or *n* is zero, then **fread** returns zero and reads nothing.

free() — Library function
(Library/general utilities/memory management)

Deallocate dynamic memory
#include <stdlib.h>
void free(void *ptr);

free deallocates a block of dynamic memory that had been allocated by **malloc**, **calloc**, or **realloc**. Deallocating memory may make it available for reuse.

ptr points to the block of memory to be freed. It must have been returned by **malloc, calloc,** or **realloc**.

free returns nothing.

Cross-references

Standard, §4.10.3.2
The C Programming Language, ed. 2, p. 167

See Also

calloc, malloc, memory management, realloc

Notes

If *ptr* does not point to a block of memory that had been allocated by **calloc**, **malloc**, or **realloc**, the behavior of **free** is undefined.

If *ptr* is equivalent to NULL, then no action occurs.

Finally, if a program attempts to access memory that has been freed, its behavior is undefined.

freestanding environment — Definition
(Environment/execution environment)

A *freestanding environment* is one in which a C program runs without an operating system. For example, a microprocessor used as a washing-machine controller is considered to be a free-standing environment.

The Standard sets minimal restrictions on a freestanding environment, as most are custom-designed for a particular task. It may call any function it wishes when the program starts up; otherwise, there are no reserved external identifiers. The implementation defines what libraries, if any, are available to the program, and what occurs when the program terminates.

Cross-reference

Standard, §2.1.2.1

See Also

execution environment, hosted environment

Notes

A strictly conforming program for a freestanding environment can use the macros and library functions that the Standard defines in the headers **float.h**, **limits.h**, and **stddef.h**. Otherwise, section 4 of the Standard, which describes the C library, does not apply to a freestanding environment. The application is expected to provide its own service functions.

freopen() — Library function
(Library/STDIO/file access)

Re-open a stream
#include <stdio.h>
FILE *freopen(const char **file***, const char ****mode***, FILE ****fp***);**

freopen opens *file* and associates it with the stream pointed to by *fp*, which is already in use. It first tries to close the file currently associated with *fp*. Then it opens *file*, and returns a pointer to the **FILE** object, through which other STDIO routines can access *file*. Under some execution environments, **freopen** can be used to access a peripheral device as well as a file. Thus, **freopen** is often used to change the device associated with the streams **stdin**, **stdout**, or **stderr**, as well as to the change the access modes for an open file.

mode indicates the manner in which *file* is to be accessed. For a table of the modes described by the Standard, see **fopen**.

freopen returns NULL if *file* could not be opened properly; otherwise, it returns *fp*.

Example
This example uses **freopen** to copy a list of files into one file.

```
#include <stddef.h>
#include <stdlib.h>
#include <stdio.h>
#include <stdarg.h>

void
fatal(char *format, ...)
{
    va_list argptr;

    /* if there is a system message, display it */
    if(errno)
        perror(NULL);

    /* if there is a user message, use it */
    if(format != NULL) {
        va_start(argptr, format);
        vfprintf(stderr, format, argptr);
        va_end(argptr);
    }
    exit(EXIT_FAILURE);
}

main(int argc, char *argv[])
{
    FILE *ifp, *ofp;
    int i, c;
```

```
        if(argc < 3)
             fatal("usage: freopen input1 input2 ... output\n");
        if((ofp = fopen(argv[argc - 1], "wb")) == NULL)
             fatal("Cannot open %s\n", argv[argc - 1]);

        ifp = stdin;
        for(i = 1; i < argc; i++) {
             if((ifp = freopen(argv[i], "rb", ifp)) == NULL)
                  fatal("Cannot open %s\n", argv[i]);

             while((c = fgetc(ifp)) != EOF)
                  fputc(c, ofp);
        }
        return(EXIT_SUCCESS);
}
```

Cross-references

Standard, §4.9.5.4
The C Programming Language, ed. 2, p. 162

See Also

fclose, fflush, file access, fopen, setbuf, setvbuf

Notes

freopen will attempt to close the file currently associated with *fp*. However, if it cannot be closed, **freopen** will still open *file* and associate *fp* with it.

frexp() — Library function
(Library/mathematics/exponent-log functions)

Fracture floating-point number
#include < math.h >
double frexp(double *real*, int **exp*);

frexp breaks a double-precision floating-point number into its mantissa and exponent. It returns the mantissa m of the argument *real*, such that $0.5 <= m < 1$ or $m=0$, and stores the binary exponent in the area pointed to by *exp*. The exponent is an integral power of two.

See **float.h** for more information about the structure of a floating-point number.

Cross-references

Standard, §4.5.4.3
The C Programming Language, ed. 2, p. 251

See Also
atof, ceil, exponent-log functions, fabs, floor, ldexp, modf

fscanf() — Library function
(Library/STDIO/input-output)
Read and interpret text from a stream
#include <stdio.h>
int fscanf(FILE *fp, const char *format, ...);

fscanf reads characters from the stream pointed to by *fp*, and uses the string pointed to by *format* to interpret what it has read into the appropriate type of data. *format* points to a string that contains one or more conversion specifications, each of which is introduced with the percent sign '%'. For a table of the conversion specifiers that may be used with **fscanf**, see **scanf**.

After *format* can come one or more arguments. There should be one argument for each conversion specification in *format*, and the argument should point to a data element of the type appropriate to the conversion specification. For example, if *format* contains conversion specifications for an **int**, a **long**, and a string, then *format* should be followed by three arguments: respectively, a pointer to an **int**, a pointer to a **long**, and an array of **chars**.

If there are fewer arguments than conversion specifications, then **fscanf**'s behavior is undefined. If there are more, then every argument without a corresponding conversion specification is evaluated and then ignored. If an argument is not of the same type as its corresponding type specification, then **fscanf** returns.

fscanf returns the number of input elements it scanned and formatted. If an error occurs while **fscanf** is reading its input, it returns **EOF**.

Example
This example reads and displays data from a file of strings with the following format:

```
ABORT     C        312    1-24-88   11:03a
ABS       C        239    1-24-88   11:03a
```

This is the output of the MS-DOS command **dir**.

```
#include <stddef.h>
#include <stdio.h>
#include <stdlib.h>
```

```
main(int argc, char *argv[])
{
    int count;
    long size;
    char fname[8], ext[3];
    FILE *ifp;

    if(argc != 2) {
        printf("usage: fscanf inputfile\n");
        exit(EXIT_FAILURE);
    }

    if((ifp = fopen(argv[1], "r")) == NULL) {
        printf("Cannot open %s\n", argv[1]);
        exit(EXIT_FAILURE);
    }

    while((count = fscanf(ifp, "%8s %3s %ld %*[^\n]",
        fname, ext, &size)) != EOF)
        if(count == 3)
            printf("%s.%s %ld\n", fname, ext, size);
    return(EXIT_SUCCESS);
}
```

Cross-references
Standard, §4.9.6.2
The C Programming Language, ed. 2, p. 245

See Also
fprintf, input-output, printf, scanf, sprintf, sscanf, vfprintf, vprintf, vsprintf

Notes
fscanf is best used to read data you are certain are in the correct format, such as strings previously written out with **fprintf**.

The character that **fscanf** recognizes as representing the decimal point is affected by the program's locale, as set by the function **setlocale**. For more information, see **localization**.

fseek() — Library function
(Library/STDIO/file positioning)
Set file-position indicator
#include <stdio.h>
int fseek(FILE **fp,* **long int** *offset,* **int** *whence***);**

fseek sets the file-position indicator for stream *fp*; this changes the point where the next read or write operation will occur.

offset and *whence* specify how the value of the file-position indicator should be reset. *offset* is the amount to move it, in bytes; this is a signed quantity. *whence* is the point from which to move it, as follows:

SEEK_CUR	the current position
SEEK_END	the end of the file
SEEK_SET	the beginning of the file

The values of these macros are set in the header **stdio.h**.

For a stream opened into binary mode, the Standard does not require an implementation to support the option **SEEK_END**. For a stream opened into text mode, *whence* should be set to **SEEK_SET**, and *offset* should be set either to zero or to a value returned by an earlier call to **ftell**. This ensures that newline characters will be correctly skipped.

Use of **fseek** clears the end-of-file indicator and undoes the effects of a previous call to **ungetc**; the next operation on *fp* may be input or output.

fseek returns a number other than zero for what the Standard calls an "improper request." Presumably, this means attempting to seek past the end or the beginning of a file, attempting to seek on an interactive device (such as a terminal), or attempting to seek on a file that does not exist.

Example
This example implements the UNIX game **fortune**. It randomly selects a line from a text file, and prints it. Multi-line fortunes, such as poems, should have '@'s embedded within them to mark line breaks.

```
#include <stddef.h>
#include <stdio.h>
#include <stdlib.h>
#include <time.h>

main(int argc, char *argv[])
{
    FILE   *ifp;
    double  randomAdj;
    int c;

    if(argc != 2) {
        printf("usage: fseek inputfile\n");
        exit(EXIT_FAILURE);
    }
```

```
if ((ifp = fopen(argv[1], "r")) == NULL) {
    printf("Cannot open %s\n", argv[1]);
    exit(EXIT_FAILURE);
}

fseek(ifp, 0L, SEEK_END);
randomAdj = (double)ftell(ifp)/((double)RAND_MAX);

/* Exercise rand() to make number more random */
srand((unsigned int)time(NULL));
for(c = 0; c < 100; c++)
    rand();

fseek(ifp, (long)(randomAdj * (double)rand()), SEEK_SET);
while('\n' != (c = fgetc(ifp)) && EOF != c)
    ;

if(c == EOF) {
    printf("File does not end with newline\n");
    exit(EXIT_FAILURE);
}

while('\n' != (c = fgetc(ifp))) {
    if(EOF == c) {
        fseek(ifp, 0L, SEEK_SET);
        continue;
    }

    /* display multi-line fortunes */
    if('@' == c)
        c = '\n';
    putchar(c);
}
return(EXIT_SUCCESS);
}
```

Cross-references
Standard, §4.9.9.2
The C Programming Language, ed. 2, p. 248

See Also
ftell, STDIO

Notes
Although the Standard does not describe the behavior of **fseek** if you attempt to seek beyond the end of a file, in some current implementations it does not result in an error condition until the corresponding read or write is attempted.

Note, too, that the Standard's definition of **fseek** allows a user to seek past the beginning of a binary file as well as past its end. *Caveat utilitor.*

fsetpos() — Library function
(Library/STDIO/file positioning)
Set file-position indicator
#include <stdio.h>
int fsetpos(FILE *fp, const fpos_t *position);

fsetpos resets the file-position indicator. *fp* points to the file stream whose indicator is being reset. *position* is a value that had been returned by an earlier call to **fgetpos**; it is of type **fpos_t**, which is defined in the header **stdio.h**.

Like the related function **fseek**, **fsetpos** clears the end-of-file indicator and undoes the effects of a previous call to **ungetc**. The next operation on *fp* may read or write data.

fsetpos returns zero if all goes well; if an error occurs, it returns nonzero and sets the integer expression **errno** to the appropriate error number.

Example
For an example of this function, see **fgetpos**.

Cross-references
Standard, §4.9.9.3
The C Programming Language, ed. 2, p. 248

See Also
fgetpos, file positioning, fseek, ftell, rewind

Notes
fsetpos is designed to be used with files whose file position cannot be represented within a **long**. For smaller files, use the related function **fseek**.

Note, too, that there is no given way to obtain the value of the file-position indicator other than by a previous call to **fgetpos**.

ftell() — Library function
(Library/STDIO/file positioning)
Get value of file-position indicator
#include <stdio.h>
long int ftell(FILE *fp);

ftell returns the value of the file-position indicator for the stream pointed to by *fp*.

The information returned by **ftell** varies, depending upon the run-time environment and whether the stream pointed to by *fp* was opened into text mode or binary mode. If *fp* has been opened into binary mode, then **ftell** returns the number of characters from the beginning of the file to the current position. If *fp* has been opened into text mode, however, **ftell** returns an implementation-defined number.

For example, in UNIX-style environments, **ftell** returns the number of characters the current position is from the beginning; whereas under MS-DOS, where lines are terminated by a carriage return-newline pair, **ftell** counts each carriage return and each newline as a character in its return value.

If an error occurs with either type of stream, **ftell** returns -1L and sets the integer expression **errno** to the appropriate value. An error will occur if, for example, you attempt to use **ftell** with a stream that is associated with a device that is not file-structured.

Example
For an example of this function, see **fseek**.

Cross-references
Standard, §4.9.9.4
The C Programming Language, ed. 2, p. 248

See Also
errno, fgetpos, file positioning, fseek, fsetpos, rewind

Notes
For a file opened into text mode, subtracting a value returned by one call to **ftell** from the value returned by a second does not necessarily yield the number of characters between the two positions.

ftell can be used only with a file whose file position can be encoded within a **long**. If this is not the case, use the function **fgetpos** to read the file-position indicator.

function — Definition
(Definitions)

A *function* is a construct that performs a task. It includes statements and related variables, including those passed to it as arguments. A C program commonly consists of many functions, each of which performs one or more tasks.

A function can be compiled and stored in a *library* or *archive*, from which it can be extracted by a linker.

Cross-references
Standard, §1.6
The C Programming Language, ed. 2, pp. 67ff

See Also
Definitions

function call — Definition
(Language/expressions/postscript operators)

A *function call* invokes a function at a particular point in a program. A function call consists of an identifier followed by a pair of parentheses '()'; between the parentheses may appear a list of arguments.

The behavior of a function call is affected by the following: a *function declaration*, a *function prototype*, and a *function definition*. Some or all of these may be visible to the translator when it interprets the function call. The translator must respond appropriately to the presence or absence of each when it translates the function call. The following paragraphs describe how these elements affect the behavior of a function call.

Function Declaration

If a function declaration is visible when function is called, then the function is assumed to return the type and to have the linkage noted in the declaration.

For example, the following declaration

```
static char *example();
```

declares that the function **example** has static linkage and returns a pointer to **char**.

If no function declaration is visible to the translator when it reads the function call, then it assumes that the function has the declaration:

```
extern int example();
```

where **example** is the name of the function being called. This action is sometimes referred to as an *implicit declaration* of a function. It declares the function to have external linkage and return type **int**.

If a declaration, whether explicit or implict, does not match what the function actually returns, the behavior is undefined.

Consider a function call of the form:

```
char *value;
value = example(argument1, argument2);
```

If the translator sees the declaration for **example**, then it knows that **example** returns a pointer to **char** and reacts accordingly. If, however, it does not see the declaration for **example**, then it implicitly declares **example** to return an **int**, and generates code appropriate for that. What happens after this error occurs may vary from implementation to implementation.

A function declaration does not check the number or the type of arguments of the function call; to check arguments, you should use a function prototype (described below). If the number and the types of the arguments to a function call do not match those that the function requires, and if no prototype is visible when the function is called, then behavior is undefined.

Function Prototype

A function prototype is a more detailed form of function declaration. A function prototype lists not only the linkage and the return value of a function, but also its parameters and the type of each. This allows the translator to check each function call to ensure that it has the correct number of arguments and that each argument has the correct type.

See **function prototype** for a full description.

Function Definition

A *function definition* defines code for a function. In effect, the function definition is where the function "lives".

A function definition begins with a *declarator*, which includes a list of the parameters the function needs. Behavior is undefined if a function call's list of arguments does not match the function declaration's list of parameters, both in number and in type, and no prototype is visible. A function call in the presence of a prototype-style function definition will be prototype-checked against this declaration.

Cross-references

Standard, §3.3.2.2
The C Programming Language, ed. 2, p. 201

See Also

(), **function declarators, function definition, function prototype, postfix operators**

Notes

C passes arguments by value; this is known as *call-by-value semantics*. This means that C always passes a *copy* of an argument to the called function. If the called function alters the value of its copy, the original argument will not change. The only way the called function can change the value of the original argument is if it is passed the address of that argument.

C does not specify the order of evaluation of arguments. Hence, for maximally portable code, you should not rely on any specific order of evaluation.

The Rationale notes that the original syntax for calling a function through a pointer to a function

```
(*example)();
```

has been augmented to allow the pointer to be automatically deferenced as:

```
example();
```

This means that pointers to functions stored in structures may be called with the syntax

```
example.funcmember();
```

instead of the more cluttered:

```
(*structure.funcmember)();
```

Such an expression cannot be used as an lvalue.

The order of evaluation of a function's arguments is undefined.

function declarators — Definition
(Language/declarations/declarators)

A *function declarator* declares a function. Its syntax is as follows; *opt* indicates *optional*:

> *function-declarator* (*parameter-type-list*$_{opt}$)
>
> *function-declarator* (*identifier-list*$_{opt}$)

As the syntax shows, a function declarator is marked by the use of parentheses '()' after the identifier. Function declarators come in two varieties.

In the first form, the parentheses enclose a list of parameters and their types. The list may end with an ellipsis '...'; this indicates that the function takes an indefinite number of arguments. The list may also consist merely of **void**, which indicates that the function takes no arguments.

This form of function declaration is called a *parameter type list*. It is also called a *function prototype,* because a succeeding call to the function can be checked against it to ensure that the call uses the correct number of arguments and that the type of each is correct. It is also referred to as a *new-style function declarator*. See **function prototype** for more information.

The second form of function declarator names the arguments to a function, but does not give their types. No prototype checking can be performed against a declarator of this sort. This form is called a *function identifier list*. It is also called an *old-style function declarator*, because the Standard states that this form is obsolescent.

Either style of function declaration will be checked against any prototype that had been declared previously and that is within scope.

Finally, a function declarator may consist simply of two parentheses with nothing between them. This indicates that the identifier names a function, but says nothing about the number or the type of arguments that the function takes.

Cross-references
Standard, §3.5.4.3
The C Programming Language, ed. 2, p. 218

See Also
(), declarators, function definition, function prototype

function definition — Definition
(Language/external definitions)

A *definition* is a declaration that reserves storage for the thing declared.

A program or its associated libraries must define exactly once each function it uses. The syntax of a function definition is as follows; *opt* indicates *optional*:

> *function-definition:*
> > *declaration-specifiers*$_{opt}$
> > > *declarator declaration-list*$_{opt}$
> > > *compound-statement*

A *compound-statement* is the code that forms the body of the function.

The *declaration-specifiers* give the function's storage class and return type. The storage class may be either **extern** or **static**. If no storage class is specified, then the function is **extern** by default. The return type may be any type except an array. This means that a function may return a structure, which was illegal under Kernighan and Ritchie's definition of C. If no return type is specified, the function is assumed to return type **int**.

The *declarator* names the function and its formal parameters. A function's parameters can be described in either of two ways. The first is to use *declaration-specifiers*. These name the function's parameters and give the type of each. For example, the function **fopen** has the following declaration:

```
FILE *fopen (const char *file, const char *mode);
```

Here, **const char *file** and **const char *mode** name **fopen**'s parameters and give the type of each.

Each declaration specifier must have both a type and an identifier. The only exception is when a function takes no parameters; then the type **void** may be used without an identifier. A declarator of this form serves as a function prototype for all subsequent calls to this function.

The second way to declare a function's parameters is to use a *declaration-list*. Here, the declarator contains only the parameter's name. Each formal parameter is then declared in a list that follows the declarator. For example, if **fopen** used a declaration list, it would appear as follows:

```
FILE *fopen (file, mode);
const char *file;
const char *mode;
```

In this example, the declaration list gives the types of the identifiers **file** and **mode**. If an identifier appears in the declarator but is not named in the following identifier list, it is assumed to be of type **int**. A declaration list can contain no storage-class specifier except **register**, and no identifier may be initialized in the identifier list.

A declarator of this type cannot be used as a function prototype for subsequent calls. The Standard considers this type of function definition to be obsolete and expects that it will disappear over time.

With either manner of definition, all parameters have automatic storage (as indicated by the fact that the only storage-class specifier allowed is **register**). When an argument is read, it is converted to an object of the type of the corresponding parameter.

Finally, every parameter is considered to be an lvalue.

Cross-references
Standard, §3.7.1
The C Programming Language, ed. 2, p. 225

See Also
conversions, definition, external definitions, function calls, function declarators, function prototypes, object definition, prototype

Notes
If a function takes an indefinite number of parameters, and its function definition does not use a list of declaration specifiers that ends with the ellipsis operator '...', the behavior is undefined.

function designator — Definition
(Language/conversions)

A *function designator* is any expression that has a function type.

A function designator whose type is "function that returns *type*" is normally converted to the type "pointer to function that returns *type*." One exception is when the function designator is the operand to the unary **&** operator. In this case, the use of **&** states explicitly that the address of the function designator is to be taken, so implicit conversion is not necessary.

Cross-references
Standard, §3.2.2.1
The C Programming Language, ed. 2, p. 201

See Also
conversions, implicit conversion

function prototype — Definition
(Language/expressions)

A *function prototype* is a sophisticated form of function declaration. A function prototype lists not only the linkage and the return value of a function, but also lists its arguments and the types of each. This allows the translator to check each argument in a function call to see that it is of the correct type.

Function prototypes are normally kept in a header. The header must be explicitly included in the source module for the prototype to be visible to the translator as it translates the module. For example, consider the following function prototype:

```
extern char *example(int argument1, long argument2);
```

This declares that the function **example** has external linkage; that it returns a pointer to **char**; and that it takes two arguments, the first of which is an **int** and the second of which is a **long**. The names of the arguments given in the function prototype are used only in the prototype. They are not visible outside of it, and so will not affect any other use of those names in your program.

A function prototype may end with an ellipsis '...'. This indicates that the function takes a variable number of arguments. For example, consider the following prototype for the function **fprintf**:

```
int fprintf(FILE *fp, const char *format, ...);
```

The prototype declares that **fprintf** takes at least two arguments, one of which is a pointer to an object of type **FILE** and the other is a pointer to **char**. The ellipsis at the end of the list of arguments indicates that a variable number of arguments may follow.

When the translator reads a call to **fprintf**, it compares the first two arguments against their declared types. All further arguments in the function call are not checked. Every function that takes a variable number of arguments must have a function prototype; otherwise, its behavior is undefined.

Another advantage of function prototypes is that arguments do not undergo the *default argument promotions*. Normally, the translator promotes arguments as follows: **char** and **short int** are promoted to **int** (if it can hold the value encoded within the variable), or to **unsigned int** (if **int** cannot hold the value). **float** is always to **double**. This is discussed more fully below.

If a function takes no arguments, its prototype should be of the form:

```
extern char *example(void);
```

The type specifier **void** between the parentheses indicates that the function takes no arguments. This is *not* the same as:

```
extern char *example();
```

This latter declaration says merely that you have nothing to say about the function's arguments.

When a function prototype is *not* visible where the function is called, then the following rules apply:

- The arguments of the function call undergo the default argument promotions. Behavior is undefined when the number of arguments does not match the number of parameters in the function definition, regardless of whether the prototype is visible where the function is defined.

- If the function prototype is *not* visible where the function is defined, then the parameters of the function definition also undergo default argument promotion. Behavior is undefined when the type of a promoted argument does not match that of its corresponding promoted parameter.

- If the function prototype *is* visible where the function is defined, then behavior is undefined either when the type of a promoted argument does not match that of its corresponding parameter, or when the function prototype ends with an ellipse '...'.

When, however, the function prototype is visible both where the function is defined and where it is called, each argument of the function call is implicitly converted to the type of its corresponding parameter. If the function prototype ends in an ellipsis, then such promotion of arguments ends with the last declared parameter; all arguments thereafter undergo default argument promotion.

For example, consider the following function call:

```
int fprintf(FILE *fp, const char *format, ...);
```

```
    . . .
float argument;
    . . .
fprintf(stderr, "%3.2f\n", argument);
```

The first two arguments in the function call are cast to the types given in the prototype. The third argument, which is indicated by the ellipsis in the function prototype, undergoes the usual promotion **double** before being passed to **fprintf**.

The last situation allows you to write code like:

```
#include <math.h>
    . . .
d = cos(2);
```

This works correctly, because the prototype

```
double cos(double d);
```

in the header tells the translator to promote the integer constant **2** to **double** rather than passing an **int** to the function, as it would do otherwise.

Cross-references
Standard, §3.1.2.1, §3.3.2.2, §3.5.4.3, §3.7.1
The C Programming Language, ed. 2, p. 202

See Also
function calls, function declarators, function definition

function types — Definition
(Language/lexical elements/identifiers/types)

A *function type* describes a function that has a set number of arguments and that returns a specific data type.

The function type is derived from the data type that the function returns. For example, if function **example()** returns type **int**, then **example** is said to have type "function that returns type **int**". The term *function type derivation* refers to the construction of a function type from the type that that function returns.

Cross-reference
Standard, §3.1.2.5

See Also
types

fwrite() — Library function
(Library/STDIO/input-output)
Write data into a stream
#include <stdio.h>
size_t fwrite(const void *buffer, **size_t** *size*, **size_t** *n*, **FILE ****fp*);

fwrite writes up to *n* items, each being *size* bytes long, from the area pointed to by *buffer* into the stream pointed to by *fp*. It increments the file-position indicator by the amount appropriate to the number of bytes written.

fwrite returns the number of items written. This will be equal to *n*, unless a write error occurs.

Example
For an example of this function, see **fgetpos**.

Cross-references
Standard, §4.9.8.2
The C Programming Language, ed. 2, p. 247

See Also
fread, input-output

Notes
If a write error occurs, the value of the file-position indicator is indeterminate.

G

general utilities — Overview
(Library)
#include < stdlib.h >

The ANSI standard describes a set of general utilities. As its name implies, this set is a grab-bag of utilities that do not fit neatly anywhere else. In accordance with the Standard's principle that every function must be declared in a header, the Committee created the header **stdlib.h** to hold the general utilities and their attendant macros and types.

The general utilities are as follows:

Environment communication

abort	End program immediately
atexit	Register a function to be performed at exit
exit	Terminate a program gracefully
getenv	Get environment variable
system	Suspend program and execute another

Integer arithmetic functions

abs	Compute absolute value of an integer
div	Perform integer division
labs	Compute absolute value of a long integer
ldiv	Perform long integer division

Memory management

calloc	Allocate and clear dynamic memory
free	De-allocate dynamic memory
malloc	Allocate dynamic memory
realloc	Reallocate dynamic memory

Multibyte character functions

mblen	Compute length of a multibyte character
mbstowcs	Convert sequence of multibyte characters to wide characters
mbtowc	Convert multibyte character to wide character
wcstombs	Convert sequence of wide characters to multibyte characters
wctomb	Convert wide character to multibyte character

Pseudo-random number functions

rand	Generate pseudo-random numbers
srand	Seed pseudo-random number generator

Searching-sorting
  bsearch Search an array
  qsort   Sort an array

String conversion functions
  atof   Convert string to floating-point number
  atoi   Convert string to integer
  atol   Convert string to long integer
  strtod Convert string to double-precision floating-point number
  strtol   Convert string to long integer
  strtoul Convert string to unsigned long integer

Cross-references
Standard, §4.10.1
The C Programming Language, ed. 2, pp. 251*ff*

See Also
div_t, EXIT_FAILURE, EXIT_SUCCESS, ldiv_t, Library, MB_CUR_MAX, MB_LEN_MAX, stdlib.h, RAND_MAX, wchar_t

getc() — Library function
(Library/STDIO/input-output)
Read a character from a stream
#include <stdio.h>
int getc(FILE **fp***);**

getc reads a character from the stream pointed to by *fp*. The character is read as an **unsigned char** converted to an **int**.

If all goes well, **getc** returns the character read. If it reads the end of file, it returns **EOF** and sets the end-of-file indicator. If an error occurs, it returns **EOF** and sets the error indicator.

Cross-references
Standard, §4.9.7.5
The C Programming Language, ed. 2, p. 247

See Also
fgetc, getchar, gets, input-output, putc, putchar, puts, ungetc

Notes
The Standard permits **getc** to be implemented as a macro. If it is implemented as a macro, *fp* could be evaluated more than once. Therefore, one should beware of the side-effects of evaluating the argument more than once, especially if the argument itself has side-effects.

getchar() — Library function
    (Library/STDIO/input-output)
Read a character from the standard input stream
#include <stdio.h>
int getchar(void)

getchar reads and returns a character from the file or device associated with
stdin. It is equivalent to:

```
getc(stdin);
```

If **getchar** reads the end of file, it returns **EOF** and sets the file's end-of-file indicator. Likewise, if an error occurs, it returns **EOF** and sets the file's error indicator.

Example

This example copies onto the standard-output device whatever is typed upon the
standard-input device. To exit, type **EOF**; what this character is depends upon the
operating system that your computer is running.

```
#include <stdio.h>
#include <stdlib.h>

main(void)
{
    int c;

    while((c = getchar()) != EOF)
        putchar(c);
    return(EXIT_SUCCESS);
}
```

Cross-references

Standard, §4.9.7.6
The C Programming Language, ed. 2, p. 247

See Also

getc, gets, input-output, putc, putchar, puts, ungetc

getenv() — Library function
    (Library/general utilities/environment communication)
Read environmental variable
#include <stdlib.h>
char *getenv(const char **variable***);**

The environment itself can make information available to a program. This information often is available in the form of an *environment variable*, which is a string that forms a definition. For example, under the UNIX operating system the environment variable **TERM** indicates the type of terminal the user has. The variable **TERM=myterm** indicates that the user is typing on a *myterm* variety of terminal. When a program reads that declaration, it knows to use the coding proper for that terminal.

The environment variables together form the *environment list*. Given the heterogeneous environments under which C is implemented, the Standard does not define the mechanism by which the environment list is passed to a program.

The function **getenv** scans the environment list and looks for the variable that is named in the string pointed to by *variable*.

getenv returns a pointer to the string that defines the variable. It returns NULL if the variable requested cannot be found.

Example
This program looks up words in the environment and displays them.

```
#include <stdio.h>
#include <stdlib.h>

main(void)
{
    for(;;) {
        char buf[80], *is;

        printf("Enter an environmental variable: ");
        fflush(stdout);

        if(gets(buf) == NULL)
            exit(EXIT_SUCCESS);

        if((is = getenv(buf)) == NULL)
            printf("Can't find %s\n", buf);
        else
            printf("%s = %s\n", buf, is);
    }

    return(EXIT_SUCCESS);
}
```

Cross-references
Standard, §4.10.4.4
The C Programming Language, ed. 2, p. 253

See Also

environment communication, environment list

Notes

getenv may use a static area to hold the environment variable requested. This buffer will be overwritten by subsequent calls to **getenv**.

An environment may not support environment variables, but it may provide another mechanism that mimics the functionality of **getenv**.

gets() — Library function
(Library/STDIO/input-output)

Read a string from the standard input stream

#include <stdio.h>
char *gets(char *buffer**);**

gets reads characters from the standard input stream and stores them in the area pointed to by *buffer*. It stops reading as soon as it detects a newline character or the end of file. **gets** discards the newline or **EOF** and appends a null character onto the string it has built.

If all goes well, **gets** returns *buffer*. When it has encountered the end of file without having placed any characters into *buffer*, it returns NULL and leaves the contents of *buffer* unchanged. If a read error occurs, **gets** returns NULL and the contents of *buffer* may or may not be altered.

Example

This example echoes whatever is typed upon the standard-input device.

```
#include <stdio.h>
#include <stdlib.h>

main(void)
{
    char buf[100];

    while(gets(buf) != NULL)
        puts(buf);
    return(EXIT_SUCCESS);
}
```

Cross-references

Standard, §4.9.7.7
The C Programming Language, ed. 2, p. 247

See Also

fgets, getc, getchar, input-output, putc, putchar, puts, ungetc

Notes

gets stops reading the input string as soon as it detects a newline character. If a previous read from the standard input stream left a newline character in the standard input buffer, **gets** will read it and immediately stop accepting characters. To the user, it will appear as if **gets** is not working at all.

For example, if **getchar** is followed by **gets**, the first character **gets** will receive is the newline character left behind by **getchar**. A simple statement will remedy this:

```
while (getchar() != '\n')
    ;
```

This discards the newline character left behind by **getchar**. **gets** will now work correctly. You should use this only when you know that a newline will be left in the buffer; otherwise, the desired line will be lost

Note, too, that in the eyes of the Committee, the role of **gets** has largely been subsumed by **fgets**.

gmtime() — Library function
(Library/date and time/time conversion)
Convert calendar time to universal coordinated time
#include <time.h>
struct tm *gmtime(const time_t *caltime);

The function **gmtime** takes the calendar time pointed to by *caltime* and breaks it down into a structure of the type **tm**, converting it into universal coordinated time.

gmtime returns a pointer to the structure **tm** that it creates. This structure is defined in the header **time.h**. If universal coordinated time cannot be computed, then **gmtime** returns NULL.

Example

This example shows Universal Coordinated Time in a message of the form "12/22/88 15:27:33".

```
#include <stdio.h>
#include <stdlib.h>
#include <time.h>
```

```
main(void)
{
    time_t now;
    char buffer[80];

    time(&now);
    strftime(buffer, sizeof(buffer),
        "%m/%d/%y %H:%M:%S\n", gmtime(&now));
    printf(buffer);
    return(EXIT_SUCCESS);
}
```

Cross-references
Standard, §4.12.3.3
The C Programming Language, ed. 2, p. 256

See Also
asctime, ctime, localtime, strftime, time conversion, tm, universal coordinated time

Notes
The name "gmtime" reflects the term "Greenwich Mean Time." the Standard prefers the term "universal coordinated time," although for all practical purposes the two are identical.

goto — C keyword
(Language/statements/jump statements)
Unconditionally jump within a function
goto *label*;

The **goto** statement forces a program's execution to jump to the point marked by *label*. A **goto** can jump only to a point within the current function. To jump beyond a function boundary, use the functions **longjmp** and **setjmp**.

The most common use for **goto** is to exit from nested control structures or go to the top of a control block. It is used most often to write "ripcord" routines, i.e., routines that are executed when a error occurs too deeply within a program for the program to disentangle itself correctly.

Example
For an example of this statement, see **name space**.

Cross-references
Standard, §4.6.6.1
The C Programming Language, ed. 2, p. 65

See Also
break, C keywords, continue, jump statements, label name, non-local jumps, return

Notes
The C Programming Language describes **goto** as "infinitely-abusable." *Caveat utilitor.*

H

header — Definition
(Library)

The Standard mandates that every function be declared in a *header*, whose contents are available to the program through the **#include** preprocessor directive. A header usually is a file, but it may also be built into the translator.

The Standard describes 15 headers, as follows:

assert.h	Run-time assertion checking
ctype.h	Character-handling functions
errno.h	**errno** and related macros
float.h	Limits to floating-point numbers
limits.h	General implementation limits
locale.h	Establish or modify a locale
math.h	Mathematics function
setjmp.h	Non-local jumps
signal.h	Signal-handling functions
stdarg.h	Handle variable numbers of arguments
stddef.h	Common definitions
stdio.h	Standard input and output
stdlib.h	General utilities
string.h	String-handling functions
time.h	Date and time functions

Each header contains only those functions described within the Standard, plus attending data types and macros. Every external identifier in every header is reserved for the implementation. Also reserved is every external identifier that begins with an underscore character '_', whether it is described in the Standard or not. If a reserved external name is redefined, behavior is undefined, even if the function that replaces it has the same specification as the original. This is done to assure the user that moving code from one implementation to another will not generate unforeseen collisions with implementation-defined identifiers. It is also done to assure the implementor that functions called by other library functions will not be derailed by user-defined external names.

Finally, every header can be included any number of times, and any number of headers can be included in any order without triggering problems.

Cross-references
Standard, §4.1.3
The C Programming Language, ed. 2, p. 241

See Also
header names, Library

Notes

In a typical operating system with tree-structured directories, standard headers generally are grouped together in a directory of their own. The implementation ascribes semantics to the two forms of the **#include** statement to locate standard headers.

An interpreter may "know" about the contents of standard headers without requiring that they be included explicitly. Other environments, such as mainframe environments, may represent headers as members of partitioned data sets. In these cases, the implementation usually maps the name used in a **#include** directive to an implementation-specific name. In either case, you need not worry about how the environment supplies the headers; you can port programs without being concerned about them.

header names — Definition
(Language/lexical elements)

A *header name* is a token that gives the name of a header. It has the following syntax:

> *header-name:*
> > < *h-char-sequence* >
> > " *q-char-sequence* "
>
> *h-char-sequence:*
> > *h-char*
> > *h-char-sequence h-char*
>
> *h-char:*
> > Any character except newline and '>'
>
> *q-char-sequence:*
> > *q-char*
> > *q-char-sequence q-char*
>
> *q-char:*
> > Any character except newline and '"'

The two varieties of header names are both searched in an implementation-defined manner.

If any of the characters ', \, or /* appear between the '<' and '>' of a bracketed header name, behavior is undefined. Likewise, if any of the characters ', \, or /* appear between the '"' and the '"' of a quoted header name, behavior is undefined.

Cross-references
Standard, §3.1.7

See Also
#include, header, lexical elements

hosted environment — Definition
(Environment/execution environment)

A *hosted environment* is one in which a C program executes under the control of an operating system. The Standard describes the behavior of a hosted environment in some detail. It does so to give programmers a "fighting chance" to write programs that can be ported from one hosted environment to another.

A hosted environment, unlike a freestanding environment, makes available to a program the full set of library functions, macros, objects, headers, and typedefs.

When a hosted environment invokes a program, control always transfers to the function **main**. A program must have one function named **main.** This function marks the beginning of program execution. See **main** for more information about this function.

Cross-reference
Standard, §2.1.2.2

See Also
argc, argv, execution environment, freestanding environment, main

HUGE_VAL — Macro
(Library/mathematics)
Represent unrepresentable object
#include < math.h >

HUGE_VAL is a macro that is defined in the header **math.h**. It represents the largest possible value of a **double**.

A mathematics function may return **HUGE_VAL** to indicate infinity, either positive or negative. For example, a system that uses IEEE representation for floating-point numbers may return **HUGE_VAL** to indicate a return of infinity for the result of **tan(PI/2)**.

Example
For an example of this macro in a program, see **sqrt**.

Cross-references
Standard, §4.5.1
The C Programming Language, ed. 2, p. 250

See Also
math.h, mathematics, range error

hyperbolic functions — Overview
(Library/mathematics)

The Standard describes three hyperbolic functions, as follows:

cosh	Hyperbolic cosine
sinh	Hyperbolic sine
tanh	Hyperbolic tangent

Cross-reference
Standard, §4.5.3

See Also
exponent-log functions, integer-value-remainder, mathematics, power functions, trigonometric functions

I

identifiers — Overview
(Language/lexical elements)

An *identifier* names one of the following lexical elements:

- Functions
- Labels
- Macros
- Members of a structure, a **union,** or an enumeration
- Objects
- Tags
- **typedefs**

Its syntax is as follows:

> *identifiers:*
> *nondigit*
> *identifier nondigit*
> *identifier digit*

nondigit: one of

```
a   b   c   d   e   f   g   h   i   j   k   l   m
n   o   p   q   r   s   t   u   v   w   x   y   z
A   B   C   D   E   F   G   H   I   J   K   L   M
N   O   P   Q   R   S   T   U   V   W   X   Y   Z
_
```

digit: one of

```
0   1   2   3   4   5   6   7   8   9
```

An identifier with internal linkage may have up to at least 31 characters, which may be in either upper or lower case. An identifier with external linkage, however, may have up to at least six characters, and it is not required to recognize both upper and lower case. These limits are defined by the implementation, and may be increased by it.

An identifier is a string of digits and non-digits, beginning with a non-digit. For a translator to know that two identifiers refer to the same entity, the identifiers must be identical. If two identifiers are meant to refer to the same entity yet differ in any character, the behavior is undefined.

Keywords in C are reserved; therefore, no identifier may match a keyword.

The Standard allows the programmer to use leading underscores '_' to name internal identifiers, but reserves for the implementation all external identifiers with leading underscores. To reduce "name space pollution," the implementor should not reserve anything that is not explicitly defined in the Standard and that does not begin with a leading underscore.

Identifiers have both *scope* and *linkage*. The scope of an identifier refers to the portion of a program to which it is "visible." An identifier can have program scope, file scope, function scope, or block scope; for more information, see the entry for **scope**. The linkage of an identifier describes whether it is joined only with its name-sakes within the same file, or can be joined to other files. Linkage can be external, internal, or none. For more information, see the entry for **linkage**.

Cross-references

Standard, §3.1.2
The C Programming Language, ed. 2, p. 192

See Also

digit, external name, function prototype, internal name, lexical elements, linkage, name space, nondigit, scope, storage duration, string literal, types

if — C keyword

(Language/statements/selection statements)

Conditionally execute an expression
if(*conditional*) *statement*;

if is a C keyword that conditionally executes an expression. If *conditional* is non-zero, then *statement* is executed. However, if *conditional* is zero, then *statement* is not executed.

conditional must use a scalar type. It may be a function call (in which case **if** evaluates what function returns), an integer, the result of an arithmetic operation, or the value returned by a relational expression.

An **if** statement can be followed by an **else** statement, which also introduces a statement. If *conditional* is nonzero, then the statement introduced by **if** is executed and the one introduced by **else** is ignored; whereas if *conditional* is equal to zero, then the statement introduced by **if** is ignored and the one introduced by **else** is executed.

Example

For an example of this statement, see **exit**.

Cross-references
Standard, §4.6.4.1
The C Programming Language, ed. 2, pp. 55*ff*

See Also
else, selection statements, switch

Notes
If the statement controlled by an **if** statement is accessed via a label, the statement controlled by an **else** statement associated with the **if** statement is not executed.

implementation — Definition
(Definitions)

An *implementation* is a program or set of programs that translates a C program under a given translation environment, and supports the execution of functions under a given execution environment.

Every implementation must be accompanied by a document that describes all implementation-defined behavior, all locale-defined behavior, and all extensions to the language.

Cross-reference
Standard, §1.6

See Also
compile, Definitions, interpret

implicit conversions — Definition
(Language/conversions)

The term *implicit conversion* means that the type of an object is changed by the translator without the direct intervention of the programmer. For a list of the rules for implicit conversion, see **conversion**.

Cross-reference
Standard, §3.2

See Also
conversions, explicit conversion

incomplete types — Definition
(Language/lexical elements/identifiers/types)

An *incomplete type* is one whose size is not known.

The set of incomplete types includes arrays of unknown size, and structures or **union**s whose content is unknown.

The type **void** is incomplete by definition and can never be completed.

With the exception of type **void**, an incomplete type must be completed before the translator reaches the end of the translation unit.

Example

An incomplete type may be a structure or **union** that is declared before its full type is specified. For example:

```
struct example1;
struct example2 {
    int member1;
    struct example1 *member2;
};

struct example1 {
    int member1;
    struct example2 *member2;
};
```

Here, the structure type **example1** is completed when its structure is fully declared.

The set of incomplete types also includes arrays of unknown size, and structures or **union**s whose content is unknown.

The type **void *** is incomplete by definition, and can never be completed.

With the exception of type **void ***, an incomplete type must be completed before the translator reaches the end of the translation unit.

Cross-references
Standard, §3.1.2.5
The C Programming Language, ed. 2, p. 212

See Also
types

initialization — Definition
(Language/declarations)

The term *initialization* refers to setting a variable to its first, or initial, value. The syntax that governs initialization is as follows:

> *initializer:*
>> *assignment-expression*
>> { *initializer-list* }
>> { *initializer-list ,* }
>
> *initializer-list:*
>> *initializer*
>> *initializer-list , initializer*

Rules of Initialization

Initializers follow the same rules for type and conversion as do assignment statements.

If a static object with a scalar type is not explicitly initialized, it is initialized to zero by default. Likewise, if a static pointer is not explicitly initialized, it is initialized to NULL by default. If an object with automatic storage duration is not explicitly initialized, its contents are indeterminate.

Initializers on static objects must be constant expressions; greater flexibility is allowed for initializers of automatic variables. These latter initializers can be arbitrary expressions, not just constant expressions. For example,

```
double dsin = sin(30);
```

is a valid initializer, where **dsin** is declared inside a function.

To initialize an object, use the assignment operator '='. The following sections describe how to initialize different classes of objects.

Scalars

To initialize a scalar object, assign it the value of a expression. The expression may be enclosed within braces; doing so does not affect the value of the assignment. For example, the expressions

```
int example = 7+12;
```

and

```
int example = { 7+12 };
```

are equivalent.

Unions and Structures

The initialization of a **union** by definition fills only its *first* member.

To initialize a **union**, use an expression that is enclosed within braces:

```
union example_u {
        int member1;
        long member2;
        float member3;
} = { 5 };
```

This initializes **member1** to five. That is to say, the **union** is filled with an **int**-sized object whose value is five.

To initialize a structure, use a list of constants or expressions that are enclosed within braces. For example:

```
struct example_s {
        int member1;
        long member2;
        union example_u member3;
};
struct example_s test1 = { 5, 3, 15 };
```

This initializes **member1** to five, initializes **member2** to three, and initializes the *first* member of **member3** to 15.

Strings and Wide Characters

To initialize a string pointer or an array of wide characters, use a string literal.

The following initializes a string:

```
char string[] = "This is a string";
```

The length of the character array is 17 characters: one for every character in the given string literal plus one for the null character that marks the end of the string.

If you wish, you can fix the length of a character array. In this case, the null character is appended to the end of the string only if there is room in the array. For example, the following

```
char string[16] = "This is a string";
```

writes the text into the array **string**, but does not include the concluding null character because there is not enough room for it.

The same rules apply to initializing an array of wide characters. For example, the following:

```
wchar_t widestring[] = L"This is a string";
```

fills **widestring** with the wide characters corresponding to the characters in the given string literal. The appropriate form of the null character is then appended to the end of the array, and the size of the array is **(17*sizeof(wchar_t))**. The prefix **L** indicates that the string literal consists of wide characters.

A pointer to **char** can also be initialized when the pointer is declared. For example:

```
char *strptr = "This is a string";    /* RIGHT */
```

initializes **strptr** to point to the first character in **This is a string**. This declaration automatically allocates exactly enough storage to hold the given string literal, plus the terminating null character.

Arrays

To initialize an array, use a list of expressions that is enclosed within braces. For example, the expression

```
int array[] = { 1, 2, 3 };
```

initializes **array**. Because **array** does not have a declared number of elements, the initialization fixes its number of elements at three. The elements of the array are initialized in the order in which the elements of the initialization list appear. For example, **array[0]** is initialized to one, **array[1]** to two, and **array[2]** to three.

If an array has a fixed length and the initialization list does not contain enough initializers to initialize every element, then the remaining elements are initialized in the default manner: static variables are initialized to zero, and other variables to whatever happens to be in memory. For example, the following:

```
int array[3] = { 1, 2 };
```

initializes **array[0]** to one, **array[1]** to two, and **array[2]** to zero.

The initialization of a multi-dimensional array is something of a science in itself. The Standard defines that the ranks in an array are filled from right to left. For example, consider the array:

```
int example[2][3][4];
```

This array contains two groups of three elements, each of which consists of four elements. Initialization of this array will proceed from **example[0][0][0]** through **example[0][0][3]**; then from **example[0][1][0]** through **example[0][1][3]**; and so on, until the array is filled.

It is easy to check initialization when there is one initializer for each "slot" in the array; e.g.,

```
int example[2][3] = {
    1,  2,  3,  4,  5,  6
};
```

or:

```
int example[2][3] = {
    { 1,  2,  3 }, { 4,  5,  6 }
};
```

The situation becomes more difficult when an array is only partially initialized; e.g.,

```
int example[2][3] = {
    { 1 }, { 2, 3 }
};
```

which is equivalent to:

```
int example[2][3] = {
    { 1, 0, 0 }, { 2, 3, 0 }
};
```

As can be seen, braces mark the end of initialization for a "cluster" of elements within an array. For example, the following:

```
int example[2][3][4] = {
    5, { 1, 2 }, { 5, 2, 4, 3 }, { 9, 9, 5 },
    { 2, 3, 7 } };
```

is equivalent to entering:

```
int example[2][3][4] = {
    { 5, 0, 0, 0 },
    { 1, 2, 0, 0 },
    { 5, 2, 4, 3 },

    { 9, 9, 5, 0 },
    { 2, 3, 7, 0 },
    { 0, 0, 0, 0 }
};
```

The braces end the initialization of one cluster of elements; the next cluster is then initialized. Any elements within a cluster that have not yet been initialized when the brace is read are initialized in the default manner.

The final entry in a list of initializers may end with a comma. For example:

```
int array[3] = { 1, 2, 3, };
```

will initialize **array** correctly. This is a departure from many current implementations of C.

ANSI C requires that the initializers of a multi-dimensional array be parsed in a top-down manner. Some implementations had parsed such initializers in a bottom-up manner. Code that expects bottom-up parsing may behave differently under ANSI C, and probably without warning. This is a quiet change that may require that some code be rewritten.

Cross-references
Standard, §3.5.7
The C Programming Language, ed. 2, pp. 218*ff*

See Also
array, declarations

initialized — Definition
(Environment/execution environment)

When a variable is *initialized*, it is set to its first, or initial, value. All objects with static duration must be initialized before the program begins execution; this rule applies both in freestanding and in hosted environments.

The translator will use its initialization rules to initialize all program variables that the program does not initialize itself. This *may* result in the generation of code to perform the initialization.

Cross-reference
Standard, §2.1.2

See Also
execution environment, initialization

input-output — Overview
(Library/STDIO)
#include <stdio.h>

The Standard describes 22 functions that perform input and output. All are declared in the header **stdio.h**. The Standard organizes them into three groups: *character*, *direct*, and *formatted*, as follows:

Character

fgetc	Read a character from a stream
fgets	Read a line from a stream
fputc	Write a character into a stream
fputs	Write a string into a stream
getc	Read a character from a stream
getchar	Read a character from the standard input stream
gets	Read a string from the standard input stream
putc	Write character into a stream
putchar	Write a character onto the standard output
puts	Write a string onto the standard output
ungetc	Push a character back into the input stream

Direct

fread	Read data from a stream
fwrite	Write data into a stream

Formatted

fprintf	Print formatted text into a stream
fscanf	Read formatted text from a stream
printf	Format and print text into standard output stream
scanf	Read formatted text from standard input stream
sprintf	Print formatted text into a string
sscanf	Read formatted text from string
vfprintf	Format and print text into a stream
vprintf	Format and print text into standard output stream
vsprintf	Format and print text into a string

Cross-references

Standard, §4.9.6, §4.9.7, §4.9.8
The C Programming Language, ed. 2, pp. 243*ff*

See Also

error handling, file access, file operations, file positioning, STDIO, stdio.h

int — C keyword
(Language/lexical elements/identifiers/types)

The type **int** holds an integer. It is usually the same size as a word (or register) on the target machine.

int is a signed integral type. This type can be no smaller than an **short** and no greater than a **long**.

A **int** can encode any number between **INT_MIN** and **INT_MAX**. These are macros that are defined in the header **limits.h**; the former can be no greater than

-32,767 and the latter no less than +32,767.

The types **signed** and **signed int** are synonyms for **int**.

Cross-references
Standard, §2.2.4.2, §3.1.2.5, §3.2.1.1, §3.5.2
The C Programming Language, ed. 2, p. 211

See Also
types

Notes
Because **int**s may be the size of **short**s on some machines and the size of **long**s on others, programs that are meant to be portable can avoid bugs by explicitly declaring all **int**s to be either **short** or **long**.

INT_MAX — Macro
(Environment/environmental considerations/limits/numerical)

INT_MAX is a macro that is defined in the header **limits.h**. It gives the largest value that can be held by an object of type **int**. It must be defined to be at least 32,767.

Example
For an example of using this macro in a program, see **abs**.

Cross-references
Standard, §2.2.4.2
The C Programming Language, ed. 2, p. 257

See Also
limits.h, numerical limits

INT_MIN — Macro
(Environment/environmental considerations/limits/numerical)

INT_MIN is a macro that is defined in the header **limits.h**. It gives the smallest value that can be held by an object of type **int**. It must be defined to be at most -32,767.

Example
For an example of using this macro in a program, see **rand**.

Cross-references
Standard, §2.2.4.2
The C Programming Language, ed. 2, p. 257

See Also
limits.h, numerical limits

integer-value-remainder — Overview
(Library/mathematics)

The Standard describes four mathematics functions that calculate nearest integer, absolute value, and remainders, as follows:

ceil	Set integral ceiling of a number
fabs	Compute absolute value
floor	Set integral floor of a number
fmod	Calculate modulus for floating-point number

Cross-reference
Standard, §4.5.5

See Also

exponent-log functions, hyperbolic functions, mathematics, power functions, trigonometric functions

integer arithmetic — Overview
(Library/general utilities)
#include < stdlib.h >

The Standard describes four functions that perform integer arithmetic, as follows:

abs	Return the absolute value of an integer
div	Perform integer division
labs	Return the absolute value of a long integer
ldiv	Perform long integer division

Some implementations of C declare **abs** or **labs** in the header **math.h**. The Standard removes them from that header, because these are the only mathematics functions that do not return a **double**.

The functions **div** and **ldiv** perform a task that has been found to be useful in FORTRAN. They return, respectively, the types **div_t** and **ldiv_t**. Each contains both the quotient and the remainder produced by integer arithmetic; the former presents them in **ints** and the latter presents them in **longs**.

Cross-reference
Standard, §4.10.6

See Also
general utilities

integer constant — Definition
(Language/lexical elements/constants)

An *integer constant* is a constant that holds an integer. Its syntax is as follows; *opt* indicates *optional*:

> *integer-constant:*
>> *decimal-constant integer-suffix*
>> *octal-constant integer-suffix$_{opt}$*
>> *hexadecimal-constant integer-suffix$_{opt}$*
>
> *decimal-constant:*
>> *nonzero-digit*
>> *decimal-constant digit*
>
> *octal-constant:*
>> 0
>> *octal-constant octal-digit*
>
> *hexadecimal-constant:*
>> 0x *hexadecimal-digit*
>> 0X *hexadecimal-digit*
>> *hexadecimal-constant hexadecimal-digit*
>
> *nonzero-digit:* one of
>> 1   2   3   4   5   6   7   8   9
>
> *octal-digit:* one of
>> 0   1   2   3   4   5   6   7
>
> *hexadecimal-digit:* one of
>> 0   1   2   3   4   5   6   7   8   9
>> a   b   c   d   e   f
>> A   B   C   D   E   F
>
> *integer-suffix:*
>> *unsigned-suffix long-suffix$_{opt}$*
>> *long-suffix unsigned-suffix$_{opt}$*
>
> *unsigned-suffix:* one of
>> u   U

long-suffix: one of
    l   L

An integer constant has the following structure:

- It begins with a digit.

- It has no period or exponent.

- It may have a prefix that indicates its base, as follows: **0X** and **0x** both indicate hexadecimal. **0** (zero) indicates octal.

- It may have a suffix that indicates its type. **u** and **U** indicate an unsigned integer; **l** and **L** indicate a long integer.

A hexadecimal number may consist of the digits '0' through '9' and the letters 'a' through 'f' or 'A' through 'F'. An octal number may consist of the digits '0' through '7'.

When an integer constant initializes a variable, the form of the constant should match that of the variable as closely as possible. For example, when an integer constant initializes a **long int**, the constant should have the suffix **l** or **L**. If the constant does not have this suffix, the variable may not be initialized correctly.

The type of an integer constant is fixed by the following rules:

- A decimal integer constant that has no suffix is given the *first* of the following types that can represent its value: **int**, **long int**, or **unsigned long int**.

- A hexadecimal or octal integer constant that has no suffix is given the first of the following types that can represent its value: **int**, **unsigned int**, **long int**, or **unsigned long int**.

- An integer constant with the prefixes **u** or **U** is given the first of the following types that can represent its value: **unsigned int** or **unsigned long int**.

- An integer constant with the prefixes **l** or **L** is given the first of the following types that can represent its value: **long int** or **unsigned long int**.

- An integer constant with both the unsigned and the long suffixes is an **unsigned long int**.

These rules, as they preserve the value of a given constant, are part of what is known as the *value-preserving rules*.

Cross-references
Standard, §3.1.3.2
The C Programming Language, ed. 2, p. 193

See Also
constants, conversions

integral promotion — Definition
(Language/conversions)

The term *integral promotion* refers to the conversion of a **char**, **short int**, an enumeration object, or a bit-field to an **int** when it is used as an operand in an expression.

This form of promotion occurs automatically when one of these smaller types is used in place of an **int**. The smaller type is promoted to an **int** if an **int** can hold all of the smaller type's possible values. If an **int** cannot hold all of possible values of the smaller type, then that type is promoted to an **unsigned int**. The conversion retains the value of the type to be promoted, including its sign.

Cross-references
Standard, §3.2.1.1
The C Programming Language, ed. 2, pp

See Also
conversions, integral types, value preserving

Notes
This scheme of conversion is called *value preserving* because it preserves the value of the promoted type. Many current implementations of C use another scheme for promotion, called *unsigned preserving*. Under this scheme, the smaller unsigned types are always promoted to **unsigned int**. Under certain circumstances, a program that depends upon unsigned-preserving promotion will behave differently when subjected to value-preserving promotion. This is a quiet change that may break some existing code.

integral types — Definition
(Language/lexical elements/identifiers/types)

The *integral types* are the set of type **char**, the signed and unsigned integer types, and the enumerated types. The integral types include the following:

char *types:*
>**char**
>**signed char**
>**unsigned char**

Signed integer types:
>   **int, signed, signed int**
>   **short, short int, signed short, signed short int**
>   **long, long int, signed long, signed long int**

Unsigned integer types:
>   **unsigned, unsigned int**
>   **unsigned short, unsigned short int**
>   **unsigned long, unsigned long int**

The types on the same line are synonyms; for example, **int** and **signed int** have the same meaning.

Whether a **char** is signed by default depends upon the implementation. The types **signed char** and **unsigned char** are supplied to give a programmer access to the appropriate, non-default type should she need it, as well as providing "hooks" for writing portable code.

The types **int, long**, and **short** are signed by default. The signed versions of their names are supplied for the sake of symmetry.

char types are included in the category of integral types because they have historically been promoted to **int**s when used in expressions. Such promotion is no longer necessary with ANSI C, according to the *as if* rule, although many translators still follow this practice.

Conversion of Integral Types

The following rules govern the conversion of one integral type to another:

- When an unsigned type is converted to another integral type, either signed or unsigned, if its value can be represented by that type, then the value is unchanged. If the value cannot be represented, the result is defined by the implementation. Thus, conversion of an integral type is *value-preserving*.

- When a non-negative, signed integer is converted to an unsigned integer that is the same size or larger (such as converting a **signed int** to an unsigned **int** or an **unsigned long**), the value of the converted integer is unchanged.

- When a negative, signed integer is converted to a larger, unsigned integer, the signed type is first promoted to the signed type that corresponds to the unsigned type. Then its value is converted to unsigned by adding to it a value that is one greater than the maximum value that can be held by the unsigned type. For example, if a negative **signed int** is being converted to an **unsigned long**, it is first promoted to a **signed long**; then it is converted to a **unsigned long** by adding to it **ULONG_MAX** plus one. The addition preserves the bit pattern of the original number, and sign-extends it to fill the extra bits of the larger integer.

- When an integer, signed or unsigned, is demoted to an unsigned type that is smaller than itself, the value of the demoted type is the remainder yielded when the value of the original type is divided by one plus the maximum value of the smaller type. For example, if a **long** is demoted to an **unsigned int**, the value of the demoted object is the remainder left when the value of the original object is divided by one plus **UINT_MAX**.

- When an integer, signed or unsigned, is demoted to a signed integer with a smaller size, or when an unsigned integer is converted to a signed integer of the same size, and its value does not fit into the new type, then the result is defined by the implementation.

Cross-references
Standard, §3.1.2.5
The C Programming Language, ed. 2, p. 196

See Also
char, conversions, floating types, int, long int, short int, types

internal name — Definition
(Language/lexical elements/identifiers)

An *internal name* is an identifier that has internal linkage. The minimum maximum for the length of an internal name is 31 characters, and an implementation must distinguish upper-case and lower-case characters.

Cross-references
Standard, §3.1.2
The C Programming Language, ed. 2, p. 35

See Also
external name, identifiers, linkage

interpret — Definition
(Definitions)

To *interpret* a program means to translate it with an interpreter. An interpreter, in turn, is a translator that, instead of producing machine instructions, reads the C program line by line and executes each as it is encountered.

An interpreter does not perform the traditional compile-and-link cycle that the Standard uses as its model of translation. However, an interpreter complies with the Standard as long as the program executes as if it had been compiled and linked by a conforming implementation of C.

See Also
compile, Definitions

isalnum() — Library function
(Library/character handling/character testing)
Check if a character is a numeral or letter
#include <ctype.h>
int isalnum(int c);

isalnum tests whether c is a letter or a numeral. A letter is any character for which **isalpha** returns true; likewise, a numeral is any character for which **isdigit** returns true. c must be a value that is representable as an **unsigned char** or **EOF**.

isalnum returns nonzero if c is a letter or a numeral, and zero if it is not.

Example
For an example of this function, see **character testing**.

Cross-references
Standard, §4.3.1.1
The C Programming Language, ed. 2, pp

See Also
character handling, character testing

Notes
The operation of this function is affected by the program's locale, as set by the function **setlocale**. See **localization** for more information.

isalpha() — Library function
(Library/character handling/character testing)
Check if a character is a letter
#include <ctype.h>
int isalpha(int c);

isalpha tests whether c is a letter. In the **C** locale, a letter is any of the characters 'a' through 'z' or 'A' through 'Z'. In any other locale, a letter is any character for which the functions **iscntrl**, **isdigit**, **ispunct**, and **isspace** all return false. c must be a value that is representable as an **unsigned char** or **EOF**.

isalpha returns nonzero if c is an alphabetic character, and zero if it is not.

Example
For an example of this function, see **character testing**.

Cross-references
Standard, §4.3.1.2
The C Programming Language, ed. 2, p. 249

See Also
character handling, character testing

Notes
The operation of this function is affected by the program's locale, as set by the function **setlocale**. See **localization** for more information.

iscntrl() — Library function
(Library/character handling/character testing)
Check if a character is a control character
#include <ctype.h>
int iscntrl(int *c*);

iscntrl tests whether *c* is a control character under the implementation's character set. The Standard defines a control character as being a character in the implementation's character that cannot be printed. *c* must be a value that is representable as an **unsigned char** or **EOF**.

iscntrl returns nonzero if *c* is a control character, and zero if it is not.

Example
For an example of this function, see **character testing**.

Cross-references
Standard, §4.3.1.3
The C Programming Language, ed. 2, p. 249

See Also
character handling, character testing

Notes
The operation of this function is affected by the program's locale, as set by the function **setlocale**. See **localization** for more information.

isdigit() — Library function
(Library/character handling/character testing)
Check if a character is a numeral
#include <ctype.h>
int isdigit(int c);

isdigit tests whether c is a numeral (any of the characters '0' through '9'). c must be a value that is representable as an **unsigned char** or **EOF**.

isdigit returns nonzero if c is a numeral, and zero if it is not.

Example
For an example of this function, see **character testing**.

Cross-references
Standard, §4.3.1.4
The C Programming Language, ed. 2, p. 249

See Also
character handling, character testing

isgraph() — Library function
(Library/character handling/character testing)
Check if a character is printable
#include <ctype.h>
int isgraph(int c);

isgraph tests whether c is a printable letter within the implementation's character set, but excluding the space character. The Standard defines a printable character as any character that occupies one printing position on an output device. c must be a value that is representable as an **unsigned char** or **EOF**.

isgraph returns nonzero if c is a printable character (except for space), and zero if it is not.

Example
For an example of this function, see **character testing**.

Cross-references
Standard, §4.3.1.5
The C Programming Language, ed. 2, p. 249

See Also
character handling, character testing

Notes
The operation of this function is affected by the program's locale, as set by the function **setlocale**. See **localization** for more information.

islower() — Library function
(Library/character handling/character testing)
Check if a character is a lower-case letter
#include <ctype.h>
int islower(int c);

islower tests whether *c* is a lower-case letter. In the **C** locale, a lower-case letter is any of the characters 'a' through 'z'. In any other locale, this is a character for which the functions **iscntrl**, **isdigit**, **ispunct**, **isspace**, and **isupper** all return false. *c* must be a value that is representable as an **unsigned char** or **EOF**.

islower returns nonzero if *c* is is a lower-case letter, and zero if it is not.

Example
For an example of this function, see **character testing**.

Cross-references
Standard, §4..1.6
The C Programming Language, ed. 2, p. 249

See Also
character handling, character set, character testing

Notes
The operation of this function is affected by the program's locale, as set by the function **setlocale**. See **localization** for more information.

isprint() — Library function
(Library/character handling/character testing)
Check if a character is printable
#include <ctype.h>
int isprint(int c);

isprint tests whether *c* is a printable letter within the implementation's character set, including the space character. The Standard defines a printable character as any character that occupies one printing position on an output device. *c* must be a value that is representable as an **unsigned char** or **EOF**.

isprint returns nonzero if *c* is a printable character, and zero if it is not.

Example
For an example of this function, see **character testing**.

Cross-references
Standard, §4.3.1.7
The C Programming Language, ed. 2, p. 249

See Also
character handling, character testing

Notes
The operation of this function is affected by the program's locale, as set by the function **setlocale**. See **localization** for more information.

ispunct() — Library function
(Library/character handling/character testing)
Check if a character is a punctuation mark
#include <ctype.h>
int ispunct(int *c*);

ispunct tests whether *c* is a punctuation mark in the implementation's character set. The Standard defines a punctuation mark as being any printable character, except the space character, for which the function **isalnum** returns false. *c* must be a value that is representable as an **unsigned char** or **EOF**.

ispunct returns nonzero if *c* is a punctuation mark, and zero if it is not.

Example
For an example of this function, see **character testing**.

Cross-references
Standard, §4.3.1.8
The C Programming Language, ed. 2, p. 249

See Also
character handling, character testing

Notes
The operation of this function is affected by the program's locale, as set by the function **setlocale**. See **localization** for more information.

isspace() — Library function
(Library/character handling/character testing)
Check if character is white space
#include <ctype.h>
int isspace(int c);

isspace tests whether *c* represents a white-space character. In the **C** locale, a white-space character is any of the following: space (' '), form feed ('\f'), newline ('\n'), carriage return ('\r'), horizontal tab ('\t'), or vertical tab ('\v'). In any other locale, a white-space character is one for which the functions **isalnum**, **iscntrl**, **isgraph**, and **ispunct** all return false. *c* must be a value that is representable as an **unsigned char** or **EOF**.

isspace returns nonzero if *c* is a space character, and zero if it is not.

Example

For an example of this function, see **character testing**.

Cross-references

Standard, §4.3.1.1
The C Programming Language, ed. 2, p. 249

See Also

character handling, character testing

Notes

The operation of this function is affected by the program's locale, as set by the function **setlocale**. For example, Middle-Eastern languages use alternate characters to denote white space. See **localization** for more information.

isupper() — Library function
(Library/character handling/character testing)
Check if a character is an upper-case letter
#include <ctype.h>
int isupper(int c);

isupper tests whether *c* is a upper-case letter. In the **C** locale, a upper-case letter is any of the characters 'A' through 'Z'. In any other locale, this is a character for which the functions **iscntrl**, **isdigit**, **islower**, **ispunct**, and **isspace** all return false. *c* must be a value that is representable as an **unsigned char** or **EOF**.

isupper returns nonzero if *c* is an upper-case letter, and zero if it is not.

Example

For an example of this function, see **character testing**.

Cross-references

Standard, §4.3.1.6
The C Programming Language, ed. 2, p. 249

See Also

character handling, character sets, character testing

Notes

The operation of this function is affected by the program's locale, as set by the function **setlocale**. See **localization** for more information.

isxdigit() — Library function
(Library/character handling/character testing)

Check if a character is a hexadecimal numeral
#include <ctype.h>
int isxdigit(int c);

isxdigit tests whether *c* is a hexadecimal numeral (any of the characters '0' through '9', any of the letters 'a' through 'd', or any of the letters 'A' through 'D'). *c* must be a value that is representable as an **unsigned char** or **EOF**.

isxdigit returns nonzero if *c* is a hexadecimal numeral, and zero if it is not.

Example

For an example of this function, see **character testing**.

Cross-references

Standard, §4.3.1.11
The C Programming Language, ed. 2, p. 249

See Also

character handling, character testing

iteration statements — Overview
(Language/statements)

An *iteration statement* executes a body of code iteratively — that is, over and over until a certain condition is met. The syntax is as follows; *opt* indicates *optional*:

iteration-statement:
>   do *statement* while(*expression*) ;
>
>   for(*expression*_{opt} ; *expression*_{opt} ; *expression*_{opt}) *statement*
>
>   while(*expression*) *statement*

An iteration statement is also called a *loop*. A loop tests its controlling expression upon each iteration. The loop continues to execute until the controlling expression is no longer true. Whether the controlling expression is tested before or after the loop executes depends upon the variety of loop being used.

An infinite loop is one that iterates forever. The following statements set up infinite loops:

>   for(;;)
>
>   while(1)
>
>   do ... while(1);

It is also possible to break out of a loop before a iteration/test cycle is completed. For more information, see **break, return,** and **goto.**

Cross-references
Standard, §3.6.5
The C Programming Language, ed. 2, p. 224

See Also
break, continue, do, for, statements, while

J

jmp_buf — Type
(Library/non-local jumps)
Type used with non-local jumps
#include <setjmp.h>

jmp_buf is a type defined in the header **setjmp.h**. It is the type used to hold the current environment to enable a non-local jump. The usual contents of the **jmp_buf** array will be the contents of registers; however, its contents are defined by the implementation.

Cross-references
Standard, §4.6
The C Programming Language, ed. 2, p. 254

See Also
non-local jumps, setjmp.h

Notes
Because **jmp_buf** usually does not contain anything except the current contents of the registers, one should not expect values of local variables or register variables to restored properly.

Historically, code has been written that calls **setjmp** and **longjmp** with an argument of type **jmp_buf**, but without taking its address. This code works because an array passed as a parameter is automatically converted to a pointer. Because structures can now be passed by value, such arguments are no longer converted to pointers. However, because both **setjmp** and **longjmp** expect a pointer argument, the type of **jmp_buf** is restricted to an array type in order to preserve existing code.

If **jmp_buf** must be a structure of heterogeneous elements, then it could be defined as a one-element array of such structures.

jump statements — Overview
(Language/statements)

A *jump statement* is one that causes the program to jump unconditionally from one point in the code to another. Jump statements have the following syntax; *opt* stands for *optional*.

jump-statement:
      `goto` *identifier* `;`
      `continue` `;`
      `break` `;`
      `return` *expression*$_{opt}$ `;`

Cross-references

Standard, §3.6.6
The C Programming Language, ed. 2, p. 224

See Also

break, continue, goto, non-local jumps, return, statements

K

keywords — Definition
(Language/lexical elements)

A *keyword* is a word that has special significance to the C language. All keywords are reserved; none may be used as an identifier.

The Standard defines the following as being C keywords:

auto	break	case	char
const	continue	default	defined
do	double	else	enum
extern	float	for	goto
if	int	long	noalias
register	return	short	signed
sizeof	static	struct	switch
typedef	union	unsigned	void
volatile	while		

Cross-references
Standard, §3.1.1
The C Programming Language, ed. 2, p. 192

See Also
lexical elements

Notes

The keywords **const, enum, noalias, signed, void,** and **volatile** are new to the C language, although some or all of these have been used as common extensions to C. A program that uses any of these words as an identifier may not translate properly under an implementation that conforms to the Standard. Likewise, the Standard eliminates the keyword **entry**, which the first edition of *The C Programming Language* defined as being unused.

The Standard recognizes that the keywords **asm** and **fortran** are common extensions to the C language, and are recognized as such by many implementations of C.

Finally, as of this writing (January 1988), the keyword **noalias** remains the subject of controversy. It may not be included within the Standard when it is published in the spring of 1988.

L

L_tmpnam — Macro
(Library/STDIO)

Define maximum size of temporary file's name
#include <stdio.h>

L_tmpnam is a macro that is defined in the header **stdio.h**. It indicates the size of the array needed to hold a name created by the function **tmpnam**.

Example
For an example of a program that uses this macro, see **tmpnam**.

Cross-reference
Standard, §4.9.1, §4.9.4.4

See Also
STDIO, stdio.h, tmpnam

label — Definition
(Language/lexical elements/identifiers/name space)

A *label* is an identifier followed by a colon ':' or that follows a **goto** statement. It marks a point within a function to which a **goto** statement can jump.

Cross-references
Standard, §3.1.2.6
The C Programming Language, ed. 2, pp. 65

See Also
goto, name space

labelled statements — Overview
(Language/statements)

Any C statement may be introduced by a label. This allows it to be accessed by a **goto** statement.

The C language includes two special labels: **case** and **default**. Both may be used only within the body of a **switch** statement. See **switch** for more information.

The syntax of a labelled statement is as follows:

labelled-statement:
      identifier : *statement*
      `case` *constant-expression* : *statement*
      `default` : *statement*

A label does not alter the flow of control in any way. Execution continues directly over it.

Cross-references

Standard, §3.6.1
The C Programming Language, ed. 2, pp. 66, 222

See Also

case, default, goto, statements

labs() — Library function
(Library/general utilities/integer arithmetic)

Compute the absolute value of a long integer
#include < stdlib.h >
int labs(long *n*);

labs computes the absolute value of the long integer *n*. The *absolute value* of a number is its distance from zero. This is *n* if *n* > = **0**, and *-n* otherwise.

Cross-references

Standard, §4.10.6.3
The C Programming Language, ed. 2, p. 253

See Also

abs, integer arithmetic

Notes

On two's complement machines, the absolute value of the most negative number may not be representable.

In some implementations, **labs** is declared in the header **math.h**. The Standard moved this function to **stdlib.h** on the grounds that it does not return **double**. This change may require that some existing code be altered.

Language — Overview
(Standard)

Section 3 of the Standard describes the C programming language. Its description of C is derived from *The C Programming Language* by Brian W. Kernighan and Dennis M. Ritchie. Additional features of the language are drawn from UNIX system V, Berkeley UNIX, and implementations on a great variety of machines.

The description of the language, both in the Standard and in this Lexicon, has the following topics, which describe completely the syntax and semantics of the language:

- constant expressions

- conversions

- declarations

- expressions

- external definitions

- lexical elements

- preprocessing

- statements

Each of these topics is introduced by its own Lexicon article.

Cross-references
Standard, §3.0
The C Programming Language, ed. 2, pp. 191*ff*

See Also
Standard, Library

LC_ALL — Macro
(Library/localization)
All locale information
#include <locale.h>

LC_ALL is a macro that is defined in the header **locale.h**. When passed to the function **setlocale**, it queries or sets all information for a given locale. Information obtained with this macro alters the operation of all functions that are affected by the program's locale, as well as the contents of the structure **lconv**. The following lists the functions affected by **LC_ALL**:

Collation
   strcoll
   strxfrm

ctype
>   **isdigit**
>   **isxdigit**

Date and time
>   **strftime**

Formatted I/O
>   **fprintf**
>   **fscanf**
>   **printf**
>   **sprintf**
>   **scanf**
>   **sscanf**
>   **vfprintf**
>   **vprintf**
>   **vsprintf**

Multibyte characters
>   **mblen**
>   **mbstowcs**
>   **mbtowc**
>   **wcstombs**
>   **wctomb**

String conversion
>   **atof**
>   **atoi**
>   **atol**
>   **strtod**
>   **strtol**
>   **strtoul**

Cross-reference
Standard, §4.4

See Also
LC_COLLATE, LC_CTYPE, LC_MONETARY, LC_NUMERIC, LC_TIME, lconv, localization, locale.h, setlocale

LC_COLLATE — Macro
>   (Library/localization)
>   Locale collation information
>   **#include <locale.h>**

LC_COLLATE is a macro that is defined in the header **locale.h**. When used with the function **setlocale**, it queries or sets collation information for a given locale.

This information can affect the operation of the functions **strcoll** and **strxfrm**.

Cross-reference
Standard, §4.4

See Also
LC_ALL, LC_CTYPE, LC_MONETARY, LC_NUMERIC, LC_TIME, localization, **locale.h,** setlocale

LC_CTYPE — Macro
(Library/localization)
Locale character-handling information
#include <locale.h>

LC_CTYPE is a macro that is defined in the header **locale.h**. When used with the function **setlocale**, it sets or queries the character-handling information for a given locale. This information helps determine the action of the functions declared in **ctype.h**, except **isdigit** and **isxdigit**, as well as the multiple-byte character functions **mblen, mbstowcs, mbtowc, wcstombs,** and **wctomb**.

Cross-reference
Standard, §4.4

See Also
LC_ALL, LC_COLLATE, LC_MONETARY, LC_NUMERIC, LC_TIME, lconv, localization, **locale.h,** setlocale

LC_MONETARY — Macro
(Library/localization)
Locale monetary information
#include <locale.h>

LC_MONETARY is a macro that is defined in the header **locale.h**. When used with the function **setlocale**, it queries or sets the monetary information for a given locale.

It affects all of the fields within the structure **lconv**, except **decimal_point**.

Cross-reference
Standard, §4.4

See Also
LC_ALL, LC_COLLATE, LC_CTYPE, LC_NUMERIC, LC_TIME, localization, locale.h, setlocale

LC_NUMERIC — Macro
(Library/localization)
Locale numeric information
#include <locale.h>

LC_NUMERIC is a macro that is defined in the header **locale.h**. When used with the function **setlocale**, it queries or sets the information for formatting numeric strings.

This information will alter the operation of the following functions:

Formatted I/O
fprintf
fscanf
printf
sprintf
scanf
sscanf
vfprintf
vprintf
vsprintf

String conversion
atof
atoi
atol
strtod
strtol
strtoul

This information also affects the following fields within the structure **lconv**:

decimal_point
thousands_sep
grouping

Cross-reference
Standard, §4.4

See Also

LC_ALL, LC_COLLATE, LC_CTYPE, LC_MONETARY, LC_TIME, lconv, localization, locale.h, setlocale

LC_TIME — Macro
(Library/localization)
Locale time information
#include < locale.h >

LC_TIME is a macro that is defined in the header **locale.h**. When used with the function **setlocale**, it queries or sets the information for formatting time strings.

This information affects the operation of the function **strftime**.

Cross-reference
Standard, §4.4

See Also

LC_ALL, LC_COLLATE, LC_CTYPE, LC_MONETARY, LC_NUMERIC, lconv, localization, locale.h, setlocale

lconv — Type
(Library/localization)
Hold monetary conversion information
#include < locale.h >

lconv is a structure that is defined in the header **locale.h**. Its members hold many details needed to format monetary and non-monetary numeric information for a given locale.

To initialize **lconv** for any given locale, use the function **localeconv**. To change any aspect of the locale information being used, use the function **setlocale.**

Any implementation of **lconv** must contain the following 17 fields:

char *currency_symbol
This points to a string that contains the symbol used locally to represent currency, e.g., the '$'. The **C** locale sets this to point to a null string.

char *decimal_point
This points to a string that contains the character used to indicate the decimal point. The **C** locale sets this to point to '.'.

char frac_digits
This is the number of fractional digits that can be displayed in a monetary string. The **C** locale sets this to **CHAR_MAX**.

char grouping
> This points to the string that indicates the grouping characteristics for nonmonetary amounts. Characters in the string can take the following values:
>
> | | |
> |---|---|
> | **0** | Use previous element for rest of digits |
> | **MAX_CHAR** | Perform no further grouping |
> | **2 through 9** | No. of digits in current group |
>
> The **C** locale sets this to **CHAR_MAX**.

char *int_curr_symbol
> This points to a string that contains the international currency symbol for the locale, as defined in the publication *ISO 4217 Codes for Representation of Currency and Funds*. The **C** locale sets this to point to a null string.

char *mon_decimal_point
> This points to a string that contains the character used to indicate a decimal point in monetary strings. The **C** locale sets this to point to a null string.

char mon_grouping
> This points to the string of characters that indicate the grouping characteristics for monetary amounts. Elements can take the following values:
>
> | | |
> |---|---|
> | **0** | Use previous element for rest of digits |
> | **MAX_CHAR** | Perform no further grouping |
> | **2 through 9** | No. of digits in current group |
>
> The **C** locale sets this to **CHAR_MAX**.

char *mon_thousands_sep
> This points to a string that contains the character used to separate groups of thousands in monetary strings. The **C** locale sets this to point to a null string.

char n_cs_precedes
> This indicates whether the symbol that indicates a negative monetary value precedes or follows the numerals in the monetary string. Zero indicates that it follows the numerals and one indicates that it precedes them. The **C** locale sets this to **CHAR_MAX**.

char n_sep_by_space
> This indicates whether a space should appear between the symbol that indicates a negative monetary value and the numerals of the monetary string. Zero indicates that it should not appear, and one indicates that it should. The **C** locale sets this to **CHAR_MAX**.

char n_sign_posn
> This indicates the position and formatting of the symbol that indicates a negative monetary value, as follows:

0	Set parentheses around numerals and monetary symbol
1	Set negative sign before currency symbol and numerals
2	Set negative sign after currency symbol and numerals
3	Set negative sign immediately before monetary symbol
4	Set negative sign immediately after monetary symbol

The **C** locale sets this to **CHAR_MAX**.

char *negative_sign
This points to a string that contains the character that indicates a negative value in a monetary string. The **C** locale sets this to point to a null string.

char p_cs_precedes
This indicates whether the currency symbol should precede or follow the numerals in the string. Zero indicates that it precedes the digits and one indicates that it follows. The **C** locale sets this to **CHAR_MAX**.

char p_sep_by_space
This indicates whether a space should appear between the monetary symbol and the numerals of the monetary string. Zero indicates that a space should not appear, and one indicates that it should. The **C** locale sets this to **CHAR_MAX**.

char p_sign_posn
This indicates the position and formatting of the symbol that indicates a positive monetary value, as follows:

0	Set parentheses around numerals and monetary symbol
1	Set positive sign before currency symbol and numerals
2	Set positive sign after currency symbol and numerals
3	Set positive sign immediately before monetary symbol
4	Set positive sign immediately after monetary symbol

The **C** locale sets this to **CHAR_MAX**.

char *positive_sign
This points to a string that contains the character that indicates a non-negative value in a monetary string. The **C** locale sets this to point to a null string.

char *thousands_sep
This points to a string that contains the character used to separate groups of thousands. The **C** locale sets this to point to a null string.

Cross-reference
Standard, §4.4, §4.4.2.1

See Also
CHAR_MAX, locale.h, localeconv, localization, setlocale

LDBL_DIG — Macro
(Environment/environmental considerations/limits/numerical)
#include <float.h>

LDBL_DIG is a macro that is defined in the header **float.h**. It is an expression that defines the number of decimal digits of precision for type **long double**. It must yield a value of at least ten.

Cross-reference
Standard, §2.2.4.2

See Also
float.h, numerical limits

LDBL_EPSILON — Macro
(Environment/environmental considerations/limits/numerical)
#include <float.h>

LDBL_EPSILON is a macro that is defined in the header **float.h**. It is an expression that yields the smallest positive floating-point number representable as a **long double**, such that 1.0 plus it does not test equal to 1.0. It must yield a value of at most 1E-9.

Cross-reference
Standard, §2.2.4.2

See Also
float.h, numerical limits

LDBL_MANT_DIG — Macro
(Environment/environmental considerations/limits/numerical)
#include <float.h>

LDBL_MANT_DIG is a macro that is defined in the header **float.h**. It is an expression that represents the number of digits in the mantissa of type **long double**, in the numeric base set by the macro **FLT_RADIX**.

Cross-reference
Standard, §2.2.4.2

See Also
float.h, numerical limits

LDBL_MAX — Macro
(Environment/environmental considerations/limits/numerical)
#include < float.h >

LDBL_MAX is a macro that is defined in the header **float.h**. It is an expression that yields the largest number that can be represented by type **long double**. It must yield a value of at least 1E+37.

Cross-reference
Standard, §2.2.4.2

See Also
float.h, numerical limits

LDBL_MAX_10_EXP — Macro
(Environment/environmental considerations/limits/numerical)
#include < float.h >

LDBL_MAX_10_EXP is a macro that is defined in the header **float.h**. It is an expression that yields the largest power, such that ten raised to it remains a floating-point number that can be encoded by type **long double**. The value this expression yields must be at least 37.

Cross-reference
Standard, §2.2.4.2

See Also
float.h, numerical limits

LDBL_MAX_EXP — Macro
(Environment/environmental considerations/limits/numerical)
#include < float.h >

LDBL_MAX_EXP is a macro that is defined in the header **float.h**. It is an expression that yields the largest power such that **FLT_RADIX** raised to it minus one remains a floating-point number that can be held by type **long double**.

Cross-reference
Standard, §2.2.4.2

See Also
float.h, numerical limits

LDBL_MIN — Macro
(Environment/environmental considerations/limits/numerical)
#include < float.h >

LDBL_MIN is a macro that is defined in the header **float.h**. It is an expression that yields the smallest number that can be represented by type **long double**. It must yield a value of at most 1E-37.

Cross-reference
Standard, §2.2.4.2

See Also
float.h, numerical limits

LDBL_MIN_10_EXP — Macro
(Environment/environmental considerations/limits/numerical)
#include < float.h >

LDBL_MIN_10_EXP is a macro that is defined in the header **float.h**. It is an expression that yields the smallest power, such that ten raised to it remains a floating-point number that can be encoded by type **long double**. It must be at most -37.

Cross-reference
Standard, §2.2.4.2

See Also
float.h, numerical limits

LDBL_MIN_EXP — Macro
(Environment/environmental considerations/limits/numerical)
#include < float.h >

LDBL_MIN_EXP is a macro that is defined in the header **float.h**. It is an expression that yields the smallest power such that **FLT_RADIX** raised to it minus one remains a floating-point number that can be held by type **long double**.

Cross-reference
Standard, §2.2.4.2

See Also
float.h, numerical limits

ldexp() — Library function
(Library/mathematics/exponent-log functions)
Load floating-point number
#include < math.h >
double ldexp(double *number*, **int** *n***);**

ldexp returns *number* times two to the *n* power.

See **float.h** for more information on the structure of a floating-point number.

Cross-references
Standard, §4.5.4.3
The C Programming Language, ed. 2, p. 251

See Also
exp, exponent-log functions, frexp, log, log10, modf

ldiv() — Library function
(Library/general utilities/integer arithmetic)
Perform long integer division
#include < stdlib.h >
ldiv_t ldiv(long int *numerator*, **long int** *denominator***);**

ldiv divides *numerator* by *denominator*. It returns a structure of the type **ldiv_t**, which consists of two **long** members, one named **quot** and the other **rem**. **ldiv** writes the quotient into one **long**, and it writes the remainder into the other.

The sign of the quotient is positive if the signs of the arguments are the same; the sign of the quotient is negative if the signs of the arguments differ. The sign of the remainder is the same as the sign of the numerator.

If the remainder is non-zero, the magnitude of the quotient is the largest integer less than the magnitude of the algebraic quotient. This is not guaranteed by the operators **/** and **%**, which merely do what the machine implements for divide.

Example
This example selects one random card out of a pack of 52.

```
#include <stddef.h>
#include <stdio.h>
#include <stdlib.h>
#include <time.h>

main(void)
{
    ldiv_t card;

    card = ldiv((unsigned long)time(NULL) % 52, 13L);
    printf("%c%c\n",
        /* note useful addressing for strings */
        "A23456789TJQK"[card.rem],
        "HCDS"[card.quot]);
    return(EXIT_SUCCESS);
}
```

Cross-references
Standard, §4.10.6.2
The C Programming Language, ed. 2, p. 253

See Also
/, div, integer arithmetic, ldiv_t

Notes
The Standard includes this function to provide a useful feature of FORTRAN. Also, on most machines, division produces a remainder. This allows a quotient and remainder to be returned from one machine-divide operation.

If the result of division cannot be represented (e.g., because *denominator* is set to zero), the behavior of **ldiv** is undefined.

ldiv_t — Type
(Library/general utilities)
Type returned by ldiv()
#include <stdlib.h>

ldiv_t is a typedef that is declared in the header **stdlib.h** and is the type returned by the function **ldiv**.

ldiv_t is a structure that consists of two **long** members, one named **quot** and the other **rem**. The Standard does not specify their order within **ldiv_t**. **ldiv** writes its quotient into **quot** and its remainder into **rem**.

Example
For an example of this type in a program, see **ldiv**.

Cross-references
Standard, §4.10.6.2
The C Programming Language, ed. 2, p. 253

See Also
general utilities, integer arithmetic, ldiv, stdlib.h

letter — Definition
(Library)

The Standard defines a *letter* as being any of the 52 printing characters that can be used to write a C program, as follows:

a	b	c	d	e	f	g	h	i
j	k	l	m	n	o	p	q	r
r	s	t	u	v	w	x	y	z
A	B	C	D	E	F	G	H	I
J	K	L	M	N	O	P	Q	R
R	S	T	U	V	W	X	Y	Z
0	1	2	3	4	5	6	7	8
9	!	"	#	%	&	'	(	)
*	+	,	-	.	/	:	;	<
=	>	?	[	\	]	^	_	{
|	}	~						

Cross-reference
Standard, §4.1.1

See Also
Library, printing character

lexical elements — Overview
(Language)

A *lexical element* is one of the elements from which a C program is built. It is the smallest unit with which a translator can work. "Lexical" refers to the fact that a program is partitioned into tokens during a translation phase that is usually called "lexical analysis."

A C program is built from the following lexical elements:

constants
header names
identifiers
keywords
operators
preprocessing numbers
punctuators
string literals

Cross-reference
Standard, §3.1

See Also
comment, constant, header name, identifier, keyword, Language, operators, preprocessing number, punctuators, string literal, token

Library — Overview
(Standard)

Library is the last of the four sections of the Standard. It defines all library functions required by the Standard, as well as attending macros and types.

A conforming hosted environment must implement all library functions the Standard describes. A conforming freestanding environment must implement only the macros, types, and functions declared in the headers **float.h**, **limits.h**, **stdarg.h**, and **stddef.h**.

Headers
Every library function is declared in a header, which is included by the **#include** preprocessor directive. Every external identifier, including function names, within every header is reserved to the implementation. Also reserved is every external identifier that begins with an underscore '_'.

These external names are reserved even if their associated header is not included. This is because the library may interact in ways unknown to the user, and to replace a function that is used by other library functions may create devastating side effects. Therefore, if a reserved external name is redefined, behavior is undefined, even if the function that replaces it is identical to the original.

Function Usage
All functions must be implemented as functions, even if they are implemented as macros. The only exceptions are **assert**, **setjmp**, **va_arg**, and **va_start**, which may be implemented *only* as macros. A function may also be implemented as a macro in the appropriate header.

If a library function expands to a macro invocation, such as for in-line code expansion, such an expansion must be "safe," in the sense that each argument is evaluated only once.

If a function is implemented as a macro, the macro version is used, assuming that the program includes the header within which the macro is defined. To force the implementation to use the function implementation of a routine instead of the macro implementation, do either of the following:

1. Enclose the function name within parentheses. For example, if the function **isupper** has been implemented as a macro as well as a library function, you can force a program to use the library version by the following:

    ```
    #include <ctype.h>
        . . .
    result = (isupper)(c);
    ```

    This also means that you can access any function by address, even if that function is also defined as a macro.

2. Turn off its macro definition by use of the **#undef** preprocessor directive. For example, the following:

    ```
    #include <ctype.h>
    #undef isupper
        . . .
    result = isupper(c);
    ```

    forces an implementation to use the library version of **isupper**, in place of an existing macro definition.

Library Functions

The Standard describes the following library functions:

assert.h

assert	Check assertion at run time

ctype.h

isalnum	Check if a character is a numeral or letter
isalpha	Check if a character is a letter
iscntrl	Check if a character is a control character
isdigit	Check if a character is a numeral
isgraph	Check if a character is printable
islower	Check if a character is a lower-case letter
isprint	Check if a character is printable
ispunct	Check if a character is a punctuation mark
isspace	Check if a character is white space
isupper	Check if a character is a upper-case letter
isxdigit	Check if a character is a hexadecimal numeral
tolower	Convert characters to lower case

	toupper	Convert characters to upper case

errno.h

	errno	External integer that holds error status

locale.h

	localeconv	Initialize **lconv** structure
	setlocale	Change or query a program's locale

math.h

	acos	Calculate inverse cosine
	asin	Calculate inverse sine
	atan	Calculate inverse tangent
	atan2	Calculate inverse tangent
	ceil	Set numeric ceiling
	cos	Calculate cosine
	cosh	Calculate hyperbolic cosine
	exp	Compute exponent
	fabs	Compute absolute value
	floor	Set a numeric floor
	fmod	Calculate modulus for floating-point number
	frexp	Fracture floating-point number
	ldexp	Multiply floating-point number
	log	Compute natural logarithm
	log10	Compute common logarithm
	modf	Separate exponent and fraction
	pow	Raise one number to the power of another
	sin	Calculate sine
	sinh	Calculate hyperbolic sine
	sqrt	Calculate the square root of a number
	tan	Calculate tangent
	tanh	Calculate hyperbolic tangent

setjmp.h

	longjmp	Perform a non-local jump
	setjmp	Save environment for non-local goto

signal.h

	raise	Send a signal
	signal	Set processing for a signal

stdarg.h

	va_arg	Return pointer to next argument in argument list
	va_end	Tidy up after traversal of argument list
	va_start	Point to beginning of argument list

stddef.h

	offsetof	Calculate offset of a field within a structure

stdio.h

clearerr	Clear error condition from a stream
close	Close a file
create	Create a file
fclose	Close a stream
feof	Examine a stream's end-of-file indicator
ferror	Examine a stream's error indicator
fflush	Flush output stream's buffer
fgetc	Read a character from a stream
fgetpos	Get value of file-position indicator
fgets	Read a line from a stream
fopen	Open a stream for standard I/O
fpos_t	Encode current position in a file
fprintf	Print formatted text into a stream
fputc	Write a character into a stream
fputs	Write a string into a stream
fread	Read data from a stream
freopen	Re-open a stream
fscanf	Read and format text from a stream
fseek	Set file-position indicator
fsetpos	Set file-position indicator
ftell	Get value of file-position indicator
fwrite	Write data into a stream
getc	Read a character from a stream
getchar	Read a character from standard input stream
gets	Read a string from standard input stream
perror	Print an error message into standard error stream
printf	Format and print text into standard output stream
putc	Write a character into a stream
putchar	Write a character into standard output stream
puts	Write a string into standard output stream
remove	Remove a file
rename	Rename a file
rewind	Reset file-position indicator
scanf	Read and format text from standard input stream
setbuf	Set alternative stream buffer
setvbuf	Set alternative stream buffer
sprintf	Print formatted text into a string
sscanf	Read and format text from a string
tmpfile	Create a temporary file
tmpnam	Generate a unique name for a temporary file
ungetc	Push a character back into the input stream
vfprintf	Print formatted text into stream
vprintf	Print formatted text into standard output stream
vsprintf	Print formatted text into string

stdlib.h

abort	End program immediately
abs	Compute the absolute value of an integer
atexit	Register a function to be performed at exit
atof	Convert string to floating-point number
atoi	Convert string to integer
atol	Convert string to long integer
bsearch	Search an array
calloc	Allocate dynamic memory
div	Perform integer division
exit	Terminate a program gracefully
free	De-allocate dynamic memory to free memory pool
getenv	Read environmental variable
labs	Compute the absolute value of a long integer
ldiv	Perform long integer division
malloc	Allocate dynamic memory
mblen	Compute length of a multibyte character
mbstowcs	Convert sequence of multibyte characters to wide characters
mbtowc	Convert multibyte character to wide character
qsort	Sort an array
rand	Generate pseudo-random numbers
realloc	Reallocate dynamic memory
strtod	Convert string to floating-point number
strtol	Convert string to long integer
strtoul	Convert string to unsigned long integer
system	Suspend a program and execute another
wcstombs	Convert sequence of wide characters to multibyte characters
wctomb	Convert wide character to multibyte character

string.h

memchr	Search a region of memory for a character
memcmp	Compare two regions
memcpy	Copy a region of memory
memmove	Copy a region of memory into one with which it may overlap
memset	Fill a buffer with a character
perror	System call error messages
strcat	Append one string onto another
strchr	Find a character in a string
strcmp	Compare two strings
strcoll	Compare two strings, using locale-specific information
strcpy	Copy one string into another
strcspn	Length one string excludes characters in another
strerror	Translate an error number into a string
strlen	Measure the length of a string
strncat	Append n characters of one string onto another
strncmp	Compare one string with a portion of another

strncpy	Copy one string into another
strpbrk	Find first occurrence of any character from another string
strrchr	Search for rightmost occurrence of character in string
strspn	Length for which a string includes characters in another
strstr	Find one string within another
strtok	Break a string into tokens
strxfrm	Transform a string

time.h

asctime	Convert broken-down time to text
clock	Get processor time used
ctime	Convert calendar time to text
difftime	Calculate difference between two times
gmtime	Convert calendar time to Universal Coordinated Time
localtime	Convert calendar time to local time
mktime	Convert broken-down time into calendar time
strftime	Format locale-specific time
time	Get current calendar time

Cross-references

Standard, §4
The C Programming Language, ed. 2, pp. 241*ff*

See Also

Environment, function, header, Language, Standard

Notes

The base document for the library section of the Standard is the *1984 /usr/group Standard*. Some functions were modelled on the UNIX System V libraries, and others from various commercial implementations.

limits — Overview
(Environment/environmental considerations)

The Standard describes two groups of limits: *environmental limits* and *numerical limits*.

Environmental limits are the limits that the environment sets upon the complexity of a C program. For example, the environment may restrict the number of **case** labels that can be contained within a **switch** statement.

Numerical limits are the limits upon the values that can be encoded within a type, e.g., the largest and smallest values that can be contained within type **int**. The implementation sets numerical limits, and every numerical limit must be recorded in a macro. Limits for integral types are recorded in the header **limits.h**, and those for floating types are recorded in the header **float.h**.

Cross-reference
Standard, §2.2.4

See Also
environmental considerations, environmental limits, float.h, limits.h, minimum maxima, numerical limits

limits.h — Header
(Environment/environmental considerations)

The header **limits.h** defines a group of macros that set the numerical limits for the translation environment.

The following table gives the macros defined in **limits.h**. Each value given is the macro's minimum maximum: a conforming implementation of C must meet these limits, and may exceed them.

CHAR_BIT
>   Number of bits in a **char**; must be at least eight.

CHAR_MAX
>   Largest value representable in an object of type **char**. If the implementation defines a **char** to be signed, then it is equal to the value of the macro **SCHAR_MAX**; otherwise, it is equal to the value of the macro **UCHAR_MAX**.

CHAR_MIN
>   Smallest value representable in an object of type **char**. If the implementation defines a **char** to be signed, then it is equal to the value of the macro **SCHAR_MIN**; otherwise, it is zero.

INT_MAX
>   Largest value representable in an object of type **int**; it must be at least 32,767.

INT_MIN
>   Smallest value representable in an object of type **int**; it must be at most -32,767.

LONG_MAX
>   Largest value representable in an object of type **long int**; it must be at least 2,147,483,647.

LONG_MIN
>   Smallest value representable in an object of type **long int**; it must be at most -2,147,483,647.

MB_LEN_MAX
Largest number of bytes in any multibyte character, for any locale; it must be at least one.

SCHAR_MAX
Largest value representable in an object of type **signed char**; it must be at least 127.

SCHAR_MIN
Smallest value representable in an object of type **signed char**; it must be at most -127.

SHRT_MAX
Largest value representable in an object of type **short int**; it must be at least 32,767.

SHRT_MIN
Smallest value representable in an object of type **short int**; it must be at most -32,767.

UCHAR_MAX
Largest value representable in an object of type **unsigned char**; it must be at least 255.

UINT_MAX
Largest value representable in an object of type **unsigned int**; it must be at least 65,535.

ULONG_MAX
Largest value representable in an object of type **unsigned long int**; it must be at least 4,294,967,295.

USHRT_MAX
Largest value representable in an object of type **unsigned short int**; it must be at least 65,535.

Cross-references
Standard, §2.2.4.2
The C Programming Language, ed. 2, p. 257

See Also
environmental considerations, header, numerical limits

line — Definition
(Library/STDIO)

A *line* is the basic unit of organization within a text stream. It consists of zero or more characters terminated by a newline character. The host environment may add or subtract characters to make the line amenable to the environment's way of storing text.

The Standard mandates that a line read from a stream will be identical to the same line written earlier into the stream only if the following conditions are met: (1) if the line consists only of printable characters, the horizontal tab character, the vertical tab character, and the form-feed character; (2) if no space characters immediately precede the terminating newline character; and (3) the last character is a newline character. Whether any space characters that immediately precede the newline character are preserved or thrown away depends upon the implementation.

Cross-references
Standard, §4.9.2
The C Programming Language, ed. 2, p. 243

See Also
buffer, BUFSIZ, file, STDIO, stream

Notes
The maximum length of a line is set by the macro **BUFSIZ**, which is defined in the header **stdio.h**. The Standard mandates that all conforming implementations of C will define **BUFSIZ** to be no less than 256.

link — Definition
(Definitions)

To *link* a program means to resolve external references among individual source files. External references may refer to data or code that reside in another translation unit.

Some function calls may be resolved by the inclusion of the code for that function from a library, which consists of implementation-defined or user-defined functions.

See Also
compile, Definitions, linkage

linkage — Definition
(Language/lexical elements/identifiers)

The term *linkage* refers to the matching of an identifier with its namesakes across blocks of code, and among files of source code, pretranslated object modules, and libraries.

Identifiers can have internal linkage, external linkage, or no linkage. An identifier with external linkage is known across multiple translation units. An identifier with internal linkage is known only within one translation unit. An identifier with no linkage has no permanent storage allocated for it and is local to a function or block.

The following describes each type of linkage in more detail:

External linkage
The following identifiers have external linkage:

- Any identifier for a function that either has no storage-class identifier or is marked with the storage-class identifier **extern**, but excluding ones marked with the storage-class identifier **static**.

- Any global identifier that either has no storage-class identifier or is marked **extern**.

Internal linkage
The following identifiers have internal linkage:

- Any identifier marked **static**.

- Any identifier for a function that has file scope and is marked **static**.

No linkage
The following identifiers have no linkage:

- An identifier for anything that is not an object or function; e.g., a structure member, a **union** member, an enumeration constant, a tag, or a label.

- Any identifier declared to be a function parameter.

- An identifier local to a block (i.e., an **auto** object), that does not have file scope and is not marked **extern**.

An identifier with internal linkage may be up to at least 31 characters long, and may use both upper- and lower-case characters. An identifier with external linkage, however, may have up to at least six characters, and is not required to use both upper- and lower-case characters. These limits are implementation defined.

An object marked **extern** will have the same linkage as any previous declaration of the same object within that translation unit. If there is no previous declaration, the object has external linkage.

If an object appears in the same source file with external and internal linkage declarations, behavior is undefined. This is called a *linkage conflict*. It may occur if an object is first declared **extern**, then later re-declared to be **static**.

Cross-references
Standard, §3.1.2.2
The C Programming Language, ed. 2, p. 228

See Also
identifiers, name space, scope

local time — Definition
(Library/date and time)

The term *local time* refers to calendar time for the current locale.

The function **localtime** returns local time in the form of broken-down time.

Cross-reference
Standard, §4.12

See Also
broken-down time, calendar time, date and time, daylight savings time, localtime

locale.h — Header
(Library/localization)
Localization functions and macros
#include <locale.h>

locale.h is a header that declares or defines all functions and macros used to manipulate a program's locale. The Standard describes the following items within this header:

Type
lconv	Structure for numeric formatting

Macros
LC_ALL	All locale information
LC_COLLATE	Locale collation information
LC_CTYPE	Locale character-handling information
LC_MONETARY	Locale monetary information
LC_NUMERIC	Locale numeric information
LC_TIME	Locale time information

Functions
localeconv	initialize **lconv** structure
setlocale	set/query locale

Cross-references
Standard, §4.4
The C Programming Language, ed. 2, pp

See Also
localization

Notes
An implementation may also define additional macros that examine the locale. All must begin with **LC_** followed by at least one capital letter. Such names are reserved, i.e., a maximally portable program should not define such names, as they may conflict with those already established within the implementation.

localeconv() — Library function
(Library/localization)

Initialize **lconv** structure

#include < locale.h >
struct lconv *localeconv(void);

localeconv initializes the structure **lconv** and returns a pointer to it. **lconv** describes the formatting of numeric strings. For more information about this structure, see **lconv**.

The function **setlocale** establishes all or part of pre-defined locale as the current locale. A call to **setlocale** with the macros **LC_ALL**, **LC_MONETARY**, or **LC_NUMERIC** may alter a portion of **lconv**.

Cross-reference
Standard, §4.4.2.1

See Also
lconv, localization, locale.h, setlocale

localization — Overview
(Library)

The Standard introduces the concept of *localization* to C programming.

The Problem
C was originally designed to implement the UNIX operating system. As such, its formatting functions assumed that the Latin alphabet would be used (that is, the only characters 'a' through 'z' and 'A' through 'Z'), assumed that no accented characters would be required, and also assumed that numeric strings would be formatted as they are in the United States. Since its invention, however, C has grown out of its original setting and its original country: it is now used internationally to write a wide range of application software.

The Standard recognizes that C internally is based on the English language. That is, C's keywords and library names reflect its origin in English, and will continue to do so. Localization, however, allows an application program to use the character set and formatting information that is specific to a given country in certain aspects of the language.

A locale can be selected when the program is run, so applications can be user-selectable. It may include things like monetary formatting, but preserve the underlying data: only the presentation differs. Locales provide a standard way for software developers to use locale-specific information without having to "reinvent the wheel" for each locale.

If an implementation of C supports various locales, then that locale information need not be gathered by programmers who write applications software. Rather than each software house writing support for European collating conventions or Japanese monetary formatting conventions, the support is provided once, by the implementor, and in a standard fashion.

Locale Functions

The Standard describes two functions that can be used to access information specific to a given locale.

setlocale can be used in either of two ways: to set the current locale, or to query the current locale settings. Either part or all of a locale's strings can be set or queried.

localeconv initializes an instance of the structure **lconv** and returns a pointer to it. This structure holds information that can be used to print numeric and monetary strings. For more information on this structure, see the entry for **lconv**.

The macros that begin with **LC_** are defined in the header **locale.h**, and represent the categories of locales (also known as *locale strings*). The following describes the areas of C that are affected by locales.

Characters

A national character set may include characters that lie outside of the Latin alphabet. Typically, these characters are not recognized as alphanumeric characters by functions like **isalpha**. To tell the translator to use the alternative character table for a given locale, use the call

```
setlocale(LC_CTYPE, locale);
```

The character-handling routines that are defined in the header **ctype.h** will use this locale information. This will also affect the functions that handle multibyte characters, as described below.

Collation

The sorting of strings that include national characters may present a problem. Normal collation functions depend upon the ASCII character order, and therefore do not know where additional, locale-specific characters go within the national character set. The Standard describes two functions, **strcoll** and **strxfrm**, that may collate strings which contain locale-specific characters. To set the locale information needed by these functions (so they know which national character order is used), use the call

```
setlocale(LC_COLL, locale);
```

strcoll and **strxfrm** will work in accordance with the current locale setting.

Date and time

Most countries have an idiomatic way to express the current date and time. To set the locale information needed by the function **strftime**, use the call:

```
setlocale(LC_TIME, locale);
```

strftime can read the locale and format date and time strings accordingly.

Decimal point

Different countries may use different characters to mark the decimal point. Occasionally, one character is used to mark the point in a numeric string and another to mark it in a string that describes money. The structure **lconv** contains the field **decimal_point**, which points to the character used to mark the decimal point in a numeric string.

To set the locale for functions that read or print the decimal point, use the call:

```
setlocale(LC_NUMERIC, locale);
```

All functions that perform string conversion, formatted output, or formatted input must interpret this information so these characters will be handled properly.

Money Each country has its own way to format monetary values. The character that represents the national currency varies from country to country, as does such aspects as whether the symbol goes before or after the numerals, how a negative value is rendered, what character is used to express a monetary decimal point (it may not be the same as the numeric decimal point), and how many digits are normally printed after the decimal point.

To set the locale information for money, use the call:

```
setlocale(LC_MONETARY, locale);
```

The structure **lconv**, which is initialized by the function **localeconv**, holds information needed to render monetary strings correctly.

Multibyte characters

Many countries, e.g., Japan and China, use systems of writing that use more characters than can be represented within one byte. Many operating systems and terminal devices, however, can receive only seven or eight bits at a time. To skirt this problem, the Standard describes two ways to encode such extensive sets of characters: with *wide characters* and *multibyte* characters.

A wide character is of type **wchar_t**. This type, in turn, is defined as being equivalent to the integral type that can describe all of the unique characters in the character set. This type is used mainly to store such characters in a device-independent manner.

A multibyte character, on the other hand, consists of two or more **chars** that together are understood by the terminal device as forming a non-alphabetic character or symbol. One wide character may map out to any number of multibyte characters, depending upon the number of systems of multibyte characters that are commonly in use.

The Standard describes five functions that manipulate wide characters and multibyte characters: **mblen**, **mbstowcs**, **mbtowc**, **wcstombs**, and **wctomb**. The actions of these functions are determined by the locale, as set by **setlocale**. To set a locale for the manipulation of multibyte characters, use the following call:

```
setlocale(LC_CTYPE, locale);
```

The Standard does not describe the mechanism by which tables of multibyte characters are made available to these functions.

Thousands

Large numbers can be broken up into groups of thousands to make them easier to read. The manner of grouping, including the number of items in each group and the character used to indicate the start of a new group, is locale specific.

The structure **lconv**, which is initialized by the function **localeconv**, contains the fields **thousands_sep**, **mon_grouping**, and **grouping**, which hold this information.

Default Locale

The only locale required of all conforming implementations is the **C** locale. This is the minimum set of locale strings needed to translate C source code. For a listing of what constitutes the **C** locale, see **lconv**.

When a C program begins, it behaves as if the call

```
setlocale(LC_ALL, "C");
```

had been issued.

Mechanism for Setting Locales

The Standard does not describe the mechanism by which **setlocale** makes locale information available to other functions, and by which the other functions use locale information. It is left to the implementation.

Cross-reference
Standard, §4.4

See Also
compliance, lconv, Library, locale.h

Notes
The Standard's section on compliance states that any program that uses locale-specific information does not conform strictly to the Standard. Therefore, a program that uses any locale other than the **C** locale is not strictly conforming. A programmer should not count on being able to port such a program to any other implementation or execution environment.

localtime() — Library function
(Library/date and time/time conversion)
Convert calendar time to local time
#include <time.h>
struct tm *localtime(const time_t *_timeptr_);

localtime takes the calendar time pointed to by _timeptr_ and breaks it down into a structure of type **tm**. Unlike the related function **gmtime**, **localtime** preserves the local time of the system.

localtime returns a pointer to the structure **tm** that it creates; this structure is defined in the header **time.h**.

Example
The following example recreates the function **asctime**.

```
#include <stdio.h>
#include <time.h>

char *month[12] = {
    "January", "February" "March", "April",
    "May", "June", "July", "August",
    "September", "October", "November", "December"
};

char *weekday[7] = {
    "Sunday", "Monday", "Tuesday", "Wednesday",
    "Thursday", "Friday", "Saturday"
};
```

```
main()
{
    char buf[20];
    time_t tnum;
    struct tm *ts;
    int hour = 0;

    /* get time from system */
    time(&tnum);

    /* convert time to tm struct */
    ts=localtime(&tnum);

    if(ts->tm_hour==0)
        sprintf(buf,"12:%02d:%02d A.M.",
            ts->tm_min, ts->tm_sec);

    else
        if(ts->tm_hour>=12) {
            hour=ts->tm_hour-12;
            if (hour==0)
                hour=12;
            sprintf(buf,"%02d:%02d:%02d P.M.",
                hour, ts->tm_min,ts->tm_sec);

        } else
            sprintf(buf,"%02d:%02d:%02d A.M.",
                ts->tm_hour, ts->tm_min, ts->tm_sec);

    printf("\n%s %d %s 19%d %s\n",
        weekday[ts->tm_wday], ts->tm_mday,
        month[ts->tm_mon], ts->tm_year, buf);

    printf("Today is the %d day of 19%d\n",
        ts->tm_yday, ts->tm_year);

    if(ts->tm_isdst)
        printf("Daylight Saving Time is in effect.\n");
    else
        printf("Daylight Saving Time is not in effect.\n");

    return(EXIT_SUCCESS);
}
```

Cross-references

Standard, §4.12.3.4
The C Programming Language, ed. 2, p. 256

See Also
asctime, ctime, gmtime, local time, strftime, time manipulation, tm

log() — Library function
(Library/mathematics/exponent-log functions)
Compute natural logarithm
#include <math.h>
double log(double z);

log computes and returns the natural (base e) logarithm of its argument z. It is the inverse of the function **exp**.

Handing **log** an argument less than zero triggers a domain error. Handing it an argument equal to zero triggers a range error.

Cross-references
Standard, §4.5.4.4
The C Programming Language, ed. 2, p. 251

See Also
exp, exponent-log functions, frexp, ldexp, log10, modf

log10() — Library function
(Library/mathematics/exponent-log functions)
Compute common logarithm
#include <math.h>
double log10(double z);

log10 computes and returns the common (base 10) logarithm of its argument z.

Handing **log10** an argument less than zero triggers a domain error. Handing it an argument equal to zero triggers a range error.

Cross-references
Standard, §4.5.4.5
The C Programming Language, ed. 2, p. 251

See Also
exp, exponent-log functions, frexp, ldexp, log, modf

logical operators — Overview
(Language/expressions)

The C language has two operators that perform logical operations: **&&** and **||**. Their syntax is as follows:

logical-AND-expression:
    inclusive-OR-expression
    logical-AND-expression && *inclusive-OR-expression*

logical-OR-expression:
    logical-AND-expression
    logical-OR-expression || *logical-AND-expression*

The operator **&&** performs a logical AND operation: if both operands are true (i.e., other than zero), the result has a value of one. However, if either operand is false (equal to zero), the result has a value of zero.

The operator **||** performs a logical OR operation: the result has a value of one if either operand is true, or if both operands are true.

Both operands must have a scalar type. The resulting expression has type **int**.

Both operators evaluate their operands from left to right. In the case of the **||** operator, if the first operand is true, then the second operand is not evaluated. In the case of the **&&** operator, however, if the first operand is false, then the second operand is not evaluated. In either case, if the second operand yields a side-effect, then the result of the expression may not be what you expect. This type of evaluation is sometimes called "short-circuit" evaluation, and is not found in some other languages (e.g., Pascal).

Cross-references
Standard, §3.3.13, §3.3.14
The C Programming Language, ed. 2, p. 207

See Also
&&, ||, expressions

Notes
Programmers who require logical operators that always generate their side effects may be tempted to use the bitwise AND and bitwise inclusive OR operators instead. You should remember, however, that the order of evaluation of the operands of the bitwise operators is not guaranteed. Hence, you will get all of the side effects, but possibly not in the order you expected.

LONG_MAX — Macro
(Environment/environmental considerations/limits)

LONG_MAX is a macro that is defined in the header **limits.h**. It gives the largest value that can be held by an object of type **long int**. It cannot be less than 2,147,483,647.

Cross-references
Standard, §2.2.4.2
The C Programming Language, ed. 2, p. 257

See Also
limits

LONG_MIN — Macro
(Environment/environmental considerations/limits)

LONG_MIN is a macro that is defined in the header **limits.h**. It gives the smallest value that can be held by an object of type **long int**. It must be at most -2,147,483,647.

Cross-references
Standard, §2.2.4.2
The C Programming Language, ed. 2, p. 257

See Also
limits

long double — Type
(Language/lexical elements/identifiers/types)

A **long double** is a data type that represents at least a double-precision floating-point number. It is defined as being at least as large as a **double**. In some environments, extra precision can be gained by representing values with it.

Like all floating-point numbers, a **long double** consists of one sign bit, which indicates whether the number is positive or negative; bits that encode the number's *exponent*; and bits that encode the number's *mantissa*, or the number upon which the exponent works. The exponent often uses a *bias*. This is a value that is subtracted from the exponent to yield the power of two by which the fraction will be increased. The structure of a **long double** and the range of values that it can encode are set in the following macros, all of which are defined in the header **limits.h**:

LDBL_DIG

This holds the number of decimal digits of precision. This must be at least ten.

LDBL_EPSILON

Where b indicates the base of the exponent (default, two) and p indicates the precision (or number of base b digits in the mantissa), this macro holds the minimum positive floating-point number x such that 1.0 + x does not equal 1.0, b^{1-p}. This must be at least 1E-9.

LDBL_MAX

This holds the maximum representable floating-point number. It must be at least 1E+37.

LDBL_MAX_EXP

This is the maximum integer such that the base raised to its power minus one is a representable finite floating-point number. No value is given for this macro.

LDBL_MAX_10_EXP

This holds the maximum integer such that ten raised to its power is within the range of representable finite floating-point numbers. It must be at least +37.

LDBL_MANT_DIG

This gives the number of digits in the mantissa. No value is given for this macro.

LDBL_MIN

This gives the minimum value encodable within a **long double**. This must be at least 1E-37.

LDBL_MIN_EXP

This gives the minimum negative integer such that when the base is raised to that power minus one is a normalized floating-point number. No value is given for this macro.

LDBL_MIN_10_EXP

This gives the minimum negative integer such that ten raised to that power is within the range of normalized floating-point numbers.

A **long double** constant is represented by the suffix l or L on a floating-point constant.

Cross-references

Standard, §2.2.4.2, §3.1.2.4, §3.1.3.1, §3.5.2
The C Programming Language, ed. 2, p. 196

See Also
double, float, types

long int — Type
(Language/lexical elements/identifiers/types)

A **long int** is a signed integral type. This type can be no closer to zero than an **int**.

A **long int** can encode any number between **LONG_MIN** and **LONG_MAX**. These are macros that are defined in the header **limits.h**; they must, respectively, be at least -2,147,483,647 and 2,147,483,647.

The types **long**, **signed long**, and **signed long int** are synonyms for **long int**.

Cross-references
Standard, §2.2.4.2, §3.1.2.5, §3.2.1.1, §3.5.2
The C Programming Language, ed. 2, p. 211

See Also
int, short int, types

longjmp() — Library function
(Library/non-local jumps)
Execute a non-local jump
#include < setjmp.h >
void longjmp(jmp_buf *environment***, int** *rval***);**

A call to **longjmp** restores the environment that the function **setjmp** had stored within the array **jmp_buf**. Execution then continues not at the point at which **longjmp** is called, but at the point at which **setjmp** was called.

environment is the environment that had been saved by an earlier call to **setjmp**. It is of type **jmp_buf**, which is defined in the header **setjmp.h**. The Standard mandates that **jmp_buf** be an array type.

longjmp returns the value *rval* to the original call to **setjmp**, as if **setjmp** had just returned. **rval** must be a number other than zero; if it is zero, then **setjmp** will return one.

Cross-references
Standard, §4.6.2.1
The C Programming Language, ed. 2, p. 254

See Also
non-local jumps, setjmp

Notes

Many user-level routines cannot be interrupted and reentered safely. For that reason, improper use of **longjmp** and **setjmp** will result in the creation of mysterious and irreproducible bugs.

longjmp will work correctly "in the contexts of interrupts, signals and any of their associated functions." Also, **longjmp**'s behavior is undefined if it is used from within a function called by signal received during the handling of a different signal.

Experience has shown that **longjmp** should not be used within an exception handler. The Standard does not guarantee that programs will work correctly when **longjmp** is used to exit interrupts and signals. Experience has shown that even if the **longjmp** terminates the signal handler and returns successfully to the context of the **setjmp**, the program can easily fail to complete the very next function call it attempts, usually because the signal interrupted an update of a non-atomic data structure. The Standard guarantees that the implementations of **setjmp**, **longjmp**, and **signal** will work together; it cannot make any promises about the interactions of these services with other library functions or with user code. *Caveat utilitor.*

lvalue — Definition
(Language/conversions)

An *lvalue* designates an object in storage. An lvalue can be of any type, complete or incomplete, other than type **void**.

A *modifiable lvalue* is any lvalue that is *not* of the following types:

- An array type.
- An incomplete type.
- Any type qualified by **const**.
- A structure or **union** with a member whose type is qualified by **const**, or with a member that is a structure or **union** with a member that is so qualified.

Only a modifiable lvalue is permitted on the left side of an assignment statement.

An lvalue normally is converted to the value that is stored in the designated object. When this occurs, it ceases to be an lvalue. For some lvalues, however, this does *not* occur, as follows:

- Any array type.

- When the lvalue is the operand of the operators **sizeof**, unary **&**, --, or ++.

- When the lvalue is the left operand of the . operator.

- When the lvalue is the left operand of any assignment operator.

An lvalue with an array type is normally converted to a pointer to the same type. The value of the pointer is the address of the first member of the array. The exceptions to this operation are as follows:

- When it is the operand of the operators **sizeof** or unary **&**.

- When it is a string literal that initializes an array of **char**.

- When it is a string literal of wide characters that initializes an array of **wchar_t**.

In addition to the restrictions listed above, the following are also *not* lvalues, and hence cannot appear on the left side of an assignment statement:

- String literals.

- Character constants.

- Numeric constants.

Cross-references
Standard, §3.2.2.1
The C Programming Language, ed. 2, p. 197

See Also
conversions, function designator, rvalue

Notes
The term itself originally came from the phrase *left value*; in an expression like

```
object = value;
```

the element to the left of the '=' is the object whose value is modified. Because the Standard distinguishes between lvalues and modifiable lvalues, it prefers to define lvalue as being a contraction of the phrase *locator value*.

M

macro replacement — Overview
(Language/preprocessing)

A *macro* is a sequence of tokens that is given a name. When a program defines a macro, the preprocessor scans the source file for the macro's name and replaces it with its tokens. This process is called *macro replacement* or *macro expansion*.

To define a macro, use the preprocessing directive **#define**. The preprocessor recognizes two varieties of macros: *object-like* and *function-like*. For more information on macro definition, see **#define**.

When the translator performs macro substitution, the translation unit has already been turned into preprocessing tokens, with all escape sequences and trigraphs resolved. After a macro has been expanded, the expanded text is scanned again to see if the expansion itself contains any macros (not including the original macro that has already been expanded). This re-scanning continues until no further replacement is possible.

Cross-references
Standard, §3.8.3
The C Programming Language, ed. 2, pp. 229*ff*

See Also
preprocessing

main — Definition
(Environment/execution environment/hosted environment)

main is the name of the function that is called when a program begins execution under a hosted environment. A program must have one function named **main.** This function is special not only because it marks the beginning of program execution, but because it is the only function that may be called with either zero arguments or two arguments:

```
int main(void) {   }
```

or

```
int main(int argc, char *argv[]) {   }
```

Some implementations of C allow **main** to take three or more arguments. Programs that use more than two arguments to **main**, however, do not conform strictly to the Standard.

The two arguments to **main** are called **argc** and **argv**. These names are used by convention; a programmer may use any names he wishes.

argv points to an array of pointers to strings. These strings can modify the operation of the program; thus, they are called *program parameters*. **argc** gives the number of strings in the array to which **argv** points.

If **main** calls **return**, it is equivalent to its calling **exit** with the same parameter. For example, the statement

```
return(EXIT_SUCCESS);
```

in **main** is equivalent to the call

```
exit(EXIT_SUCCESS);
```

If **main** returns without returning a value to the host environment, the value that is returned to the host environment is undefined.

Cross-references
Standard, §2.1.2.2
The C Programming Language, ed. 2, pp. 6, 164

See Also
argc, argv, hosted environment

malloc() — Library function
(Library/general utility/memory management)
Allocate dynamic memory
#include <stdlib.h>
void *malloc(size_t *size*);

malloc allocates a block of memory *size* bytes long.

malloc returns a pointer to the block of memory it has allocated. The pointer is aligned for any type of object. If it could not allocate the amount of memory requested, it returns NULL.

Example
For an example of this function, see **realloc**.

Cross-references
Standard, §4.10.3.3
The C Programming Language, ed. 2, p. 167

See Also
alignment, calloc, free, memory management, realloc

Notes
If *size* is set to zero, the behavior of **malloc** is implementation defined: **malloc** returns either NULL or a unique pointer. This is a quiet change that may silently break some existing code.

manifest constant — Definition
(Definitions)

A *manifest constant* is a value that has been given a name. Although this term is commonly used by programmers, the Standard prefers to call it a *macro*.

The following demonstrates the definition of a manifest constant:

```
#define MAXFILES 9
```

Here, the constant **MAXFILES** is defined as having the value of nine. During the preprocessing phase of translation, the translator will substitute the character '9' for **MAXFILES** wherever it appears — or behave as if it had made such a substitution.

These constants serve two purposes within a C program: First, a constant can be changed throughout the program simply by changing its definition. Second, a programmer who reads the program will find it easier to understand the meaning of a well-named manifest constant than to understand its numeric analogue; for example, it is easy to grasp that **MAXFILES** represents the maximum number of files, but it is not nearly as easy to understand what **9** means.

Manifest constants have file scope, unless undefined with an **#undef** directive.

Cross-reference
The C Programming Language, ed. 2, p. 230

See Also
Definitions, macro, scope

Notes
The C Programming Language calls these constants *symbolic constants*.

math.h — Header
(Library/mathematics)
Header for mathematics functions
#include < math.h >

math.h is the header file that declares and defines mathematical functions and macros.

The Standard describes three macros to be included in **math.h**, as follows:

EDOM	Domain error
ERANGE	Range error
HUGE_VAL	Unrepresentable object

The first two macros are used to set the global variable **errno** to an appropriate value when, respectively, a domain error or a range error occurs. **HUGE_VAL** is returned when any mathematics function attempts to calculate a number that is too large to be encoded into a **double**.

The Standard also describes 22 mathematics functions that are to be included with every implementation of C. For a listing of them, see **mathematics**.

Cross-references
Standard, §4.5
The C Programming Language, ed. 2, p. 250

See Also
header, mathematics

mathematics — Overview
(Library)

The Standard describes 22 mathematics functions that are to be included with every conforming implementation of C, as follows:

Exponent-log functions

exp	Compute exponential
frexp	Fracture floating-point number
ldexp	Load floating-point number
log	Compute natural logarithm
log10	Compute common logarithm
modf	Separate floating-point number

Hyperbolic functions

cosh	Calculate hyperbolic cosine
sinh	Calculate hyperbolic sine
tanh	Calculate hyperbolic tangent

Integer, value, remainder

ceil	Set integral ceiling of a number
fabs	Compute absolute value
floor	Set integral floor of a number
fmod	Calculate modulus for floating-point number

Power functions

pow	Raise one number to the power of another
sqrt	Calculate the square root of a number

Trigonometric functions

acos	Calculate inverse cosine
asin	Calculate inverse sine
atan	Calculate inverse tangent
atan2	Calculate inverse tangent
cos	Calculate cosine
sin	Calculate sine
tan	Calculate tangent

The Standard reserves all names that match those in this section and have a suffix of **f** or **l**, e.g., **ftan** or **ltan**. A future version of the Standard may provide additional library support for functions that manipulate **float**s or **long double**s.

Some existing implemetations may, on detection of domain or range errors, or other exceptional conditions, allow the function in question to call a user-specified exception handler, **matherr**. UNIX implementations have traditionally behaved this way. The Standard, in trying to accommodate a wide range of floating-point implementations, does not allow this behavior.

Cross-references
Standard, §4.5
The C Programming Language, ed. 2, p. 250

See Also
domain error, range error, HUGE_VAL, Library, math.h

Notes
The Standard excludes the functions **ecvt**, **fcvt**, and **gcvt**, on the grounds that everything they do can be done more easily by the function **sprintf**.

MB_CUR_MAX — Macro
(Library/general utilities)
Largest size of a multibyte character in current locale
#include < stdlib.h >

MB_CUR_MAX is a macro that is defined in the header **stdlib.h**. It expands into an expression that indicates the maximum number of bytes contained in a multibyte character in the current locale.

The value that **MB_CUR_MAX** yields is affected by the current locale, as set by the function **setlocale**. For more information on locales, see **localization**. Note, however, that its value is never greater than that of the macro **MB_MAX_LEN**, which is also defined in the header **stdlib.h**.

Cross-references
Standard, §4.10.7
The C Programming Language, ed. 2, pp

See Also
MB_MAX_LEN, mblen, mbtowc, multibyte characters, wctomb

MB_LEN_MAX — Macro
(Environment/environmental considerations/limits)
Maximum size of MB_CUR_MAX

MB_LEN_MAX is a macro that is defined in the header **limits.h**. It gives the maximum number of bytes in any multibyte character, for any locale. It must be defined to be at least one. The macro **MB_CUR_MAX** will never be set to a value larger than that of **MB_LEN_MAX**.

Cross-reference
Standard, §2.2.4.2

See Also
limits, MB_CUR_MAX, multibyte characters

mblen() — Library function
(Library/general utilities/multibyte characters)
Return length of a string of multibyte characters
#include < stdlib.h >
int mblen(const char *address, size_t number);

The function **mblen** checks to see if the *number* or fewer bytes of storage pointed to by *address* form a legitimate multibyte character. If they do, it returns the number of bytes that comprise that character. This function is equivalent to the call

```
mbtowc((wchar_t *)0, address, number);
```

If *address* is equivalent to NULL, then **mblen** returns zero if the current multibyte character set does not have state-dependent encodings and nonzero if it does. If *ad-*

dress is not NULL, then **mblen** returns the following: (1) If *address* points to a null character, then **mblen** returns zero. (2) If the *number* or fewer bytes pointed to by *address* forms a legitimate multibyte character, then **mblen** returns the number of bytes that comprise the character. (3) Finally, if the *number* bytes pointed to by *address* do not form a legitimate multibyte character, **mblen** returns -1. In no instance is the value returned by **mblen** greater than *number* or the value of the macro **MB_CUR_MAX**, whichever is less.

Cross-reference
Standard, §4.10.7.1

See Also
MB_CUR_MAX, mbtowc, multibyte characters, wchar_t, wctomb

Notes
The operation of this function is affected by the program's locale, as set by the function **setlocale**. See **localization** for more information.

mbstowcs() — Library function
(Language/general utilities/multibyte characters)
Convert sequence of multibyte characters to wide characters
#include <stdlib.h>
size_t mbstowcs(wchar_t **widechar*, **const char** **multibyte*, **size_t** *number*);

The function **mbstowcs** converts a sequence of multibyte characters to their corresponding wide characters. It is the same as a series of calls of the type:

```
mbtowc(widechar, multibyte, MB_LEN_MAX);
```

except that the call to **mbstowcs** does not affect the internal state of **mbtowc**.

multibyte points to the base of the sequence of multibyte characters to be converted to wide characters. *widechars* points to the area where the converted characters are written, and *number* is the number of characters to convert. **mbstowcs** converts characters until either it reads a null character, or until it has converted *number* characters. In the latter case, then, no null character is written onto the end of the sequence of wide characters.

mbstowcs returns -1 cast to **size_t** if it encounters an invalid multibyte character before it has converted *number* multibyte characters. Otherwise, it returns the number of multibyte characters it converted to wide characters, excluding the null character that ends the sequence.

Cross-reference
Standard, §4.10.7.2

See Also
multibyte characters, wcstombs

Notes
The operation of this function is affected by the program's locale, as set by the
function **setlocale**. See **localization** for more information.

mbtowc() — Library function
(Library/general utilities/multibyte characters)
Convert a multibyte character to a wide character
#include <stdlib.h>
int mbtowc(wchar_t *charptr, const char *address, size_t number);

The function **mbtowc** converts *number* or fewer bytes at *address* from a multibyte
character to a wide character and stores the result in the area pointed to by
charptr.

The behavior of **mbtowc** varies depending upon the values of *address* and *charptr*,
as follows:

1. If *address* and *charptr* each point to a value other than NULL, then **mbtowc**
    reads the area pointed to by *address* and checks to see if *number* or fewer
    bytes comprise a legitimate multibyte character.

    If they do, then **mbtowc** stores the wide character that corresponds to that
    multibyte character in the area pointed to by *charptr* and returns the number
    of bytes that form the multibyte character.

    If *address* does not point to the beginning of a legitimate multibyte character,
    then **mbtowc** returns -1.

    Finally, if *address* points to a null character, **mbtowc** returns zero.

    In no instance does the value returned by **mbtowc** exceed *number* or value of
    the macro **MB_CUR_MAX**, whichever is less.

2. If *charptr* is set to NULL and *address* is set to a value other than NULL, then
    mbtowc behaves exactly like the function **mblen**: it examines the area
    pointed to by *address* but does not convert the multibyte character to a wide
    character.

3. If *address* is set to NULL, or both *address* and *charptr* are set to NULL, then
    mbtowc checks to see if the current multibyte character set have state-depen-
    dent encodings. **mbtowc** returns zero if the set does not have state-depen-
    dent encodings, and a number greater than zero if it does. It does not store

anything in the area pointed to by *charptr*.

Cross-reference
Standard, §4.10.7.3

See Also
MB_CUR_MAX, mblen, multibyte characters, wchar_t, wctomb

Notes
The operation of this function is affected by the program's locale, as set by the
function **setlocale**. See **localization** for more information.

member — Definition
(Language/lexical elements/identifiers/name space)

A *member* names an element within a structure or a **union**. It can be accessed via
the member-selection operators '.' or '->'. For example, consider the following:

```
struct example {
      int member1;
      long member2;
      example *member3;
};
struct example object;
struct example *pointer = &object;
```

To read the contents of **member1** within **object**, use the '.', as follows:

```
object.member1
```

On the other hand, to read the contents of **member1** via **pointer**, use the '->'
operator:

```
pointer->member1
```

The same is true for a **union**, but with the following restriction: if a value is stored
in one member of a **union**, then attempting to read another member of the **union**
generates implementation-defined behavior. This restriction has one exception. If
the **union** consists of several structures that have a common initial sequence, then
that common sequence can be read when a value is written into any of the structures.

Cross-references
Standard, §3.1.2.6, §3.3.2.3
The C Programming Language, ed. 2, p. 128

See Also
->, ., **name space, struct, union**

memchr() — Library function
(Library/string handling/string searching)
Search a region of memory for a character
#include <string.h>
void *memchr(const void **region***, int** *character***, size_t** *n***)**

memchr searches the first *n* characters in *region* for *character*. It returns a pointer to *character* if it is found, or NULL if it is not.

Unlike the string-search function **strchr**, **memchr** searches a portion of a region. Therefore, it does not stop when it encounters a null character.

Example
The following example deals a random hand of cards from a standard deck of 52. The command line takes one argument, which indicates the size of the hand you want dealt. It uses an algorithm published by Bob Floyd in the September 1987 *Communications of the ACM.*

```
#include <stddef.h>
#include <stdio.h>
#include <stdlib.h>
#include <string.h>
#include <time.h>
#define DECK 52

main(int argc, char *argv[])
{
     char deck[DECK], *fp;
     int  deckp, n, j, t;

     if(argc != 2 ||
        52 < (n = atoi(argv[1])) ||
        1 > n) {
            printf("usage: memchr n # where 0 < n < 53\n");
          exit(EXIT_FAILURE);
     }

     /* exercise rand() to make it more random */
     srand((unsigned int)time(NULL));
     for(j = 0; j < 100; j++)
          rand();
```

```
        deckp = 0;
        /* Bob Floyd's algorithm */
        for(j = DECK - n; j < DECK; j++) {
                t = rand() % (j + 1);
                if((fp = memchr(deck, t, deckp)) != NULL)
                        *fp = (char)j;
                deck[deckp++] = (char)t;
        }

        for(t = j = 0; j < deckp; j++) {
                div_t card;

                card = div(deck[j], 13);
                t += printf("%c%c   ",
                        /* note useful string addressing */
                        "A23456789TJQK"[card.rem],
                        "HCDS"[card.quot]);

                if(t > 50) {
                        t = 0;
                        putchar('\n');
                }
        }

        putchar('\n');
        return(EXIT_SUCCESS);
}
```

Cross-references
Standard, §4.11.5.1
The C Programming Language, ed. 2, p. 250

See Also
strchr, strcspn, string searching, strpbrk, strrchr, strspn, strstr, strtok

memcmp() — Library function
(Library/string handling/string comparison)
Compare two regions
#include < string.h >
int memcmp(const void *region1, const void *region2, size_t count)

memcmp compares *region1* with *region2* character by character for *count* characters.

If every character in *region1* is identical to its corresponding character in *region2*, then **memcmp** returns zero. If it finds that a character in *region1* has a numeric value greater than that of the corresponding character in *region2*, then it returns a number greater than zero. If it finds that a character in *region1* has a numeric value less than less that of the corresponding character in *region2*, then it returns a number less than zero.

For example, consider the following code:

```
char region1[13], region2[13];
strcpy(region1, "Hello, world");
strcpy(region2, "Hello, World");
memcmp(region1, region2, 12);
```

memcmp scans through the two regions of memory, comparing **region1[0]** with **region2[0]**, and so on, until it finds two corresponding "slots" in the arrays whose contents differ. In the above example, this will occur when it compares **region1[7]** (which contains 'w') with **region2[7]** (which contains 'W'). It then compares the two letters to see which stands first in the character table used in this implementation, and returns the appropriate value.

Cross-references

Standard, §4.11.4.1
The C Programming Language, ed. 2, p. 250

See Also

strcmp, strcoll, string comparison, strncmp, strxfrm

Notes

memcmp differs from the string comparison routine **strcmp** in the following ways:

First, **memcmp** compares regions of memory rather than strings; therefore, it does not stop when it encounters a null character.

Second, **memcmp** takes two pointers to **void**, whereas **strcmp** takes two pointers to **char**. The following code illustrates how this difference affects these functions:

```
char carray[10];
int iarray[10];
char *s = "hi";
      . . .
strcmp(carray, s)       /* RIGHT */
memcmp(carray, s, 3)    /* RIGHT */
strcmp(iarray, s)       /* WRONG, 1st arg not char * */
memcmp(iarray, s, 3)    /* RIGHT, args converted to void * */
```

It is wrong to use **strcmp** to compare an **int** array with a **char** array because this function compares strings. Using **memcmp** to compare an **int** array with a **char** array is permissible because **memcmp** simply compares areas of data.

memcpy() — Library function
(Library/string handling/string copying)
Copy one region of memory into another
#include < string.h >
void *memcpy(void **region1***, const void ****region2***, size_t** *n***)**

memcpy copies *n* characters from *region2* into *region1*. Unlike the routines **strcpy** and **strncpy**, **memcpy** copies from one region to another. Therefore, it will not halt automatically when it encounters a null character.

memcpy returns *region1*.

Example

The following example copies a structure and displays it.

```
#include <string.h>
#include <stdio.h>

struct stuff {
    int a, b, c;
} x, y;

main(void)
{
    x.a = 1;
    /* this would stop strcpy or strncpy. */
    x.b = 0;
    x.c = 3;

    /* y = x; would do the same */
    memcpy(&y, &x, sizeof(y));
    printf("a =%d, b =%d, c =%d\n", y.a, y.b, y.c);
    return(EXIT_SUCCESS);
}
```

Cross-references

Standard, §4.11.2.1
The C Programming Language, ed. 2, p. 250

See Also

memmove, strcpy, string copying, strncpy

Notes

If *region1* and *region2* overlap, the behavior of **memcpy** is undefined. *region1* should point to enough reserved memory to hold *n* bytes of data; otherwise, code or data will be overwritten.

memmove() — Library function
(Library/string handling/string copying)
Copy one region of memory into another with which it may overlap
#include < string.h>
void *memmove(void ***region1, const void ***region2**, size_t** *count***);**

memmove copies *count* characters from *region2* into *region1*. Unlike **memcpy**,
memmove correctly copies the region pointed to by *region2* into that pointed by
region1 even if they overlap. To "correctly copy" means that the overlap does not
propagate, not that the moved data stay intact. Unlike the string-copying routines
strcpy and **strncpy**, **memmove** continues to copy even if it encounters a null
character.

memmove returns *region1*.

Example
The following example rotates a block of memory by one byte.

```
#include <string.h>
#include <stddef.h>
#include <stdio.h>

char *
rotate_left(char *region, size_t len)
{
    char sav;

    sav = *region;
    /* with memcpy this might propagate the last char */
    memmove(region, region + 1, --len);
    region[len] = sav;
    return(region);
}

char nums[] = "0123456789";
main(void)
{
    printf(rotate_left(nums, strlen(nums)));
    return(EXIT_SUCCESS);
}
```

Cross-references
Standard, §4.11.2.2 *The C Programming Language*, ed. 2, p. 250

See Also
memcpy, strcpy, string copying, strncpy

Notes
region1 should point to enough reserved memory to hold the contents of *region2*; otherwise, code or data will be overwritten.

memory management — Overview
(Library/general utilities)
#include <stdlib.h>

Memory management refers to the dynamic allocation and deallocation of memory within a program.

Dynamic memory allocation can be contrasted with static allocation. Static allocation of memory occurs when the program is translated and the translator reserves space for objects declared within the program. When the program is run, these objects may live in memory, on the stack, or in registers.

Dynamic allocation occurs as the program is run. Objects that are allocated dynamically may be located in a separate area of memory, which may be called the *heap* or the *arena*. One common application that uses dynamic memory is a linked-list structure.

The Standard describes four routines that allocate and deallocate memory, as follows:

calloc	Allocate and clear dynamic memory
free	De-allocate dynamic memory
malloc	Allocate dynamic memory
realloc	Reallocate dynamic memory

calloc, **malloc**, and **realloc** each returns a pointer to the block of memory allocated; the pointer is aligned for any type of object. They return NULL if the requested amount of memory cannot be allocated. **calloc** also fills with zeroes the space it allocates. **realloc** is used to change the size of a block already allocated.

free deallocates memory to make it available for reuse. Using **free** to deallocate a block of memory that had not been allocated with one of the above functions produces undefined behavior.

Cross-references
Standard, §4.10.3
The C Programming Language, ed. 2, p. 167

See Also
alignment, general utilities

Notes
If you attempt to allocate a block of memory that is zero bytes long, the behavior of **calloc, malloc,** and **realloc** is implementation-defined: they return either NULL or a unique pointer. This is a quiet change that may silently break some existing code.

memset() — Library function
(Library/string handling/string miscellaneous)
Fill an area with a character
#include <string.h>
void *memset(void * *buffer***, int** *character***, size_t** *n***);**

memset fills the first *n* bytes of the area pointed to by *buffer* with copies of *character*. It casts *character* to an **unsigned char** before filling *buffer* with copies of it.

memset returns the pointer *buffer*.

Example
The following example fills an area with 'X', and prints the result.

```
#include <stdio.h>
#include <string.h>
#define BUFSIZ 20

main(void)
{
     char buffer[BUFSIZ];

     /* fill buffer with 'X' */
     memset(buffer, 'X', BUFSIZ);

     /* append null to end of buffer */
     buffer[BUFSIZ-1] = '\0';

     /* print the result */
     printf("%s\n", buffer);
     return(EXIT_SUCCESS);
}
```

Cross-references
Standard, §4.11.6.1
The C Programming Language, ed. 2, p. 250

See Also

memchr, memcmp, memcpy, memmove, string miscellaneous

minimum maxima — Definition
(Rationale)

The Standard, unlike *The C Programming Language,* sets numerical limits for some aspects of C. The range of each numeric type, the number of **#include** files that can be opened, the depth of function nesting — each is given a minimum value that every implementation must meet. The term *minimum maxima* (singular, "minimum maximum") refers to the fact that most of the Standard's limits are minimal; that is, an implementation may exceed these limits.

For example, a byte is defined as having at least eight bits. Here, "eight" is the Standard's *minimum maximum* for byte: a byte may have any number of bits, as long as it does not have fewer than eight.

Cross-reference

Rationale, §1.1

See Also

limits.h, Rationale

mktime() — Library function
(Library/date and time/time manipulation)

Turn broken-down time into calendar time
#include <time.h>
time_t mktime(struct tm *timeptr);

mktime reads broken-down time from the structure pointed to by *timeptr* and converts it into calendar time of the type **time_t**. It does the opposite of the functions **localtime** and **gmtime**, which turn calendar time into broken-down time.

mktime manipulates the structure **tm** as follows:

1.   It reads the contents of the structure, but ignores the fields **tm_wday** and **tm_yday**.

2.   The original values of the other fields within the **tm** structure need not be restricted to the values described in the article for **tm**. This allows you, for example, to increment the field **tm_hour** to discover the calendar time one hour hence, even if that forces the value of **tm_hour** to be greater than 23, its normal limit.

3. When calculation is completed, the values of the fields within the **tm** structure are reset to within their normal limits to conform to the newly calculated calendar time. The value of **tm_mday** is not set until after the values of **tm_mon** and **tm_year**.

4. The calendar time is returned.

If the calendar time cannot be calculated, **mktime** returns -1 cast to **time_t**.

Example
This example gets the date from the user and writes it into a **tm** structure.

```
#include <math.h>
#include <stddef.h>
#include <stdio.h>
#include <stdlib.h>
#include <time.h>
#define BAD_TIME ((time_t)-1)

/* ask for a number and return it. */
int
askint(char * msg)
{
    char buf[20];

    printf("Enter %s ", msg);
    fflush(stdout);

    if(gets(buf) == NULL)
        exit(EXIT_SUCCESS);
    return(atoi(buf));
}

main(void)
{
    struct tm t;

    for(;;) {
        t.tm_mon  = askint("month");
        t.tm_mday = askint("day");
        t.tm_year = askint("year");
        t.tm_hour = t.tm_min = t.tm_sec = 1;

        if(BAD_TIME == mktime(&t)) {
            printf("Invalid date\n");
            continue;
        }
```

```
        printf("Day of week is %d\n", t.tm_wday);
        break;
    }
    return(EXIT_SUCCESS);
}
```

Cross-references
Standard, §4.12.2.3
The C Programming Language, ed. 2, p. 256

See Also
clock, difftime, time, time manipulation

Notes
The above description may appear to be needlessly complex. However, the Committee intended that **mktime** be used to implement a portable mechanism for determining time and for controlling time-dependent loops. This function is needed because not every environment describes time internally as a multiple of a known time unit.

modf — Library function
(Library/mathematics/exponent-log functions)
Separate floating-point number
#include < math.h >
double modf(double *real*, **double** **ip*);

modf breaks the floating-point number *real* into its integer and fraction.

modf stores the integer in the location pointed to by *ip*, and returns the fraction *real*. Both the integer and the fraction have the same sign. f in the range $0 <= f < 1$.

Cross-references
Standard, §4.5.4.6
The C Programming Language, ed. 2, p. 251

See Also
exp, exponent-log functions, frexp, ldexp, log, log10, modf

multibyte characters — Overview
(Library/general utilities)

C was invented at Bell Laboratories as a portable language for implementing the UNIX operating system. Since then, C has grown into a language used throughout the world, for both operating systems and applications.

The character sets of many nations are too large to be encoded within one eight-bit byte. The Japanese Kanji characters form one such set; the ideograms of Mandarin Chinese form another. For the sake of brevity, the following discussion will call such sets *large-character sets*. A character from a large character set will be called a *large character*.

Wide Characters

The Standard describes two ways to encode a large character: by using a *multibyte character* or a *wide character*.

wchar_t is a typedef that is declared in the header **stdlib.h**. It is defined as the integral type that can represent all characters of given national character set.

The following restrictions apply to objects of this type: (1) The null character still has the value of zero. (2) The characters of the standard C character set must have the same value as they would when used in ordinary **char**s. (3) **EOF** must have a value that is distinct from every other character in the set.

wchar_t is a typedef of an integral type, whereas a multibyte character is a bundle of one or more one-byte characters. The format of a multibyte character is defined by the implementation, whereas a **wchar_t** can be used across implementations.

Wide characters are used to store large character sets in a device-independent manner. Multibyte characters are used most often to pass large characters to a terminal device. Most terminal devices can receive only one byte at a time. Thus, passing the pieces of a wide character to a terminal would undoubtedly create problems; the individual characters of a multibyte character, however, can be passed safely. This is also important because the Standard does not describe any function that reads more than one byte from a stream at any time — there is no Standard version of **fgetw** or **fputw**.

Multibyte Characters

The Standard describes multibyte characters as follows:

- A multibyte character may not contain a null character or 0xFF (-1, or **EOF**) as one of its bytes.

- All of the characters in the C character set must be present in any set of multibyte characters.

- An implementation of multibyte characters may use a *shift state* or a special sequence of characters that marks when a sequence of multibyte characters begins and when it ends. Depending upon the shift state, the bytes of a multibyte character may either be read as individual characters or as forming one multibyte character. Note, too, that a shift state may allow *state-dependent coding*, by which one of a number of possible sets of multibyte characters is indicated by the shift state.

- A comment, string literal, or character constant must begin and end in the same shift state. For example, a comment cannot consist of multibyte characters mixed with single-byte characters; it must be all one or all the other. If a comment, string literal, or character constant is built of multibyte characters, each such character must be valid.

Multibyte Character Functions

The support added to the C language for multibyte characters thus far is limited to character constants, string literals, and comments. The Standard describes five functions that handle multibyte characters:

mblen	Compute length of a multibyte character
mbstowcs	Convert sequence of multibyte characters to wide characters
mbtowc	Convert multibyte character to wide character
wcstombs	Convert sequence of wide characters to multibyte characters
wctomb	Convert a wide character to a multibyte character

As mentioned above, a wide character is encoded using type **wchar_t**. The macro **MB_CUR_MAX** holds the largest number of characters of any multibyte character for the current locale. It is never greater than the value of the macro **MB_LEN_MAX**. **wcstombs** and **mbstowcs** convert sequences of characters from one type to the other.

All of the above are defined in the header **stdlib.h**.

Localization

The sets of multibyte characters and wide characters recognized by the above functions are determined by the program's locale, as set by the function **setlocale**.

To load the appropriate sets of multibyte characters and wide characters, use the call

```
setlocale(LC_CTYPE, locale);
```

or

```
setlocale(LC_ALL, locale);
```

See the entry for **localization** for more information.

Cross-reference

Standard, §2.2.1.2, §4.10.7

See Also

general utilities

Notes

Because compiler vendors are active in Asia, and because there is an active Japanese standards organization, a future version of the Standard may include more extensive support for multibyte characters, such as additional library functions. The support added to the C language for multibyte characters thus far is limited to character constants, string literals, and comments.

At present, all function names that begin with **wcs** are reserved. They should not be used if you wish your code to be maximally portable.

multiplicative operators — Overview
(Language/expressions)

C includes the following multiplicative operators:

*	Multiply two operands
/	Divide two operands and return the quotient
%	Divide two operands and return the remainder

Their syntax is as follows:

multiplicative expressions:
>   *cast-expression*
>   *multiplicative-expression* * *cast-expression*
>   *multiplicative-expression* / *cast-expression*
>   *multiplicative-expression* % *cast-expression*

The operands for the * and / operations must have arithmetic type; those for the % operation must have integral type. Each operand undergoes normal arithmetic conversion. The result of each operation has the type to which the operands are promoted.

In the operations / or %, the behavior is undefined if the right operand is zero. In the / operation, if either operand is negative the implementation defines the method of rounding, i.e., whether the result is the largest integer that is less than the algebraic quotient, or the smallest integer that is greater than the algebraic quotient. In the % operation, the implementation defines the sign of the result if either operand is negative.

Finally, if the result of **X/Y** can be represented, **(X/Y)*Y+(X%Y)** must equal **X**.

Cross-references

Standard, §3.3.5
The C Programming Language, ed. 2, p. 205

See Also
expressions

Notes
The order of evaluation of these operators is undefined. For example,

```
function1() * function2();
```

may call either **function1** or **function2** first.

```
(0 * function1());
```

may legally never call **function1** as the result may be determined without it. You should avoid expressions in which the order of evaluation is important.

N

name space — Definition
(Language/lexical elements/identifiers)

The term *name space* refers to the "list" where the translator records an identifier. Each name space holds a different set of identifiers. If two identifiers are spelled exactly the same and appear within the same scope but are not in the same name space, they are *not* considered to be identical.

The four varieties of name space, as follows:

Label names
> The translator treats every identifier followed by a colon ':' or that follows a **goto** statement as a label.

Tags   A tag is the name that follows the keywords **struct, union,** or **enum**. It names the type of object so declared.

Members
> A member names a field within a structure or a **union**. A member can be accessed via the operators '.' or '->'. Each structure or **union** type has a separate name space for its members.

Ordinary identifiers
> These name ordinary functions and variables. For example, the expression

```
int example;
```

> declares the ordinary identifier **example** to name an object of type **int**.

The Standard reserves external identifiers with leading underscores to the implementor. To reduce "name-space pollution," the implementor should not reserve anything that is not explicitly defined in the Standard (macros, **typedef**s, etc.) and that does not begin with a leading underscore.

Example

The following program illustrates the concept of name space. It shows how the identifier **foo** can be used numerous times within the same scope yet still be distinguished by the translator. This is extremely poor programming style. Please do not write programs like this.

```
#include <stdio.h>
#include <stdlib.h>
```

```
/* structure tag */
struct foo {
    /* structure member */
    struct foo *foo;
    int bar;
};
main()
{
    /* ordinary identifier */
    struct foo *foo;
    int i = 0;

    foo = (struct foo *)malloc(sizeof(foo));
    foo->bar = ++i;
    foo->foo = NULL;
/* label */
foo: printf("Chain, chain, chain -- chain of \"foo\"s.\n");
    if (foo->foo == NULL) {
        foo->foo = (struct foo *)malloc(sizeof(foo));
        foo->foo->foo = NULL;
        foo->foo->bar = ++i;
        goto foo;
    }

    printf("The foo loop executed %d times\n", foo->foo->bar);
    return(EXIT_SUCCESS);
}
```

Cross-references

Standard, §3.1.2.3

See Also

identifiers, linkage, scope

Notes

Pre-ANSI implementations disagree on the name spaces of structure/**union** members. The Standard adopted the "Berkeley" rules, which state that every unique structure/**union** type has its own name space for its members. It rejected the rules of the first edition of *The C Programming Language*, which state that the members of all structures/**unions** reside in a common name space.

NDEBUG — Macro
(Library/diagnostics)
Turn off assert()

NDEBUG is a macro that is referenced in the header **assert.h**.

NDEBUG can be defined from the command line, or from another header that is included prior to including **assert.h**. Defining it will turn off assertion checking in your program.

When it is defined before the header **assert.h** is included, the macro **assert** is redefined as

```
#define assert(ignore)
```

This, in effect, turns off the **assert** macro.

If an expression tested by **assert** has side effects, then using the **NDEBUG** macro as described here will change the behavior of the program.

Cross-references
Standard, §4.2
The C Programming Language, ed. 2, p. 254

See Also
assert, assert.h, diagnostics

noalias — C keyword
(Language/declarations/type qualifier)
Qualify an identifier as having no aliases

The type qualifier **noalias** marks a variable as having no aliases. This means that there is no way to modify the given object other than through explicitly assigned pointers to the object itself. See **alias** for more information on aliasing under C.

If a variable is marked **noalias**, the translator may properly copy it into a register or any other portion of fast memory and read only the copy without checking whether the original object has changed.

Cross-reference
Standard, §3.5.3

See Also
alias, const, type qualifier, volatile

Notes

As of this writing (January 1988), **noalias** remains the subject of much controversy. It may not be adopted into the Standard when it is formally published.

non-local jumps — Overview
(Library)

At times, exceptional conditions arise in a program that make it desirable to jump to a previous point within the program. **goto** can jump from one point to another within the same function, but it does not permit a jump from one function to another. The **setjmp/longjmp** mechanism was created to allow a program to jump immediately from one function to another, i.e., to perform a non-local jump.

The macro **setjmp** reads the machine environment and stores the environment in the array **jmp_buf**, which must be an array. The "machine environment" consists of the elements that determine the behavior of the machine, e.g., the contents of machine registers. What constitutes the machine environment will vary greatly from machine to machine. It may be impossible on some machines to save such elements of the machine environment as register variables and the contents of the stack or to restore the machine environment from within an extraordinarily complex computation.

For example, consider the following:

```
{
      int status[3][3][3], fn();
      jmp_buf buf;
      status[fn(1)][fn(2)][fn(3)] = setjmp(buf);
}
```

Here, the translator is trying to store the return value of **setjmp** into an array element with extremely complex index computations. It cannot be guaranteed that on every machine, the proper array element will be overwritten on reentry. For this reason, the Standard states that **setjmp** can be expected to save the machine environment only if used in a simple expression, such as in an **if** or **switch** statement.

The function **longjmp** jumps back to the point marked by the earlier invocation of **setjmp**. It restores the machine environment that **setjmp** had saved. This allows **longjmp** to perform a non-local jump.

A non-local jump can be dangerous. For example, many user-level routines cannot be interrupted and reentered safely. Thus, improper use of **longjmp** and **setjmp** with them will create mysterious and irreproducible bugs.

The Standard mandates that **longjmp** work correctly "in the contexts of interrupts, signals and any of their associated functions." Experience has shown, however, that **longjmp** should not be used within an exception handler that interrupts STDIO routines.

longjmp must not restore the machine environment of a routine that has already returned.

Cross-references
Standard, §4.6
The C Programming Language, ed. 2, p. 254

See Also
jmp_buf, jump statements, Library, setjmp.h

Notes
longjmp's behavior is undefined if it is invoked from within a function that is called by a signal that is received during the handling of another signal. See **signal handling** for more information on signals.

nondigit – Definition
(Language/lexical elements/identifiers)

In the context of identifiers, a *nondigit* is any one of the following characters:

_	a	b	c	d	e	f	g	h
i	j	k	l	m	n	o	p	q
r	s	t	u	v	w	x	y	z
A	B	C	D	E	F	G	H	I
J	K	L	M	N	O	P	Q	R
S	T	U	V	W	X	Y	Z	

Cross-reference
Standard, §3.1.2

See Also
digit, identifiers

NULL – Macro
(Library)
Null pointer
#include <stddef.h>

NULL is a macro that is defined in the header **stddef.h**. It defines the null pointer constant.

The Rationale notes that NULL can be defined as being equivalent to zero, 0L, or **(void *)0**. The last is necessary under environments where a pointer is not the same size as any existing integer type.

The Rationale also cautions against using NULL as an explicit argument to any function that expects a pointer on the grounds that, under some environments, pointers to different data types may be of different lengths. All such problems will be avoided if a function prototype is within the scope of the function call. Then, NULL will be transformed automatically to the proper type of pointer. See *function prototype* for more information.

Cross-references
Standard, §4.1.5
The C Programming Language, ed. 2, p. 102

See Also
Library, null pointer constant, pointer, stddef.h

Notes
Because much existing code assumes that NULL is of type **char ***, the Standard requires objects of type **void *** to have the same representation as objects of type **char ***.

null character — Definition
(Definitions)

The *null character* is a character with a value of zero. C uses it to mark the end of a string.

See Also
Definitions, string

null directive — Definition
(Language/preprocessing)
Directive that does nothing

A *null directive* is a preprocessing directive that consists only of a '#' followed by **<newline>**. It does nothing.

Cross-reference
Standard, §3.8.7

See Also
preprocessing

null pointer constant — Definition
(Language/conversions)

A *null pointer constant* is an integral constant expression with the value of zero, or such a constant that has been cast to type **void ***. When the null pointer constant is compared with a pointer for equality, it is converted to the same type as the pointer before they are compared.

The null pointer constant always compares unequal to a pointer to an object or function. Two null pointers will always compare equal, regardless of any casts.

Cross-references
Standard, §3.2.2.3
The C Programming Language, ed. 2, p. 102

See Also
conversions, NULL

null statement — Definition
(Language/statements)

A *null statement* is one that consists only of a semicolon ';'. Its syntax is as follows:

> *null statement:*
> ;

A null statement performs no operations.

Cross-references
Standard, §3.6.3
The C Programming Language, ed. 2, p. 222

See Also
expression statement, statements

numerical limits — Overview
(Environment/environmental considerations/limits)

The Standard describes numerical limits for every arithmetic type. For integral types, it sets the largest and smallest values that can be held in the given environment. For floating types, it also gives values for the manner in which a floating-point number is encoded.

These limits are recorded in two groups of macros: one for integral types, and the other for floating types. The groups of macros are kept, respectively, in the headers **limits.h** and **float.h**. The Lexicon entries for these headers lists the Standard's numerical limits.

Cross-references
Standard, §2.2.4.2
The C Programming Language, ed. 2, p. 257

See Also
environmental considerations

Notes
The ANSI Committee has tried to keep its numerical limits compatible with those given in IEEE document 754, which describes a floating-point standard for binary number systems.

O

object — Definition
(Definitions)

An *object* is an area of memory that can contain one or more values. With the exception of a bit-field, an object consists of a byte or a contiguous group of bytes. The significance of each byte's value is defined by the program or the implementation. Objects that are variables are interpreted according to their type.

Cross-references
Standard, §1.6
The C Programming Language, ed. 2, p. 197

See Also
Definitions

object definition — Definition
(Language/external definitions)

A *definition* is a declaration that reserves storage for the thing declared. An *object definition* defines an object and makes it available throughout either the translation unit (if it has internal linkage) or throughout the program (if it has external linkage).

The term "tentative definition" refers to a definition to which more information is added by a later re-definition of the same object. The extra information may be a storage-class specifier, or it may initialize the object. The term, although somewhat misleading, is meant to show that every object has only one definition, but that definition can be refined during the course of translation.

Only one definition can contain an initializer. If an object is not initialized by the end of a file, it is initialized to zero.

A tentative definition of a static, incomplete object is disallowed semantically:

```
static int array[];
    . . .
int array[] = {3, 4, 5, 6};   /* Non-portable */
```

Because the Standard does not forbid an implementation to support such code, it may not generate an error message; however, this code is not portable.

The following *is* allowed semantically:

```
int array[];
     . . .
static int array[] = {3, 4, 5, 6};    /* RIGHT */
```

However, it may create a linker conflict in some implementations, such as in one-pass compilers.

To be assured that your code is maximally portable, declare the storage class and size of each object before you use it.

Cross-references
Standard, §3.7.2
The C Programming Language, ed. 2, p. 197

See Also
definition, external definitions, function definition, linkage, object

object types — Definition
(Language/lexical elements/identifiers/types)

The *object types* are the set of types that describe objects. This set includes the **integral types**, the **floating types**, the **pointer types**, and the **aggregate types**.

Cross-reference
Standard, §3.1.2.5

See Also
function type, incomplete type, pointer, types

obsolescent — Definition
(Definitions)

The term *obsolescent* refers to any feature of the C language that is widely used, but that may be withdrawn from future editions of the Standard. For example, consider the practice of first defining a function and then following the definition with a list of parameter declarations:

```
int example(parm1, parm2, parm3)
long parm1;
char *parm2;
int parm3;
{
     . . .
}
```

The Standard regards this as obsolete, and may eventually withdraw recognition of it in favor of the following syntax:

```
int example(long parm1, char *parm2, int parm3)
{
        .  .  .
}
```

The Standard regards three features of the language as being obsolete. The first is the use of separate lists of parameters identifiers and declaration lists, as described above. The second is the use of function declarators with empty parentheses; if a function takes no arguments, the word **void** should appear between the parentheses. The third is the placing of storage-class specifier at any point other than at the beginning of the declaration specifiers.

Cross-reference
Standard, §1.8, §3.9

See Also
Definitions, function declarators, storage-class specifiers

offsetof() — Macro
(Library)
Offset of a field within a structure
#include < stddef.h >
size_t offsetof(*structname*, *fieldname*);

offsetof is a macro that is defined in the header **stddef.h**. It returns the number of bytes that the field *fieldname* is offset from the beginning of the the structure *structname*.

offsetof may return an offset for *fieldname* that is larger than the sum of the sizes of all the members that precede it. This will be due to the fact that some implementations insert padding into a structure to ensure that they are properly aligned.

Cross-reference
Standard, §4.1.5

See Also
Library, stddef.h

open — Definition
(Library/STDIO)
Open a file or device

To *open* a file means to establish a stream for the file or device. The stream governs the way data are accessed for that file or device. The information the stream needs to access the file is encoded within a **FILE** object. Because environments vary greatly in the information needed to access a file, the Standard does not describe the internals of the **FILE** object.

To open a file, use the functions **fopen** or **freopen**. The former function simply opens a file and assigns a stream to it. The latter reopens a file; that is, it takes the stream being used to access one file, assigns it to another, and attempts to close the original file. **freopen** can also be used to change the manner in which a file is accessed.

Cross-references
Standard, §4.9.3
The C Programming Language, ed. 2, p. 241

See Also
buffer, close, file, FILE, STDIO, stream

operators — Overview
(Language/lexical elements)

An *operator* specifies an operation performed upon one or two operands. The operation yields a value, performs designation, produces a side effect, or performs any combination of these.

The C language uses the following operators:

!	Not
!=	Compare two arithmetic operands for inequality
#	Substitute preprocessor token ("stringize")
##	Token-paste preprocessor tokens
%	Modulus operation on two arithmetic operands
%=	Modulus operation and assign result
&	Bitwise AND operation
&&	Logical AND for two expressions
&=	Bitwise AND operation and assign result
()	Cast operators
*	Multiply two arithmetic operands
*=	Multiply two arithmetic operands and assign result
+	Add two arithmetic operands

++	Increment a scalar operand
+=	Add two operands and assign result
,	Evaluate an *rvalue*
-	Subtract two scalar operands, unary minus
--	Decrement a scalar operand
-=	Subtract two operands and assign result
->	Offset from structure/**union** pointer
.	Select member from structure/**union**
/	Divide two arithmetic operands
/=	Divide two arithmetic operands and assign result
<	Less than
<<	Bitwise left shift
<<=	Bitwise left shift and assign result
<=	Less than or equality
=	Assignment operator
==	Equality
>	Greater than
>=	Greater than or equal
>>	Bitwise right shift
>>=	Bitwise right shift and assign result
?:	Perform if/else operation
[]	Array subscript
^	Perform bitwise exclusive OR operation
^=	Perform bitwise exclusive OR and assign result
defined	Check if a macro is defined
sizeof	Size of operand in bytes
|	Perform bitwise OR operation
|=	Perform bitwise OR and assign result
||	Logical OR for two expressions
~	One's complement

The term *precedence* refers to the default order in which the operators in an expression are evaluated. The following list gives the default precedence of operators. Precedence is always overridden by the operators (), which, by default, enclose a primary expression:

Operator								Associativity
() [] -> .								Left to right
! ~ ++ -- - (operand) * & sizeof								Right to left
* / %								Left to right
+ -								Left to right
<< >>								Left to right
< <= > >=								Left to right

== !=	Left to right
&	Left to right
^	Left to right
|	Left to right
&&	Left to right
||	Left to right
? :	Right to left
= += -= *= /= %=	Right to left
,	Left to right

Cross-references
Standard, §3.1.5
The C Programming Language, ed. 2, pp. 41*ff*

See Also
additive operators, assignment operators, bitwise operators, cast operators, equality operators, lexical elements, logical operators, multiplicative operators, postfix operators, punctuators, unary operators

ordinary identifier — Definition
(Language/lexical elements/identifiers/name space)

An *ordinary identifier* names all identifiers *except* labels, tags, and members. For example, the expression

```
int example;
```

declares the ordinary identifier **example** to name an object of type **int**.

Cross-references
Standard, §3.1.2.6
The C Programming Language, ed. 2, p. 192

See Also
name space

P

parameter — Definition
(Definitions)

The term *parameter* refers to an object that is declared with a function or a function-like macro.

With a function, a parameter is declared within a function declaration or definition. It acquires a value when the function is entered. For example, in the following declaration

```
FILE *fopen (const char *file, const char *mode);
```

file and **mode** are both objects that are declared within the function declaration. Both parameters will acquire their values when **fopen** is called.

With a function-like macro, a parameter is one of the identifiers that is bracketed by parantheses and separated by commas. For example, in the following example:

```
#define getchar(parameter) getc(stdin, parameter)
```

parameter is the identifier used with the macro **getchar**.

The scope of a function parameter is the block within which it is enclosed. The scope of a parameter to a function-like macro is the logical source line of the macro's definition.

Cross-references
Standard, §1.6
The C Programming Language, ed. 2, p. 202

See Also
argument, Definitions, function definition, scope

Notes
The Standard uses the term "argument" when it refers to the actual arguments of a function call or macro invocation; it uses the term "parameter" to refer to the formal parameters given in the definition of the function or macro.

perror() — Library function
(Library/STDIO/error handling)
Write error message into standard error stream
#include <stdio.h>
void perror(const char *string);

perror checks the integer expression **errno**, then writes the standard error message associated with the value of **errno** into the standard error stream.

string points to a string that will prefix the error message, followed by a colon. For example, the call

```
perror("example");
```

ensures that the string

```
example:
```

will appear before any message that **perror** writes. If *string* is set to NULL, then the message will have no prefix.

Example

For an example of this function, see **feof**.

Cross-references

Standard, §4.9.10.4
The C Programming Language, ed. 2, p. 248

See Also

clearerr, error handling, feof, ferror, strerror

Notes

perror differs from the related function **strerror** in that it writes the error message directly into the standard error stream, instead of returning a pointer to the message.

The text of the message returned by **strerror** and the error-specific part of the message produced by **perror** should be the same for any given error number.

pointer — Definition
(Language/lexical elements/identifiers/types)

A *pointer* is an object whose value is the address of another object. The name "pointer" derives from the fact that its contents "point to" another object. A pointer may point to any type, complete or incomplete, including another pointer. It may also point to a function, or to nowhere.

The term *pointer type* refers to the object of a pointer. The object to which a pointer points is called the *referenced type*. For example, an **int *** ("pointer to **int**") is a pointer type; the referenced type is **int**. Constructing a pointer type from a referenced type is called *pointer type derivation*.

The Null Pointer

A pointer that points to nowhere is a *null pointer*. The macro **NULL**, which is defined in the header **stddef.h**, defines the null pointer for a given implementation. The null pointer is an integer constant with the value zero, or such a constant cast to the type **void ***. It compares unequal to a pointer to any object or function.

Declaring a Pointer

To declare a pointer, use the indirection operator '*****'. For example, the declaration

```
int *pointer;
```

declares that the variable **pointer** holds the address of an **int**-length object.

Likewise, the declaration

```
int **pointer;
```

declares that **pointer** holds the address of a pointer whose contents, in turn, point to an **int**-length object. See **declarations** for more information.

Wild Pointers

Pointers are omnipresent in C. C also allows you to use a pointer to read or write the object to which the pointer points; this is called *pointer dereferencing*. Because a pointer can point to any place within memory, it is possible to write C code that generates unpredictable results, corrupts itself, or even obliterates the operating system if running in unprotected mode. A pointer that aims where it ought not is called a *wild pointer*.

When a program declares a pointer, space is set aside in memory for it. However, this space has not yet been filled with the address of an object. To fill a pointer with the address of the object you wish to access is called *initializing* it. A wild pointer, as often as not, is one that is not properly initialized.

Normally, to initialize a pointer means to fill it with a meaningful address. For example, the following initializes a pointer:

```
int number;
int *pointer;
   . . .
pointer = &number;
```

The address operator '**&**' specifies that you want the address of an object rather than its contents. Thus, **pointer** is filled with the address of **number**, and it can now be used to access the contents of **number**.

The initialization of a string is somewhat different than the initialization of a pointer to an integer object. For example,

```
char *string = "This is a string."
```

declares that **string** is a pointer to a **char**. It then stores the string literal **This is a string** in memory and fills **string** with the address of its first character. **string** can then be passed to functions to access the string, or you can step through the string by incrementing **string** until its contents point to the null character at the end of the string.

Another way to initialize a pointer is to fill it with a value returned by a function that returns a pointer. For example, the code

```
extern void *malloc(size_t variable);
char *example;
    . . .
example = (char *)malloc(50);
```

uses the function **malloc** to allocate 50 bytes of dynamic memory and then initializes **example** to the address that **malloc** returns.

Reading What a Pointer Points To

The indirection operator '*' can be used to read the object to which a pointer points. For example,

```
int number;
int *pointer;
    . . .
pointer = &number;
    . . .
printf("%d\n", *pointer);
```

uses **pointer** to access the contents of **number**.

When a pointer points to a structure, the elements within the structure can be read by using the structure offset operator '->'. See the entry for **->** for more information.

Pointers to Functions

A pointer can also contain the address of a function. For example,

```
char *(*example)();
```

declares **example** to be a pointer to a function that returns a pointer to a **char**.

This declaration is quite different from:

```
char **different();
```

The latter declares that **different** is a function that returns a pointer to a pointer to a **char**.

The following demonstrates how to call a function via a pointer:

```
(*example)(arg1, arg2);
```
Here, the '*' takes the contents of the pointer, which in this case is the address of the function, and uses that address to pass to a function its list of arguments.

A pointer to a function can be passed to another function as an argument. The library functions **bsearch** and **qsort** both take function pointers as arguments. A program may also use of arrays of pointers to functions.

*void ***

void * is the generic pointer; it replaces **char *** in that role. A pointer may be cast to **void *** and then back to its original type without any change in its value. **void *** is also aligned for any type in the execution environment.

For more information on the use of the generic pointer, see **void**.

Pointer Conversion

One type of pointer may be converted, or *cast*, to another. For example, a pointer to a **char** may be cast to a pointer to an **int**, and vice versa.

Any pointer may be cast to type **void *** and back again without its value being affected in any way. Likewise, any pointer of a scalar type may be cast to its corresponding **const** or **volatile** version. The qualified pointers are equivalent to their unqualified originals.

Pointers to different data types are compatible in expressions, but only if they are cast appropriately. Using them without casting produces a *pointer-type mismatch*. The translator should produce a diagnostic message when it detects this condition.

Pointer Arithmetic

Arithmetic may be performed on all pointers to scalar types. Pointer arithmetic is quite limited and consists of the following:

1. One pointer may be subtracted from another.

2. An **int** or a **long**, either variable or constant, may be added to a pointer or subtracted from it.

3. The operators **+ +** or **--** may be used to increment or decrement a pointer.

No other pointer arithmetic is permitted.

Cross-references

Standard, §3.1.2.5, §3.2.2.1, §3.2.2.3, §3.3.2.2-3, §3.5.4.1
The C Programming Language, ed. 2, pp. 93*ff*

See Also
NULL, types, void

Notes

The Rationale cautions against using NULL as an explicit argument to any function that expects a pointer on the grounds that, under some environments, pointers to different data types may be of different lengths. All such problems will be avoided if a function prototype is within the scope of the function call. Then, NULL will be transformed automatically to the proper type of pointer. See *function prototype* for more information.

pointer declarators — Definition
(Language/declarations/declarators)

A *pointer declarator* declares a pointer. It has the following syntax; *opt* indicates *optional*:

* *type-qualifier-list*$_{opt}$ *declarator*

As shown, the asterisk '*****' marks an identifier as being a pointer. For example:

```
int *example;
```

states that **example** is a pointer to **int**. Likewise, the use of two asterisks marks an identifier as being a pointer to a pointer. For instance,

```
int **example;
```

declares a pointer to a pointer to an **int**. It is sometimes helpful to read a C declarator backwards, i.e., from right to left, to decipher it.

A pointer declarator may be modified by the type qualifiers **const** or **volatile**. For example, the declarator

```
int *const example;
```

declares that **example** is a constant pointer to a variable value of type **int**, whereas the declaration

```
const int *example;
```

declares that **example** is a variable pointer to a constant integer value. The same syntax applies to **volatile**. The declaration

```
const int *const example;
```

declares a constant pointer to a constant **int**.

Cross-references
Standard, §3.5.4.1
The C Programming Language, ed. 2, p. 94

See Also
*, declarators, pointer

portability — Definition
(Definitions)

The term *portability* refers to a program's ability to be translated and executed under more than one environment. The Standard is designed so that if you adhere to it strictly, you will, in the words of the Rationale, "have a 'fighting chance' to make powerful C programs that are also highly portable ...."

Although true portability is an ideal that is difficult to realize, you can take a number of practical steps to ensure that your code is portable:

* Do not assume that an integer and a pointer have the same size. Remember that undeclared functions are assumed to return an **int**.

* Do not write routines that depend on a particular order of code evaluation, particular byte ordering, or particular length of data types, except for those specified within the Standard.

* Do not write routines that play tricks with a machine's "magic characters". For example, writing a routine that depends on a file's ending with <**ctrl-Z**> instead of **EOF** ensures that that code can run only under operating systems that recognize this magic character.

* Always use constant such as **EOF** and make full use of **#define** statements.

* Use headers to hold all machine-dependent declarations and definitions.

* Declare everything explicitly. In particular, be sure to declare functions as **void** if they do not return a value. This avoids unforeseen problems with undefined return values.

* Do not assume that all varieties of pointer are the same or can point anywhere. On some machines, for example, a **char *** is longer than an **int ***. On others, a function pointer aims at a different space than does a data pointer.

* NULL should not be used as an explicit argument to any function that expects a pointer because, under some environments, pointers to different data types may be of different lengths. All such problems are avoided if a function prototype is within the scope of the function call. Then, NULL is transformed automatically to the proper type of pointer.

- Always exit or return explicitly from **main**, even when the program has run successfully to its end.

- **int** is the register size of the machine. Use **short** or **long** wherever size is a consideration.

- Inevitably, you will have code that is not 100% portable. Try to separate code that is machine-specific or operating-system specific into its own file.

Cross-reference
The C Programming Language, ed. 2, p. 3

See Also
behavior, Definitions

postfix operators — Overview
(Language/expressions)

A *postfix operator* is an operator that appears immediately after its operand.

The postfix operators have the following syntax; *opt* indicates *optional*:

postfix-expression:
    primary expression
    postfix-expression [*expression*]
    postfix-expression (*argument-expression-list$_{opt}$*)
    postfix-expression . *identifier*
    postfix-expression -> *identifier*
    postfix-expression ++
    postfix-expression - -

argument-expression-list:
    assignment-expression
    argument-expression-list , *assignment-expression*

The following can be used as postfix operators:

[]	Define an array/read an element in an array/dereference a pointer
()	Call a function
.	Read a member of a structure or **union**
->	Read a member via a pointer
++	Increment the operand
--	Decrement the operand

Some of these operators may have other meanings when used in other contexts.

Cross-reference
Standard, §3.3.2

See Also
(), + +, --, - >, [], ., **expressions, function calls**

pow() — Library function
(Library/mathematics/power functions)
Raise one number to the power of another
#include < math.h >
double pow(double z, double x);

pow calculates and returns *z* raised to the power of *x*.

Cross-references
Standard, §4.5.5.1
The C Programming Language, ed. 2, p. 251

See Also
power functions, sqrt

Notes
A domain error occurs if *z* equals zero, if *x* is less than or equal to zero, or if *z* is less than zero and *x* is not an integer.

power functions — Overview
(Library/mathematics)

The Standard describes two functions that deal with powers of numbers. They are as follows:

pow	Raise one number to the power of another
sqrt	Calculate the square root of a number

Cross-reference
Standard, §4.5.5

See Also
exponent-log functions, hyperbolic functions, integer-value-remainder, mathematics, trigonometric functions

preprocessing — Overview
(Language)

Preprocessing encompasses all tasks that logically precede the translation of a program. The preprocessor is part of the translator, but uses a syntax that differs from that of C itself. The preprocessor processes headers, expands macros, and conditionally includes or excludes source code.

Directives

The preprocessor recognizes the following directives:

#if	Include code if a condition is true
#elif	Include code if directive is true
#else	Include code if preceding directives fail
#endif	End of code to be included conditionally
#ifdef	Include code if a given macro is defined
#ifndef	Include code if a given macro is not defined
#define	Define a macro
#undef	Undefine a macro
#include	Read another file and include it
#line	Reset current line number
#pragma	Perform implementation-defined task
#error	Flag an error

Their syntax is as follows; *opt* means *optional*:

preprocessing-file:
> *group*$_{opt}$

group:
> *group-part*
> *group group-part*

group-part:
> *preprocessing-tokens*$_{opt}$ *newline*
> *if-section*
> *control-line*

if-section:
> *if-group elif-groups*$_{opt}$ *else-group*$_{opt}$ *endif-line*

if-group:
> `#if`   *constant-expression newline group*$_{opt}$
> `#ifdef`   *identifier newline group*$_{opt}$
> `#ifndef` *identifier newline group*$_{opt}$

elif-groups:
    elif-group
    elif-groups elif-group

elif-group:
    #elif   *constant-expression newline group$_{opt}$*

else-group:
    #else   *newline group$_{opt}$*

endif-line:
    #endif   *newline*

control-line:
    #include *preprocessing-tokens newline*
    #define   *identifier replacement-list newline*
    #define   *identifier lparen identifier-list$_{opt}$) replacement-list newline*
    #undef   *identifier newline*
    #line   *preprocessing-tokens newline*
    #error   *preprocessing-tokens$_{opt}$ newline*
    #pragma *preprocessing-tokens$_{opt}$ newline*
    #   *newline*

lparen:
    left-parenthesis without preceding white space

replacement-list:
    preprocessing-tokens$_{opt}$

preprocessing-tokens:
    preprocessing-token
    preprocessing-tokens preprocessing-token

newline:
    newline character

A preprocessing directive is always introduced by the '#' character. The '#' must be the first non-white space character on a line, but it may be preceded by white space and it may be separated from the directive name that follows it by one or more white space characters.

Program Translation

As noted in the article on **translation phases**, the Standard's description of translation breaks it into eight discreet phases. Several of these phases deal with preprocessing tasks. Phase 3, among other things, partitions a source file into preprocessing tokens. Phase 4 processes preprocessor directives, such as performing macro substitution and processing include files.

Preprocessing Operators

The Standard defines two operators that are recognized by the preprocessor: the "stringize" operator #, and the "token-paste" operator ##. It also defines a new keyword associated with preprocessor statements: **defined**.

The operator # indicates that the following argument is to be replaced by a string literal; this literal names the preprocessing token that replaces the argument. For example, consider the macro:

```
#define display(x) show((long)(x), #x)
```

When the preprocessor reads the line

```
display(abs(-5));
```

it replaces it with the following:

```
show((long)(abs(-5)), "abs(-5)");
```

The ## operator performs "token pasting" — that is, it joins two tokens together, to create a single token. For example, consider the macro:

```
#define printvar(x) printf("%d\n", variable ## x)
```

When the preprocessor reads the line

```
printvar(3);
```

it translates it into:

```
printf("%d\n", variable3);
```

In the past, token pasting had been performed by inserting a comment between the tokens to be pasted. This no longer works.

Predefined Macros

The Standard describes the following macros that must be recognized by the preprocessor:

- _ _DATE_ _ date of translation
- _ _FILE_ _ source-file name
- _ _LINE_ _ current line within source file
- _ _STDC_ _ conforming translator and level
- _ _TIME_ _ time of translation

For more information on any one of these macros, see its entry.

Conditional Inclusion

The preprocessor will conditionally include lines of code within a program. The directives that include code conditionally are defined in such a way that you can construct a chain of inclusion directives to include exactly the material you want.

The keyword **defined** determines whether a symbol is defined to the **#if** preprocessor directive. For example,

```
#if defined(SYMBOL)
```

or

```
#if defined SYMBOL
```

is equivalent to

```
#ifdef SYMBOL
```

except that it can be used in more complex expressions, such as

```
#if defined FOO && defined BAR && FOO==10
```

defined is recognized only in lines beginning with **#if** or **#elif**.

Macro Definition and Replacement

The preprocessor performs simple types of macro replacement. To define a macro, use the preprocessor directive **#define** *identifier value*. The preprocessor scans the translation unit for preprocessor tokens that match *identifier*; when one is found, the preprocessor substitutes *value* for it.

For more information, see **macro replacement**.

Cross-references

Standard, §3.8
The C Programming Language, ed. 2, pp. 223*ff*

See Also

conditional inclusion, Language, macro replacement, preprocessing numbers, translation phases, token

Notes

Although preprocessing logically precedes parsing, a translator is not obliged to execute all preprocessing tasks before it begins to parse a program. Many compilers combine the preprocessing and parsing phases to increase the speed of translation.

preprocessing numbers — Definition
(Language/lexical elements)

A *preprocessing number* is one of the intermediate lexical elements handled during translation phases 1 through 6. As semantic analysis occurs in translation phase 7, the set of valid preprocessing numbers forms a superset of valid C numeric tokens.

A preprocessing number is any floating constant or integer constant. It has the following syntax:

preprocessing-number:
    digit
    . digit
    preprocessing-number digit
    preprocessing-number letter
    preprocessing-number e *sign*
    preprocessing-number E *sign*
    preprocessing-number .

A preprocessing number begins with either a digit or a period '.', and may consist of digits, letters, periods, and the character sequences **e+**, **e-**, **E+**, or **E-**.

Cross-reference
Standard, §3.1.8

See Also
lexical elements, preprocessing, token, translation phases

primary expressions — Definition
(Language/expressions)

A *primary expression* is an expression that needs no further evaluation. Primary expressions are the "bricks" from which more complex expressions are built. The syntax of primary expressions is as follows:

primary-expression:
    identifier
    constant
    string-literal
    (*expression*)

An identifier is a primary expression if it names an object or a function. Constants and string literals are primary expressions by definition. An expression within parentheses is considered a primary expression because the translator must resolve it before it considers any expression outside of the parentheses.

Cross-references
Standard, §3.3.1
The C Programming Language, ed. 2, p. 200

See Also
expressions

printf() — Library function
(Library/STDIO/input-output)
Format and print text into the standard output stream
#include <stdio.h>
int printf(const char *_format_ ...);

printf constructs a formatted string and writes it into the standard output stream.

format points to a string that can contain text, character constants, and one or more _conversion specifications_. A conversion specification describes how a particular type is to be converted into text.

Each conversion specification is introduced by the percent sign '%', and is followed, in order, by one or more of the following:

- A flag, which modifies the meaning of the conversion specification.

- An integer, which sets the minimum width of the field upon which the text is printed.

- A period and an integer, which sets the precision with which a number is printed.

- One of the following modifiers: **h**, **l**, or **L**. Their use is discussed below.

- Finally, a character that specifies the type of conversion to be performed. These are given below. This is the only element required after a '%'.

After _format_ can come one or more arguments. There should be one argument for each conversion specification within _format_ of the type appropriate to its conversion specifier. For example, if _format_ contains conversion specifications for an **int**, a **long**, and a string, then _format_ should be followed by three arguments, being, respectively, an **int**, a **long**, and a pointer to **char**.

If there are fewer arguments than conversion specifications, then **printf**'s behavior is undefined. If there are more, then every argument without a corresponding conversion specification is evaluated and then ignored. If an argument is not of the same type as its corresponding conversion specifier, then the behavior of **printf** is undefined.

If it writes the formatted string correctly, **printf** returns the number of characters written; otherwise, it returns a negative number. The Standard mandates that **printf** must be able to generate a string that is up to at least 509 characters long.

The following sections describe in detail the elements of the conversion specification.

Conversion Specifiers

The following lists the conversion specifiers described by the Standard. If *format* includes any conversion specifiers other than the ones shown below, the behavior is undefined. Using a **union**, an aggregate, or a pointer to a **union** or an aggregate as an argument produces undefined behavior.

c   Convert the **int** or **unsigned int** argument to a character.

d   Convert the **int** argument to signed decimal notation.

e   Convert the **double** argument to exponential form. The format is

> *[-]d.dddddd**e**+/-dd*

At least one digit always appears to the left of the decimal point and as many as *precision* digits to the right of it (default, six). If the precision is zero, then no decimal point is printed.

E   Same as **e**, except that 'E' is used instead of 'e'.

f   Convert the **double** argument to a string of the form

> *[-]d.dddddd*

At least one digit always appears to the left of the decimal point, and as many as *precision* digits to the right of it (default, six). If the precision is zero, then no decimal point is printed.

g   Convert the **double** argument to either of the formats **e** or **f**. The number of significant digits is equal to the precision set earlier in the conversion specification. Normally, this conversion selects conversion type **f**. It selects type **e** only if the exponent that results from such a conversion is either less than -4 or greater than the precision.

G   Same as **g**, except that it selects between conversion types **E** and **f**.

i   Same as **d**.

n   This conversion specification takes a pointer to an integer, into which it writes the number of characters **printf** has generated to the current point within *format*. It does not affect the string **printf** generates.

o   Convert the **int** argument to unsigned octal digits.

p   This conversion sequence takes a pointer to **void**. It translates the pointer into a set of characters and prints them. What it generates is defined by the implementation.

s   Print the string to which the corresponding argument points; the argument must point to a C string. It prints either the number of characters set by the precision, or to the end of the string, whichever is less. If no precision is specified, then the entire string is printed.

u   Convert the **int** argument to unsigned decimal digits.

x   Convert the **int** argument to unsigned hexadecimal characters. The values 10, 11, 12, 13, 14, and 15 are represented, respectively, by 'a', 'b', 'c', 'd', and 'e'.

X   Same as **x**, except that the values 10, 11, 12, 13, 14, and 15 are represented, respectively, by 'A', 'B', 'C', 'D', and 'E'.

The description of each conversion specifier assumes that it will be used with an argument whose type matches the type that the specifier expects. If the argument is of another type, it is cast to the type expected by the specifier. For example,

```
float f;
printf("%d\n", f);
```

will truncate **f** to an **int** before printing its value.

Flags

The '%' that introduces a conversion specification may be followed immediately by one or more of the following flags:

-   Left-justify text within its field. The default is to right-justify all output text within its field.

+   Precede a signed number with a plus or minus sign. For example,

```
printf("%+d %+d\n", -123, 123);
```

yields the following when executed:

-123 +123

<space>
If the first character of a signed number is its sign, then that sign is appended to the beginning of the text string generated; if it is not a sign, then a space is appended to the beginning of the text string. For example,

```
printf("% d\n", -123);
printf("% d\n",  123);
```

generates the following:

```
-123
 123
```

This flag can be used with every conversion specifier for a numeric data type. It forces **printf** to use a special format that indicates what numeric type is being printed. The following gives the effect of this flag on each appropriate specifier:

    e   always retain decimal point
    E   always retain decimal point

> f   always retain decimal point
> F   always retain decimal point
> g   always retain decimal point; keep trailing zeroes
> G   always retain decimal point; keep trailing zeroes
> x   print '0x' before the number
> X   print '0X' before the number

Any specified precision is expanded by the appropriate amount to allow for the printing of the extra character or characters. Using '#' with any other conversion specifier yields undefined results.

0   When used with the conversion specifiers **d, e, E, f, g, G, i, o, u, x,** or **X,** a leading zero indicates that the field width is to be padded with leading zeroes instead of spaces. If precision is indicated with the specifiers **d, i, o, u, x, X,** then the **0** flag is ignored; it is also ignored if it is used with the - flag. If this flag is used with any conversion specifier other than the ones listed above, behavior is undefined.

Field width

The field width is an integer that sets the minimum field upon which a formatted string is printed.

If a field width is specified, then that many characters-worth of space is reserved within the output string for that conversion. When the text produced by the conversion is *smaller* than the field width, spaces are appended to the beginning of the text to fill out the difference; this is called *padding*. Beginning the field width with a zero makes the padding character a '0' instead of a space. When the text is *larger* than the allotted field width, then the text is given extra space to allow it to be printed. Setting the field width never causes text to be truncated.

By default, text is set flush right within its field; using the '-' flag sets the text flush left within its field.

Using an asterisk '*' instead of an integer forces **printf** to use the corresponding argument as the field width. For example,

```
char *string = "Here's a number:";
int    width = 12;
int  integer = 123;
printf("%s%*d\n", string, width, integer);
```

produces the following text:

```
Here's a number:            123
```

Here, **width** was used to set the field width, so 12 spaces were used to pad the formatted integer.

Precision

The precision is indicated by a decimal point followed by a number. If a decimal point is used without a following number, then it is regarded as equivalent to '.0'.

The precision sets the number of characters to be printed for each conversion specifier. Setting the precision to n affects each conversion specifier as follows:

d	print at least n digits
e	print n digits after decimal point
E	print n digits after decimal point
f	print n digits after decimal point
g	print no more than n significant digits
G	print no more than n significant digits
i	print at least n digits
o	print at least n digits
s	print no more than n characters
u	print at least n digits
x	print at least n digits
X	print at least n digits

The precision differs from the field width in that the field width controls the amount of space set aside for the text, whereas the precision controls the number of characters to be printed. If the amount of padding called for by the precision conflicts with that called for by the field width, the amount called for by the precision is used.

Using an asterisk '*' instead of an integer forces **printf** to use the corresponding argument as the precision.

For example, this code

```
int   foo = 12345;
float bar = 12.345;
char *baz = "Hello, world";

printf("Example 1: %7.6d\n", foo);
printf("Example 2: %7.6f\n", bar);
printf("Example 3: %7.6s\n", baz);
```

produces the following text when executed:

```
Example 1:  012345
Example 2: 12.345000
Example 3:  Hello,
```

Modifiers

The following three modifiers may be used before a conversion specifier:

h   When used before the specifiers **d, i, o, u, x,** or **X,** it specifies that the corresponding argument is a **short int** or an **unsigned short int**. When used before **n,** it indicates that the corresponding argument is a **short int**. In implementations where **short int** and **int** are synonymous, it is not needed; however, it is useful in writing portable code.

l   When used before **d, i, o, u, x,** or **X,** it specifies that the corresponding argument is a **long int** or an **unsigned long int**. When used before 'n', it indicates that the corresponding argument is a **long int**. In implementations where **long int** and **int** are synonymous, it is not needed; however, it is useful in writing portable code.

L   When used before **e, E, f, F,** or **G,** it indicates that the corresponding argument is a **long double**.

Using **h, l,** or **L** before a conversion specifier other than the ones mentioned above results in undefined behavior.

Default argument promotions are performed on the arguments. There is no way to suppress this.

Example

This example implements a mini-interpreter for **printf** statements. It is a convenient tool for seeing exactly how some of the **printf** options work. To use it, type a **printf** conversion specification at the prompt. The formatted string will then appear. To reuse a format identifier, simply type **<return>**.

```
#include <math.h>
#include <stddef.h>
#include <stdio.h>
#include <stdlib.h>
#include <string.h>

/* the replies go here */
static char reply[80];

/* ask for a string and echo it in reply. */
char *
askstr(char *msg)
{
    printf("Enter %s ", msg);
    fflush(stdout);

    if(gets(reply) == NULL)
        exit(EXIT_SUCCESS);
    return(reply);
}
```

```
main(void)
{
    char fid[80], c;

    /* initialize to an invalid format identifier */
    strcpy(fid, "%Z");

    for(;;) {
        askstr("format identifier");
        /* null reply uses previous FID */
        if(reply[0])
            /* leave the '%' */
            strcpy(fid + 1, reply);

        switch(c = fid[strlen(fid) - 1]) {
        case 'd':
        case 'i':
            askstr("signed number");
            if(strchr(fid, 'l') != NULL)
                printf(fid, atol(reply));
            else
                printf(fid, atoi(reply));
            break;

        case 'o':
        case 'u':
        case 'x':
        case 'X':
            askstr("unsigned number");
            if(strchr(fid, 'l') != NULL)
                printf(fid, atol(reply));
            else
                printf(fid, (unsigned)atol(reply));
            break;

        case 'f':
        case 'e':
        case 'E':
        case 'g':
        case 'G':
            printf(fid, atof(askstr("real number")));
            break;

        case 's':
            printf(fid, askstr("string"));
            break;
```

```
        case 'c':
            printf(fid, *askstr("single character"));
            break;
        case '%':
            printf(fid);
            break;
        case 'p':
            /* print pointer to format id */
            printf(fid, fid);
            break;
        case 'n':
            printf("n not implemented");
            break;
        default:
            printf("%c not valid", c);
        }
    printf("\n");
    }
}
```

Cross-references
Standard, §4.9.6.3
The C Programming Language, ed. 2, p. 244

See Also
fprintf, input-output, scanf, sprintf, vfprintf, vprintf, vsprintf

Notes
printf must be able to construct and output a string at least 509 characters long.

The conversion specifier 'r', which is used by many implementations to pass an array of arguments to **printf**, is specifically excluded by the Standard. To achieve the functionality of the 'r' specifier, use **vprintf**.

The character that **printf** prints to represent the decimal point is affected by the program's locale, as set by the function **setlocale**. For more information, see **localization**.

printing character — Definition
(Library/character handling)

A *printing character* is any character in a locale-defined character set that, when printed, occupies one printing position on a display device.

Cross-references
Standard, §4.3
The C Programming Language, ed. 2, p. 249

See Also
character handling, control character

program execution — Overview
(Environment/execution environment)

The Standard describes *program execution* in terms of an abstract implementation that executes every instruction literally as it is described by the program. A real implementation is allowed to take short-cuts to speed execution, as long as the result is the same as if it had executed in the same manner as the abstract implementation.

The Standard divides program execution into a series of *sequence points*. A sequence point is any point where all *side effects* are resolved. A side effect, in turn, is any change to the execution environment that is caused by the program accessing a volatile object, modifying an object, modifying a file, or calling a function that performs any of these tasks. An expression may generate side effects; a void expression exists just for the side effects it generates.

At every sequence point, the environment of the actual machine must match that of the abstract machine. That is, whatever optimizations or short-cuts an implementation may take, at every sequence point it must be as if the machine executed every instruction as it appeared literally in the program. Sequence points cause the program's actual behavior to be synchronized with the abstract behavior that the code describes.

The sequence points are as follows:

- When all arguments to a function call have been evaluated.

- When the *first* operand of the following operators has been evaluated: logical AND '&&', logical OR '||', conditional '?', and comma ','.

- When a variable is initialized.

- When the controlling expression or expressions are evaluated for the following statements: **do**, **for**, **if**, **return**, **switch**, and **while**.

If the execution of a program is interrupted by a signal, the program cannot assume that the value of any object has been updated since the last sequence point.

An automatic variable is recreated every time the program re-enters the block within which the variable is declared. The variable holds its last-stored value while the block is executed, and retains it whenever the block is suspended by a signal or a function call.

Interactive devices must be accessed through a buffer. For a fuller description of buffering, see **STDIO**.

Finally, when the program terminates, the contents of any file that it writes must be the same as if the abstract implementation had been executed.

Cross-reference
Standard, §2.1.2.3

See Also
execution environment, sequence point, side effect

Notes
The difference between the abstract and real implementations required that the keyword **volatile** be created. It exists to warn the implementation that taking short-cuts with a particular variable may be dangerous. If an implementation followed each instruction literally, of course, no such warning would be needed.

program startup — Definition
(Environment/execution environment)

Program startup occurs when the execution environment invokes the program. Execution begins, and continues until program termination occurs. A program's execution may be suspended by the environment and resumed at a later time. The program, however, only starts once.

Cross-reference
Standard, §2.1.2

See Also
execution environment, program termination

program termination — Definition
(Environment/execution environment)

Program termination occurs when a program stops executing and returns control to the execution environment. Program termination may be triggered when the program calls either of the functions **abort** or **exit**, when **main** returns, when the environment or hardware raises a signal, or when program termination has been requested by some other program or event.

There are two types of termination: *unsuccessful* and *successful*.

Unsuccessful termination occurs either when a program aborts due to a significant problem in its operation (such as memory violation or division by zero), or when the program did not function as expected (such as when a requested file cannot be found).

A program indicates unsuccessful termination either by calling the function **exit** with the argument **EXIT_FAILURE**, by calling the function **abort**, or by using the function **raise** to generate the signal **SIGABRT**. **exit** is used to stop a program that cannot perform correctly, but does not threaten the integrity of the environment. **abort** and **raise** are used to stop a program that has gone seriously wrong.

Successful termination is declared to occur when the program runs to its conclusion correctly. A program indicates successful termination by calling the function **exit** with the argument **EXIT_SUCCESS**, or when **main** returns **EXIT_SUCCESS**.

Cross-reference
Standard, §2.1.2, §4.10.4.1, §4.10.4.3

See Also
abort, environment communication, execution environment, exit, EXIT_FAILURE, EXIT_SUCCESS, main, program startup, signal

Notes
On some operating systems, a program may be stopped, blocked, or suspended without causing it to terminate. In these cases, the program may be later unstopped, unblocked, or resumed. This does not qualify as program termination, even though execution has stopped and control has been returned to the environment.

pseudo-random numbers — Overview
(Library/general utilities)

The following functions generate a list of pseudo-random numbers. These numbers are called "pseudo-random" because the same set of random numbers is generated every time.

The function **rand** generates and returns a pseudo-random number. This number is an integer between zero and **RAND_MAX**, which must set to at least 32,767.

The function **srand** "seeds" the random-number generator used by **rand**. This forces **rand** to begin at a point in its set of random numbers other than where it normally begins.

Cross-reference
Standard, §4.10.2

See Also
general utilities

Notes
The Standard recognizes that there is no best algorithm to generate pseudo-random numbers on all machines. However, it offers the following example that generates an acceptable series of pseudo-random numbers on all machines:

```
static unsigned long int number = 1;
int rand(void)
{
     number = number * 1103515245 + 12345;
     return(unsigned int)(number/65536) % 32768;
}
void srand(unsigned int seed)
{
     number = seed;
}
```

This is a version of the algorithm offered by Knuth in volume 2 of *The Art of Computer Programming*. This sort of generator is called the "linear congruential method," which is a fancy term for a simple algorithm. One begins by choosing four parameters that determine all the random numbers to generated:

start	the initial value, nonnegative
multiplier	the multiplier, nonnegative
inc	increment, nonnegative
mod	modulus, nonnegative

The sequence of random numbers is defined by:

```
next = (multiplier * previous + inc) % mod;
```

rand stores **previous**, the last random number it returned, in a static variable and simply calculates **next** from **previous**, without reference to **start**.

ptrdiff_t — Type
(Library)
Numeric difference between two pointers
#include <stddef.h>

ptrdiff_t is a type that is defined in the header **stddef.h**. It is the signed integral type that can hold the result of subtracting one pointer from another.

Cross-references
Standard, §4.1.5
The C Programming Language, ed. 2, p. 206

See Also
Library, stddef.h

punctuators — Overview
(Language/lexical elements)

A *punctuator* is a symbol that has syntactic meaning but does not represent an operation that yields a value. All lexical elements that do not fall into another meaningful category are lumped together as punctuators.

Most often, a punctuator is used to mark or delimit an identifier or a portion of code, rather than modify it.

The set of punctuators consists of the following:

[]	Mark an array/delimit its size
()	Mark a parameter/argument list
{}	Delimit a block of code or a function
*	Identify a pointer type in a declaration
,	Delimit a function argument
:	Delimit a label
;	Mark end of a statement
...	(ellipsis) Indicate function takes flexible number of arguments
#	Indicate a preprocessor directive

The punctuators { }, [ ], and ( ) must be used in pairs.

A symbol that acts as a punctuator may also act as an operator, depending upon its context.

Cross-reference
Standard, §3.1.6

See Also
lexical elements, operators, statements

putc() — Library function
(Library/STDIO/input-output)
Write a character into a stream
#include <stdio.h>
int putc(int *character*, **FILE** *fp)**;**

putc writes *character* into the stream pointed to by *fp*.

putc returns *character* if it was written correctly; otherwise, it sets the error indicator for *fp* and returns **EOF**.

Example
This example writes newline characters into a file until the disk is full. Because this example uses the function **tmpfile**, the file it writes will disappear when the program terminates. It is not recommended that you run this program on a multi-user system.

```
#include <stddef.h>
#include <stdio.h>
#include <stdlib.h>

main(void)
{
    long count;
    FILE *tmp;

    if((tmp = tmpfile()) == NULL) {
        fprintf(stderr, "Can't open tmp file\n");
        exit(EXIT_FAILURE);
    }

    for(count = 0; putc('\n', tmp) != EOF; count++)
        ;

    fprintf(stderr, "We wrote %ld characters\n", count);
    return(EXIT_SUCCESS);
}
```

Cross-references
Standard, §4.9.7.8
The C Programming Language, ed. 2, p. 247

See Also
getc, getchar, gets, input-output, putchar, puts, ungetc

Notes
The Standard permits **putc** to be implemented as a macro. If it is implemented as a macro, *fp* may be read more than once. Therefore, one should beware of the side-effects of evaluating the argument more than once, especially if the argument itself has side-effects. See the entry for **macro** for more information. Use **fputc** if this behavior is not acceptable.

putchar() — Library function
(Library/STDIO/input-output)
Write a character into the standard output stream
#include <stdio.h>
int putchar(int *character***);**

putchar writes a character into the standard output stream. It is equivalent to:

```
putc(character, stdout);
```

putchar returns *character* if it was written correctly. If *character* could not be written, **putchar** sets the error indicator for the stream associated with stdout and returns **EOF**.

Example
This example prints all of the printable ASCII characters. It will work only under implementations that use ASCII characters.

```
#include <stdio.h>
#include <stdlib.h>

main(void)
{
    char c;

    for(c = ' '; putchar(c) <= '}'; c++)
        ;

    return(EXIT_SUCCESS);
}
```

Cross-references
Standard, §4.9.7.9
The C Programming Language, ed. 2, p. 247

See Also
getc, getchar, gets, input-output, puts, ungetc

puts() — Library function
(Library/STDIO/input-output)

Write a string into the standard output stream
#include <stdio.h>
int puts(char **string***);**

puts replaces the null character at the end of *string* with a newline character, and writes the result into the standard output stream.

puts returns a non-negative number if it could write *string* correctly; otherwise, it returns **EOF**.

Example

This example uses **puts** to print a string into the standard output stream.

```
#include <stdio.h>
#include <stdlib.h>

main(void)
{
    puts("Hello world.");
    return(EXIT_SUCCESS);
}
```

Cross-references
Standard, §4.9.7.10
The C Programming Language, ed. 2, p. 247

See Also
getc, getchar, gets, input-output, putc, putchar, ungetc

Notes

For historical reasons, **fputs** writes *string* unchanged, whereas **puts** appends a newline character.

Note, too, that in some implementations, **puts** does not return anything useful. Under the Standard, this has been made obsolete.

Q

qsort() — Library function
(Library/general utilities/searching-sorting)
Sort an array
void qsort(void *`array`, size_t `number`, size_t `size`, int (*`comparison`)
(const void *`arg1`, const void *`arg2`));

qsort sorts the elements within an array. *array* points to the base of the array being sorted; it has *number* members, each of which is *size* bytes long. In practice, *array* is usually an array of pointers and *size* is the **sizeof** the object to which each points.

comparison points to the function that compares two members of *array*. *arg1* and *arg2* each point to a member within *array*. The comparison routine must return a negative number, zero, or a positive number, depending upon whether *arg1* is, respectively, less than, equal to, or greater than *arg2*. If two or more members of *array* are identical, their ordering within the sorted array is unspecified.

Example
This example prints the command-line arguments in alphabetical order.

```
#include <stddef.h>
#include <stdio.h>
#include <stdlib.h>
#include <string.h>

int
compar(char *cp1[], char *cp2[])
{
    return(strcmp(*cp1, *cp2));
}

main(int argc, char *argv[])
{
    qsort((void *)++argv, (size_t)--argc, sizeof(*argv), compar);

    while(argc--)
        printf("%s ", *argv++);
    return(EXIT_SUCCESS);
}
```

Cross-references
Standard, §4.10.5.2
The C Programming Language, ed. 2, p. 87
The Art of Computer Programming, vol. 3

See Also

bsearch, searching-sorting

Notes

The name "qsort" reflects the fact that most implementations of this function use C. A. R. Hoare's "quicksort" algorithm. This algorithm is recursive and makes heavy use of the stack. It is also specified by the Association for Computing Machinery's algorithm 271.

Quicksort works on the basis of partitioning its input, and is highly dependent on the first element that starts the partitioning process. Given appropriate data, it can have a worst-case performance of $O(n^2)$.

qualified types — Definition
(Language/lexical elements/identifiers/types)

A *qualified type* is one whose top type is modified with the qualifiers **const**, **noalias**, or **volatile**. Types so qualified are called, respectively, *const-qualified types*, *noalias-qualified types*, and *volatile-qualified types*.

An *unqualified type* is one that is not so qualified.

Cross-references

Standard, §3.1.2.6
The C Programming Language, ed. 2, pp. 208, 211

See Also

const, noalias, types, volatile

Notes

As of this writing, **noalias** is the center of controversy. It may not be included in the Standard when it is finally published.

quiet change — Definition
(Rationale)

A *quiet change* occurs when an valid element of a C program behaves one way under a pre-ANSI implementation of C, and another way under ANSI C. The Committee attempted to avoid quiet changes, but some were unavoidable and are labelled as such in the Rationale.

The following lists the quiet changes noted within the Rationale:

Array initialization (§3.5.6)

Initialization of multi-dimensional arrays, such as

```
example[2][3][3];
```

can vary from implementation to implementation. The situation is clear when the initialization contains an entry for every "slot" in the array; e.g.,

```
example[2][3] = {
     1,   2,   3,   4,   5,   6
};
```

or:

```
example[2][3] = {
     { 1,   2,   3 }, { 4,   5,   6 }
};
```

The situation becomes more difficult when an array is only partially initialized; e.g.,

```
example[2][3] = {
     { 1 }, { 2, 3 }
};
```

Here, the programmer depends upon the set of initializers being parsed in a particular manner so that an initializers is written into the correct slot within the array.

The Standard mandates that that initialization of aggregates is always done in "top-down" fashion. A program will not be initialized correctly if it depends upon initialization being performed from the "bottom up". For more information, see **initialization**.

Bit shifting (§3.3.7)

Under many implementations of C, bit-shifting an **int** by a value set in a **long** requires that the **int** be widened to **long**. For example,

```
int example = 5000;
long bar = 3;
example << bar;
```

would, under many current implementations of C, result in **example**'s being widened to a **long** before the shift operation was performed. This does not have to happen under ANSI C.

Character constants (§3.1.3.4)

Some implementations of C would allow programmers to use octal character constants that included non-octal characters, e.g., '\078'. The Standard forbids this practice. Under the standard, '\078' is now interpreted as signifying octal value 7 and the ASCII character '8' (octal value 070). For more information, see **escape sequences**.

Escape sequences (§3.1.3.4)

The Standard now assigns values to the escape sequences \a and \x. The former represents an alert (such as ringing the bell), and the latter introduces a hexadecimal character constant. Some implementations of C defined these sequences differently; programs written for them will behave differently under ANSI C. For more information, see **escape sequences**.

Floating-point arithmetic (§3.2.1.1)

An expression that involves two variables of type **float** may now be calculated in single precision; an implementation is no longer required to promote both variables to type **double** before performing calculations. This rule holds as long as the implementation produces the same result as it would have if both variables had been promoted to **doubles** and the result truncated to **float**. This is an example of the *as if* rule. See **float** for more information.

Function definitions (§3.7.1)

Existing practice, in accordance with *The C Programming Language,* has always dictated that certain "default argument promotions" occur. For instance, objects of type **char** were always promoted to type **int** when passed as parameters.

With function prototypes, you can now pass the "narrow type," if a prototype is within the function's scope when the function is called. For example, you can pass a **float** as a **float**. To pass a **float** as a **double**, your prototype should give a **double** parameter type in this argument's position. If a **float** is passed internally as a **double**, it must be truncated back to a **float** within the function. Hence, you may find that a function no longer promotes arguments as it once did.

#if *statements* (§3.4)

The Standard thoroughly defines the C preprocessor. In general, the Standard forbids the use of environmental inquiries with **#if** statements, such as

```
#if (1<<16)==0
```

to check if the program is running on a machine whose word size is 16 bits. All preprocessor statements must be entirely resolved when the program is translated. Therefore, a program that uses an **#if** statement to determine aspects of the execution environment may not work the same under ANSI C as it does under some current implementations. Environmental limits are set in the header **limits.h**.

Internal identifiers (§3.1.2)

The Standard mandates that internal identifiers must be case-sensitive and must be significant for at least 31 characters. Thus, a conforming implementation of ANSI C will recognize that the identifiers

```
this_is_very_long_identifier_A
this_is_very_long_identifier_a
```

are, in fact, different. Hence, a program that relies on these two identifiers being equivalent may no longer translate correctly. See **identifiers** for more information.

Macro parameter substitution (§3.8.3.2)

The Standard introduces a new preprocessor operator, '#', to perform string substitutions within a preprocessor macro. Macros that depend upon parameter substitution within strings will not work the same under ANSI C.

Memory-management functions (§4.10.3)

The Standard requires that all memory-allocation functions return NULL when asked to allocate zero bytes. All programs that depend on such a request returning a non-NULL address may no longer work. For more information, see **memory management**.

Scope (§3.1.2.1)

The Standard states that the scope of an external declaration is confined to the block of code within which it is declared. Granting file scope to an external identifier is a common extension to the C language, as noted in §6.5.4. Under ANSI C, programs that depend upon all external declarations being available throughout a file, regardless of whether they were made within a block or globally, either may not work or may work differently. See **scope** and **linkage** for more information.

String constants (§2.2.1.1)

The Standard reserves the sequence "??" to introduce a *trigraph sequence*. This will be interpreted even within a string constant. For example, the expression

```
printf("Are you kidding??!\n");
```

under ANSI C will generate the string:

```
Are you kidding|
```

See **trigraph** and **translation phase** for more information.

Structure definition (§3.5.2.2)

One difficulty with C is writing a pair of structures that refer to each other. A typical solution is to write a pair of structures of the form:

```
struct example { struct bar *x; };
struct bar { struct example *y; };
```

Given ANSI C's block-scope rules, however, if **bar** was previously defined within **example**'s current block (or an outer one), then **example** will use that previous definition of **bar** rather than the subsequent one. This can, of course, create problems. To get around this, the Standard allows you to write a declaration of the form

```
struct bar;
```

to mask the previous declaration of **bar**. The quiet change in this situation arises if the program already uses "empty" declarations of this form. Such a declaration may have unexpected effects under ANSI C.

switch *statement labels* (§3.7.1)

In most present implementations of C, the labels in a switch statement are truncated to **int**. Under ANSI C, a label may now be of any integral type. If a program depends upon a case label being truncated to **int**, it may work differently under ANSI C. For more information, see **case** and **switch**.

Type promotion §3.2.1.1)

The Standard mandates that a variable of type **unsigned char** or **unsigned short** be promoted within an expression to an **int** if that type can hold the value of the variable that is being promoted. If an **int** cannot hold the value of the **unsigned char** or **unsigned short** being promoted, then it must be promoted to an **unsigned int**. Expressions that depend upon an **unsigned char** or **unsigned short** being promoted to an **unsigned int** in all circumstances will behave differently under ANSI C, and probably without warning.

Cross-reference
Rationale, §1.1

See Also
Rationale

R

raise() — Library function
(Library/signal handling)
Send a signal
#include < signal.h >
int raise(int *signal***);**

raise sends *signal* to the program that is currently being executed. If called from within a signal handler, the processing of this signal may be deferred until the signal handler exits.

Example
This example sets a signal, raises it itself, then allows the signal to be raised interactivly. Finally, it clears the signal and exits.

```
#include <stddef.h>
#include <stdio.h>
#include <stdlib.h>
#include <signal.h>

void gotcha(void);

void
setgotcha(void)
{
    if(signal(SIGINT, gotcha) == SIG_ERR) {
        printf("Couldn't set signal\n");
        abort();
    }
}

void
gotcha(void)
{
    char buf[10];

    printf("Do you want to quit this program? <y/n> ");
    fflush(stdout);
    gets(buf);

    if(tolower(buf[0]) == 'y')
        abort();

    setgotcha();
}
```

```
main(void)
{
    char buf[80];

    setgotcha();
    printf("Set signal; let's pretend we get one.\n");
    raise(SIGINT);

    printf("Returned from signal\n");
    /* <ctrl-c> may not work on all operating systems */
    printf("Try typing <ctrl-c> to signal <enter> to exit");
    fflush(stdout);
    gets(buf);

    if(signal(SIGINT, SIG_DFL) == SIG_ERR) {
        printf("Couldn't lower signal\n");
        abort();
    }

    printf("Signal lowered\n");
    exit(EXIT_SUCCESS);
}
```

Cross-references
Standard, §4.7.2.1
The C Programming Language, ed. 2, p. 255

See Also
signal, signal handling, signal.h

Notes
This function is derived from the UNIX function **kill**.

rand() — Library function
(Library/general utilities/pseudo-random numbers)
Generate pseudo-random numbers
#include <stdlib.h>
int rand(void)

rand generates and returns a pseudo-random number. The number generated is in the range of zero to **RAND_MAX**, which must equal at least 32,767.

rand will always return the same series of random numbers unless you change its *seed*, or beginning-point, with **srand**. Without having first called **srand**, it is as if you had initially set *seed* to one.

Example

This example produces a **char** that consists of random bits. The Standard's description of **rand** produces random **ints**, not random bits.

```
#include <limits.h>
#include <stdio.h>
#include <stdlib.h>

unsigned char
bitrand(void)
{
    register int i, r;

    for(i = r = 0; i < CHAR_BIT; i++) {
        r <<= 1;
        if(((long)rand() << 1) < (long)RAND_MAX)
            r++;
    }
    return(r);
}

main(void)
{
    printf("Random stuff %02x %02x %02x\n",
        bitrand(), bitrand(), bitrand());
    return(EXIT_SUCCESS);
}
```

Cross-references

Standard, §4.10.2.2
The C Programming Language, ed. 2, p. 252

See Also

pseudo-random numbers, RAND_MAX, srand

RAND_MAX — Macro
(Library/general utilities)
Largest size of a pseudo-random number
#include <stdlib.h>

RAND_MAX is a macro that is defined in the header **stdlib.h**. It indicates the largest pseudo-random number that can be returned by the function **rand**.

Example
For an example of using this macro in a program, see **rand**.

Cross-references
Standard, §4.10.2.1
The C Programming Language, ed. 2, p. 252

See Also
general utilities, rand, stdlib.h

Notes
The value of **RAND_MAX** is at least 32,767, which is also the minimum maximum of a **short int**.

range error — Definition
(Library/mathematics)

The *range* of a function is that set of values over which the function can take a value. It is thought of as the set of possible output values for the function. If a function evaluates to a value that is outside its defined range, or calculates a value not representable by a **double**, it may set **errno** to the value of the macro **ERANGE**, which indicates that a range error occurred.

When a number is too small to be encoded within a **double**, a function always returns zero. Whether **errno** is set to **ERANGE**, however, is up to the implementation.

Cross-reference
Standard, §4.5.1

See Also
ERANGE, errno, HUGE_VAL, math.h, mathematics

Rationale — Overview
(Standard)

The Standard is accompanied by a Rationale, which describes the reasoning behind the decisions by the ANSI committee. The Rationale also points out many of the changes, quiet or vocal, that have been incorporated into the Standard, and how they might affect current programs or implementations.

The Rationale is not part of the Standard *per se*, but is useful in helping readers to understand the Standard.

See Also
as if rule, minimum maxima, quiet change, spirit of C

realloc() — Library function
(Library/general utility/memory management)
Reallocate dynamic memory
#include <stdlib.h>
void *realloc(void **ptr***, size_t** *size***);**

realloc reallocates a block of memory that had been allocated with the functions **calloc** or **malloc**. This function is often used to change the size of a block of allocated memory.

ptr points to the block of memory to reallocate. If *ptr* is set to NULL, then **realloc** behaves exactly the same as **malloc**: it allocates the requested amount of memory and returns a pointer to it. *size* is the new size of the block. If *size* is zero and *ptr* is not NULL, then the memory pointed to is freed.

realloc returns a pointer to the block of *size* bytes that it has reallocated. The pointer it returns is aligned for any type of object. If it cannot reallocate the memory, it returns NULL.

Example
This example concatenates two strings that had been created with **malloc**.

```
#include <stddef.h>
#include <stdio.h>
#include <stdlib.h>
#include <string.h>
char *
combine(char **a, char **b)
{
     if(NULL == *a) {
          *a = *b;
          *b = NULL;
          return(*a);
     }
     else if(NULL == *b)
          return(*a);

     if((*a = realloc(*a, strlen(*a) + strlen(*b))) == NULL)
          return(NULL);
     return(strcat(*a, *b));
}
```

```
/* Copy a string into a malloc'ed hole. */
char *
copy(char *s)
{
      size_t len;
      char *ret;

      if(!(len = strlen(s)))
          return(NULL);
      if((ret = malloc(len)) == NULL)
          return(NULL);
      return(strcpy(ret, s));
}

main(void)
{
      char *a, *b;

      a = copy("A fine string. ");
      b = copy("Another fine string. ");

      puts(combine(&a, &b));
      return(EXIT_SUCCESS);
}
```

Cross-references
Standard, §4.10.3.4
The C Programming Language, ed. 2, p. 252

See Also
alignment, calloc, free, malloc, memory management

Notes
If *size* is larger than the size of the block of memory that is currently allocated, the
value of the pointer that **realloc** returns is indeterminate — it may point to the old
block of memory, or it may not. If it is not, the contents of the old block of memory
is copied to the new block.

register — C keyword
  (Language/declarations/storage-class specifiers)
  Quick access required
  register *type identifier*

The storage-class specifier **register** declares that *identifier* is to be accessed as
quickly as possible. In many computing environments, this indicates that *identifier*
should be kept in a machine register. The translator, however, is not required to

do this. It is a *hint* by the programmer to the translator, in the hope of obtaining more efficient code.

It is not permissible to take the address of an object declared with the **register** designator, regardless of whether the implementation stores such an object in a machine register or not.

Example

For an example of using this specifier in a program, see **srand**.

Cross-references

Standard, §3.5.1
The C Programming Language, ed. 2, p. 83

See Also

storage-class identifiers

Notes

An implementation must document how it handles variables declared to be **register**. Practice currently ranges from ignoring register declarations completely, to allowing a few register declarations for objects of an appropriate type (typically integer or pointer), to ignoring the designator and implementing a full global register allocation scheme.

relational operators — Overview
(Language/expressions)

A *relational operator* is one that compares two operands, to discover which has the greater value. The syntax is as follows:

> *relational-expression:*
> > *shift-expression*
> > *relational-expression < shift-expression*
> > *relational-expression <= shift-expression*
> > *relational-expression > shift-expression*
> > *relational-expression >= shift-expression*

The operands must be one of the following:

- Two objects with arithmetic type.

- Two pointers to compatible types of objects, regardless of whether they are qualified.

- Two pointers to compatible, incomplete types.

If both operands are arithmetic types, then both undergo the usual arithmetic conversions before they are compared.

If both operands are pointers, the following rules apply:

- If the pointers point to members of the same structure, the pointer to the member that is declared later will compare higher.

- If the pointers point to the same array, then the pointer whose member has the higher subscript will compare higher.

- All pointers to the members of a **union** will compare equal.

- If the two pointers do not point to the same aggregate object, the behavior is undefined, with the following exception: If the pointer **X** points to the last member of an array, the pointer expression **X+1** will compare higher than **X** even though it lies just beyond the end of the array.

The result of a relational operator always has type **int**. It has a value of zero if the condition is not satisfied, non-zero if it is.

Cross-references
Standard, §3.3.8
The C Programming Language, ed. 2, pp. 41, 206

See Also
!=, <, < =, = =, >, > =, **equality operators, expressions**

remove() — Library function
(Library/STDIO/file operations)
Remove a file
#include < stdio.h >
int remove(const char **filename***);**

remove breaks the link between between *filename* and the actual file that it represents. In effect, it removes a file. Thereafter, any attempt to use *filename* to open that file will fail.

remove returns zero if it could remove *filename*, and nonzero if it could not.

Example
This example removes the file named on the command line.

```
#include <stdio.h>
#include <stdlib.h>
main(int argc, char *argv[])
{
     if(argc != 1) {
          fprintf(stderr, "usage: remove filename\n");
          exit(EXIT_FAILURE);
     }

     if(remove(argv[1])) {
          perror("remove failed");
          exit(EXIT_FAILURE);
     }
     return(EXIT_SUCCESS);
}
```

Cross-references
Standard, §4.9.4.1
The C Programming Language, ed. 2, p. 242

See Also
file operations, rename, tmpfile, tmpnam

Notes
remove is equivalent to the UNIX function **unlink**.

If you attempt to remove a file that is currently open, the behavior is implementation-defined.

rename() — Library function
(Library/STDIO/file operations)
Rename a file
#include <stdio.h>
rename(const char **old**; const char ****new**);**

rename changes the name of a file, from the string pointed to by *old* to the string pointed to by *new*. Both *old* and *new* must point to a valid file name. If *new* points to the name of a file that already exists, the behavior is implementation-defined.

rename returns zero if it could rename the file, and nonzero if it could not. If **rename** could not rename the file, its name remains unchanged.

Example

This example renames the file named in the first command-line argument to the name given in the second argument.

```
#include <stdio.h>
#include <stdlib.h>

main(int argc, char *argv[])
{
    if(argc != 3) {
        fprintf(stderr, "usage: rename from to\n");
        exit(EXIT_FAILURE);
    }

    if(rename(argv[1], argv[2])) {
        perror("rename failed");
        exit(EXIT_FAILURE);
    }
    return(EXIT_SUCCESS);
}
```

Cross-references

Standard, §4.9.4.2
The C Programming Language, ed. 2, p. 242

See Also

file operations, remove, tmpfile, tmpnam

Notes

rename will fail if the file it is asked to rename is open, or if its contents must be copied in order to rename it.

return — C keyword

(Language/statements/jump statements)
Return to calling function
return;
return *expression*;

return is a statement that forces a function to return immediately to the function that called it.

return may also evaluate *expression* and pass its value to the calling function; the calling function regards this value as the value of the called function.

return can return a value to the calling function only if the called function was *not* declared to have a return type of **void**. The calling function is, of course, free to ignore the value **return** hands it.

If the called function is declared to return a type other than what **return** is actually returning, the value passed by **return** will be altered to conform to what the function was declared to return. For example,

```
main()
{
      printf("%s\n", example());
}
char *example(void)
{
      return "This is a string";
}
```

the pointer returned by **example** will be changed to an **int** before being returned to **main**. This is because **example** is declared implicitly within **main**, and a function that is declared implicitly is assumed to return an **int**. In environments where an **int** and a pointer are the same length, this code will work correctly. However, it will fail in environments where an **int** and a pointer have different lengths.

A function may have any number of **return** statements within it; however, a function can return only one value to the function that called it.

Finally, reaching the last '}' in a function is equivalent to calling **return** without an expression.

Cross-references
Standard, §3.6.6.4
The C Programming Language, ed. 2, p. 70

See Also
break, C keywords, continue, goto, jump statements

Notes
If a program uses what is returned by a function as a value, and that function uses **return** without an expression, the behavior of the program is undefined.

rewind() — Library function
(Standard/STDIO/file positioning)
Reset file-position indicator
#include <stdio.h>
void rewind(FILE *fp);

rewind resets the file-position indicator to the beginning of the file associated with stream *fp*. It is equivalent to:

```
(void)fseek(fp, OL, SEEK_SET);
```

rewind, unlike **fseek**, clears the error indicator for *fp*.

Cross-references
Standard, §4.9.9.5
The C Programming Language, ed. 2, p. 248

See Also
fgetpos, file positioning, fseek, fsetpos, ftell

Notes
In many current implementations, **rewind** returns an **int**. In the Standard's description, **rewind** returns nothing.

rvalue — Definition
(Definitions)

An *rvalue* is the value of an expression. The name comes from the assignment expression **E1 = E2;** in which the right operand is an rvalue.

Unlike an lvalue, an rvalue can be either a variable or a constant.

Although the term "rvalue" is commonly used among programmers, the Standard prefers the term "value of an expression".

Cross-references
The C Programming Language, ed. 2, pp

See Also
Definitions, lvalue

Notes
All non-void expressions have an rvalue.

S

scalar types — Definition
(Language/lexical elements/identifiers/types)

The *scalar types* are the set of all arithmetic types and pointer types. They do not include the aggregate types, structures, or arrays.

Cross-reference
Standard, §3.1.2.5

See Also
types

scanf() — Library function
(Library/STDIO/input-output)
Read and interpret text from standard input stream
#include <stdio.h>
int scanf(const char *format, ...);**

scanf reads characters from the standard input stream and uses the string *format* to interpret what it has read into the appropriate types of data.

format is a string that consists of one or more conversion specifications, each of which describes how a portion of text is to be interpreted. *format* is followed by zero or more arguments. There should be one argument for each conversion specification within *format*, and each should point to the data type that corresponds to the conversion specifier within its corresponding conversion specification. For example, if *format* contains three conversion specifications that convert text into, respectively, an **int**, a **float**, and a string, then *format* should be followed by three arguments that point, respectively, to an **int**, a **float**, and an array of **chars** that is large enough to hold the string being input. If there are fewer arguments than conversion specifications, then **scanf**'s behavior is undefined. If there are more, then every argument without a corresponding conversion specification is evaluated and then ignored. If an argument is not of the same type as its corresponding type specification, then **scanf** returns.

scanf organizes the text read into a series of tokens. Each token is delimited by white space. White space usually is thrown away, except in the case of the 'c' or '[' conversion specifiers, which are described below.

If an input error occurs during input or if **EOF** is read, **scanf** returns immediately. If it reads an inappropriate character (e.g., an alphabetic character where it expects a digit), it returns immediately. **scanf** returns the number of conversions it accomplished; if it could accomplish no conversions, it returns **EOF**.

Conversion Specifications

The percent sign character '%' marks the beginning of a conversion specification. The '%' will be followed by one or more of the following:

- An asterisk '*', which tells **scanf** to skip the next conversion; that is, read the next token but do not write it into the corresponding argument.

- A decimal integer, which tells **scanf** the maximum width of the next field being read. How the field width is used varies among conversion specifier. See the table of specifiers below for more information.

- One of the three modifiers **h**, **l**, or **L**, whose use is described below.

- A conversion specifier, whose use is described below.

Modifiers

The following three modifiers may be used before a conversion specifier:

h   When used before **d**, **i**, **o**, **u**, **x**, or **X**, it specifies that the corresponding argument points to a **short int** or an **unsigned short int**. When used before **n**, it indicates that the corresponding argument points to a **short int**. In implementations where **short int** and **int** are synonymous, it is not needed. However, it is useful in writing portable code.

l   When used before **d**, **i**, **o**, **u**, **x**, or **X**, it specifies that the corresponding argument points to a **long int** or an **unsigned long int**. When used before **n**, it indicates that the corresponding argument points to a **long int**. In implementations where **long int** and **int** are synonymous, it is not needed. However, it is useful in writing portable code.

L   When used before **e**, **E**, **f**, **F**, or **G**, it indicates that the corresponding argument points to a **long double**.

If **h**, **l**, or is used before a conversion specifier other than the ones mentioned above, it is ignored.

Conversion Specifiers

The Standard describes the following conversion specifiers:

c   Convert into **chars** the number of characters specified by the field width, and write them into the array pointed to by the corresponding argument. The default field width is one. **scanf** does not write a null character at the end of the array it creates. This specifier forces **scanf** to read and store white-space characters and numerals, as well as letters.

d   Convert the token to a decimal integer; the format should be equivalent to that expected by the function **strtol** with a base argument of ten. The corresponding argument should point to an **int**.

e   Convert the token to a floating-point number. The format of the token should be that expected by the function **strtod** for a floating-point number that uses exponential notation. The corresponding argument should point to a **double**.

E   Same as **e**.

f   Convert the token to a floating-point number. The format of the token should be that expected by the function **strtod** for a floating-point number that uses decimal notation. The corresponding argument should point to a **double**.

g   Convert the token to a floating-point number. The format of the token should of that expected by the function **strtod** for a floating-point number that uses either exponential notation or decimal notation. The corresponding argument should point to a **double**.

G   Same as **g**.

i   Convert the token to a decimal integer. The format should be equivalent to that expected by the function **strtol** with a base argument of zero. The corresponding argument should point to an **int**.

n   Do not read any text. Write into the corresponding argument the number of characters that **scanf** has read up to this point. The corresponding argument should point to an **int**.

o   Convert the token to an octal integer. The format should be equivalent to that expected by the function **strtol** with a base argument of eight. The corresponding argument should point to an **int**.

p   Pointer format: read a sequence of implementation-defined characters, convert them in an implementation-defined way, and write them in an implementation-defined manner. The vagueness of this description is unavoidable, because the pointer format will vary between machines, and even on the same machine. The corresponding argument should point to a **void ***. The sequence of characters recognized should be identical with that written by **printf**'s **p** conversion specifier.

s   Read a string of non-white space characters, copy them into the area pointed to by the corresponding argument, and append a null character to the end. The argument should be of type **char ***, and should point to enough allocated memory to hold the string being read plus its terminating null character.

u   Convert the token to an unsigned integer. The format should be equivalent to that expected by the function **strtoul** with a base argument of ten. See **strtoul** for more information. The corresponding argument should point to an **unsigned int**.

x   Convert the token from hexadecimal notation to a signed integer. The format should be equivalent to that expected by the function **strtol** with a base argument of 16. See **strtol** for more information. The corresponding argument should point to an **unsigned int**.

X   Same as **x**.

%   Match a single percent sign '%'. Make no conversion or assignment.

[/]   Scan a *scanset*, which is a set of characters enclosed by brackets. A character that matches any member of the scanset is copied into the area pointed to by the corresponding argument, which should be a **char *** that points to enough allocated memory to hold the maximum number of characters that may be copied, plus the concluding null character. Appending a circumflex '^' to the scanset tells **scanf** to copy every character that does *not* match a member of the scanset (i.e., *complements* the scanset). If the format string begins with ']' or '^]', then ']' is included in the scanset, and the set specifier is terminated by the next ']' in the format string. If a hyphen appears within the scanset, the behavior is implementation-defined; often, it indicates a range of characters, as in **[a-z]**.

      For example, passing the string **hello, world** to

```
char array[50];
scanf("[^abcd]", array);
```

      writes the string **hello, worl** into **array**.

Cross-references
Standard, §4.9.6.4
The C Programming Language, ed. 2, p. 246

See Also
fscanf, input-output, printf, sscanf

Notes
scanf will read up to, but not through, a newline character. The newline remains in the standard input device's buffer until you dispose of it. Programmers have been known to forget to empty the buffer before calling **scanf** a second time, which leads to unexpected results.

Experience has shown that **scanf** should not be used directly to obtain a string from the keyboard: use **gets** to obtain the string, and **sscanf** to format it.

The character that **scanf** recognizes as representing the decimal point is affected by the program's locale, as set by the function **setlocale**. For more information, see **localization**.

SCHAR_MAX — Macro
(Environment/environmental considerations/limits/numerical)

SCHAR_MAX is a macro that is defined in the header **limits.h**. It gives the largest value that can be held in an object of type **signed char**. It must be defined to be at least 127.

Cross-references
Standard, §2.2.4.2
The C Programming Language, ed. 2, p. 257

See Also
limits.h, numerical limits

SCHAR_MIN — Macro
(Environment/environmental considerations/limits/numerical)

SCHAR_MIN is a macro that is defined in the header **limits.h**. It gives the smallest value that can be held in an object of type **signed char**. It must be defined to be at most -127.

Cross-references
Standard, §2.2.4.2
The C Programming Language, ed. 2, p. 257

See Also
limits.h, numerical limits

scope — Definition
(Language/lexical elements/identifiers)

The term *scope* describes the portion of the program in which a given identifier is recognized, or *visible*. Scope is similar to, but not identical to, linkage. Linkage refers to whether an identifier can be joined, or *linked*, across files. Scope refers to the portion of a program that can recognize an identifier.

There are four varieties of scope: *block*, *file*, *function*, and *function prototype*.

An identifier with block scope is visible only within the block of code where it is declared. When the program reaches the '}' that ends that block of code, then the identifier is no longer visible, and so no longer "within scope".

An identifier with file scope is visible throughout the translation unit within which it is declared. The only identifiers that have file scope are those that are declared globally, i.e., that are declared outside the braces that enclose any function. If a function in one file uses an identifier that is defined in another file, it must mark that identifier as being external, by using the storage-class specifier **extern**.

An identifier with function scope is visible throughout a function, no matter where in the function it is declared. A label is the only variety of identifier that has function scope.

An identifier with function-prototype scope is visible only within the function prototype where it is declared. For example, consider the following function prototype:

```
void va_end(va_list listptr);
```

The identifier **listptr** has function-prototype scope. It is recognized only within that prototype, and is used only for purposes of documentation.

If an identifier is redeclared but is within an enclosing scope, it "hides" the outermost identifier and renders it inaccessible. This condition is called "information hiding", and it holds true as long as the inner declaration is within scope.

Example

The following program demonstrates scope, and shows how to hide information.

```
/* global i */
int i = 13;

void
function1(void)
{
     /* local i; hides global i */
     int i = 23;

     for(;;) {
          /* block-scope i; hides local and global i's */
          int i = 33;
          /* print block-scope i */
          printf ("block-scope i: %d\n", i);
          break;
     }
     /* block-scope i has disappeared; print local i */
     printf ("local i: %d\n", i);
}
```

```
void
function2(void)
{
    /* local i has disappeared; print global i */
    printf("global i: %d\n", i);
}

main(void)
{
    function1();
    function2();
    return(EXIT_SUCCESS);
}
```

Cross-references

Standard, §3.1.2.1
The C Programming Language, ed. 2, p. 227

See Also

extern, identifiers, storage duration

Notes

If an identifier is declared both within a block and with the storage-class identifier **extern**, it has block scope. An external declaration made within one block of code is not available outside that block. If an identifier that is declared external within one block is referenced within another, behavior is undefined.

A common extension to C automatically promotes to file scope all external identifiers that are declared within a block. Under such implementations, the following will work correctly:

```
/* non-ANSI code! */
function1()
{
    extern float example();
        . . .
}

function2()
{
    float variable;
        . . .
    variable = example();
        . . .
}
```

Under the Standard, however, this code will not work correctly: the declaration of the function **example** has block scope; therefore, it cannot be seen in **function2**. In **function2**, therefore, the translator properly assumes that **example** returns an **int**. The **float** that **example** actually returns is altered, causing undefined behavior. ANSI C causes this code to behave differently than expected, and an implementation may not issue a warning message. This is a quiet change that may break existing code.

searching-sorting — Overview
(Library/general utilities)
#include < stdlib.h >

The Standard describes two functions that perform searching and sorting. They are as follows:

bsearch	Perform binary search
qsort	Sort an array

Cross-references
Standard, §4.10.5
The C Programming Language, ed. 2, p. 118

See Also
general utilities

SEEK_CUR — Macro
(Library/STDIO)
Seek from current position of file-position indicator
#include < stdio.h >

SEEK_CUR is a macro that is defined in the header **stdio.h**. When used as an argument to the function **fseek**, it indicates that seeking should be performed relative to the current position of the file-position indicator.

Cross-references
Standard, §4.9.1, §4.9.9.2
The C Programming Language, ed. 2, p. 248

See Also
fseek, SEEK_END, SEEK_SET, STDIO, stdio.h

SEEK_END — Macro
(Library/STDIO)
Seek from the end of a file
#include <stdio.h>

SEEK_END is a macro that is defined in the header **stdio.h**. When used as an argument to the function **fseek**, it indicates that seeking should be performed relative to the end of the file.

Cross-references
Standard, §4.9.1, §4.9.9.2
The C Programming Language, ed. 2, p. 248

See Also
fseek, SEEK_CUR, SEEK_SET, STDIO, stdio.h

SEEK_SET — Macro
(Library/STDIO)
Seek from beginning of a file
#include <stdio.h>

SEEK_SET is a macro that is defined in the header **stdio.h**. When used as an argument to the function **fseek**, it indicates that seeking should be performed relative to the beginning of the file.

Cross-references
Standard, §4.9.1, §4.9.9.2
The C Programming Language, ed. 2, p. 248

See Also
fseek, SEEK_CUR, SEEK_END, STDIO, stdio.h

selection statements — Overview
(Language/statements)

C includes two mechanisms by which a program can execute code conditionally: the **if** statement and the **switch** statement. The **if** statement evaluates a condition, and then selects either of two possible actions. A **switch** statement evaluates a condition, and then selects from among many possible actions.

The syntax of the **if** statement is as follows:

selection-statement:
        if (*expression*) *statement*
        if (*expression*) *statement* else *statement*

The **if** statement executes its *statement* if *expression* is true (i.e., a value other than zero). If *expression* is false (i.e., equal to zero), then *statement* is not executed.

An **if** statement may be followed by an **else** statement. If *expression* is *false*, the statements that follow the **else** statement are executed. If *expression* is true, however, the statements that follow the **else** statement are skipped.

The syntax of the **switch** statement is as follows:

```
switch ( expression ) {
    case expression :
        statement

        . . .
    default :
        statement
}
```

The **switch** statement evaluates *expression*, then jumps to the **case** label whose *expression* is equivalent to the value of *expression*. Execution then proceeds from that point.

A **switch** statement may be thought of as a multi-way branch statement. **if/else** allows the program to select between two alternatives. **switch** allows the program to select from among as many as 257 alternatives — or more, if the implementation allows.

Cross-references
Standard, §3.6.4
The C Programming Language, ed. 2, p. 223

See Also
else, if, statements, switch

sequence point — Definition
(Environment/execution environment/program execution)

A sequence point is any point in a program where all side effects are resolved. At every sequence point, the environment of the actual machine must match that of the abstract machine. That is, whatever optimizations or short-cuts an implementation may take, at every sequence point it must be as if the machine executed every instruction as it appeared literally in the program. Sequence points cause the program's actual behavior to be synchronized with the abstract behavior that the source code describes.

The sequence points are as follows:

- When all arguments to a function call have been evaluated.

- When the *first* operand of the following operators has been evaluated: logical AND '&&', logical OR '||', conditional '?', and comma ','.

- When a variable is initialized.

- When the controlling expression or expressions are evaluated for the following statements: **do, for, if, return, switch,** and **while.**

Cross-reference
Standard, §2.1.2.3

See Also
program execution, side effect

setbuf() — Library function
(Library/STDIO/file access)
Set alternative stream buffer
#include < stdio.h >
void setbuf(FILE *fp, char *buffer);

When the functions **fopen** and **freopen** open a stream, they automatically establish a buffer for it. The buffer is **BUFSIZ** bytes long. **BUFSIZ** is a macro that is defined in the header **stdio.h**; it cannot be less than 256.

setbuf changes the buffer for the stream pointed to by *fp* from its default buffer to *buffer*. It sets *buffer* to be **BUFSIZ** bytes long. To create a buffer of a size other than **BUFSIZ**, use **setvbuf.**

You should use **setbuf** after *fp* has been opened, but before any data have been read from or written to it.

If *buffer* is set to NULL, then *fp* will be unbuffered. For example, the call

```
setbuf(stdout, NULL);
```

ensures that all output to the standard output stream is unbuffered.

Cross-references
Standard, §4.9.5.5
The C Programming Language, ed. 2, p. 243

See Also
BUFSIZ, fclose, fflush, file access, freopen, setbuf, setvbuf

setjmp() — Macro

(Library/non-local jumps)
Save environment for non-local jump
#include < setjmp.h >
int setjmp(jmp_buf *environment***);**

setjmp copies the current environment into the array **jump_buf**. The environment can then be restored by a call to the function **longjmp**.

environment is of type **jmp_buf**, which is defined in the header **setjmp.h**. **jmp_buf** must be an array type so that it will conform to current usage.

setjmp returns zero if it is called directly. When it returns after a call to **longjmp**, however, it returns **longjmp**'s argument *rval*. If *rval* is set to zero, then **setjmp** returns one. See **longjmp** and **non-local jumps** for more information.

Cross-references
Standard, §4.6.1.1
The C Programming Language, ed. 2, p. 254

See Also
longjmp, jmp_buf, non-local jumps

Notes
Many user-level routines cannot be interrupted and reentered safely. For that reason, improper use of **setjmp** and **longjmp** will result in the creation of mysterious and irreproducible bugs. The use of **longjmp** to exit interrupt, exception, or signal handlers is particularly hazardous.

setjmp must be used as the controlling operand in a **switch** statement, as the controlling expression in an **if** statement, or as an operand in an equality expression. Any other use generates undefined behavior.

The Standard mandates that **setjmp** be implemented only as a macro, not as a library function. The intent is to have it be a simple expression that expands in line, without requiring local or temporary variables.

setjmp.h — Header

(Library/non-local jump)
Declarations for non-local jump
#include < setjmp.h >

setjmp.h is the header that contains declarations for the elements that perform a non-local jump. It contains the prototype for the function **longjmp**, and it defines the macro **setjmp** and the type **jmp_buf**.

Cross-references
Standard, §4.6
The C Programming Language, ed. 2, p. 254

See Also
header, jmp_buf, longjmp, non-local jump, setjmp

setlocale() — Library function
(Library/localization)
Set or query a program's locale
#include < locale.h >
char *setlocale(int *portion*, **const char ****locale***);**

setlocale is a function that lets you set all or a portion of the locale information used by your program or query for information about the current locale.

portion is the portion of the locale that you wish to set or query. The Standard defines a number of macros for this purpose, as follows:

LC_ALL
Set or query all locale-specific information. Setting the locale affects all of the following locale categories.

LC_COLLATE
Set or query information that affects collating functions. This affects the operation of the functions **strcoll** and **strxfrm**.

LC_CTYPE
Set or query information about character handling. This affects he operation of all character-handling functions, except for **isdigit** and **isxdigit**. It also affects the operation of the functions that handle multibyte characters, i.e., **mblen, mbtowc, mbstowcs**, and **wcstombs, wctomb**.

LC_MONETARY
Set or query all monetary-specific information as used in the structure **lconv**, which is initialized by the function **localeconv**.

LC_NUMERIC
Set or query information for formatting numeric strings. This may change the decimal-point character used by string conversion functions and functions that perform formatted input and output. This may also affect the contents of the structure **lconv**.

LC_TIME
> Set or query information for formatting time strings. This changes the operation of the function **strftime**.

Setting *locale* to NULL tells **setlocale** that you wish to query information about the current locale rather than set a new locale.

setlocale returns a pointer to a string that contains the information needed to set or examine the locale. For example, the call

```
setlocale(LC_TIME, "");
```

returns a string that can be used to modify the time and date functions to conform to the requirements of the native locale. **setlocale** returns NULL if it does not recognize either *portion* or *locale*.

Cross-reference
Standard, §4.4.1.1

See Also
lconv, localeconv, localization

Notes
The Standard does not describe the mechanism by which **setlocale** modifies the action of other library functions. It mandates only that the modification be done in such a way as to alter the action of the functions at run time rather than at translation time. An implementation need only supply the information required by the **C** locale.

There are many possible approaches to supporting locales. The Rationale suggests that the string returned by **setlocale** could be the name of a file that would contain locale information used by the appropriate functions. Another approach would be to set environment variables.

The locales supported by any implementation are all implementation-defined. Hence, to find out what specific locales are supported by an implementation, consult the documentation for your implementation.

Because support of any particular locale is intimately entwined with the translator and its library, only those locales actually supported by the implementation can be used.

Finally, the Standard's section on compliance states that any program that uses locale-specific information does not strictly comply with the Standard. Therefore, any program that uses a locale other than the **C** locale *cannot* be assumed to be portable to every environment for which a conforming implementation of C has been written. *Caveat utilitor.*

setvbuf() — Library function
(Library/STDIO/file access)

Set alternative stream buffer
#include < stdio.h >
int setvbuf(FILE **fp***, char ****buffer***, int** *mode***, size_t** *size***);**

When the functions **fopen** and **freopen** open a stream, they automatically establish a buffer for it. The buffer is **BUFSIZ** bytes long. **BUFSIZ** is a macro that is
defined in the header **stdio.h**; it cannot be less than 256.

setvbuf alters the buffer used with the stream pointed to by *fp* from its default
buffer to *buffer*. Unlike the related function **setbuf**, it also allows you set the size of
the new buffer as well as the form of buffering.

buffer is the address of the new buffer. *size* is its size, in bytes. *mode* is the manner in which you wish the stream to be buffered, as follows:

_IOFBF	Fully buffered
_IOLBF	Line-buffered
_IONBF	No buffering

These macros are defined in the header **stdio.h**. For more information on what
these terms mean, see **buffering**.

You should call **setvbuf** after a stream has been opened but before any data have
been written to or read from the stream. For example, the following give *fp* a 50-
byte buffer that is line-buffered:

```
char buffer[50];
FILE *fp;

fopen(fp, "r");
setvbuf(fp, buffer, _IOLBF, sizeof(buffer));
```

On the other hand, the following turns off buffering for the standard output
stream:

```
setvbuf(stdout, NULL, _IONBF, 0);
```

setvbuf returns zero if the new buffer could be established correctly. It returns a
number other than zero if something went wrong or if an invalid parameter is
given for *mode* or *size*.

Example

This example uses **setvbuf** to turn off buffering and echo.

```
#include <stdio.h>
#include <stddef.h>
#include <stdlib.h>
main(void)
{
    int c;

    if(setvbuf(stdin,  NULL, _IONBF, 0))
        fprintf(stderr, "Couldn't turn off stdin buffer\n");

    if(setvbuf(stdout,  NULL, _IONBF, 0))
        fprintf(stderr, "Couldn't turn off stdout buffer\n");

    while((c = getchar()) != EOF)
        putchar(c);
    return(EXIT_SUCCESS);
}
```

Cross-references
Standard, §4.9.5.6
The C Programming Language, ed. 2, p. 243

See Also
BUFSIZ, fclose, fflush, file access, fopen, freopen, setbuf

short int — Type
(Language/lexical elements/identifiers/types)

A **short int** is a signed integral type. This type can be no smaller than a **char**, and no larger than an **int**.

A **short int** can encode any number between **SHRT_MIN** and **SHRT_MAX**. These are macros that are defined in the header **limits.h**. The former can be no greater than -32,767, and the latter no less than +32,767.

The types **short**, **signed short**, and **signed short int** are all synonyms for **short int**.

Cross-references
Standard, §2.2.4.2, §3.1.2.5, §3.2.1.1, §3.5.2
The C Programming Language, ed. 2, p. 211

See Also
int, long int, types

SHRT_MAX — Macro
  (Environment/environmental considerations/limits/numerical)

> **SHRT_MAX** is a macro that is defined in the header **limits.h**. It gives the largest value that can be held in an object of type **short int**. It must be defined to be at least 32,767.

> *Cross-references*
> Standard, §2.2.4.2
> *The C Programming Language*, ed. 2, p. 257

> *See Also*
> **limits.h, numerical limits**

SHRT_MIN — Macro
  (Environment/environmental considerations/limits/numerical)

> **SHRT_MIN** is a macro that is defined in the header **limits.h**. It gives the smallest value that can be held in an object of type **short int**. It must be defined to be at most -32,767.

> *Cross-references*
> Standard, §2.2.4.2
> *The C Programming Language*, ed. 2, p. 257

> *See Also*
> **limits.h, numerical limits**

side effect — Definition
  (Environment/execution environment/program execution)

> A *side effect* is any change to the execution environment that is caused by the program that accesses a volatile object, modifies an object, modifies a file, or calls a function that performs any of these tasks. An expression may generate side effects; a void expression exists just for the side effects it generates.

> *Cross-references*
> Standard, §2.1.2.3
> *The C Programming Language*, ed. 2, p. 53

See Also
program execution, sequence point

sig_atomic_t — Type
(Library/signal handling)
Type that can be updated despite signals

sig_atomic_t is an integral data type that is defined in the header **signal.h**. It defines the type of "atomic" object that can be accessed properly even if an asynchronous interrupt occurs.

The details of what constitutes this type are implementation-specific.

Cross-reference
Standard, §4.7.1

See Also
signal handling, signal.h, volatile

Notes
When declaring objects of this type, you should use the type qualifier **volatile**; for example:

```
volatile sig_atomic_t save_state;
```

The **volatile** declaration tells the translator to re-read the object's value from memory each time it is used in an expression. When the program says to store the object, it should be stored immediately.

SIG_DFL — Macro
(Library/signal handling)
Pointer to default signal-handling function

SIG_DFL is a macro that is defined in the header **signal.h**. It is a special constant that will never be equal to a real function pointer. Although it is cast to be a function pointer, calling it will result in the most unpleasant sort of undefined behavior.

SIG_DFL is passed to the function **signal** to request that default signal handling be performed, and is returned by **signal** to indicate that default signal handling is being performed.

Example
For an example of its use in a program, see **raise**.

Cross-references
Standard, §4.7
The C Programming Language, ed. 2, p. 255

See Also
SIG_ERR, SIG_IGN, signal handling

SIG_ERR – Macro
(Library/signal handling)
Pointer to error-handling function

SIG_ERR is a macro that is defined in the header **signal.h**. It is a special constant that will never be equal to a real function pointer. Though it is cast to be a function pointer, calling it will result in the most unpleasant sort of undefined behavior. It is returned by the function **signal** to indicate that an error prevented the signal request from being honored.

Example
For an example of its use in a program, see **raise**.

Cross-references
Standard, §4.7
The C Programming Language, ed. 2, p. 255

See Also
SIG_DFL, SIG_IGN, signal handling,

SIG_IGN – Macro
(Library/signal handling)
Pointer to function that ignores signals

SIG_IGN is a macro that is defined in the header **signal.h**. It is a special constant that will never be equal to a real function pointer. Although it is cast to be a function pointer, calling it will result in the most unpleasant sort of undefined behavior. It is passed to the function **signal** to request that a signal be ignored, and is returned by **signal** to indicated that a signal is being ignored.

Cross-references
Standard, §4.7
The C Programming Language, ed. 2, p. 255

See Also
SIG_DFL, SIG_IGN, signal handling,

SIGABRT — Macro
(Library/signal handling)
Abort signal

SIGABRT is a macro that is defined in the header **signal.h**. It is an integer that signals that the program is aborting itself.

Cross-references
Standard, §4.7.1
The C Programming Language, ed. 2, p. 255

See Also
raise, SIGFPE, SIGILL, SIGINT, signal, signal handling, SIGSEGV, SIGTERM

SIGFPE — Macro
(Library/signal handling)
Signal error in floating-point arithmetic

SIGFPE is a macro that is defined in the header **signal.h**. Its name stands for "signal floating-point exception." It is an integer that, when detected as a signal, indicates that an error in floating-point arithmetic has occurred.

Depending upon the type and severity of the error, the signal handler might restart the computation with adjusted operands, terminate the computation to seek advice from the user, or abort the process.

Cross-references
Standard, §4.7.1
The C Programming Language, ed. 2, p. 255

See Also
SIGABRT, SIGILL, SIGINT, signal handling, signal.h, SIGSEGV, SIGTERM

SIGILL — Macro
(Library/signal handling)
Illegal instruction signal

SIGILL is a macro that is defined in the header **signal.h**. It is an integer that, when detected as a signal, indicates that an invalid instruction has been encountered. This may be an instruction that is reserved, privileged, or bad.

Cross-references
Standard, §4.7.1
The C Programming Language, ed. 2, p. 255

See Also
SIGABRT, SIGFPE, SIGINT, signal handling, signal.h, SIGSEGV, SIGTERM

SIGINT — Macro
(Library/signal handling)
Process asynchronous interrupt signal

SIGINT is a macro that is defined in the header **signal.h**. It is an integer that, when received as a signal, indicates that the program has received an interrupt. For example, under the MS-DOS operating system, typing **<ctrl-C>** normally causes a program to terminate immediately.

By setting up a handler for the **SIGINT** signal, a program may be able to "catch" this signal and terminate itself gracefully.

Example
For an example of its use in a program, see **raise**.

Cross-references
Standard, §4.7.1
The C Programming Language, ed. 2, p. 255

See Also
SIGABRT, SIGFPE, SIGILL, signal handling, signal.h, SIGSEGV, SIGTERM

signal() — Library function
(Library/signal handling)
Set processing for a signal
#include <signal.h>
void (*signal(int *signame*, **void (****function***)(int)))(int);**

signal is a function that tells the environment what to do when it detects a given interrupt, or "signal." *signame* names the signal to be handled, and *function* points to the signal handler (the function to be executed when *signame* is detected). *signame* may be generated by the environment itself (when it detects an error condition, for example), by the hardware (to indicate a bus error, timer event, or other hardware error condition), or by the program itself (by using the function **raise**).

If **signal** is successful, it returns a pointer to the function that the environment previously used to handle *signame*. If an error occurred, **signal** returns **SIG_ERR** and the global variable **errno** is set to an appropriate value.

signal is commonly used in multi-user environments, such as the UNIX operating system. Each environment has unique requirements, and therefore a unique set of signals to be handled. The Standard describes a skeletal form of **signal** that should be portable to most environments under which C has been implemented. For a list of the signals recognized, see **signal handling**.

signal can establish the following ways of handling a *signame*:

1.   If it sets *function* to **SIG_DFL**, it tells the environment to execute the default signal-handling function for *signame*.

2.   Then, the equivalent of

```
(*function)(signame)
```

is executed, where function is the user-defined function installed with **signal** to handle *signame*.

3.   If it sets *function* to point to a user-defined function, then it tells the environment to execute that function when it detects *signame*.

If **signal** is used to establish a user-defined *function* for a particular signal, then the following occurs when that signal is detected:

1.   The equivalent of

```
signal(signame, SIG_DFL);
```

is executed. If *signame* is equivalent to **SIGILL** (which indicates that an illegal instruction has been found), then this step is optional, depending upon the implementation.

2.   Then, the equivalent of

```
(*function)(signame)
```

is executed, where *function* points to a user-defined function. Some signals are reset to **STD_DFL**, some are not. The exception handler should be reset by another call to **signal** if subsequent signals are expected for that condition.

3.   *function* can terminate either by returning to the calling function, or by calling **abort**, **exit**, or **longjmp**. If *function* returns and *signame* indicates that a computational exception had occurred (e.g., division by zero), then the behavior is undefined. Otherwise, the program which responded to the signal will continue to execute.

Cross-references
Standard, §4.7.1.1
The C Programming Language, ed. 2, p. 255

See Also
raise, signal handling, signal.h

Notes
The signal handler pointed to by *function* should not be another library function.
Also, the signal handler should not attempt to modify external data other than
those declared as type **volatile sig_atomic_t.**

signal.h — Header
(Library/signal handling)
Signal-handling routines
#include <signal.h>

signal.h is the header that defines or declares all elements used to handle
asynchronous interrupts, or *signals.*

Signals vary from environment to environment. Therefore, the contents of **sig-
nal.h** will also vary greatly from environment to environment, and from implementation to implementation. The Standard mandates that it define the following
elements to create a skeletal, portable suite of signal-handling routines:

Type

sig_atomic_t	Type that can be accessed atomically

Macros

SIG_DFL	Default signal-handling indicator
SIG_ERR	Indicate error in setting a signal
SIG_IGN	Indicate ignore a signal
SIGABRT	Abort signal
SIGFPE	Erroneous arithmetic signal
SIGILL	Illegal instruction
SIGINT	Interrupt signal
SIGSEGV	Invalid access to storage signal
SIGTERM	Program termination signal

Functions

raise	Generate a signal
signal	Set processing for a signal

Cross-references
Standard, §4.7
The C Programming Language, ed. 2, p. 255

See Also
signal handling

signal handling — Overview
(Library)
#include <signal.h>

A *signal* is an asynchronous interrupt in a program. Its use allows a program to be notified of and react to external conditions, such as errors that would otherwise force it either to abort or to continue despite erroneous conditions.

To respond to a signal, a program uses a *signal handler*, which is a function that performs the actions appropriate to a given signal. A signal handler usually is installed early in a program. It is invoked either when the condition arises for which the signal handler was installed, or when the program uses the function **raise** to raise a signal explicitly. A signal handler can be thought of as a "daemon," or a process that lives in the background and waits for the right conditions to occur for it to spring to life. Once the signal has been handled, the program may continue to execute.

Every conforming implementation of C must include at least a skeletal facility for handling signals. The Standard describes two functions: **raise**, which generates (or "raises") a signal; and **signal**, which tells the environment what function to execute in response to a given signal.

The suite of signals that can be handled varies from environment to environment. At a minimum, the following signals must be recognized:

SIGABRT	Abort
SIGFPE	Erroneous arithmetic
SIGILL	Illegal instruction
SIGINT	Interrupt
SIGSEGV	Invalid access to storage
SIGTERM	Program termination request

All of these are positive integral expressions. An implementation is obliged to respond only if one of these signals is raised explicitly via the function **raise**. This limitation is imposed because in some environments it may be impossible for an implementation to "sense" the presence of such conditions.

signal tells the environment which function to execute in response to a signal by passing it a pointer to that function. The Standard describes three macros that expand to constant expressions that point to functions, as follows:

SIG_DFL	Default signal-handling indicator
SIG_ERR	Indicate error in setting a signal
SIG_IGN	Indicate ignore a signal

The Standard describes a new data type, called **sig_atomic_t**. An object of this type can be updated or read correctly, even if a signal occurs while it is being updated or read. Accesses to objects of this type are atomic, i.e., uninterruptable.

All of the above are defined or declared in the header **signal.h**.

Cross-references
Standard, §4.7, §2.2.3
The C Programming Language, ed. 2, p. 255

See Also
Library, signal.h, sequence points

Notes
The name *signal* is derived from the electrical model of having a wire connected to the central processing unit for an interrupt. When the level on the wire would rise, an interrupt would be generated and the central processing unit would service the device that "raised" its "signal."

signals/interrupts — Definition
(Environment/environmental considerations)

The Standard mandates the following restrictions upon the manner in which functions are implemented. First, a signal must be able to interrupt a function at any time. Second, a signal handler must be able to call a function without affecting the value of any object with automatic duration created by any earlier invocation of the function. Third, the function image (that is, the set of instructions that constitutes the executable image of the function) cannot be altered in any way as it is executed. All variables must be kept outside of the function image.

Cross-reference
Standard, §2.2.3

See Also
environmental considerations, signal handling

signed — Definition
(Language/lexical elements/identifiers/types)

The modifier **signed** indicates that a data type can contain both positive and negative values. In some representations, the sign of a signed object is indicated by a bit set aside for the purpose. For this reason, a signed object can encode an absolute value only half that of its unsigned counterpart.

The four integral data types can be marked as signed: **char, short int, int**, and **long int**.

The implementation defines whether a **char** is signed or unsigned by default. The Standard describes the types **signed char** and **unsigned char**. These let the programmer use the type of **char** other than that supplied by the implementation. **short int, int**, and **long int** are signed by default; the declarations **signed short int, signed int**, and **signed long int** were created for the sake of symmetry.

For information about converting one type of integer to another, see **integral types**.

If **signed** is used by itself, the translator assumes that it is a synonym for **int**.

Cross-references
Standard, §3.1.2.5, §3.2.1.2
The C Programming Language, ed. 2, p. 211

See Also
integral type, types, unsigned

signed char — Type
(Language/lexical elements/identifiers/types)

A **signed char** is a type that has the same size and the same alignment requirements as a plain **char**. The Standard created this type for implementations whose **char** type is unsigned by default.

A **signed char** can encode values from **SCHAR_MIN** to **SCHAR_MAX**. These are macros that are defined in the header **limits.h**. The former must be set to at most -127, and the latter to at least +127.

Cross-references
Standard, §2.2.4.2, §3.1.2.5, §3.5.2
The C Programming Language, ed. 2, p. 44

See Also
char, types, unsigned char

SIGSEGV — Macro
(Library/signal handling)
Signal invalid reference to memory

SIGSEGV is a macro that is defined in the header **signal.h**. It is an integral constant expression that, when received as a signal, indicates that storage has been accessed illegally. This can be an illegal address, an odd address, non-existent memory, or an access violation.

Cross-references
Standard, §4.7.1
The C Programming Language, ed. 2, p. 255

See Also
SIGABRT, SIGFPE, SIGILL, signal handling, signal.h, SIGTERM

Notes
The name **SIGSEGV** comes from the phrase "signal segmentation violation." It is historical, and derives from machines with segmented architecture.

SIGTERM — Macro
(Library/signal handling)
Program-termination signal

SIGTERM is a macro defined in the header **signal.h**. It is an integral constant expression that, when received as a signal, indicates that the program has been ordered to terminate itself immediately.

Cross-references
Standard, §4.7.1
The C Programming Language, ed. 2, p. 255

See Also
SIGABRT, SIGFPE, SIGILL, SIGINT, signal handling, signal.h, SIGSEGV

sin() — Library function
(Library/mathematics/trigonometric functions)
Calculate sine
#include < math.h >
double sin(double *radian***);**

sin calculates and returns the sine of its argument *radian*, which must be in radian measure.

Example

This examples checks the accuracy of **sin** and **cos** on your implementation. It verifies the identity **sin(2*x) = = 2*sin(x)*cos(x)** over a range of values. Then, it scans the range of the worst error in smaller and smaller increments, until the precision of your implementation's floating point will not allow any more.

```
#include <float.h>
#include <math.h>
#include <stddef.h>
#include <stdio.h>
#include <stdlib.h>
#define PI 0.31415926535897932e+01

main(void)
{
    int ct;
    double a, e, i, worstp;
    double worste=0.0;
    double f=-PI;

    printf("Verify sin(2*x) == 2*sin(x)*cos(x)\n");
    for(i = (PI / 100.0); (f + i) > f; i *= 0.01) {
        for(ct = 200, a = f; --ct; a += i) {
            e = fabs(sin(a+a)-(2.0*sin(a)*cos(a)));
            if(e > worste) {
                worste = e;
                worstp = a;
            }
        }
        f = worstp - i;
    }

    printf("Worst error %.17e at %.17e\n", worste, worstp);
    printf("sin(2x)=%.17e 2*sin(x)*cos(x)=%.17e\n",
        f=sin(worstp+worstp), 2.0*sin(worstp)*cos(worstp));
    printf("Epsilon is %.17e\n", fabs(f) * DBL_EPSILON);
    return(EXIT_SUCCESS);
}
```

Cross-references

Standard, §4.5.2.6
The C Programming Language, ed. 2, p. 251

408 sinh() — size_t

See Also
acos, asin, atan, atan2, cos, tan, trigonometric functions

sinh() — Library function
(Library/mathematics/hyperbolic functions)
Calculate hyperbolic sine
#include < math.h >
double sinh(double *value*);

sinh calculates and returns the hyperbolic sine of *value*. A range error will occur if the argument is too large.

Cross-references
Standard, §4.5.3.2
The C Programming Language, ed. 2, p. 251

See Also
cosh, hyperbolic functions, tanh

size_t — Type
(Library)
Type returned by sizeof operator
#include < stddef.h >

size_t is a type that is defined in the header **stddef.h**. It is the unsigned integral type returned by the operator **sizeof**. This must be an existing integral type; thus, it cannot be larger than an **unsigned long**.

size_t sets a limit on the number of elements that can be placed in an array. For any array *X* with *n* elements, the following must be true:

```
n == sizeof(X)/sizeof(X[0]);
```

Cross-references
Standard, §3.3.3.4, §4.1.5
The C Programming Language, ed. 2, p. 135

See Also
Library, sizeof, stddef.h

Notes
If an implementation defines **sizeof** as returning anything other than an **int**, then code that assumes that **sizeof** returns an **int** will not work.

The Standard lists **size_t** as being declared in both **stddef.h** and **stdlib.h**.

sizeof — C keyword
(Language/expressions/unary operators)

The operator **sizeof** yields the size of its argument, in bytes. Its argument can be the name of a type, an array, a function, a structure, or an expression that yields an object.

When the name of a type is used as the operand to **sizeof**, it must be enclosed within parentheses. If any of the types **char**, **signed char**, or **unsigned char** are used as the argument to **sizeof**, the result by definition is always one. When any complete type is used (i.e., a type whose size is known by the translator), the result is the size of that type, in bytes. For example,

```
sizeof (long double);
```

returns the size of a **long double** in bytes.

If **sizeof** is given the name of an array, it returns the size of the array. For example, the code

```
int example[5];
     . . . /* example[] is filled with some things */
sizeof example[] / sizeof int;
```

yields the number of members in **example[]**.

When **sizeof** is given the name of a structure or a **union**, it returns the size of that object, including padding used to align the objects within the structure, if any. This is especially useful when allocating memory for a linked list; for example:

```
struct example {
    int member1;
    example *member2;
};
struct example *variable;
variable=(struct example *)malloc(sizeof(struct example));
```

If **sizeof** is used to measure either a function or an array that has been passed as an argument to a function, it returns the size of a *pointer* to the appropriate object. This is because when an array name or function name is passed as an argument to a function, it is converted to a pointer. See **function definition** for more information.

sizeof always returns an object of type **size_t**; this type is defined in the header **stddef.h**. It is intended to be an unsigned integral type.

sizeof must not be used with a function, with an object whose type is incomplete, or a bit-field.

Example

For an example of using this operator in a program, see **bsearch**.

Cross-references

Standard, §3.3.3.4
The C Programming Language, ed. 2, p. 204

See Also

expressions, operators, size_t, unary operators

source file — Definition
(Environment/translation environment)

A *source file* is any file of C source text.

Cross-reference

Standard, §2.1.1.1

See Also

translation environment, translation unit

spirit of C — Definition
(Rationale)

The term *spirit of C* refers to the programming principles that underlie C. These principles are not formally defined, but the ANSI committee gave much thought to preserving the spirit of C as it drew up the Standard.

The Rationale offers the following mottoes as expressing part of the spirit of C:

- "Trust the programmer."

- "Don't prevent the programmer from doing what needs to be done."

- "Keep the language small and simple."

- "Provide only one way to do an operation."

- "Make it fast, even if it is not guaranteed to be portable."

The last motto means that the Standard will not prevent the programmer from writing code that is tailored to a particular machine's architecture.

The Standard invokes the spirit of C on numerous occasions. Like all matters spiritual, the spirit of C is not easily defined. C has traditionally been considered a "structured assembly language". The Committee sought to keep the language flexible enough for low-level machine-specific code, yet give users a "fighting chance" to write truly portable code.

Cross-reference
Rationale, §1.1

See Also
as if rule, Rationale

sprintf() — Library function
(Library/STDIO/input-output)
Print formatted text into a string
#include <stdio.h>
int sprintf(char *_string_, const char *_format_, ...);

sprintf constructs a formatted string in the area pointed to by *string*, and appends a null character onto the end of what it constructs. It translates integers, floating-point numbers, and strings into a variety of text formats.

format points to a string that can contain text, character constants, and one or more *conversion specifications*. A conversion specification describes how to convert a particular data type into text. Each conversion specification is introduced with the percent sign '%'. (To print a literal percent sign, use the escape sequence "%%".) See **printf** for further discussion of the conversion specification, and for a table of the type specifiers that can be used with **sprintf**.

After *format* can come one or more arguments. There should be one argument for each conversion specification in *format*. The argument should be of the type appropriate to the conversion specification. For example, if *format* contains conversion specifications for an **int**, a **long**, and a string, then *format* should be followed by three arguments, respectively, an **int**, a **long**, and a **char ***.

If there are fewer arguments than conversion specifications, then **sprintf**'s behavior is undefined. If there are more, then every argument without a corresponding conversion specification is evaluated and then ignored. If an argument is not of the same type as its corresponding conversion specifier, then the behavior of **sprintf** is undefined. Thus, presenting an **int** where **sprintf** expects a **char *** may generate unwelcome results.

sprintf returns the number of characters written into *string*, not counting the terminating null.

Cross-references
Standard, §4.9.6.5
The C Programming Language, ed. 2, p. 245

See Also
fprintf, fscanf, input-output, printf, scanf, sscanf, vfprintf, vprintf, vsprintf

Notes

string must point to enough allocated memory to hold the string **sprintf** constructs, or you may overwrite unallocated memory.

The Standard does not include the conversion specifier 'r', which is used by many implementations to pass an array of arguments to **sprintf**. To achieve the functionality of the 'r' specifier, use **vsprintf**.

The character that **sprintf** uses to represent the decimal point is affected by the program's locale, as set by the function **setlocale**. For more information, see **localization**.

sqrt() — Library function
(Library/mathematics/power functions)

Calculate the square root of a number
#include < math.h >
double sqrt(double *z*);

sqrt calculates and returns the square root of *z*.

Example

This example calculates the time an object takes to fall to the ground at sea level. It ignores air friction and the inverse square law.

```
#include <errno.h>
#include <math.h>
#include <stdio.h>
#include <stdlib.h>

double
fallingTime(double meters)
{
        double time;
```

```
        errno = 0;
        time = sqrt(meters * 2 / 9.8);
        /*
         * it would be simpler to test for (meters < 0) first,
         * but this way shows how sqrt() sets errno
         */
        if(errno) {
            printf("Sorry, but you can't fall up\n");
            return(HUGE_VAL);
        }
        return(time);
}

main(void)
{
    for(;;) {
        char buf[80];
        double height;

        printf("Enter height in meters ");
        fflush(stdout);
        if(gets(buf) == NULL || !strcmp(buf, "quit"))
            break;

        errno = 0;
        height = strtod(buf, (char **)NULL);

        if(errno) {
            printf("%s: invalid floating-point number\n");
            continue;
        }

        printf("It takes %3.2f sec. to fall %3.2f meters\n",
            fallingTime(height), height);

    }

    return(EXIT_SUCCESS);
}
```

Cross-references
Standard, §4.5.5.2
The C Programming Language, ed. 2, p. 251

See Also
domain error, pow, power functions

Notes
If *z* is negative, a domain error occurs.

srand() — Library function
  (Library/general utilities/pseudo-random numbers)
Seed pseudo-random number generator
#include <stdlib>
void srand(unsigned int *seed*);

srand uses *seed* to initialize the sequence of pseudo-random numbers returned by
rand. Different values of *seed* produce different sequences.

Example
This example uses the random-number generator to encrypt or decrypt a file. This
example is for illustration only. Do *not* use it if any serious attack is expected.
This example also demonstrates a simple form of hashing.

```
#include <stdio.h>
#include <stdlib.h>

/* Ask for a string and echo it. */
char *
ask(char *msg)
{
     static char reply[80];

     printf("Enter %s ", msg);
     fflush(stdout);

     if(gets(reply) == NULL)
          exit(EXIT_SUCCESS);
     return(reply);
}

main(void)
{
     register char *kp;
     register int c, seed;
     FILE *ifp, *ofp;

     if((ifp = fopen(ask("input filename"), "rb")) == NULL)
          exit(EXIT_FAILURE);
     if((ofp = fopen(ask("output filename"), "wb")) == NULL)
          exit(EXIT_FAILURE);
```

```
     /* hash encryption key into an int */
     seed = 0;
     for(kp = ask("encryption key"); c = *kp++; ) {
         /* don't lose any bits */
         if((seed <<= 1) < 0)
             /* a number picked at random */
             seed ^= 0xE51B;
         seed ^= c;
     }

     /* initialize random-number stream */
     srand(seed);

     while((c = fgetc(ifp)) != EOF)
         /*
          * Use only the high byte of rand;
          * its low-order bits are very non-random
          */
         fputc(c ^ (rand() >> 8), ofp);

     return(EXIT_SUCCESS);
}
```

Cross-references
Standard, §4.10.2.2
The C Programming Language, ed. 2, p. 252

See Also
pseudo-random numbers, rand

sscanf() — Library function
(Library/STDIO/input-output)
Read and interpret text from a string
#include < stdio.h >
int sscanf(const char ***string, const char ***format**, ...);**

sscanf reads characters from *string* and uses the string pointed to by *format* to interpret what it has read into the appropriate type of data. *format* points to a string that contains one or more conversion specifications, each of which is introduced with the percent sign '%'. For a table of the conversion specifiers that can be used with **sscanf**, see **scanf**.

After *format* can come one or more arguments. There should be one argument for each conversion specification in *format*, and the argument should point to a data element of the type appropriate to the conversion specification. For example, if *format* contains conversion specifications for an **int**, a **long**, and a string, then *format* should be followed by three arguments, pointing, respectively, to an **int**, a **long**, and an array of **chars**.

If there are fewer arguments than conversion specifications, then **sscanf**'s behavior is undefined. If there are more, then every argument without a corresponding conversion specification is evaluated and then ignored. If an argument is not of the same type as its corresponding type specification, then **sscanf** returns.

sscanf returns the number of input elements it scanned and formatted. If an error occurs while **sscanf** is reading its input, it returns **EOF**.

Example
This example reads a list of hexadecimal numbers from the standard input and adds them.

```
#include <stddef.h>
#include <stdio.h>
#include <stdlib.h>
#include <string.h>

main(void)
{
    long h[5], total;
    char buf[80];
    int  count, i;

    printf("Enter a list of up to five hex numbers or quit\n");
    while(gets(buf) != NULL) {
        if(!strcmp("quit", buf))
            break;
        count = sscanf(buf, "%lx %lx %lx %lx %lx",
            h, h+1, h+2, h+3, h+4);

        for(i = total = 0; i < count; i++)
            total += h[i];
        printf("Total 0x%lx %ld\n", total, total);
    }

    return(EXIT_SUCCESS);
}
```

Cross-references
Standard, §4.9.6.6
The C Programming Language, ed. 2, p. 246

See Also
fscanf, input-output, printf, scanf

Notes
sscanf is best used to read data you are certain are in the correct format, such as data previously written with **sprintf**.

The character that **sscanf** recognizes as representing the decimal point is affected by the program's locale, as set by the function **setlocale**. For more information, see **localization**.

Standard — Overview

The *Standard* is the document written by the American National Standards Institute committee X3J11 to describe the programming language C. It is based on the following documents:

- Kernighan, B. W., Ritchie, D. M.: *The C Programming Language*. Englewood Cliffs, NJ: Prentice-Hall Inc., 1978. The Standard bases its description of C syntax upon Appendix A of this book.

- /usr/group Standard Committee: *1984 /usr/group Standard*. Santa Clara, Calif.: /usr/group, 1984. This document was the basis for the Standard's description of the C library.

- *American National Dictionary for Information Processing Systems*. Information Processing Systems Technical Report ANSI X3/TR-1-82. 1982.

- ISO 646-1983 Invariant Code Set. This was used to help describe the C character set, and to select the characters that need to be represented by trigraphs.

- *IEEE Standard for Binary Floating-Point Arithmetic*. ANSI/IEEE Standard 754-1985. This is the basis for the Standard's description of floating-point numbers.

- ISO 4217 Codes for Representation of Currency and Funds. This is the target for the Standard's description of locale-specific ways to represent money.

The first two, due to their fundamental effect upon the Standard, are referred to as the "base documents".

Using this Lexicon
The Standard itself is organized into chapters, sections, and sub-sections.

This Lexicon re-describes the Standard to clarify what the Standard says and make the Standard more accessible to programmers. The Lexicon's logical structure follows closely that of the Standard. For an overview of the Lexicon's logical structure, see Appendix A. Unlike the Standard, however, this Lexicon discusses each topic in a separate article and presents all of the articles in alphabetical order. This makes it much easier for you to find the discussion of any given topic.

Each article shows its place in the Lexicon in two ways. First, the header for each article (except this one) gives a "path name", which indicates the article's place in the Lexicon's logical structure. Second, each article cross-references articles on related topics. By following either the path name or the cross-references, you can move from any article within the Lexicon to any other.

Cross-reference
Standard, §1.3, §1.5

See Also
Definitions, Environment, Language, Library, Rationale

Notes
The description of the Standard contained in this manual is based on the draft of January 11, 1988, which is the second Public Review of the draft. At this time of this writing, the Standard has not yet been released officially, nor have all topics been resolved. If a topic has not yet been resolved, its article will warn you of that fact.

standard error — Definition
(Library/STDIO)

When a C program begins, it opens three text streams by default: the standard error, the standard input, and the standard output. The *standard error* is the stream into which error messages are written. In most implementations, the standard error stream is associated with the user's terminal.

The macro **stderr** points to the **FILE** object through which the standard error device is accessed. It is defined in the header **stdio.h**.

Cross-references
Standard, §4.9.3
The C Programming Language, ed. 2, pp. 151*ff*

See Also
standard input, standard output, std‑rr, STDIO

standard input — Definition
(Library/STDIO)

When a C program begins execution, it opens three text streams by default: the standard error, the standard input, and the standard output. The *standard input* is the stream from which the program receives input by default. In most implementations, the standard input stream is associated with the user's terminal.

The macro **stdin** points to the **FILE** object that accesses the standard input stream. It is defined in the header **stdio.h**.

Cross-references
Standard, §4.9.3
The C Programming Language, ed. 2, pp. 151*ff*

See Also
standard error, standard output, stdin, STDIO

standard output — Definition
(Library/STDIO)

When a C program begins execution, it opens three text streams by default: the standard output, the standard input, and the standard error. The *standard output* is the stream into which a program's non-diagnostic output is written. In most implementations, the standard output stream is associated with the user's terminal.

The macro **stdout** points to the **FILE** object that accesses the standard output device. It is defined in the header **stdio.h**.

Cross-references
Standard, §4.9.3
The C Programming Language, ed. 2, pp. 151*ff*

See Also
standard error, standard input, STDIO, stdout

statements — Overview
(Language)

A *statement* specifies an action to be performed. Unless otherwise specified, statements are executed in the order in which they appear in the program.

The actions of some statements may be controlled by a *full expression*; this is an expression that is not part of another expression. For example, **do, if, for, switch,** and **while** introduce statements that are controlled by one or more full expressions. The **return** statement may also use a full expression.

The Standard describes the following varieties of statements:

Compound statement

Expression statement

Iteration statements
> **do**
> **for**
> **while**

Jump statements
> **break**
> **continue**
> **goto**
> **return**

Labelled statements
> **case**
> **default**

Null statement

Selection statements
> **if**
> **else**
> **switch**

The set of compound, iteration, and selection statements is the foundation upon which many programming languages are based. From these alone, a programmer can construct many useful and interesting programs.

Cross-references
Standard, §3.6
The C Programming Language, ed. 2, pp. 222*ff*

See Also
Language

static — C keyword
(Language/declarations/storage-class specifiers)
Internal linkage
static *type identifier*

The storage-class specifier **static** declares that *identifier* has internal linkage. This specifier may not be used to declare a function that has block scope.

Cross-references
Standard, §3.5.1
The C Programming Language, ed. 2, p. 83

See Also
linkage, storage-class identifiers

stdarg.h — Header
(Library/variable arguments)
Header for variable numbers of arguments
#include < stdarg.h >

The header **stdarg.h** declares and defines routines that are used to traverse a variable-length argument list. It declares the type **va_list** and the function **va_end**, and it defines the macros **va_start** and **va_arg**.

Cross-references
Standard, §4.8
The C Programming Language, ed. 2, p. 254

See Also
header, variable arguments

stddef.h — Header
(Library)
Header for standard definitions
#include < stddef.h >

The header **stddef.h** defines three types and one macro that are used through the library. They are as follows:

NULL	Null pointer
offsetof	Offset of a field within a structure
ptrdiff_t	Numeric difference between two pointers
size_t	Type returned by **sizeof** operator
wchar_t	Typedef for wide **chars**

Cross-reference
Standard, §4.1.5

See Also
header, Library

stderr — Macro
(Library/STDIO)
Pointer to standard error stream
#include < stdio.h >

When a C program begins, it opens three text streams by default: the standard error, the standard input, and the standard output. **stderr** points to the **FILE** object through which the standard error stream is accessed; this is the stream into which error messages are written. In most implementations, the standard error stream is associated with the user's terminal.

stderr is defined in the header **stdio.h**.

stderr is not fully buffered when it is opened.

Example
For an example of **stderr** in a program, see **fprintf**.

Cross-references
Standard, §4.9.1, §4.9.3
The C Programming Language, ed. 2, p. 243

See Also
stdin, stdout, standard error, STDIO, stdio.h

stdin — Macro
(Library/STDIO)
Pointer to standard input stream
#include < stdio.h >

When a C program begins, it opens three text streams by default: the standard error, the standard input, and the standard output. **stdin** points to the **FILE** object that accesses the standard input stream; this is the stream from which the program receives input by default. In most implementations, the standard input stream is associated with the user's terminal.

stdin is defined in the header **stdio.h**.

Example
For an example of **stdin** in a program, see **setvbuf**.

Cross-references
Standard, §4.9.1, §4.9.3
The C Programming Language, ed. 2, p. 243

See Also
stderr, stdout, standard input, STDIO, stdio.h

STDIO — Overview
(Library)
Standard input and output
#include < stdio.h >

STDIO is an acronym for *standard input and output*. Input-output can be performed on text files, binary files, or interactive devices. It can be either buffered or unbuffered.

The Standard describes 41 functions that perform input and output, as follows:

Error handling
clearerr	Clear a stream's error indicator
feof	Examine a stream's end-of-file indicator
ferror	Examine a stream's error indicator
perror	Write error message into standard error stream

File access
fclose	Close a stream
fflush	Flush an output stream's buffer
fopen	Open a stream
freopen	Close and reopen a stream
setbuf	Set an alternate buffer for a stream
setvbuf	Set an alternate buffer for a stream

File operations
remove	Remove a file
rename	Rename a file
tmpfile	Create a temporary file
tmpnam	Generate a unique name for a temporary file

File positioning
fgetpos	Get value of stream's file-position indicator (**fpos_t**)
fseek	Set stream's file-position indicator
fsetpos	Set stream's file-position indicator (**fpos_t**)
ftell	Get the value of the file-position indicator
rewind	Reset stream's file-position indicator

Input-output
    By character

fgetc	Read a character from a stream
fgets	Read a line from a stream
fputc	Write a character into a stream
fputs	Write a string into a stream
getc	Read a character from a stream
getchar	Read a character from the standard input stream
gets	Read a string from the standard input stream
putc	Write character into a stream
putchar	Write a character into the standard output
puts	Write a string into the standard output
ungetc	Push a character back into the input stream

    Direct

fread	Read data from a stream
fwrite	Write data into a stream

    Formatted

fprintf	Print formatted text into a stream
fscanf	Read formatted text from a stream
printf	Format and print text into standard output stream
scanf	Read formatted text from standard input stream
sprintf	Print formatted text into a string
sscanf	Read formatted text from string
vfprintf	Format and print text into a stream
vprintf	Format and print text into standard output stream
vsprintf	Format and print text into a string

The prototypes for these functions appear in the header **stdio.h**, along with definitions for the types and macros they use.

The Standard does not mention the low-level functions **read**, **write**, **open**, **close**, and **lseek**. The Committee concluded that these functions were too implementation-specific to be included within the Standard. Implementations may still support these functions as extensions to the Standard. However, programs that use them are not guaranteed to be portable to every implementation of ANSI C.

All STDIO functions access a file or device through a *stream*. A stream is accessed via an object of type **FILE**; this object contains all of the information needed to access the file or device under the given environment. Because of the heterogeneous environments under which C has been implemented, the Standard does not describe the interior workings of the **FILE** object. It states only that this object contain all information needed to access a stream under the given environment.

Cross-references
Standard, §4.9
The C Programming Language, ed. 2, pp. 151*ff*, 241*ff*

See Also
close, create, file, file-position indicator, Library, line, open, stdio.h, stream

stdio.h — Header
(Library/STDIO)
Declarations and definitions for STDIO

stdio.h is the header that holds the definitions, declarations, and function prototypes used by the STDIO routines.

The following lists the types, macros, and functions defined in **stdio.h**:

Types
FILE	Hold descriptor for a stream
fpos_t	Hold current position within a file

Macros
_IOFBF	Indicates stream is fully buffered
_IOLBF	Indicates stream is line-buffered
_IONBF	Indicates stream is unbuffered
BUFSIZ	Default size of buffer for STDIO stream
EOF	Indicates end of file when returned by STDIO routine
FILENAME_MAX	Maximum length of a file name, in bytes
FOPEN_MAX	Maximum number of files that can be opened at once
L_tmpnam	Maximum length of temporary file name, in bytes
SEEK_CUR	Seek from current position (**fseek**)
SEEK_END	Seek from the end of a file (**fseek**)
SEEK_SET	Seek from beginning of a file (**fseek**)
stderr	Pointer to standard error stream
stdin	Pointer to standard input stream
stdout	Pointer to standard output stream
TMP_MAX	Maximum number of calls to **tmpnam**

Functions
clearerr	Clear a stream's error indicator
fclose	Close a stream
feof	Examine a stream's end-of-file indicator
ferror	Examine a stream's error indicator
fflush	Flush an output stream's buffer
fgetc	Read a character from a stream

fgetpos	Get value of stream's file-position indicator (**fpos_t**)
fgets	Read a line from a stream
fopen	Open a stream
fprintf	Print formatted text into a stream
fputc	Write a character into a stream
fputs	Write a string into a stream
fread	Read data from a stream
freopen	Close and reopen a stream
fscanf	Read formatted text from a stream
fseek	Set stream's file-position indicator
fsetpos	Set stream's file-position indicator (**fpos_t**)
ftell	Get the value of the file-position indicator
fwrite	Write data into a stream
getc	Read a character from a stream
getchar	Read a character from the standard input stream
gets	Read a string from the standard input stream
perror	Write error message into standard error stream
printf	Format and print text into standard output stream
putc	Write character into a stream
putchar	Write a character into the standard output stream
puts	Write a string into the standard output stream
remove	Remove a file
rename	Rename a file
rewind	Reset stream's file-position indicator
scanf	Read formatted text from standard input stream
setbuf	Set an alternate buffer for a stream
setvbuf	Set an alternate buffer for a stream
sprintf	Print formatted text into a string
sscanf	Read formatted text from string
tmpfile	Create a temporary file
tmpnam	Generate a unique name for a temporary file
ungetc	Push a character back into the input stream
vfprintf	Format and print text into a stream
vprintf	Format and print text into standard output stream
vsprintf	Format and print text into a string

Cross-references

Standard, §4.9.1
The C Programming Language, ed. 2, pp. 151*ff*, 241*ff*

See Also
header, STDIO

stdlib.h — Header

(Library/general utilities)
General utilities
#include <stdlib.h>

stdlib.h is a header that declares the Standard's set of general utilities and defines attending macros and data types, as follows:

Types

div_t	Type of object returned by **div**
ldiv_t	Type of object returned by **ldiv**

Macros

EXIT_FAILURE	Value to indicate that program failed to execute properly
EXIT_SUCCESS	Value to indicate that program executed properly
MB_CUR_MAX	Largest size of multibyte character in current locale
MB_LEN_MAX	Largest overall size of multibyte character in any locale
RAND_MAX	Largest size of pseudo-random number

Functions

abort	End program immediately
abs	Compute the absolute value of an integer
atexit	Register a function to be executed at exit
atof	Convert string to floating-point number
atoi	Convert string to integer
atol	Convert string to long integer
bsearch	Search an array
calloc	Allocate dynamic memory
div	Perform integer division
exit	Terminate a program gracefully
free	De-allocate dynamic memory to free memory pool
getenv	Read environmental variable
labs	Compute the absolute value of a long integer
ldiv	Perform long integer division
malloc	Allocate dynamic memory
mblen	Compute length of a multibyte character
mbstowcs	Convert multibyte-character sequence to wide characters
mbtowc	Convert multibyte character to wide character

qsort	Sort an array
rand	Generate pseudo-random numbers
realloc	Reallocate dynamic memory
strtod	Convert string to floating-point number
strtol	Convert string to long integer
strtoul	Convert string to unsigned long integer
system	Suspend a program and execute another
wcstombs	Convert wide-character sequence to multibyte characters
wctomb	Convert wide character to multibyte character

Cross-references
Standard, §4.10.1
The C Programming Language, ed. 2, p. 251

See Also
general utilities

stdout — Macro
(Library/STDIO)
Pointer to standard output stream
#include <stdio.h>

When a C program begins, it opens three text streams by default: the standard error, the standard input, and the standard output. **stdout** points to the **FILE** object that accesses the standard output stream; this is the stream into which non-diagnostic output is written. In most implementations, the standard output stream is associated with the user's terminal.

stdout is defined in the header **stdio.h**.

Example
For an example of **stdout** in a program, see **setvbuf**.

Cross-references
Standard, §4.9.1, §4.9.3
The C Programming Language, ed. 2, p. 243

See Also
stdin, stderr, standard output, STDIO, stdio.h

storage-class specifiers — Overview
(Language/declarations)

A *storage-class specifier* specifies the manner in which an object is to be stored in memory. There are five such specifiers:

auto	Automatic storage duration
extern	External linkage
register	Quick access required
static	Internal linkage
typedef	Synonym for another type

Only one storage-class specifier is allowed per declaration. The Standard declares as "obsolescent" any declaration that does not have its storage class as the first specifier in a declaration.

Strictly speaking, **typedef** is not a storage-class specifier. The Standard bundles it into this group for the sake of convenience.

Cross-references
Standard, §3.5.1
The C Programming Language, ed. 2, p. 210

See Also
declarations, storage class, storage duration

storage duration — Definition
(Language/lexical elements/identifiers)

The term *storage duration* refers to how long a given object is retained within memory. There are two varieties of storage duration: *static* and *automatic*.

An object with static storage duration is retained throughout program execution. Its storage is reserved, and the object is initialized only when the program begins execution. All string literals have static duration, as do all objects that are declared globally — that is, declared outside of any function.

An object with automatic duration is declared within a block of code. It endures within memory only for the life of that block of code. Memory is allocated for the variable whenever that block is entered and deallocated when the block is terminated, either by encountering the '}' that closes the block, or by exiting the block with **goto**, **longjmp**, or **return**.

A common practice is to declare all automatic variables at the beginning of a function. These variables endure as long as the function is operating. If the function calls another function, then these functions are stored away (usually in an special area of memory called the "stack"), but they cannot be accessed until the called function returns.

Automatic variables can be allocated on a stack, a heap, or in machine registers. Function parameters, as well as objects declared within a function, are automatic. Some mainframe systems do not have a stack; on these machines, variables with automatic storage reside in a separate area of memory.

Cross-references
Standard, §3.1.2.4
The C Programming Language, ed. 2, p. 195

See Also
auto, identifiers, scope, static

strcat() — Library function
(Library/string handling/string concatenation)
Append one string onto another
char *strcat(char **string1***, const char ****string2***)**

strcat copies all characters in *string2*, including the terminating null character, onto the end of the string pointed to by *string1*. The null character at the end of *string1* is overwritten by the first character of *string2*.

strcat returns the pointer *string1*.

Example
The following example concatenates two strings.

```
#include <stdio.h>
#include <string.h>

char string1[80] = "The first string. ";
char string2[] = "The second string.";

main(void)
{
    printf("result = %s\n", strcat(string1, string2));
    return(EXIT_SUCCESS);
}
```

Cross-references
Standard, §4.11.3.1
The C Programming Language, ed. 2, p. 250

See Also
string concatenation, strncat

Notes
string1 should point to enough reserved memory to hold itself and *string2*; otherwise, data or code will be overwritten.

strchr() — Library function
(Library/string handling/string searching)
Find a character in a string
#include < string.h >
char *strchr(const char ***string, int** *character***);**

strchr searches for *character* within *string*. The null character at the end of *string* is included within the search. Internally, **strchr** converts *character* from an **int** to a **char** before searching for it within *string*.

strchr returns a pointer to the first occurrence of *character* within *string*; if *character* is not found, it returns NULL.

Example
The following example creates functions called **replace** and **trim. replace** finds and replaces every occurrence of an item within a string and returns the altered string. **trim** removes all trailing spaces from a string, and returns a pointer to the altered string.

```
#include <stdlib.h>
#include <stddef.h>
#include <string.h>
#include <stdio.h>

char *
replace(char *string, char item, char newitem)
{
    char *start;

    /* replacing 0 is too dangerous */
    if ((start = string) == NULL || item == '\0')
        return(start);
    while ((string = strchr(string, item)) != NULL)
        *string = newitem;
    return(start);
}
```

```
char *
trim(char * str)
{
     register char *endp;

     if(str == NULL)
          return(str);

     /* start at end of string while in string and spaces */
     for(endp  = strchr(str, '\0');
         endp != str && *--endp == ' '; )
          *endp = '\0';
     return(str);
}
char string1[] = "Remove trailing spaces          ";
char string2[] = "Spaces become dashes.";
main(void)
{
     printf("\"%s\"\n", trim(string1));
     printf("%s\n", replace(string2, ' ', '-'));
     return(EXIT_SUCCESS);
}
```

Cross-references
Standard, §4.11.5.2
The C Programming Language, ed. 2, p. 249

See Also
memchr, strcspn, string searching, strpbrk, strrchr, strspn, strstr, strtok

Notes
This is equivalent to the function **index**, which is described in the first edition of *The C Programming Language*, page 67.

strcmp() — Library function
(Library/string handling/string comparison)
Compare two strings
#include < string.h >
int strcmp(const char **string1**, const char ****string2**)**

strcmp lexicographically compares the string pointed to by *string1* with the one pointed to by *string2*. Comparison ends when a null character is encountered.

strcmp compares the two strings character by character until it finds a pair of characters that are not identical. It returns a number less than zero if the character in *string1* is less (i.e,. occurs earlier in the character table) than its counterpart in *string2*. It returns a number greater than zero if the character in *string1* is greater (i.e,. occurs later in the character table) than its counterpart in *string2*. If no characters are found to differ, then the strings are identical and **strcmp** returns zero.

Example
For an example of this function, see **fflush**.

Cross-references
Standard, §4.11.4.2
The C Programming Language, ed. 2, p. 250

See Also
memcmp, strcmp, strcoll, string comparison, strncmp, strxfrm

Notes
strcmp differs from the memory-comparison routine **memcmp** in the following ways:

First, **strcmp** compares strings rather than areas of memory; therefore, it stops when it encounters a null character.

Second, **memcmp** takes two pointers to **void**, whereas **strcmp** takes two pointers to **char**. The following code illustrates how this difference affects these functions:

```
char carray[10];
int iarray[10];
char *s = "hi";
    . . .
strcmp(carray, s)      /* RIGHT */
memcmp(carray, s, 3)   /* RIGHT */
strcmp(iarray, s)      /* WRONG, 1st arg not char * */
memcmp(iarray, s, 3)   /* RIGHT, args cast to void * */
```

It is wrong to use **strcmp** to compare an **int** array with a **char** array, because this function compares strings. Using **memcmp** to compare an **int** array with a **char** array is permissible because **memcmp** simply compares areas of data.

strcoll() — Library function
(Library/string handling/string comparison)
Compare two strings, using locale-specific information
#include < string.h >
int strcoll(const char *string1, const char *string2);

strcoll lexicographically compares the string pointed to by *string1* with one pointed to by *string2*. Comparison ends when a null character is read. **strcoll** differs from *strcmp* in that it uses information concerning the program's locale, as set by the function **setlocale**, to help compare strings. It can be used to provide locale-specific collating. See **localization** for more information about setting a program's locale.

strcoll compares the two strings character by character until it finds a pair of characters that are not identical. It returns a number less than zero if the character in *string1* is less (i.e,. occurs earlier in the character table) than its counterpart in *string2*. It returns a number greater than zero if the character in *string1* is greater (i.e,. occurs later in the character table) than its counterpart in *string2*. If no characters are found to differ, then the strings are identical and **strcoll** returns zero.

Cross-references
Standard, §4.11.4.3
The C Programming Language, ed. 2, p. 250

See Also
localization, memcmp, strcmp, string comparison, strncmp, strxfrm

Notes
The string-comparison routines **strcoll**, **strcmp**, and **strncmp** differ from the memory-comparison routine **memcmp** in that they compare strings rather than regions of memory; they stop when they encounter a null character, but **memcmp** does not. **memcmp** performs the same when run on ASCII or EBCDIC machines, whereas the string-comparison routines do not.

strcpy() — Library function
    (Library/string handling/string copying)
    Copy one string into another
    #include <string.h>
    char *strcpy(char *string1, const char *string2)

strcpy copies the string pointed to by *string2*, including the null character, into the area pointed to by *string1*.

strcpy returns *string1*.

Example
For an example of this function, see **realloc**.

Cross-references
Standard, §4.11.2.3
The C Programming Language, ed. 2, p. 249

See Also
memcpy, memset, string copying, strncpy

Notes
If the region of memory pointed to by *string1* overlaps with the string pointed to by *string2*, the behavior of **strcpy** is undefined.

string1 should point to enough reserved memory to hold *string2*, or code or data will be overwritten.

strcspn() — Library function
(Library/string handling/string searching)
Return length for which one string excludes characters in another
#include < string.h >
size_t strcspn(const char **string1***, const char ****string2***)**

strcspn compares *string1* with *string2*. It then returns the length, in characters, for which *string1* consists of characters *not* found in *string2*.

Example
The following example returns a pointer to the first white-space character in a string. White space is defined as space, tab, or newline.

```
#include <stdlib.h>
#include <string.h>
#include <stdio.h>

char *
nextwhite(char *string)
{
     size_t skipcount;

     if(string == NULL)
          return NULL;
     skipcount = strcspn(string, "\t \n");
     return(string + skipcount);
}

char string1[] = "My love is like a red, red, rose";
```

```
main(void)
{
    printf(nextwhite(string1));
    return(EXIT_SUCCESS);
}
```

Cross-references
Standard, §4.11.5.3
The C Programming Language, ed. 2, p. 250

See Also
memchr, strchr, string searching, strpbrk, strrchr, strspn, strstr, strtok

stream — Definition
(Library/STDIO)

The term *stream* is a metaphor for the flow of data between a C program and either an external I/O device (e.g., a terminal) or a file stored on a semi-permanent medium (e.g., disk or tape). A program can read data from a stream, write data into it, or (in the case of a file) directly access any named portion of it.

The Standard describes two types of stream: the *binary* stream and the *text* stream.

A binary stream is simply a sequence of bytes. The Standard requires that once a program has written a sequence of bytes into a stream, it should be able to read back the same sequence of bytes unchanged from that stream — with the sole exception that, in some environments, one or more null characters may be appended to the end of the mass.

A text stream, on the other hand, consists of characters that have been organized into lines. A *line* in turn, consists of zero or more characters terminated by a newline character. The Standard declines to describe in detail how a text stream is manipulated; it simply mandates that reading, writing, and seeking be done in a consistent manner.

When data are written into a binary file, the file is not truncated. Whether a text file is truncated when data are written into it depends upon the implementation.

The Standard also mandates that an implementation should be able to handle a line that is **BUFSIZ** characters long, which includes the terminating newline character. **BUFSIZ** is a macro that is defined in the header **stdio.h**, and must be defined to be equal to at least 256.

The maximum number of streams that can be opened at any one time is given by the macro **FOPEN_MAX**. This must be at least eight, including **stdin**, **stdout**, and **stderr**.

Cross-references
Standard, §4.9.2
The C Programming Language, ed. 2, p. 241

See Also
buffer, file, line, STDIO, stdio.h

strerror() — Library function
(Library/string handling/string miscellaneous)
Translate an error number into a string
#include <string.h>
char *strerror(int *error***);**

strerror helps to generate an error message. It takes the argument *error*, which presumably is an error code generated by an error condition in a program, and may return a pointer to the corresponding error message.

The error numbers recognized and the texts of the corresponding error messages all depend upon the implementation.

Example
This example prints the user's error message and the standard error message before exiting.

```
#include <stdio.h>
#include <math.h>
#include <string.h>
#include <stddef.h>

fatal(char * msg)
{
     int save;

     save = errno;
     /* this may clobber errno */
     fprintf(stderr, "%s", msg);
     if (save)
          fprintf(stderr, ": %s", strerror(save));
     fprintf(stderr, "\n");
     exit(save);
}
```

```
main(void)
{
    /* guaranteed wrong */
    sqrt(-1.0);
    fatal("What does sqrt say to -1?");
    return(EXIT_SUCCESS);
}
```

Cross-references
Standard, §4.11.6.2
The C Programming Language, ed. 2, p. 250

See Also
errors, perror, string miscellaneous

Notes
strerror returns a pointer to a static array that may be overwritten by a subsequent call to **strerror**.

strerror differs from the related function **perror** in the following ways: **strerror** receives the error number through its argument *error*, whereas **perror** reads the global constant **errno**. Also, **strerror** returns a pointer to the error message, whereas **perror** writes the message directly into the standard error stream.

The error numbers recognized and the texts of the messages associated with each error number depend upon the implementation. However, **strerror** and **perror** must return the same error message when handed the same error number.

strftime() — Library function
(Library/date and time/time conversion)
Format locale-specific time
#include <time.h>
**size_t strftime(char *string, size_t maximum, const char *format,
    const struct tm *brokentime);**

The function **strftime** provides a locale-specific way to print the current time and date. It also gives you an easy way to shuffle the elements of date and time into a string that suits your preferences.

strftime references the portion of the locale that is affected by the calls

```
setlocale(LC_TIME, locale);
```

or

```
setlocale(LC_ALL, locale);
```

For more information on setting locales, see the entry for **localization**.

string points to the region of memory into which **strftime** writes the date and time string it generates. *maximum* is the maximum number of characters that can be written into *string*. *string* should point to an area of allocated memory at least *maximum* + 1 bytes long; if it does not, reserved portions of memory may be overwritten.

brokentime points to a structure of type **tm**, which contains the broken-down time. This structure must first be initialized by either of the functions **localtime** or **gmtime**.

Finally, *format* points to a string that contains one or more conversion specifications, which guide **strftime** in building its output string. Each conversion specification is introduced by the percent sign '%'. When the output string is built, each conversion specification is replaced by the appropriate time element. Characters within *format* that are not part of a conversion specification are copied into *string*; to write a literal percent sign, use "%%".

strftime recognizes the following conversion specifiers:

a   The locale's abbreviated name for the day of the week.

A   The locale's full name for the day of the week.

b   The locale's abbreviated name for the month.

B   The locale's full name for the month.

c   The locale's default representation for the date and time.

d   The day of the month as an integer (01 through 31).

H   The hour as an integer (00 through 23).

I   The hour as an integer (01 through 12).

j   The day of the year as an integer (001 through 366).

m   The month as an integer (01 through 12).

M   The minute as an integer (00 through 59).

p   The locale's way of indicating morning or afternoon (e.g, in the United States, "AM" or "PM").

S   The second as an integer (00 through 59).

U   The week of the year as an integer (00 through 53); regard Sunday as the first day of the week.

w   The day of the week as an integer (0 through 6); regard Sunday as the first day of the week.

W   The day of the week as an integer (0 through 6); regard Monday as the first day of the week.

x   The locale's default representation of the date.

X   The locale's default representation of the time.

y   The year within the century (00 through 99).

Y   The full year, including century.

Z   The name of the locale's time zone. If no time zone can be determined, print a null string.

Use of any conversion specifier other than the ones listed above will result in undefined behavior.

If the number of characters written into *string* is less than or equal to *maximum*, then **strftime** returns the number of characters written. If, however, the number of characters to be written exceeds *maximum*, then **strftime** returns zero and the contents of the area pointed to by *string* are indeterminate.

Cross-references
Standard, §4.12.3.5
The C Programming Language, ed. 2, p. 256

See Also
asctime, ctime, gmtime, localtime, time conversion, time_t, tm

Notes
strftime is modelled after the UNIX command **date**.

string — Definition
(Library)

A *string* is an array of characters that is terminated by a null character. For example:

```
This is a string.\0
```

When you declare a pointer to a string, you can initialize it by enclosing the desired text with quotation marks and using the assignment operation '='. This initializes the pointer to the address of the first byte in the string. For example,

```
char *stringptr = "This is a string.";
```

initializes the pointer **stringptr** to point to the first character in the string. It is not necessary to append a null character onto the end of the string; the translator does this automatically.

Finally, the length of a string is defined as being the number of bytes in it, from its beginning through the one that immediately precedes the null character. For example, the string

```
This is a string.\0
```

has a length of 17. Each space character is each counted as a byte, but the null character at the end of the string is not.

Cross-references
Standard, §4.1.1
The C Programming Language, ed. 2, p. 30

See Also
Library

string.h — Header
(Library/string handling)
#include < string.h >

string.h is the header that holds the declarations and definitions of all routines that handle strings and buffers. For a list of these routines, see **string handling**.

Cross-references
Standard, §4.11
The C Programming Language, ed. 2, p. 249

See Also
header, string handling

string comparison — Overview
(Library/string handling)

The Standard describes five routines that compare two strings or two regions of memory. All are declared in the header **string.h**. They are as follows:

memcmp	Compare two regions
strcmp	Compare two strings
strcoll	Compare two strings, using locale collating information
strncmp	Compare one string with first n bytes of another
strxfrm	Transform a string using locale information

Every comparison routine works on a character-by-character basis: each compares two strings or regions character by character either until it finds two that differ, or it reaches a specified limit.

memcmp differs from the other functions in that it examines areas of memory rather than a strings. Because C defines a string as being an sequence of characters terminated by a null character, the string-comparison routines will not look past the first null character encountered; **memcmp**, however, will.

Cross-references
Standard, §4.11.4
The C Programming Language, ed. 2, p. 250

See Also
string, string handling, string.h

Notes
strxfrm appears to belong properly with the group of string conversion routines, but the Standard includes it here apparently because it is coupled with **strcoll**, which compares strings that use locale-specific information.

string concatenation — Overview
(Library/string handling)

The Standard describes two routines that concatenate strings: **strcat** and **strncat**. The former copies one string onto the end of another; the latter copies up to the first *n* characters from one string onto another. Both routines are declared in the header **string.h**.

Cross-reference
Standard, §4.11.3

See Also
string, string handling, string.h

string conversion — Overview
(Library/general utilities)
#include <stdlib.h>

The Standard describes six functions that convert string to numbers. These are as follow:

atof	Convert string to floating-point number
atoi	Convert string to integer
atol	Convert string to long integer
strtod	Convert string to double-precision floating-point number
strtol	Convert string to long integer
strtoul	Convert string to unsigned long integer

Cross-reference
Standard, §4.10.1

See Also
general utilities

Notes
The functions **atof** and **strtod**, which convert a string to a floating-point number, are affected by the locale under which the program is run, as set by the function **setlocale**. Specifically, the character they recognize as marking the decimal point will change from locale to locale. See **localization** for more information.

The functions **atof**, **atoi**, and **atol** have been rendered obsolete, and are retained in the Standard only because they are used widely. Their functionality has been subsumed by **strtod**, **strtol**, and **strtoul**. Their names are derived from their use in ASCII-based environments.

string copying — Overview
(Library/string handling)

The Standard describes four routines that copy strings or regions of memory, as follows:

memcpy	Copy one region into another
memmove	Copy one region into another with which it may overlap
strcpy	Copy one string into another
strncpy	Copy *count* characters from one string into another

These routines, like all of the string-handling routines, are defined in the header **string.h**.

The Standard describes four such routines. **strcpy** and **strncpy** copy strings. They differ in that **strcpy** copies an entire string, regardless of its length, whereas **strncpy** copies only up to *n* bytes of a string. The behavior of each is undefined if the string being copied overlaps with the area to which it is being copied.

By contrast, **memcpy** and **memmove** copy regions of memory rather than strings. Thus, they will always copy a specified number of bytes, instead of quitting if they encounter a null character. These functions differ in that **memmove** works correctly if the region being copied from overlaps with the region being copied to, whereas **memcpy** does not.

Cross-reference
Standard, §4.11.2

See Also
string, string handling, string.h

string handling — Overview
(Library)
#include <string.h>

The Standard includes 22 routines for handling strings and regions of memory. All are declared in the header **string.h**. The routines are as follows:

String comparison

memcmp	Compare two regions
strcmp	Compare two strings
strcoll	Compare two strings, using locale information
strncmp	Compare one string with first n bytes of another
strxfrm	Transform a string using locale information

String concatenation

strcat	Concatenate two strings
strncat	Concatenate one string with n bytes of another

String copying

memcpy	Copy one region into another
memmove	Copy one region into another with which it may overlap
strcpy	Copy one string into another
strncpy	Copy n bytes from one string into another

String miscellaneous

memset	Fill a region with a character
strerror	Return the text of a pre-defined error message
strlen	Return the length of a string

String searching

memchr	Find first occurrence of a character in a region
strchr	Find first occurrence of a character in a string
strcspn	Find how much of the initial portion of a string consists of characters *not* found in another string
strpbrk	Find first occurrence in one string of any character from another string
strrchr	Find *last* occurrence of a character within a string
strspn	Find how much of the initial portion of string consists only of characters from another string
strstr	Find one string within another string
strtok	Break a string into tokens

Cross-references
Standard, §4.11
The C Programming Language, ed. 2, p. 249

See Also
Library, string, string.h

string literal — Definition
(Language/lexical elements)

A *string literal* consists of zero or more characters that are enclosed by quotation marks "". For example, the following is a string literal:

```
"This is a string literal."
```

The syntax of a string literal is as follows; *opt* indicates *optional*.

string-literal:
    "*s-char-sequence*_{opt} "

s-char-sequence:
    s-char
    s-char-sequence s-char

s-char:
    any character in the source character set except
        the quotation mark ", the backslash \, or
        the newline character
    escape-sequence

Each character within a string literal is handled exactly as if it were within a character constant, with the following exceptions: The apostrophe ' ' ' may be represented either by itself or by the escape sequence \', and the quotation mark ' " ' must be represented by the escape sequence '\"'.

A string literal has **static** duration. Its type is array of **char** which is initialized to the string of characters enclosed within the quotation marks.

If string literals are adjacent, the translator will concatenate them. For example, the string literals

```
"Here's a string literal" "Here's another string literal"
```

are automatically concatenated into one string literal.

If a string literal is not followed by another string literal, then the translator appends a null character to the end of the string as a terminator.

If two or more string literals within the same scope are identical, then the translator may store only one of them in memory and redirect to that one copy all references to any of the duplicate literals. For this reason, a program's behavior is undefined whenever it modifies a string literal.

A *wide-character literal* is a string literal that is formed of wide characters rather than ordinary, one-byte characters. It is marked by the prefix 'L'. For example, the following

```
L"This is a wide-character literal"
```

is stored in the form of a string of wide characters. See **multibyte characters** for more information about wide characters.

Cross-references
Standard, §3.1.4
The C Programming Language, ed. 2, p. 194

See Also
", escape sequences, lexical elements, string, trigraphs

Notes
Because trigraph sequences are interpreted in translation phase 1, before string literals are parsed, a string literal that contains trigraph sequences will be translated to a different string. This is a quiet change that may break existing code.

string miscellaneous — Overview
(Library/string handling)

The Standard describes three string-handling functions that are termed "miscellaneous". They are as follows:

memset	Fill a region of memory with a character
strerror	Return a pre-defined error message
strlen	Return the length of a string

Cross-reference
Standard, §4.11.6

See Also
string, string handling, string.h

string searching — Overview
(Library/string handling)

The Standard describes eight functions that search for a character or string within a string or a region of memory. They are as follows:

memchr	Find first occurrence of a given character within a region.
strchr	Find first occurrence of a given character within a string.
strcspn	Find how much of the initial portion of a string consists of characters *not* found in another string.
strpbrk	Find first occurrence in a string of any character from another string.
strrchr	Find *last* occurrence of a given character within a string.
strspn	Find how much of the initial portion of a string consists only of characters from another string.
strstr	Find whether one string occurs within another.
strtok	Break a string into tokens.

Cross-reference
Standard, §4.11.5

See Also
string, string handling, string.h

strlen() — Library function
(Library/string handling/string miscellaneous)
Measure the length of a string
size_t strlen(const char **string***)**

strlen counts the number of characters in *string* up to the null character that ends it. It returns the number of characters in *string*, excluding the null character that ends it.

Example

The following example prints the length of an entered string. Because **size_t** may be **unsigned long** or smaller, it is cast to **unsigned long** for **printf**.

```
#include <stddef.h>
#include <string.h>
#include <stdio.h>

main(void)
{
    char buf[132];

    printf("Enter something\n");
    if(gets(buf) != NULL)
        printf("You entered %lu characters\n",
            (unsigned long)strlen(buf));
    return(EXIT_SUCCESS);
}
```

Cross-references

Standard, §4.11.6.3
The C Programming Language, ed. 2, p. 250

See Also

string miscellaneous

strncat() — Library function
(Library/string handling/string concatenation)

Append *n* characters of one string onto another
#include < string.h >
char *strncat(char *string1, const char *string2, size_t n)

strncat copies up to *n* characters from the string pointed to by *string2* onto the end of the one pointed to by *string1*. It stops when *n* characters have been copied or it encounters a null character in *string2*, whichever occurs first. The null character at the end of *string1* is overwritten by the first character of *string2*.

strncat returns the pointer *string1*.

Example

The following example concatenates two strings to make a file name. It works for an operating system in which a file name can have no more than eight characters, and a suffix of no more than three characters.

```
#include <string.h>
#include <stdio.h>

char *
dosfilen(char *dosname, char *filename, char *filetype)
{
    *dosname = '\0';
    /* strncpy() doesn't guarantee a NULL */
    strncat(dosname, filename, 8);
    strcat(dosname, ".");
    return(strncat(dosname, filetype, 3));
}

main(void)
{
    char dosname[13];

    puts(dosfilen(dosname, "A_LONG_FILENAME",
        "A_LONG_FILETYPE"));
    return(EXIT_SUCCESS);
}
```

Cross-references
Standard, §4.11.3.2
The C Programming Language, ed. 2, p. 250

See Also
strcat, string concatenation

Notes
strncat always appends a null character onto the end of the concatenated string. Therefore, the number of characters appended to the end of *string1* could be as many as $n+1$. *string1* should point to enough allocated memory to hold itself plus $n+1$ characters; if it does not, data or code will be overwritten.

strncmp() — Library function
(Library/string handling/string comparison)
Compare one string with a portion of another
#include < string.h >
int strncmp(const char *string1, const char *string2, size_t n)

strncmp compares *string1* with *n* bytes of *string2*. Comparison ends when a null character is read.

strncmp compares the two strings character by character until it finds a pair of characters that are not identical. It returns a number less than zero if the character in *string1* is less (i.e,. occurs earlier in the character table) than its counterpart in *string2*. It returns a number greater than zero if the character in *string1* is greater (i.e,. occurs later in the character table) than its counterpart in *string2*. If no characters are found to differ, then the strings are identical and **strncmp** returns zero. Comparison ends either when *n* bytes have been compared or a null character has been encountered in either string. The null character is compared before **strncmp** terminates.

Example

The following example searches for a word within a string. It is a simple implementation of the function **strstr**.

```c
#include <stdio.h>
#include <stdlib.h>
#include <string.h>

void fatal(const char *string)
{
    fprintf(stderr, "%s\n", string);
    exit(EXIT_FAILURE);
}

main(int argc, char *argv[])
{
    int word, string, i;

    if (--argc != 2)
        fatal("Usage: example word string");

    word = strlen(argv[1]);
    string = strlen(argv[2]);
    if (word >= string)
        fatal("Word is longer than string being searched.");

    /* walk down "string" and search for "word" */
    for (i = 0; i < string - word; i++)
        if (strncmp(argv[2]+i, argv[1], word) == 0) {
            printf("%s is in %s.\n", argv[1], argv[2]);
            exit(EXIT_SUCCESS);
        }

    /* if we get this far, "word" isn't in "string" */
    printf("%s is not in %s.\n", argv[1], argv[2]);
    exit(EXIT_SUCCESS);
}
```

Cross-references
Standard, §4.11.4.4
The C Programming Language, ed. 2, p. 250

See Also

memcmp, strcmp, strcoll, string comparison, strxfrm

Notes

The string-comparison routines **strcoll**, **strcmp**, and **strncmp** differ from the memory-comparison routine **memcmp** in that they compare strings rather than regions of memory. They stop when they encounter a null character, but **memcmp** does not. **memcmp** performs the same when run on ASCII or EBCDIC machines, whereas the string-comparison routines do not.

strncpy() — Library function
(Library/string handling/string copying)

Copy one string into another
#include < string.h >
char *strncpy(char *string1, const char *string2, size_t n)

strncpy copies *n* characters from the string pointed to by *string2* into the area pointed to by *string1*. Copying ends when *n* bytes have been copied or a null character is encountered in *string2*.

If *string2* is less than *n* characters long, **strncpy** pads *string1* with null characters until *n* characters have been deposited.

strncpy returns *string1*.

Example

This example reads a file of names and changes them from the format

        first_name [middle_initial] last_name

to the format:

        last_name, first_name [middle_initial]

```
#include <stdio.h>
#include <stdlib.h>
#include <string.h>
```

```
#define NNAMES 512
#define MAXLEN 60
#define PERIOD '.'
#define SPACE ' '
#define COMMA ','
#define NEWLINE '\n'

char *array[NNAMES];
char gname[MAXLEN], lname[MAXLEN];

main(int argc, char *argv[])
{
    FILE *fp;
    int count, num;
    char  *name, string[MAXLEN], *cptr, *eptr;
    unsigned glength, length;

    /* check number of arguments */
    if (--argc != 1) {
        fprintf (stderr, "Usage: example filename\n");
        exit(EXIT_FAILURE);
    }

    /* open file */
    if ((fp = fopen(argv[1], "r")) == NULL) {
        fprintf(stderr, "Cannot open %s\n", argv[1]);
        exit(EXIT_FAILURE);
    }
    count = 0;

    /* get line and examine it */
    while (fgets(string, MAXLEN, fp) != NULL) {
        if ((cptr = strchr(string, PERIOD)) != NULL) {
            cptr++;
            cptr++;
        } else if ((cptr=strchr(string, SPACE))!=NULL)
            cptr++;
        else continue;

        strcpy(lname, cptr);
        eptr = strchr(lname, NEWLINE);
        *eptr = COMMA;

        strcat(lname, " ");
        glength = (unsigned)(strlen(string)-strlen(cptr));
        strncpy(gname, string, glength);
```

```
            name = strncat(lname, gname, glength);
            length = (unsigned)strlen(name);
            array[count] = (char *)malloc(length + 1);

            strcpy(array[count],name);
            count++;
        }
        for (num = 0; num < count; num++)
            printf("%s\n", array[num]);
        return(EXIT_SUCCESS);
    }
```

Cross-references
Standard, §4.11.2.4
The C Programming Language, ed. 2, p. 249

See Also
memcpy, memset, strcpy, string copying

Notes
string1 should point to enough reserved memory to hold *n* characters; otherwise, code or data will be overwritten.

If the region of memory pointed to by *string1* overlaps with the string pointed to by *string2*, then the behavior of **strncpy** is undefined.

strpbrk() — Library function
(Library/string handling/string searching)
Find first occurrence in a string of any character from another string
#include < string.h >
char *strpbrk(const char **string1***, const char ****string2***)**

strpbrk returns a pointer to the first character in *string1* that matches any character in *string2*. It returns NULL if no character in *string1* matches a character in *string2*. The set of characters that *string2* points to is sometimes called the "break string". For example,

```
    char *string = "To be, or not to be: that is the question.";
    char *brkset = ",;";
    strpbrk(string, brkset);
```

returns the value of the pointer **string** plus six. This points to the comma, which is the first character in the area pointed to by **string** that matches any character in the string pointed to by **brkset**.

Example

This example finds the first white-space character or punctuation character in a
string and returns a pointer to it. White space is defined as tab, space, and
newline. Punctuation is defined as the following characters:

```
! @ # $ % ^ & * ( ) - + = ' ~
{ } [ ] : ; ' " | / , . ?
```

```c
#include <stdlib.h>
#include <string.h>
#include <stdio.h>

char *
findseparator(char *string)
{
    static char separators[] =
        " \n\t!@#$%^&*()-+=''~{}[]:;\"|\\/,.?";

    if(string == NULL)
        return(NULL);

    return strpbrk(string, separators);
}

char string1[]="I shall arise and go now/And go to Innisfree."

main(void)
{
    printf(findseparator(string1));
    return(EXIT_SUCCESS);
}
```

Cross-references

Standard, §4.11.5.4
The C Programming Language, ed. 2, p. 250

See Also

**memchr, strchr, strcspn, string searching, strpbrk, strrchr, strspn, strstr,
strtok**

Notes

strpbrk resembles the function **strtok** in functionality, but unlike **strtok**, it
preserves the contents of the strings being compared. It also resembles the function **strchr**, but lets you search for any one of a group of characters, rather than
for one character alone.

strrchr() — Library function
>   (Library/string handling/string searching)
>   Search for rightmost occurrence of a character in a string
>   **#include < string.h >**
>   **char *strrchr(const char ****string***, int** *character***);**

>   **strrchr** looks for the last, or rightmost, occurrence of *character* within *string*. *character* is declared to be an **int**, but is handled within the function as a **char**. Another way to describe this function is to say that it performs a reverse search for a character in a string.

>   **strrchr** returns a pointer to the rightmost occurrence of *character*, or NULL if *character* could not be found within *string*.

Example

This example truncates a string by replacing the character after the last terminating character with a zero. It returns the truncated string.

```
#include <stddef.h>
#include <stdlib.h>
#include <string.h>
#include <stdio.h>

char *
truncate(char *string, char endat)
{
      char *endchr;

      if(string!=NULL && (endchr=strrchr(string, endat))!=NULL)
          *++endchr = '\0';
      return(string);
}

char string1[] = "Here we go gathering nuts in May.";

main(void)
{
      puts(truncate(string1, ','));
      return(EXIT_SUCCESS);
}
```

Cross-references

Standard, §4.11.5.5
The C Programming Language, ed. 2, p. 249

See Also
memchr, strchr, strcspn, string searching, strpbrk, strspn, strstr, strtok

Notes
strrchr is identical to the function **rindex**, which is included with many implementations of C.

strspn() — Library function
(Library/string handling/string searching)
Return length for which one string includes characters in another
#include <string.h>
size_t strspn(const char *_string1_, const char *_string2_)

strspn returns the length for which _string1_ initially consists only of characters that are found in _string2_. For example,

```
char *s1 = "hello, world";
char *s2 = "kernighan & ritchie";
strcspn(s1, s2);
```

returns two, which is the length for which the first string initially consists of characters found in the second.

Example
This example returns a pointer to the first non-white-space character in a string. White space is defined as a space, tab, or newline character.

```
#include <stdlib.h>
#include <string.h>
#include <stddef.h>
#include <stdio.h>

char *
skipwhite(char *string)
{
    size_t skipcount;

    if (string == NULL)
        return NULL;
    skipcount = strspn(string, "\t \n");
    return(string+skipcount);
}

char string1[] = "\t  Inventor: One who makes an intricate\n";
char string2[] = "arrangement of wheels, levers, and springs,\n;
char string3[] = "         and calls it civilization.\n";
```

```
main(void)
{
     printf("%s", skipwhite(string1));
     printf("%s", skipwhite(string2));
     printf("%s", skipwhite(string3));
     return(EXIT_SUCCESS);
}
```

Cross-references

Standard, §4.11.5.6
The C Programming Language, ed. 2, p. 250

See Also

memchr, strchr, strcspn, string searching, strpbrk, strrchr, strstr, strtok

strstr() — Library function
(Library/string handling/string searching)
Find one string within another
#include <string.h>
char *strstr(const char **string1***, const char ****string2***)**

strstr looks for *string2* within *string1*. The terminating null character is not considered part of *string2*.

strstr returns a pointer to where *string2* begins within *string1*, or NULL if *string2* does not occur within *string1*.

For example,

```
char *string1 = "Hello, world";
char *string2 = "world";
strstr(string1, string2);
```

returns **string1** plus seven, which points to the beginning of **world** within **Hello, world**. On the other hand,

```
char *string1 = "Hello, world";
char *string2 = "worlds";
strstr(string1, string2);
```

returns NULL because **worlds** does not occur within **Hello, world**.

Example

This function counts the number of times a pattern appears in a string. The occurrences of the pattern can overlap.

```
#include <stdlib.h>
#include <string.h>
#include <stddef.h>
#include <stdio.h>

size_t
countpat(char *string, char *pattern)
{
     size_t found_count = 0;
     char *found;

     if((found = string)==NULL || pattern==NULL)
          return 0;

     while((found = strstr(found, pattern)) != NULL) {
          /* move past beginning of this one */
          found++;
          /* count it */
          found_count++;
     }
     return(found_count);
}

char string1[] = "Badges, Badges -- we need no stinking Badges.";
char string2[] = "Badges";

main(void)
{
     printf("%s occurs %d times in %s\n",
          string2, countpat(string1, string2), string1);
     return(EXIT_SUCCESS);
}
```

Cross-references
Standard, §4.11.5.7
The C Programming Language, ed. 2, p. 250

See Also
memchr, strchr, strcspn, string searching, strpbrk, strrchr, strspn, strtok

strtod() — Library function
(Library/general utilities/string conversion)
Convert string to floating-point number
#include < stdlib.h >
double strtod(const char **string***, char *****tailptr***);**

strtod converts the string pointed to by *string* to a double-precision floating-point number.

strtod reads the string pointed to by *string*, and parses it into three portions: beginning, subject sequence, and tail.

The *beginning* consists of zero or more white-space characters that begin the string.

The *subject sequence* is the portion of the string that will be converted into a floating-point number. It begins when **strtod** reads a sign character, a numeral, or a decimal-point character. It can include at least one numeral, at most one decimal point, and may end with an exponent marker (either 'e' or 'E') followed by an optional sign and at least one numeral. Reading continues until **strtod** reads either a second decimal-point character or exponent marker, or any other non-numeral.

The *tail* continues from the end of the subject sequence to the null character that ends the string.

strtod ignores the beginning portion of the string. It then converts the subject sequence to a double-precision number and returns it. Finally, it sets the pointer pointed to by *tailptr* to the address of the first character of the string's tail.

strtod returns the **double** generated from the subject sequence. If no subject sequence could be recognized, it returns zero. If the number represented by the subject sequence is too large to fit into a **double**, then **strtod** returns **HUGE_VAL** and sets the global constant **errno** to **ERANGE**. If the number represented by the subject sequence is too small to fit into a **double**, then **strtod** returns zero and again sets **errno** to **ERANGE**.

Example
For an example of using this function in a program, see **sqrt**.

Cross-references
Standard, §4.10.4
The C Programming Language, ed. 2, p. 251

See Also
atof, atoi, atol, errno, string conversion, strtol, strtoul

Notes
The character that **strtod** recognizes as representing the decimal point depends upon the program's locale, as set by the function **setlocale**. See **localization** for more information.

Initial white space in the string pointed to by *string* is ignored. White space is defined as being all characters so recognized by the function **isspace**; the current locale setting may affect the operation of **isspace**.

strtok() — Library function
(Library/string handling/string searching)
Break a string into tokens
#include <string.h>
char *strtok(char **string1***, const char ****string2***);**

strtok helps to divide a string into a set of tokens. *string1* points to the string to be divided, and *string2* points to the character or characters that delimit the tokens.

strtok divides a string into tokens by being called repeatedly.

On the first call to **strtok**, *string1* should point to the string being divided. **strtok** searches for a character that is *not* included within *string2*. If it finds one, then **strtok** regards it as the beginning of the first token within the string. If one cannot be found, then **strtok** returns NULL to signal that the string could not be divided into tokens. When the beginning of the first token is found, **strtok** then looks for a character that *is* included within *string2*. When one is found, **strtok** replaces it with a null character to mark the end of the first token, stores a pointer to the remainder of *string1* within a static buffer, and returns the address of the beginning of the first token.

On subsequent calls to **strtok**, set *string1* to NULL. **strtok** then looks for subsequent tokens, using the address that it saved from the first call. With each call to **strtok**, *string2* may point to a different delimiter or set of delimiters.

Example
The following example breaks **command_string** into individual tokens and puts pointers to the tokens into the array **tokenlist[]**. It then returns the number of tokens created. No more than **maxtoken** tokens will be created. **command_string** is modified to place '\0' over token separators. The token list points into **command_string**. Tokens are separated by spaces, tabs, commas, semicolons, and newlines.

```
#include <stdlib.h>
#include <string.h>
#include <stddef.h>
#include <stdio.h>

tokenize(char *command_string, char *tokenlist[],
     size_t maxtoken)
{
     static char tokensep[]="\t\n ,;";
     int tokencount;
     char *thistoken;
```

```
        if(command_string == NULL || !maxtoken)
            return 0;

        thistoken = strtok(command_string, tokensep);

        for(tokencount = 0; tokencount < maxtoken &&
                thistoken != NULL;) {
            tokenlist[tokencount++] = thistoken;
            thistoken = strtok(NULL, tokensep);
        }

        tokenlist[tokencount] = NULL;
        return tokencount;
}
#define MAXTOKEN 100
char *tokens[MAXTOKEN];
char buf[80];

main(void)
{
        for(;;) {
            int i, j;

            printf("Enter string ");
            fflush(stdout);
            if(gets(buf) == NULL)
                exit(EXIT_SUCCESS);

            i = tokenize(buf, tokens, MAXTOKEN);
            for(j = 0; j < i; j++)
                printf("%s\n", tokens[j]);
        }
        return(EXIT_SUCCESS);
}
```

Cross-references
Standard, §4.11.5.8
The C Programming Language, ed. 2, p. 250

See Also
memchr, strchr, strcspn, string searching, strpbrk, strrchr, strspn, strstr

strtol() — Library function
(Library/general utilities/string conversion)
Convert string to long integer
#include <stdlib.h>

long strtol(const char *sptr, char **tailptr, int base);

strtol converts the string pointed to by *sptr* into a **long**.

base gives the base of the number being read, from 0 to 36. This governs the form of the number that **strtol** expects. If *base* is zero, then **strtol** expects a number in the form of an integer constant. See **integer constant** for more information. If *base* is set to 16, then the string to be converted may be preceded by **0x** or **0X**.

strtol reads the string pointed to by *sptr* and parses it into three portions: beginning, subject sequence, and tail.

The *beginning* consists of zero or more white-space characters that begin the string.

The *subject sequence* is the portion of the string that will be converted into a **long**. It is introduced by a sign character, a numeral, or an alphabetic character appropriate to the base of the number being read. For example, if *base* is set to 16, then **strtol** will recognize the alphabetic characters 'A' through 'F' and 'a' to 'f' as indicating numbers. It continues to scan until it encounters any alphabetic character outside the set recognized for the setting of *base*, or the null character.

The *tail* continues from the end of the subject sequence to the null character that ends the string.

strtol ignores the beginning portion of the string. It then converts the subject sequence to a **long**. Finally, it sets the pointer pointed to by *tailptr* to the address of the first character of the string's tail.

strtol returns the **long** that it has built from the subject sequence. If it could not build a number, for whatever reason, it returns zero. If the number it builds is too large or too small to fit into a **long**, it returns, respectively, **LONG_MAX** or **LONG_MIN** and sets the global variable **errno** to the value of the macro **ERANGE**.

Cross-references
Standard, §4.10.1.5
The C Programming Language, ed. 2, p. 252

See Also
atof, atoi, atol, errno, string conversion, strtod, strtoul

Notes
Initial white space in the string pointed to by *string* is ignored. White space is defined as being all characters so recognized by the function **isspace**; the current locale setting may affect the operation of **isspace**.

strtoul() — Library function
(Library/general utilities/string conversion)
Convert string to unsigned long integer
#include <stdlib.h>
unsigned long strtoul(const char *sptr, **char *****tailptr*, **int** *base*);

strtoul converts the string pointed to by *sptr* into an **unsigned long**.

base gives the base of the number being read, from 0 to 36. This governs the form of the number that **strtoul** expects. If *base* is zero, then **strtoul** expects a number in the form of an integer constant. See **integer constant** for more information. If *base* is set to 16, then the string to be converted may be preceded by **0x** or **0X**.

strtoul reads the string pointed to by *sptr* and parses it into three portions: beginning, subject sequence, and tail.

The *beginning* consists of zero or more white-space characters that begin the string.

The *subject sequence* is the portion of the string that will be converted into an **unsigned long**. It is introduced by a sign character, a numeral, or an alphabetic character appropriate to the base of the number being read. For example, if *base* is set to 16, then **strtoul** will recognize the alphabetic characters 'A' through 'F' and 'a' to 'f' as indicating numbers. It continues to scan until it encounters any alphabetic character outside the set recognized or the setting of *base*, or the null character.

The *tail* continues from the end of the subject sequence to the null character that ends the string.

strtoul ignores the beginning portion of the string. It then converts the subject sequence to an **unsigned long**. Finally, it sets the pointer pointed to by *tailptr* to the address of the first character of the string's tail.

strtoul returns the **unsigned long** that it has built from the subject sequence. If it could not build a number, for whatever reason, it returns zero. If the number it builds is too large to fit into an **unsigned long**, it returns **ULONG_MAX** and sets the global variable **errno** to the value of the macro **ERANGE**.

Example

This example uses **strtoul** as a hash function for table lookup. It demonstrates both hashing and linked lists. Hash-table lookup is the most efficient when used to look up entries in large tables; this is an example only.

```
#include <stddef.h>
#include <stdio.h>
#include <stdlib.h>
#include <string.h>
```

```
/*
 * For fastest results, use a prime about 15% bigger
 * than the table. If short of space, use a smaller prime.
 */
#define HASHP 11
struct symbol {
    struct symbol *next;
    char *name;
    char *descr;
} *hasht[HASHP], codes[] = {
    NULL,      "a286",        "frogs togs",
    NULL,      "xy7800",      "doughnut holes",
    NULL,      "z678abc",     "used bits",
    NULL,      "xj781",       "black-hole varnish",
    NULL,      "h778a",       "table hash",
    NULL,      "q167",        "log(-5.2)",
    NULL,      "18888",       "quid pro quo",
    NULL,      NULL,          NULL  /* end marker */
};

void
buildTable(void)
{
    long h;
    register struct symbol *sym, **symp;

    for(symp = hasht; symp != (hasht + HASHP); symp++)
        *symp = NULL;

    for(sym = codes; sym->descr != NULL; sym++) {
        /*
         * hash by converting to base 36. There are
         * many ways to hash, but use all the data.
         */
        h = strtoul(sym->name, NULL, 36) % HASHP;
        sym->next = hasht[h];
        hasht[h] = sym;
    }
}

struct symbol *
lookup(char *s)
{
    long h;
    register struct symbol *sym;
```

```
        h = strtoul(s, NULL, 36) % HASHP;
        for(sym = hasht[h]; sym != NULL; sym = sym->next)
                if(!strcmp(sym->name, s))
                        return(sym);
        return(NULL);
}
main(void)
{
        char buf[80];
        struct symbol *sym;

        buildTable();
        for(;;) {
                printf("Enter name ");
                fflush(stdout);

                if(gets(buf) == NULL)
                        exit(EXIT_SUCCESS);

                if((sym = lookup(buf)) == NULL)
                        printf("%s not found\n", buf);

                else
                        printf("%s is %s\n", buf, sym->descr);
        }
        return(EXIT_SUCCESS);
}
```

Cross-references

Standard, §4.10.1.5
The C Programming Language, ed. 2, p. 252

See Also

atof, atoi, atol, string conversion, strtod, strtol

Notes

This function has no historical usage, but provides greater functionality than does **strtol**.

Initial white space in the string pointed to by *string* is ignored. White space is defined as being all characters so recognized by the function **isspace**. The current locale setting may affect the operation of **isspace**.

struct — C keyword
(Language/lexical elements/identifiers/types)

The keyword **struct** introduces a *structure*. This is an aggregate data type that consists of a number of fields, or *members*, each of which can have its own name and type.

The members of a structure are stored sequentially. Unlike the related type **union**, the elements of a **struct** do not overlap. Thus, the size of a **struct** is the total of the sizes of all of its members, plus any bytes used for alignment (if the implementation requires them). Aligning bytes may not be inserted at the beginning of a **struct**, but may appear in its middle, or at the end. For this reason, it is incorrect to assume that any two members of a structure abut each other in memory.

Any type may be used within a **struct**, including bit-fields. No incomplete type may be used; thus, a **struct** may not contain a copy of itself, but it may contain a pointer to itself. A **struct** is regarded as incomplete until its closing '}' is read.

The members of a **struct** are stored in the order in which they are declared. Thus, a pointer to a **struct** also points to the beginning of the **struct**'s first member.

The following is an example of a structure:

```
struct person {
    char name[30];
    char st_address[25];
    char city[20];
    char state[2];
    char zip[9];
    char id_number[9];
} MYSELF;
```

This example defines a structure type **person**, as well as an instance of this type, called **MYSELF**.

Cross-references
Standard, §3.1.2.5, §3.5.2.1
The C Programming Language, ed. 2, pp. 127*ff*

See Also
alignment, member name, tag, types, union

strxfrm() — Library function
(Library/string handling/string comparison)
Transform a string
#include < string.h >
size_t strxfrm(char * string1 **, const char *** string2 **, size_t** n **);**

strxfrm transforms *string2* using information concerning the program's locale, as set by the function **setlocale**. See **localization** for more information about setting a program's locale.

strxfrm writes up to *n* bytes of the transformed result into the area pointed to by *string1*. It returns the length of the transformed string, not including the terminating null character. The transformation incorporates locale-specific material into *string2*.

If *n* is set to zero, **strxfrm** returns the length of the transformed string.

strxfrm transforms strings in such a manner that if two strings return a given result when compared by **strcoll** before transformation, they will return the same result when compared by **strcmp** after transformation.

Cross-references
Standard, §4.11.4.5
The C Programming Language, ed. 2, p. 250

See Also
localization, memcmp, strcmp, strcoll, string comparison, strncmp

Notes
If **strxfrm** returns a value equal to or greater than *n*, the contents of the area pointed to by *string1* are indeterminate.

switch — C keyword
(Language/statements/selection statements)
Select an entry in a table
switch (*expression* **)** *statement*

switch evaluates *expression*, then jumps to the **case** label whose expression is equal to *expression* and continues execution from there. *expression* may evaluate to any integral type, not just an **int**; every **case** label's *expression* is cast to the type of *conditional* before it is compared with *expression*.

If no **case** expression matches *expression*, **switch** jumps to the point marked by the **default** label. If there is no default label, then **switch** does not jump and no statement is executed; execution continues from the '}' that marks the end of the

switch statement.

The program continues its execution from the point to which **switch** jumps, either until a **break, continue, goto,** or **return** statement is read, or until the '}' that encloses all of the **case** statements is encountered.

All **case** labels are subordinate to the closest enclosing **switch** statement. No two **case** labels can have expressions with the same value. However, if a **case** label introduces a secondary **switch** statement, then that **switch** statement's suite of **case** labels may duplicate the values used by the **case** labels of the outer **switch** statement.

Example
For an example of this statement, see **printf**.

Cross-references
Standard, §3.6.4.2
The C Programming Language, ed. 2, pp. *58ff*

See Also
break, case, default, if, selection statements

Notes
It is good programming practice always to use a **default** label with a **switch** statement. There may be only one **default** label with any **switch** statement.

The number of **case** labels that can be included with a **switch** statement may vary from implementation to implementation. The Standard requires that every conforming implementation allow a **switch** statement to have up to at least 257 **case** labels.

The first edition of *The C Programming Language* requires that *conditional* may evaluate to an **int**. The Standard lifts this requirement: *conditional* may now be any integral type, from **short** to **unsigned long**. Every *expression* associated with a **case** label will be altered to conform to the type of *conditional*. Therefore, if a program depends upon *conditional* or any *expression* being an **int**, it may work differently under a conforming translator. This is a quiet change that may break existing code.

system() — Library function
(Library/general utilities/environment communication)
Suspend a program and execute another
#include <stdlib.h>
int system(const char *program);

system provides a way to execute another program from within a C program. It suspends the program currently being run, and passes the name pointed to by *program* to the environment's command processor, should there be one. When *program* has finished executing, the environment returns to the current program, which then continues its operation.

If *program* is set to NULL, **system** checks to see if a command processor exists. In this case, **system** returns zero if a command processor does not exist and nonzero if it does. If *program* is set to any value other than NULL, then what **system** returns is defined by the implementation.

Example
This example execute system commands on request.

```
#include <stdio.h>
#include <stdlib.h>

syscmds(char * prompt)
{
    for(;;) {
        char buf[80];

        printf(prompt);
        fflush(stdout);
        if(gets(buf) == NULL || !strcmp(buf, "exit"))
            return;
        system(buf);
    }
}

main(void)
{
    printf("Enter system commands: ");
    syscmds(">");
    return(EXIT_SUCCESS);
}
```

Cross-references
Standard, §4.10.4.5
The C Programming Language, ed. 2, p. 253

See Also
command processor, environment communication, exit

Notes

system is not guaranteed to work if it is nested. That is, if you suspend a program and call another with **system**, suspending that second program with **system** and calling a third may not work.

The Rationale describes three ways that a program can communicate with the program it invokes with **system**: (1) through a string that is passed to the program as its command-line arguments; (2) by setting environmental variables; or (3) by writing data into a file that the secondary program reads. The last is considered to be the most portable. Likewise, the secondary program can return information to the program that called it through the following means: (1) through a return value (as defined by the implementation); (2) through the status code that is returned to the environment by the function **exit**; or (3) through a file. Again, the last mechanism is said to be the most portable.

The Rationale suggests that all open files be closed before **system** calls the subordinate program.

T

tag — Definition
(Language/lexical elements/identifiers/name space)

A *tag* is a name that follows the keywords **struct**, **union**, or **enum**. It names the type of object so declared. For example, in the following code

```
struct STR {
            . . .
};
```

the identifier **STR** is a tag. It defines a new type of structure called **STR**. It does not, however, allocate any storage for any instance of this type.

Cross-references
Standard, §3.1.2.6
The C Programming Language, ed. 2, pp. 212*ff*

See Also
member, name space

tan() — Library function
(Library/mathematics/trigonometric functions)
Calculate tangent
#include <math.h>
double tan(double *radian***);**

tan calculates and returns the tangent of its argument *radian*, which must be in radian measure.

Cross-references
Standard, §4.5.2.7
The C Programming Language, ed. 2, p. 251

See Also
acos, asin, atan, atan2, cos, sin, trigonometric functions

tanh() — Library function
(Library/mathematics/hyperbolic functions)
Calculate hyperbolic tangent
#include <math.h>
double tanh(double *value***);**

tanh calculates the hyperbolic tangent of *radian*.

Cross-references
Standard, §4.5.3.3
The C Programming Language, ed. 2, p. 251

See Also
cosh, hyperbolic functions, sinh

time() — Library function
(Library/date and time/time manipulation)
Get current calendar time
#include <time.h>
time_t time(time_t *tp);

The function **time** returns the current calendar time. If *tp* is set a value other than NULL, then **time** also writes the result to the object pointed to by *tp*.

time returns an object of the type **time_t**, which is defined in the header **time.h**. If the current calendar time is not available, **time** returns -1 cast to type **time_t**.

Example
This example displays the time, if it is available.

```
#include <stdio.h>
#include <stdlib.h>
#include <time.h>

main(void)
{
    time_t t;

    /* get the time */
    if(-1 == time(&t))
        printf("The time is unavailable?");
    else
        /* display it */
        printf(ctime(&t));
    return(EXIT_SUCCESS);
}
```

Cross-references
Standard, §4.12.2.4
The C Programming Language, ed. 2, p. 256

See Also

clock, difftime, mktime, time manipulation, time_t

time.h — Header

(Library/date and time)

Header for date and time
#include <time.h>

time.h is the header that declares the function and defines the types used to represent time. It contains prototypes for the following nine functions:

asctime	Convert broken-down time into text
clock	Get processor time used by the program
ctime	Convert calendar time to text
difftime	Calculate difference between two times
gmtime	Convert calendar time to Universal Coordinated Time
localtime	Convert calendar time to local time
mktime	Convert broken-down time into calendar time
strftime	Format locale-specific time
time	Get current calendar time

It also contains definitions for the following data types:

clock_t	Encode system time
time_t	Encode calendar time
tm	Encode broken-down time

It contains a definition for the macro **CLK_TCK**, which is used to convert the value returned by the function **clock** into seconds of real time.

Cross-references

Standard, §4.12
The C Programming Language, ed. 2, p. 255

See Also

date and time, header

time_t — Type

(Library/date and time)

Calendar time
#include <time.h>

time_t is a data type that is defined in the header **time.h**. It is an arithmetic type that can represent time.

time_t is used to hold the calendar time, as computed from the system time by the function **time**. The functions **localtime** and **gmtime** use **time_t** to generate broken-down time, and the function **ctime** uses it to create a string that states the current date and time. The function **mktime** reads broken-down time and returns calendar time of type **time_t**.

Example
For an example of using this type in a program, see **difftime**.

Cross-references
Standard, §4.12.1
The C Programming Language, ed. 2, p. 255

See Also
broken-down time, calendar time, clock_t, date and time

time conversion — Overview
(Library/date and time)
#include <time.h>

The Standard's repertoire of date and time functions includes five functions that convert time from one form to another, as follows:

asctime	Convert broken-down time to text
ctime	Convert calendar time to text
gmtime	Convert calendar time to Universal Coordinated Time
localtime	Convert calendar time to local time
strftime	Format locale-specific time

The operation of **strftime** is affected by the locale, as set by the function **setlocale**. For more information see **localization**.

With the exception of **strftime**, all of these functions return the converted value in one of two static buffers: a text buffer and a buffer of the type **tm**. The text buffer holds the strings created by the functions **asctime** and **ctime**; and the **tm** buffer holds the broken-down time generated by the functions **gmtime** and **localtime**. These buffers may be overwritten by a subsequent call to a time function. For example, the output of a call to **localtime** can be overwritten by a subsequent call to either **localtime** or **gmtime**.

Cross-reference
Standard, §4.12.3

See Also
date and time, time manipulation

time manipulation — Overview
(Library/date and time)
#include <time.h>

The Standard's repertoire of date and time functions include four functions that manipulate the date and time, as follows:

clock	Get processor time used
difftime	Calculate difference between two times
mktime	Convert broken-down time into calendar time
time	Get current calendar time

Cross-reference
Standard, §4.12.2

See Also
date and time, time conversion

tm — Type
(Library/date and time)
Encode broken-down time
#include <time.h>

tm is the structure that holds the elements of broken-down time. It must contain at least the following fields. (The values representable are shown within parentheses):

int tm_sec	second (0-59)
int tm_min	minute (0-59)
int tm_hour	hour (0-23): 0 = = midnight
int tm_mday	day of the month (1-31)
int tm_mon	month (0-11): 0 = = January
int tm_year	year since 1900 A.D.
int tm_wday	day of week (0-6): 0 = = Sunday
int tm_yday	day of the year (0-366)
int tm_isdst	daylight savings time flag

The field **tm_isdst** indicates whether daylight saving time is currently in effect. It is set to a positive number if daylight saving time is in effect, to zero if it is not, and to a negative number if information concerning daylight saving time is not available.

The functions **localtime** and **gmtime** read the calendar time, as returned by the function **time**, and use it initialize **tm**; they then return a pointer to the structure.

The function **strftime** reads **tm** and uses it to build strings that present the date and time in a locale-specific manner. Finally, the function **mktime** reads **tm** and uses its contents to compute the corresponding calendar time.

Example
For an example of using this structure in a program, see **localtime**.

Cross-references
Standard, §4.12.1
The C Programming Language, ed. 2, p. 255

See Also
broken-down time, calendar time, clock_t, date and time, time_t

TMP_MAX — Macro
(Library/STDIO)
Maximum number of calls to **tmpnam**
#include <stdio.h>

TMP_MAX is a macro that is defined in the header **stdio.h**. It expands to an integer expression that defines the maximum number of unique file names that the function **tmpnam** can to generate. It cannot be defined to be less than 25.

Example
For an example of a program that uses this macro, see **tmpnam**.

Cross-references
Standard, §4.9.1, §4.9.4.4
The C Programming Language, ed. 2, p. 243

See Also
STDIO, stdio.h, tmpnam

tmpfile() — Library function
(Library/STDIO/file operations)
Create a temporary file
#include <stdio.h>
FILE *tmpfile(void);

tmpfile creates a file to hold data temporarily. The file is opened into binary update mode (**wb+**) and is removed automatically when it is closed or when the program ends. There is no way to access the temporary file by name. If your program needs to do so, it should open a file explicitly.

tmpfile returns NULL if it could not create the temporary file; if it could, it returns a pointer to the **FILE** associated with the temporary file. The function **exit** removes all files created by **tmpfile**.

Example

This example implements a primitive file editor that can edit large files. It uses two temporary files to keep all changes. The editor accepts the following commands:

dn	delete; **d52** deletes line 52
in	insert; **i7** inserts line before line 7
pn	print; **p17** prints line 17
p	print the entire file
w	write the edited file and quit
q	quit without writing the file

The entire temporary file is copied with each command.

```
#include <stdio.h>
#include <stddef.h>
#include <stdlib.h>
#include <stdarg.h>

FILE *fp, *tmp[2];
int linecount;

void
fatal(char *format, ...)
{
    va_list argptr;

    /* if there is a system message, display it */
    if(errno)
        perror(NULL);

    /* if there is a user message, use it */
    if(format != NULL) {
        va_start(argptr, format);
        vfprintf(stderr, format, argptr);
        va_end(argptr);
    }
    exit(EXIT_FAILURE);
}
```

```
/*
 * Copy up to line number or EOF.
 * Return number of lines copied.
 */
static int
copy(int line, FILE *ifp, FILE *ofp)
{
    int i, c, count;

    count = 0;
    for(c=i=1; (i<line || line==-1) && c!=EOF; i++) {
        while((c = fgetc(ifp)) != EOF && c != '\n')
            fputc(c, ofp);

        if(c == '\n') {
            count++;
            fputc('\n', ofp);
        }
    }
    return(count);
}

/*
 * Read a file until line number is read.
 * Return 1 if line is found before EOF.
 */
static int
find(int line, FILE *ifp)
{
    int i, c;

    for(c=i=1; i<line && c!=EOF; i++)
        while((c = fgetc(ifp)) != EOF && c != '\n')
            ;
    return(c != EOF);
}

main(int argc, char *argv[])
{
    int i, line, args;
    char c, cmdbuf[80];

    if(argc != 2)
        fatal("usage: tmpfile filename\n");

    if((tmp[0]=tmpfile())==NULL||(tmp[1]=tmpfile())==NULL)
        fatal("Error opening tmpfile\n");
```

```
if((fp = fopen(argv[1], "r")) == NULL)
    fatal("Error opening %s\n", argv[1]);
linecount = copy(-1, fp, tmp[i = 0]);
fclose(fp);

/* one file pass per command */
for(;;) {
    if(gets(cmdbuf) == NULL)
        fatal("EOF on stdin\n");

    if(!(args = sscanf(cmdbuf, "%c%d", &c, &line)))
        continue;
    fseek(tmp[i], 0L, SEEK_SET);

    switch(c) {
    /* Write edited file */
    case 'w':
        if((fp = fopen(argv[1], "w")) ==  NULL)
            fatal("Error opening %s\n", argv[1]);
        copy(linecount + 1, tmp[i], fp);
        fclose(fp);

    /* Quit */
    case 'q':
        exit(EXIT_SUCCESS);

    /* Print entire file */
    case 'p':
        if(args == 1) {
            copy(linecount + 1, tmp[i], stdout);
            continue;
        }
        if(find(line, tmp[i]))
            copy(2, tmp[i], stdout);
        continue;

    /* Delete a line */
    case 'd':
        if(args == 1)
            printf("dn where n is a number\n");
        else if(line > linecount)
            printf("only %d lines\n", linecount);

        else {
            copy(line, tmp[i], tmp[i^1]);
            if(find(2, tmp[i]))
                copy(-1, tmp[i], tmp[i^1]);
```

```
                    linecount--;
                    fseek(tmp[i], OL, SEEK_SET);
                    i ^= 1;
                }
                continue;
        /* Insert a line */
        case 'i':
            if(1 == args)
                printf("in where n is a number\n");
            else if(line > linecount)
                printf("only %d lines\n", linecount);

            else {
                copy(line, tmp[i], tmp[i^1]);
                printf("Enter inserted line\n");
                copy(2, stdin, tmp[i^1]);
                copy(-1, tmp[i], tmp[i^1]);
                linecount++;

                fseek(tmp[i], OL, SEEK_SET);
                i ^= 1;
            }
            continue;

        default:
            printf("Invalid request\n");
            continue;
        }
    }
}
```

Cross-references
Standard, §4.9.4.3
The C Programming Language, ed. 2, p. 243

See Also
file operations, remove, rename, tmpnam

Notes
The Standard requires that the temporary file created by **tmpfile** work as if it were a file written onto a mass-storage device; however, the implementor is not required to do so literally.

The implementation determines whether a temporary file is removed when a program exits abnormally.

tmpnam() — Library function
(Library/STDIO/file operations)
Generate a unique name for a temporary file
#include <stdio.h>
char *tmpnam(char **name***);**

tmpnam constructs a unique name for a file. The names returned by **tmpnam** generally are mechanical concatenations of letters, and therefore are mostly used to name temporary files, which are never seen by the user. Unlike a file created by **tmpfile**, a file named by **tmpnam** does not automatically disappear when the program exits. It must be explicitly removed before the program ends if you want it to disappear.

name points to the buffer into which **tmpnam** writes the name it generates. If *name* is set to NULL, **tmpnam** writes the name into an internal buffer that may be overwritten each time you call this function.

tmpnam returns a pointer to the temporary name.

Example
The following example uses **tmpnam** to generate some file names, opens one, and writes the rest of the names into it.

```
#include <stdio.h>
#include <stdlib.h>

void fatal(const char *string)
{
    fprintf(stderr, "%s\n", string);
    exit(EXIT_FAILURE);
}

main()
{
    int i, files;
    FILE *fp;
    char buffer[L_tmpnam];

    if ((fp = fopen(tmpnam(buffer), "w")) == NULL)
        fatal("Cannot open temporary file");
    printf("Temporary file name is %s\n", buffer);

    /* put realistic limit on number of names */
    100 > TMP_MAX ? files = TMP_MAX : files = 100;
    for(i = 0; i < files; i++)
        fprintf(fp, "%s\n", tmpnam(NULL));
```

```
fclose(fp);
return(EXIT_SUCCESS);
}
```

Cross-references
Standard, §4.9.4.4
The C Programming Language, ed. 2, p. 243

See Also
file operations, remove, rename, tmpfile

Notes
If you want the file name to be written into *buffer,* you should allocate at least **L_tmpnam** bytes of memory for it; **L_tmpnam** is defined in the header **stdio.h**.

tmpnam can be called at least **TMP_MAX** times to return unique file names. **TMP_MAX** is also set in **stdio.h**; it cannot be set to less than 25.

token — Definition
(Language/lexical elements)

A *token* is the basic, indivisible unit of text that is processed by the translator.

There are two varieties of token: *lexical token* and *preprocessing token*. When the Standard uses the term "token," it refers to what is here called a "lexical token." Note, too, that the term "preprocessing token" does not mean a token that is manipulated only by the preprocessor.

Preprocessing tokens form the following varieties of lexical elements:

- Character constant.
- Header name.
- Identifier.
- Operator.
- Preprocessing number.
- Punctuator.
- String literal.
- Each non-white space character that does not fall into one of the above categories

White-space characters can appear only within a header name, a character constant, or a string literal; in all other instances, white space separates tokens.

Preprocessing tokens are processed during phases 3 through 6 of translation. For details on translation, see the entry for **translation phases**. In brief, all preprocessing directives are executed: **#include** states are expanded, code is conditionally included, and macros are expanded. Each comment is replaced with one white-space character.

Adjacent string literals are concatenated and clusters of text that are not separated by white space are parsed. A cluster of text is always parsed into the longest possible sequence of characters that forms a valid token. For example, the text

    a+++++b

must be parsed into:

    a ++ ++ + b

The preprocessor passes unchanged what it does not recognize as being a preprocessor token.

Lexical tokens (which the Standard calls simply "tokens") form the following types of lexical elements:

- Constant.

- Identifier.

- Keyword.

- Operator.

- Punctuator.

- String literal.

Lexical tokens are parsed, analyzed, and linked.

Cross-references
Standard, §3.1
The C Programming Language, ed. 2, pp. 191, 229

See Also
lexical elements, translation phase

tolower() — Library function
(Library/character handling/case mapping)
Convert character to lower case
int tolower(int c);

tolower converts the upper-case character c to its corresponding lower-case character, as defined by the locale's character set. The Standard defines an upper-case character as one for which the function **isupper** returns true. *c* must be a value that is representable as an **unsigned char** or **EOF**.

If *c* is an upper case letter, then **tolower** returns the corresponding lower-case letter. If *c* is not a letter or is already lower case, then **tolower** returns it unchanged.

Example

The following example demonstrates **tolower** and **toupper**. It reverses the case of every character in a text file.

```
void fatal(const char *message)
{
    fprintf(stderr, "%s\n", message);
    exit(EXIT_FAILURE);
}
```

```
#include <ctype.h>
#include <stdio.h>
void fatal(const char *string);
```

```
main(int argc, char *argv[])
{
    FILE *fp;
    int ch;

    if (argc != 2)
        fatal("usage: example filename");

    if ((fp = fopen(argv[1], "r")) == NULL)
        fatal("cannot open text file");

    while ((ch = fgetc(fp)) != EOF)
        putchar(isupper(ch) ? tolower(ch) : toupper(ch));
    }
}
```

Cross-references

Standard, §4.3.2.1
The C Programming Language, ed. 2, p. 249

See Also

case mapping, toupper

Notes

The operation of this function is affected by the program's locale, as set by the function **setlocale**. See **localization** for more information.

top type — Definition
(Language/lexical elements/identifiers/types)

The term *top type* refers to the most basic form of a type, stripped of all specifiers and qualifiers. For any basic type, the top type is the type itself. For a derived type, however, the top type is the *first* term used to describe it. For example, the type **int *** is described as a "pointer to **int**"; therefore, its top type is pointer.

Cross-reference
Standard, §3.1.2.5

See Also
basic type, qualifiers, specifiers, types

toupper() — Library function
(Library/character handling/case mapping)
Convert character to upper case
int toupper(int c);

toupper converts the lower-case character *c* to its corresponding upper-case character. The Standard defines an lower-case character as one for which the function **islower** returns true. *c* must be either a value that is representable as an **unsigned char** or **EOF**.

If **c** is an lower-case letter, then **toupper** returns the corresponding upper-case letter for the locale's character set. If *c* is not a letter or is already upper case, then **toupper** returns it unchanged.

Example
For an example of this function, see **character-case mapping**.

Cross-references
Standard, §4.3.2.2
The C Programming Language, ed. 2, p. 249

See Also
case mapping, tolower

Notes
The operation of this function is affected by the program's locale, as set by the function **setlocale**. See **localization** for more information.

translation — Definition
(Definitions)

The term *translation* refers to the task of turning one or more files of C source code into a set of executable instructions.

The Standard assumes that translation is done by *compiling* source code into files of data and instructions, and then *linking* these files with functions drawn from libraries to form an executable program. The Standard, however, does not require that a translator conform to this model. It only requires that the translator produce the same behavior from source code as if it had been compiled and linked.

See Also
compile, Definitions, interpret, link

translation environment — Overview
(Environment)

The *translation environment* is the environment in which a program is translated (i.e., compiled or interpreted). It does not have to be the same environment as the one within which the program is executed.

The limits for the translation environment may be *greater* than those for the execution environment, but they may not be less. For example, the precision of a floating-point number at translation time may exceed the precision available in the execution environment, but it may not be less than that available in the execution environment.

Preprocessing directives and expressions are always evaluated in the translation environment, in full 32-bit arithmetic. The rest of the source file is interpreted here according to the specification of the language; if the program is compiled, all code generated by the compiler is executed in the **execution environment**.

Cross-reference
Standard, §2.1.1

See Also
Environment, execution environment

translation limits — Definition
(Environment/environmental considerations/limits)

A *translation limit* is a limit that must be met by every implementation of C that conforms to the Standard. The following lists the translation limits that must be met by a conforming implementation. Each limit is a minimum maximum; the implementation must at least meet the limit, but it is free to exceed it.

- Levels of nesting for compound statements: **15.**
- Levels of nesting for iteration control structures (**for, while,** and **do**): **15.**
- Levels of nesting for selection control structures (**if, switch**): **15.**
- Levels of nesting for conditional inclusion (**#if, #ifdef, #ifndef**): **8.**
- Pointer, array, and function declarators that can modify the declaration of an arithmetic type, a structure type, a **union** type, or an incomplete type: **12.**
- Declarators that can be nested by parentheses within a full declarator: **31.**
- Expressions that can be nested by parentheses within a full expression: **32.**
- Initial characters that are significant in an internal identifier or a macro name: **31.**
- Initial characters that are significant in an external identifier: **6.**
- External identifiers that can appear in one translation unit: **511.**
- Identifiers with block scope that can appear in a block: **127.**
- Macro identifiers that have been defined within one translation unit: **1,024.**
- Parameters in a function definition: **31.**
- Arguments in a function call: **31.**
- Parameters in a macro invocation: **31.**
- Characters in a logical line of source code (i.e., the line that is created when the "escaped" newline character that separates two lines of code is removed): **509.**
- Characters in a string literal or wide-character literal, after all adjacent string literals and wide-character literals have been concatenated: **509.**
- Bytes in an object, under a hosted environment: **32,767.**
- Levels of nesting for files called with **#include** directives: **8.**
- Number of **case** labels in a **switch** statement, included those in nested **switch** statements: **257.**
- Members in a structure or **union**: **127.**
- Enumeration constants in an enumeration: **127.**
- Levels of nesting for structure or **union** definitions within one structure declaration list: **15.**

Cross-reference
Standard, §2.2.4.1

See Also
limits

translation phases — Definition
(Environment/translation environment)

To *translate* a program means to take the source code typed by the programmer, and generate a corresponding set of instructions that can be executed by the computer. The translator must perform a number of tasks as it translates a program. The Standard describes eight *translation phases* that specify the order in which these tasks must be performed.

The translation phases are as follows:

1. The translator maps the source code to the C character set. It replaces every trigraph with its corresponding character.

2. The translator removes every newline character that is preceded by a backslash '\'. This splices the two lines of code that had been separated by the "escaped" newline character into one line of source code. Every source file must end with a newline character that is *not* preceded by a backslash.

3. The translator then "decomposes" the source file into preprocessing tokens, white space, and comments. This may not involve any physical change to the source file. A source file may not end within a comment or with a partial preprocessing token. The translator then replaces each comment with one space character. The translator must retain all newline characters, but the implementation defines whether it keeps other white-space characters or replaces them with space characters.

4. The translator then executes all preprocessing directives and expands every macro found throughout the source file. For every **#include** directive, it reads the appropriate header and executes translation phases 1 through 4 upon it.

5. The translator finds all escape sequences that are within character constants and string literals, and converts them to the appropriate character in the execution character set.

6. The translator concatenates adjacent string literals and adjacent wide-string literals.

7. The translator ceases to regard white-space characters as significant. It transforms preprocessing tokens into tokens. This may not cause any change to the tokens. It then analyzes the tokens syntactically and semantically, and trans-

forms them into processor-executable instructions. This is the portion of translation ordinarily called *compiling*.

8.   The translator resolves all references to external objects and functions. When an external function is stored in a library, the translator finds it and makes it available to the program. This is the portion of translation ordinarily called *linking*. Finally, the translator creates a *program image* that contains all of its output plus all other information the program needs to be run in its execution environment.

Although the tasks described in these phases must be logically executed in the order described here, any or all of them may be combined. Also, a portion of the program source text may be processed through phases 1 through 7 before later parts are scanned. Likewise, the program image that the translator creates may be written into a file (in the case of a compiler), or simply retained in memory for execution (in the case of an interpreter).

Cross-references
Standard, §2.1.1.2
The C Programming Language, ed. 2, p. 229

See Also
compile, link, translation environment

translation unit — Definition
(Environment/translation environment)

A *translation unit* is the basic unit of code that is translated into executable form. It consists of a source file, plus all headers that are requested with the preprocessing directive **#include**, and excluding all code that is skipped by preprocessing conditional inclusion.

Cross-references
Standard, §2.1.1.1
The C Programming Language, ed. 2, p. 191

See Also
#include, conditional inclusion, source file, translation environment

trigonometric functions — Overview
(Library/mathematics)

The Standard describes seven trigonometric functions, as follows:

acos	Calculate inverse cosine
asin	Calculate inverse sine
atan	Calculate inverse tangent
atan2	Calculate inverse tangent
cos	Calculate cosine
sin	Calculate sine
tan	Calculate tangent

Cross-reference
Standard, §4.5.2

See Also
exponent-log functions, hyperbolic functions, integer-value-remainder, mathematics, power functions

Notes
The inverse trigonometric functions are also sometimes called by the prefix "arc", e.g., **arcsine**.

trigraph sequences — Definition
(Environment/environmental considerations)

A *trigraph sequence* is a set of three characters that represents one character in the C character set. The set of trigraph sequences was created to allow users to use the full range of C characters, even if their keyboards do not implement the full C character set. Trigraph sequences are also useful with input devices that reserve one or more members of the C character set for internal use.

Each trigraph sequence is introduced by two question marks. The third character in the sequence indicates which character is being represented. The following table gives the set of trigraph sequences:

Trigraph Sequence	Character Represented
??=	#
??(	[
??/	\
??)	]
??'	^
??<	{
??!	|
??>	}
??-	~

The characters represented are the ones used in the C character set but not included in the ISO 646 character set. ISO 646 describes an invariant sub-set of the ASCII character set.

Trigraph sequences are interpreted even if they occur within a string literal or a character constant. This is because they are interpreted before the source code is tokenized; see **translation phases** for more information. Thus, strings that uses a literal "??" will not work the same as under a non-ANSI implementation of C. For example, the function call

```
printf("Feel lucky, punk??!\n");
```

would print:

```
Feel lucky, punk|
```

This is a silent change that may break existing code.

To print a pair of questions marks, use the escape sequence '\?\?'. For example:

```
printf("Feel lucky, punk\?\?!\n");
```

Cross-references
Standard, §2.2.1.1
The C Programming Language, ed. 2, p. 229

See Also
environmental considerations

true — Definition
(Definitions)

In the context of a C program, an expression is *true* if it yields nonzero.

See Also
Definitions, false

typedef — C keyword
(Language/declarations/storage-class specifiers)
Synonym for another type

The storage-class specifier **typedef** names a synonym for a type. Its syntax is as follows:

typedef-name:
     identifier

The new synonym must include all qualifiers and storage-class specifiers. For example, the declaration

```
typedef volatile unsigned long int giant;
```

states that the type **giant** is a synonym for **volatile unsigned long int**. Thus, the declaration

```
giant example();
```

declares, in effect, that the function **example** returns an **volatile unsigned long int**. An object declared to be type **giant** and one declared to be type **volatile unsigned long int** behave exactly the same.

typedef is often used to declare a structure type. For example, the structure declaration

```
typedef struct {
    int member1, member2;
    long member3;
} EXAMPLE;
```

declares that **EXAMPLE** is a type name, and that it is a synonym for the structure that precedes it.

Cross-references
Standard, §3.5.6
The C Programming Language, ed. 2, p. 146

See Also
storage-class specifiers, type names, types

Notes
The term *typedef* also describes a type that is defined in a **typedef** statement.

The Standard does not allow benign redeclarations of typedefs. For example, if the declaration

```
typedef int SINT;
```

were included in a header and the same declaration appeared in a source file that included this header, a diagnostic message should appear during translation.

type names — Definition
(Language/declarations)

A *type name* is the name of an object or function, omitting the identifier. It is what its name implies: the name of a type.

Type names have the following syntax; note that *opt* indicates *optional*:

type-name:
        specifier-qualifier-list abstract-declarator$_{opt}$

abstract-declarator:
        pointer
        pointer$_{opt}$ *direct-abstract-declarator*

direct-abstract-declarator:
        (*abstract-declarator*)
        direct-abstract-declarator$_{opt}$ [*constant-expression*]
        direct-abstract-declarator$_{opt}$ (*parameter-type-list*)

Cross-references
Standard, §3.5.5
The C Programming Language, ed. 2, p. 220

See Also
declarations, punctuators, storage-class specifiers, type definitions, type specifiers, types

type qualifier — Overview
(Language/declarations)

A *type qualifier* is, as its name implies, a keyword that alters the nature of a type in a significant way.

There are three type qualifiers:

const	Qualify an identifier as not modifiable
noalias	Qualify an identifier as having no aliases
volatile	Qualify an identifier as changing frequently

The changes affected by a type qualifier take effect only in expressions that yield an lvalue.

No type qualifier may modify an identifier more than once, either directly or via a **typedef**. Also, two types are considered to be compatible only if their qualifiers match.

Many quirks surround the use of qualifiers. For example:

```
const int *cip;
int *ip;

cip = ip;    /* RIGHT */
ip = cip;    /* WRONG */
```

In effect, assignments that serve to "hide" the qualified object must be diagnosed. Although the above examples uses the qualifier **const**, the same restrictions apply to any combination of qualifiers on an object.

Cross-references
Standard, §3.5.3
The C Programming Language, ed. 2, p. 211

See Also
declarations

Notes
Because type qualifiers can alter the manner in which an object is accessed, they can be considered to be "access modifiers".

As of this writing (January 1988), the type qualifier **noalias** remains a subject of controversy. It may not be included in the final Standard when it is published.

types — Overview
(Language/lexical elements/identifiers)

Type determines the meaning of a value stored in an object or returned by a function. For example, if an object four bytes long were declared to be type **long**, the meaning of its contents is quite different than if it were declared to be of type **long ***, or a pointer to a **long**. In the former instance, the contents are regarded as an absolute value; in the latter, the contents are regarded as an address of another object.

The Standard organizes types into a number of varieties and categories, as follows:

Aggregate types
        All array and structure types.

Arithmetic types
        The set of integral and floating types.

Array types
        A set of objects that have the same type and are in contiguous memory.

Basic types
        The set of **char**, the signed and unsigned integer types, and the floating types; i.e., arithmetic types but not enumerated types.

Composite type
        A type constructed from two compatible types, one of which has additional type information. For example, the declarations

```
int example;
```

```
      . . .
      const int example;
```

together form a composite type.

Derived declarator types
> The set of array, function, and pointer types.

Derived types
> The set of array, function, pointer, structure, and **union** types that are derived from the basic types.

Enumerated type
> A set of named integer constant values that comprise an enumeration.

Floating types
> The types **float, double,** or **long double.**

Function types
> The type that describes a given function with a specified return type and specified number and types of parameters.

Incomplete types
> A type for which the translator does not possess all necessary information. Examples are an array of unknown size, or a structure or **union** of unknown content. An incomplete type must be completed by the end of translation.

Integral types
> The set of type **char**, the signed and unsigned integer types, and the enumerated types.

Object types
> The set of types that describe objects, rather than functions.

Pointer type
> A type that describes the type of object to which a pointer points. The two classes of pointers are object pointers and function pointers. Object pointers are referred to by the type of object to which they point.

Qualified type
> A type whose top type is qualified with some combination of the type qualifiers **const, noalias,** or **volatile.**

Scalar types
> The set of arithmetic types and pointer types.

Signed integer types
> Any of the types **signed char, int, long int,** or **short int.** Any of the last three types may also use the prefix **signed,** but the addition of this prefix does not change them in any way.

Structure type

> A type that describes a group of data objects that are contiguous; each object may have its own specified type and its own name.

Top type

> The top type of a basic type is the type itself. The top type of a derived type is the first type used to describe the type; for example, the type **int *** is described as "pointer to **int**"; therefore, its top type is pointer.

union *type*

> A type that describes a set of objects that overlap in memory. Each object may have its own type and its own name.

Unqualified type

> Any type whose top type is *not* qualified with the type qualifiers **const**, **noalias**, or **volatile**.

Unsigned integer types

> Any of the types **unsigned char, unsigned int, unsigned long int**, and **unsigned short int**.

Basic Types

The following is the set of basic types. Those on the same line are synonyms:

> **char**
> **double**
> **float**
> **int, signed int**
> **long double**
> **long int, long, signed long, signed long int**
> **signed char**
> **short int, short, signed short int, signed short**
> **unsigned char**
> **unsigned int**
> **unsigned long int, unsigned long**
> **unsigned short int, unsigned short**

Cross-references

Standard, §3.1.2.5
The C Programming Language, ed. 2, p. 195

See Also

aggregate types, arithmetic types, array types, basic types, composite types, enumerated types, derived types, floating types, function types, incomplete types, integral types, identifiers, object types, pointer types, qualified types, scalar types, signed, struct, union, unsigned

Notes

On some machines, **char** is a synonym for **signed char**. On others, it is a synonym for **unsigned char**. You should declare a **char** variable to be **signed** or **unsigned** if its behavior when promoted to **int** is significant.

type specifier — Overview
(Language/declarations)

A *type specifier* specifies the type of an object or function when it is declared.

The following lists the legal C type specifiers:

> **char**
> **double**
> **enum** *tag-name*
> **float**
> **int**
> **long**
> **signed**
> **short**
> **struct** *tag-name*
> **unsigned**
> **union** *tag-name*
> **void**

The type specifiers can be combined into any one of the following combinations. Those on the same line are synonyms:

> **char**
> **double**
> **enum** *type-name*
> **float**
> **int, signed, signed int**
> **long double**
> **long int, long, signed long, signed long int**
> **signed char**
> **short int, short, signed short int, signed short**
> **struct** *type-name*
> **typedef** *name*
> **union** specifier
> **unsigned char**
> **unsigned int, unsigned**
> **unsigned long int, unsigned long**
> **unsigned short int, unsigned short**
> **void**

Cross-references
Standard, §3.5.2
The C Programming Language, ed. 2, p. 211

See Also
char, compatible types, declarations, double, enum, float, int, long double, long int, signed char, short int, struct, type equivalence, type qualifier, typedef, union, unsigned char, unsigned int, unsigned long int, unsigned short int, void

U

UCHAR_MAX — Macro
(Environment/environmental considerations/limits/numerical)

UCHAR_MAX is a macro that is defined in the header **limits.h**. It gives the largest value that can be held in an object of type **unsigned char**. It must be defined to be at least 255. The smallest value is, of course, zero.

Cross-references
Standard, §2.2.4.2
The C Programming Language, ed. 2, p. 257

See Also
limits.h, numerical limits

UINT_MAX — Macro
(Environment/environmental considerations/limits/numerical)

UINT_MAX is a macro that is defined in the header **limits.h**. It gives the largest value that can be held by an object of type **unsigned int**. It must be defined to be at least 65,535. The smallest value that can be held by this type is, of course, zero.

Cross-references
Standard, §2.2.4.2
The C Programming Language, ed. 2, p. 257

See Also
limits.h, numerical limits

ULONG_MAX — Macro
(Environment/environmental considerations/limits/numerical)

ULONG_MAX is a macro that is defined in the header **limits.h**. It gives the largest value that can be held by an object of type **unsigned long int**. It must be defined to be at least 4,294,967,295. The smallest value that can be held by this type is, of course, zero.

Cross-references
Standard, §2.2.4.2
The C Programming Language, ed. 2, p. 257

See Also
limits.h, numerical limits

unary operators — Overview
(Language/expressions)

A *unary operator* is one that takes only one operand. It takes the following syntax:

unary-expression:
    postfix-expression
    ++ *unary-expression*
    -- *unary-expression*
    unary-operator cast-expression
    sizeof *unary-expression*
    sizeof (*unary-expression*)

unary-operator: one of
        &   *   +   -   ~   !

The Standard describes the following suite of unary operators:

&	Yield address of operand
*	Yield value of object to which pointer operand points
+	Yield value of operand
++	Increment operand by one
-	Yield negated value of operand
--	Decrement operand by one
~	Yield bitwise complement of operand
!	Negate logical value of operand
sizeof	Yield size of operand, in bytes

Some of these operators have a different meaning when used with two operands. See the entry for each for a fuller description.

Cross-references
Standard, §3.3.3
The C Programming Language, ed. 2, p. 203

See Also
expressions, postfix operators

ungetc() — Library function
(Library/STDIO/input-output)
Push a character back into the input stream
#include <stdio.h>
int ungetc(int *character*, **FILE** **fp***);**

ungetc converts *character* to an **unsigned char** and pushes it back into the stream pointed to by *fp*, where the next call to an input function will read it as the next character available from the stream. **ungetc** clears the end-of-file indicator for the stream.

The Standard only guarantees that one character can safely be pushed back into *fp* at any given time. A subsequent call to **fflush**, **fseek**, **fsetpos**, or **rewind** will discard the "ungotten" character.

ungetc returns *character* if it could be pushed back onto *fp*; otherwise, it returns **EOF**. If *character* is equivalent to **EOF**, **ungetc** will fail.

Cross-references
Standard, §4.9.7.11
The C Programming Language, ed. 2, p. 247

See Also
fgetc, fgets, fputc, fputs, getc, getchar, gets, input-output, putc, putchar, puts

Notes
ungetc may be called before a character is read from *fp*. How this feature is handled is up to the implementor.

How **ungetc** affects the file-position indicator will vary, depending upon whether *fp* was opened into text mode or binary mode. If *fp* was opened into binary mode, then its file-position indicator is decremented with every successful call to **ungetc**. If, however, it was opened into text mode, then the value of the file-position indicator after a successful call to **ungetc** is unspecified; the Standard specifies only that when a character is pushed back and then re-read, the file position indicator has same value as it did when the character was first read.

union — Type
(Language/lexical elements/identifiers/type)

A **union** is a data type whose members occupy the same region of storage. It is used when one value may be used in a number of different circumstances. This is in contrast with a **struct**, which is a set of data elements that are laid adjacent to each other. Each object within a **union** may have its own name and distinct type.

Any object type may be contained within a **union**, including a bit-field. No incomplete object may be used. Thus, a **union** may not contain a copy of itself, but it may contain a pointer to itself. A **union** is regarded is incomplete until its closing '}' is read.

The size of a **union** is that of its largest member. Thus, a pointer to a **union** can, if correctly cast, be used as a pointer to each of the **union**'s members.

In effect, a **union** is a multiple declaration of a variable. For example, a **union** may be declared to consist of an **int**, a **double**, and a **char ***. Any one of these three elements can be held by the **union** at a time, and will be handled appropriately by it. For example, the declaration

```
union {
     int number;
     double bignumber;
     char *stringptr;
} EXAMPLE;
```

allows **EXAMPLE** to hold either an **int**, a **double**, or a pointer to a **char**, whichever is needed at the time. The elements of a **union** are accessed like those of a **struct**: for example, to access **number** from the above example, type **EXAMPLE.number**.

unions are helpful in dealing with heterogeneous data, especially within structures. However, the programmer must keep track of what data type the **union** is holding at any given time. Assigning to a **double** within a **union** and then reading the **union** as though it held an **int** will yield results that are defined by the implementation.

A **union** initializer may only initialize the *first* member of the **union**.

Example

The following example uses a **union** to demonstrate the byte ordering of the machine upon which the program is run. It assumes that an **int** is two bytes long, and a **long** is four bytes long.

```
main()
{
     union {
          char bytes[4];
          int words[2];
          long longs;
     } u;
     u.l = 0x12345678L;

     printf("%x %x %x %x\n",
          u.bytes[0], u.bytes[1], u.bytes[2], u.bytes[3]);
     printf("%x %x\n", u.words[0], u.words[1]);
     printf("%lx\n", u.longs);
}
```

Cross-references
Standard, §3.1.2.5, §3.5.2.1
The C Programming Language, ed. 2, pp. 212*ff*

See Also
bit-field, member name, struct, tag, types

Notes
Oftentimes, **union** will be a member of a structure, and the preceding structure member will be a "tag" field, whose value indicates the type of object the **union** currently has stored. Though such a tag is required in some languages (such as Pascal), it is not required in C.

universal coordinated time — Definition
(Library/date and time)

Universal coordinated time (*universel temps coordonne*, or UTC) is a universal standard of time that is based on study of an atomic clock, as corrected by comparison with pulsars. It is, for all practical purposes, identical to Greenwich Mean Time, which is the mean solar time recorded at the Greenwich Observatory in England, where by international convention the Earth's zero meridian is fixed.

Standard local time is usually calculated as an offset of UTC. For example, the time zone for Chicago is six hours (360 minutes) behind UTC, so the standard time for Chicago is calculated by subtracting 360 minutes from UTC. Calculating local time may not always be so easy, however. For example, some Islamic countries calculate local time by dividing the time between sunrise and sunset into 12 hours.

The function **gmtime** returns a pointer to the structure **tm** that has been initialized to hold the current UTC. The name of this function reflects the older practice of referring to Greenwich Mean Time instead of UTC.

Cross-reference
Standard, §4.12.1

See Also
broken-down time, calendar time, date and time, gmtime, local time, localtime

unsigned — C keyword
(Language/lexical elements/identifiers/type)

When a declaration includes the modifier **unsigned**, it indicates that the type can hold only a non-negative value.

There are four **unsigned** data types: **unsigned char, unsigned int, unsigned long int**, and **unsigned short int**. If the modifier **unsigned** is not used, the translator assumes that **int, long int**, and **short int** are signed. The implementation defines whether **char** is signed or unsigned by default.

An unsigned data type takes the same amount of storage as the corresponding signed type, and has the same alignment requirements.

Any value that can be represented by both a signed and an unsigned type will be represented the same way in both. An unsigned type, however, cannot represent a negative value. If the implementation uses a "sign bit" to indicate the sign of a number, that bit is freed to hold a value. In this instance, an unsigned type can store a value of twice what can be stored in its signed counterpart.

Arithmetic that involves unsigned types will never overflow. If an arithmetic operation produces a value that is too large to fit into a particular unsigned type, that value is divided by one plus the largest value that can be held in that unsigned type, and the remainder is then stored in the unsigned type.

For information about converting one type of integer to another, see **integral types**.

When **unsigned** is used by itself, it is regarded as a synonym for **unsigned int**.

Cross-references
Standard, §3.1.2.5
The C Programming Language, ed. 2, p. 211

See Also
char, signed, types, unsigned

unsigned char — Type
(Language/lexical elements/identifiers/types)

An **unsigned char** is an unsigned integral type. It takes the same amount of storage as a **char**, and has the same alignment requirements.

An **unsigned char** has the minimum value of zero, and a maximum value of **UCHAR_MAX**. The last is a macro that is defined in the header **limits.h**; it must be at least 255.

Cross-references
Standard, §2.2.4.2, §3.1.2.5, §3.2.1.1, §3.5.2
The C Programming Language, ed. 2, p. 44

See Also
char, signed char, types, unsigned

unsigned int — Type
(Language/lexical elements/identifiers/types)

An **unsigned int** is an unsigned integral type. It requires the same amount of storage as a **int** and has the same alignment requirements.

An **unsigned int** has the minimum value of zero, and a maximum value of **UINT_MAX**. The last is a macro that is defined in the header **limits.h**; it must be at least 65,535.

The type **unsigned** is a synonym for **unsigned int**.

Cross-references
Standard, §2.2.4.2, §3.1.2.5, §3.2.1.1, §3.5.2
The C Programming Language, ed. 2, p. 211

See Also
int, types, unsigned

unsigned long int — Type
(Language/lexical elements/identifiers/types)

An **unsigned long int** is an unsigned integral type. It requires the same amount of storage as a **long int**, and has the same alignment requirements.

An **unsigned long int** has the minimum value of zero, and a maximum value **ULONG_MAX**. The last is a macro that is defined in the header **limits.h**; it must be at least 4,294,967,295.

Cross-references
Standard, §2.2.4.2, §3.1.2.5, §3.2.1.1, §3.5.2
The C Programming Language, ed. 2, p. 211

See Also
long int, types, unsigned

unsigned short int — Type
(Language/lexical elements/identifiers/types)

An **unsigned short int** is an unsigned integral type. It requires the same amount of storage as a **short int**, and has the same alignment requirements.

An **unsigned short int** has the minimum value of zero, and a maximum value of **USHRT_MAX**. The last is a macro that is defined in the header **limits.h**; it must be at least 65,535.

Cross-references
Standard, §2.2.4.2, §3.1.2.5, §3.2.1.1, §3.5.2
The C Programming Language, ed. 2, p. 211

See Also
short int, types, unsigned

USHRT_MAX — Macro
(Environment/environmental considerations/limits/numerical)

USHRT_MAX is a macro that is defined in the header **limits.h**. It gives the maximum value that can be held by an object of type **unsigned short int**. It must be defined to be at least 65,535.

Cross-references
Standard, §2.2.4.2
The C Programming Language, ed. 2, p. 257

See Also
limits.h, numerical limits

V

va_arg() — Macro
(Library/variable arguments)
Return pointer to next argument in argument list
#include <stdarg.h>
typename ***va_arg(va_list** *listptr*, *typename*)

va_arg returns a pointer to the next argument in an argument list. It can be used with functions that take a variable number of arguments, such as **printf** or **scanf**, to help write such functions portably. It is always used with **va_end** and **va_start** within a function that takes a variable number of arguments.

listptr is of type **va_list**, which is an object defined in the header **stdarg.h**. It must first be initialized by the macro **va_start**.

typename is the name of the type for which **va_arg** is to return a pointer. For example, if you wish **va_arg** to return a pointer to an integer, *typename* should be of type **int**.

va_arg can only handle "standard" data types, i.e., those data types that can be transformed to pointers by appending an asterisk '*****'.

Example
For an example of this macro, see the entry for **variable arguments**.

Cross-references
Standard, §4.8.1.2
The C Programming Language, ed. 2, p. 254

See Also
va_end, va_start, variable arguments

Notes
If there is no next argument for **va_arg** to handle, or if *typename* is incorrect, then the behavior of **va_arg** is undefined.

va_arg must be implemented only as a macro. If its macro definition is suppressed within a program, the behavior is undefined.

va_end() — Library function
(Library/variable arguments)
Tidy up after traversal of argument list
#include <stdarg.h>
void va_end(va_list *listptr*);

va_end helps to tidy up a function after it has traversed the argument list for a function that takes a variable number of arguments. It can be used with functions that take a variable number of arguments, such as **printf** or **scanf**, to help write such functions portably. It should be used with the routines **va_arg** and **va_start** from within a function that takes a variable number of arguments.

listptr is of type **va_list**, which is declared in header **stdarg.h**. *listptr* must first have been initialized by macro **va_start**.

The manner of "tidying up" that **va_end** performs will vary from one computing environment to another. In many computing environments, **va_end** is not needed, and it may be implemented as an empty function.

Example
For an example of this function, see the entry for **variable arguments**.

Cross-references
Standard, §4.8.1.3
The C Programming Language, ed. 2, p. 254

See Also
va_arg, va_start, variable arguments

Notes
If **va_list** is not initialized by **va_start**, or if **va_end** is not called before a function with variable arguments exits, then behavior is undefined.

va_list — type
(Library/variable arguments)
Type used to handle argument lists of variable length

va_list is a **typedef** declared in the header **stdarg.h**. Although its type is selected by the implementor, commonly it will be either an array or a pointer. Its elements can be of various types. No programmer should assume anything about this type, and no program should use it for anything else.

va_list is used to help implement functions like **printf** and **scanf**, which can take an indeterminate number of arguments.

Example
For an example of this type, see the entry for **variable arguments**.

See Also
va_arg, va_end, va_start, variable arguments

va_start() — Macro
(Library/variable arguments)
Point to beginning of argument list
#include <stdargs.h>
void va_start(va_list *listptr, type rightparm***)**

va_start is a macro that points to the beginning of a list of arguments. It can be used with functions that take a variable number of arguments, such as **printf** or **scanf**, to help implement them portably. It is always used with **va_arg** and **va_end** from within a function that takes a variable number of arguments.

listptr is of type **va_list**, which is a type defined in the header **stdarg.h**.

rightparm is the rightmost parameter defined in the function's parameter list — that is, the last parameter defined before the **...** punctuator. Its type is set by the function that is using **va_start**. Undefined behavior results if any of the following conditions apply to **rightparm**: if it has storage class **register**; if it has a function type or an array type; or if its type is not compatible with the type that results from the default argument promotions.

Example
For an example of this macro, see the entry for **variable arguments**.

Cross-references
Standard, §4.8.1.1
The C Programming Language, ed. 2, p. 254

See Also
va_arg, va_end, va_list, variable arguments

Notes
The implementation is not obliged to use *rightparm* when implementing **va_start**.

va_start must be implemented only as a macro. If the macro definition of **va_start** is suppressed within a program, the behavior is undefined.

value preserving — Definition
(Language/conversions)

With respect to integral promotions, the Standard has adopted *value-preserving rules*. This may quietly break some existing code that depended on unsigned-preserving rules, as many UNIX implementations have done.

In most cases, there will be no difference in the results produced by unsigned-preserving rules and those produced by value-preserving rules. There are, however, several instances in which different results will be seen. For example:

```
long l;
unsigned int ui;
    . . .
l = ui + 1;
```

In this operation, before the addition is performed, **ui** will first be promoted to type **long** if a **long** can hold the value contained in the **unsigned int**. The operation will then be performed as long addition, assigning the result to the variable l.

If a **long** is not large enough to represent the value contained in **ui**, which may occur under an implementation where **int**s and **long**s are the same size, then *both* **ui** and l are first converted to **unsigned long** before the addition is performed. Because conversion is needed to preserve the value (as opposed to the sign) of the operand as well as the result, the term "value preserving" is appropriate.

As usual, code may have to be generated to perform the conversion, and a high-quality implementation will usually issue a diagnostic message in such a case.

Cross-references
Standard, §3.2
The C Programming Language, ed. 2, pp

See Also
conversions, integral promotions

variable arguments — Overview
(Library)

The Standard mandates the creation of a set of routines to help implement functions, such as **printf** and **scanf**, that take a variable number of arguments. These routines are called from within another function to help it handle its arguments. If the ellipsis punctuator '...' appears at the end of the list of arguments in a function's prototype, then that a function can take a variable number of arguments.

These routines are declared or defined in the header **stdarg.h**, and are as follows:

va_arg	Return pointer to next argument in argument list
va_end	Tidy up after an argument list has been traversed
va_start	Initialize object that holds function arguments

va_arg and **va_start** must be implemented as macros; **va_end** must be implemented as a library function. All three use the special type **va_list**, which is an object that holds the arguments to the function being implemented.

Example

The following example concatenates multiple strings into a common allocated string and returns the string's address.

```
#include <stdarg.h>
#include <stdlib.h>
#include <stddef.h>
#include <stdio.h>

char *
multcat(int numargs, ... )
{
    va_list argptr;
    char *result;
    int i, siz;

    /* get size required */
    va_start(argptr, numargs);
    for(siz = i = 0; i < numargs; i++)
        siz += strlen(va_arg(argptr, char *));

    if ((result = calloc(siz + 1, 1)) == NULL) {
        fprintf(stderr, "Out of space\n");
        exit(EXIT_FAILURE);
    }
    va_end(argptr);

    va_start(argptr, numargs);
    for(i = 0; i < numargs; i++)
        strcat(result, va_arg(argptr, char *));
    va_end(argptr);
    return(result);
}
```

```
int
main(void)
{
    printf(multcat(5, "One ", "two ", "three ",
        "testing", ".\n"));
    return(EXIT_SUCCESS);
}
```

Cross-references
Standard, §4.8
The C Programming Language, ed. 2, p. 254

See Also
Library, stdarg.h, va_list

Notes
These macros, functions, and types allow a program to pass, in a portable way, variable numbers and variable types of arguments. The programmer need have no knowledge of the mechanism by which a particular implementation performs the passing.

The mechanism by which an implementation passes variable numbers of arguments may differ from the mechanism by which it passes a fixed number of arguments. Therefore, a programmer should take care not to mix a forward declaration for a variable number of arguments with an implementation that uses fixed numbers of arguments.

vfprintf() — Library function
(Library/STDIO/input-output)
Print formatted text into stream
#include <stdarg.h>
#include <stdio.h>
int vfprintf(FILE**fp***, const char ****format***, va_list** *arguments***);**

vfprintf constructs a formatted string and writes it into the stream pointed to by *fp*. It translates integers, floating-point numbers, and strings into a variety of text formats. Unlike the related function **fprintf**, **vfprintf** can handle a variable list of arguments of various types. It is roughly equivalent to the 'r' conversion specifier, which under some implementations, is used to pass an array of arguments to **fprintf**.

format points to a string that can contain text, character constants, and one or more *conversion specifications*. A conversion specification describes how particular data type is converted into a particular text format. Each conversion specification is introduced with the percent sign '%'. (To print a literal percent sign, use the escape sequence "%%".) See **printf** for further discussion of the conversion specification, and for a table of the type specifiers that can be used with **vfprintf.**

After *format* comes *arguments*. This is of type **va_list**, which is defined in the header **stdarg.h**. It has been initialized by the macro **va_start** and points to the base of the list of arguments used by **vfprintf**. For more information, see **variable arguments**. *arguments* should access one argument for each conversion specification in *format*, of the type appropriate to its conversion specification.

For example, if *format* contains conversion specifications for an **int**, a **long**, and a string, then *arguments* access three arguments, being, respectively, an **int**, a **long**, and a **char ***. *arguments* can take only the data types acceptable to the macro **va_arg**; namely, basic types that can be converted to pointers simply by adding a '*' after the type name. See **va_arg** for more information on this point.

If there are fewer arguments than conversion specifications, then **vfprintf**'s behavior is undefined. If there are more, then every argument without a corresponding conversion specification is evaluated and then ignored. If an argument is not of the same type as its corresponding conversion specifier, then the behavior of **vfprintf** is undefined. Thus, presenting an **int** where **vfprintf** expects a **char *** may generate unwelcome results.

If it writes the formatted string correctly, **vfprintf** returns the number of characters written; otherwise, it returns a negative number.

Example
This example sets up a standard multiargument error message. It is the source of the function **fatal**, which is used throughout this manual.

```
#include <math.h>
#include <stdarg.h>
#include <stddef.h>
#include <stdio.h>
#include <stdlib.h>

void
fatal(char *format, ...)
{
    va_list argptr;

    /* if there is a system message, display it */
    if(errno)
        perror(NULL);
```

```
        /* if there is a user message, use it */
        if(format != NULL) {
            va_start(argptr, format);
            vfprintf(stderr, format, argptr);
            va_end(argptr);
        }
        exit(EXIT_FAILURE);
    }

main(void)
{
    /*
     * This is guaranteed to be wrong.  It should push
     * an error code into errno.
     */
    sqrt(-1.0);

    /* Now, show the messages */
    fatal("A %s error message%c", "complex", '\n');

    /* If we get this far, something is wrong */
    return(EXIT_FAILURE);
}
```

Cross-references
Standard, §4.9.6.7
The C Programming Language, ed. 2, p. 245

See Also
fprintf, fscanf, input-output, printf, scanf, sprintf, sscanf, vprintf, vsprintf

Notes
vfprintf must be able to construct a string up to at least 509 characters long.

The character that **vfprintf** uses to represent the decimal point is affected by the program's locale, as set by the function **setlocale**. For more information, see **localization**.

void — C keyword
(Language/lexical elements/identifiers/types)
Empty type

The term **void** indicates the empty type. The following sections describe the ways it is used.

Function Type

void can be used in a function prototype or definition to indicate that a function returns no value. For example, the declaration

```
void example();
```

indicates that the function **example** returns nothing. It would be an error for **example** to attempt to return a value to a function that calls it, or for the calling function to use its value in an expression.

Function Arguments

void can also be used in a function prototype or function declaration to indicate that a function has no arguments. For example, the declaration

```
void example(void);
```

indicates that the function **example** not only returns nothing, but it takes no arguments as well. The older practice of writing **example()** remains legal. But as before, it indicates merely that nothing is said about arguments.

Void Expression

void can be used to indicate that the value of an expression is to be ignored. This is done by casting the expression to type **void**. Prefacing an expression with the cast **(void)** throws away its value (i.e., casts it into the void), although the expression is evaluated for possible side-effects.

void *

A **void *** ("pointer to void") is a generic pointer. It is used in much the same way that **char *** ("pointer to **char**") was used in earlier descriptions of C. The new generic pointer type eliminates the earlier confusion between a pointer to **char** (e.g., a string pointer) and a generic pointer.

Because by definition the **void** type includes no objects, a pointer to **void** may not be dereferenced. That is, you should not directly access the object to which it points by using the indirection operator '*****'. In the code

```
void *voidp;
    . . .
if (*voidp > 0)
    . . .
```

the behavior of dereferencing the pointer to **void** is undefined. It may or may not generate an error; if it does not, the results may be unpredictable.

It is correct, however, to cast a pointer to **void** to a standard object pointer type and then dereference it. For example, the code

```
void *voidp;
    . . .
if (*(char *)voidp > 0)
    . . .
```

is permitted.

The Standard guarantees that a pointer to **void** may be converted to a pointer to any incomplete type or object type. It also guarantees that a pointer to any incomplete type or object type may be converted into a pointer to **void**. Moreover, converting the result back to the original type results in a pointer equal to the original pointer. That is, conversion of any object pointer type to **void *** and back again does not change the representation of the pointer. However, if an object pointer is converted to **void *** and then converted to a pointer to a type whose alignment is stricter than that of the original type, behavior is undefined.

The Standard also guarantees that the pointer types **char *** and **void *** have the same representation. This prevents the Standard from breaking existing code for functions with generic-pointer arguments (previously defined using type **char *** but now defined with type **void ***).

The introduction of the generic pointer **void *** by the Standard serves several purposes in addition to those noted above. The Standard no longer allows comparison between pointers of different types, except that any object pointer may be compared to a **void ***. Casting object pointers with the expression

```
(void *)
```

allows comparisons that would otherwise be illegal. Library functions that have commonly been written with pointers of various types as arguments (such as **fread**) can be defined with a prototype **void *** argument, which allows the arguments to be quietly converted to the correct type.

The generic pointer **void *** is also used as the type of the value returned by some functions (e.g., **malloc**), to indicate that the returned value is a pointer to something of indeterminate type.

Cross-references
Standard, §3.1.2.5, §3.2.2.2-3, §3.3.4, §3.5.2, §3.5.3.1, §3.5.4.3
The C Programming Language, ed. 2, pp. 199, 218

See Also
incomplete type, NULL, pointer, precedence, types

void expression — Definition
(Language/conversions)

A *void expression* is any expression that has type **void**. By definition, it has no value; therefore, its value cannot be assigned to any other expression. Normally, a void expression is used for its side-effects.

If an expression of any other type is used in a situation that requires a void expression, the value of that expression is discarded.

Cross-reference
Standard, §3.2.2.2

See Also
conversions

volatile — C keyword
(Language/declarations/type qualifier)
Qualify an identifier as frequently changing

The type qualifier **volatile** marks an identifier as being frequently changed, either by other portions of the program, by the hardware, by other programs in the execution environment, or by any combination of these. This alerts the translator to re-fetch the given identifier whenever it encounters an expression that includes the identifier. In addition, an object marked as **volatile** must be stored at the point where an assignment to this object takes place.

Cross-references
Standard, §3.5.3
The C Programming Language, ed. 2, p. 211

See Also
const, noalias, type qualifier

Notes
volatile was created by the Committee for systems' programs that deal with memory-mapped I/O or ports where the program is not the only task that may modify the given port in memory. **volatile** tells the translator that it does not know everything that is happening to the object.

Another use for **volatile** is for translators that perform optimizations, such as deferring storage of registers or peephole optimization. **volatile** requires that the object be read and stored at exactly those points where the program has specified these actions.

vprintf() — Library function
(Library/STDIO/input-output)
Print formatted text into standard output stream
#include <stdarg.h>
#include <stdio.h>
int vprintf(const char *format, va_list arguments);

vprintf constructs a formatted string and writes it into the standard output
stream. It translates integers, floating-point numbers, and strings into a variety of
text formats. Unlike the related function **printf**, **vprintf** can handle a variable list
of arguments of various types. It is roughly equivalent to the 'r' conversion
specifier under some implementations of **printf**.

format points to a string that can contain text, character constants, and one or
more *conversion specifications*. A conversion specification defines how a particular
data type is converted into a particular text format. Each conversion specification is
introduced with the percent sign '%'. (To print a literal percent sign, use the escape sequence "%%".) See **printf** for further discussion of the conversion specification and for a table of the type specifiers that can be used with **vprintf**.

After *format* comes *arguments*. This is of type **va_list**, which is defined in the
header **stdarg.h**. It has been initialized by the macro **va_start** and points to the
base of the list of arguments used by **vprintf**. For more information, see **variable
arguments**. *arguments* should access one argument for each conversion specification in *format* of the type appropriate to conversion specification.

For example, if *format* contains conversion specifications for an **int**, a **long**, and a
string, then *arguments* access three arguments, being, respectively, an **int**, a **long**,
and a **char ***.

If there are fewer arguments than conversion specifications, then **vprintf**'s behavior is undefined. If there are more, every argument without a corresponding
conversion specification is evaluated and then ignored. If an argument is not of the
same type as its corresponding type specification, then the behavior of **vprintf** is
undefined; thus, accessing an **int** where **vprintf** expects a **char *** may generate
unwelcome results.

If it writes the formatted string correctly, **vprintf** returns the number of characters
written; otherwise, it returns a negative number.

Cross-references
Standard, §4.9.6.8
The C Programming Language, ed. 2, p. 245

See Also
fprintf, fscanf, input-output, printf, scanf, sprintf, sscanf, vfprintf, vsprintf

Notes
vprintf must be able to construct a string up to at least 509 characters long.

The character that **vprintf** uses to represent the decimal point is affected by the program's locale, as set by the function **setlocale**. For more information, see **localization**. *8

Each *argument* must have basic type, which can be converted to a pointer simply by adding an '*' after the type name. This is the same restriction that applies to the arguments to the macro **va_arg**.

vsprintf() — Library function
(Library/STDIO/input-output)
Print formatted text into string
#include <stdarg.h>
#include <stdio.h>
int vsprintf(char *string, const char *format, va_list arguments);

vsprintf constructs a formatted string in the area pointed to by *string*. It translates integers, floating-point numbers, and strings into a variety of text formats. Unlike the related function **printf**, **vsprintf** can handle a variable list of arguments of various types. It is roughly equivalent to the 'r' conversion specifier under some implementations of **sprintf**.

format points to a string that can contain text, character constants, and one or more *conversion specifications*. A conversion specification describes how to convert a particular data type into a particular text format. Each conversion specification is introduced with the percent sign '%'. (To print a literal percent sign, use the escape sequence "%%".) See **printf** for further discussion of the conversion specification and for a table of the type specifiers that can be used with **vsprintf**.

After *format* comes *arguments*. This is of type **va_list**, which is defined in the header **stdarg.h**. It has been initialized by the macro **va_start** and points to the base of the list of arguments used by **vsprintf**. For more information, see **variable arguments**. *arguments* should access one argument for each conversion specification in *format* of the type appropriate to the conversion specification.

For example, if *format* contains conversion specifications for an **int**, a **long**, and a string, then *arguments* access three arguments, being, respectively, an **int**, a **long**, and a **char ***.

If there are fewer arguments than conversion specifications, then **vsprintf**'s behavior is undefined. If there are more, then every argument without a corresponding conversion specification is evaluated and then ignored. If an argument is not of the same type as its corresponding type specification, then the behavior of

vsprintf is undefined; thus, accessing an **int** where **vsprintf** expects a **char *** may generate unwelcome results.

If it writes the formatted string correctly, **vsprintf** returns the number of characters written; otherwise, it returns a negative number.

Cross-references

Standard, §4.9.6.7
The C Programming Language, ed. 2, p. 245

See Also

fprintf, fscanf, input-output, printf, scanf, sprintf, sscanf, vprintf, vsprintf

Notes

vsprintf must be able to construct a string up to at least 509 characters long.

The character that **vsprintf** uses to represent the decimal point is affected by the program's locale, as set by the function **setlocale**. For more information, see **localization**.

W

wchar_t — Type
(Library/general utilities)
Typedef for a wide character
#include <stddef.h>

wchar_t is a typedef that is declared in the header **stdlib.h**. It is defined as the integral type that can represent all characters of given national character set.

The following restrictions apply to objects of this type: (1) The null character has a value of zero. (2) The characters of the standard C character set must have the same value as they would when used in ordinary **chars**. (3) **EOF** must have a value that is distinct from every other character in the set.

wchar_t is a typedef of an integral type, whereas a multibyte character is a bundle of one or more one-byte characters. The format of a multibyte character is defined by the implementation, whereas a **wchar_t** can be used across implementations.

The functions **mblen**, **mbstowcs**, **mbtowc**, **wcstombs**, and **wctomb** manipulate objects of type **wchar_t**.

Cross-references
Standard, §4.10
The C Programming Language, ed. 2, p. 193

See Also
ASCII, character sets, general utilities, multibyte characters, stdlib.h

Notes
The name **wchar_t** comes from the term "wide character".

The Standard lists **wchar_t** as being declared in both **stddef.h** and **stdlib.h**.

wcstombs() — Library function
(Language/general utilities/multibyte characters)
Convert sequence of wide characters to multibyte characters
#include <stdlib.h>
size_t wcstombs(wchar_t *multibyte, const char *widechar, size_t number);

The function **wcstombs** converts a sequence of wide characters to their corresponding multibyte characters. It is the same as a series of calls of the type:

```
wctomb(multibyte, *widechar);
```

except that the call to **wcstombs** does not affect the internal state of **wctomb**.

widechars points to the base of the sequence of wide characters to be converted to multibyte characters. *multibyte* points to the area into which the characters will be written; the sequence begins and ends in an initial shift state. *number* is the number of characters to be converted. **wcstombs** converts characters either until it reads and converts the null character that ends the sequence, or until it has converted *number* characters. In the latter case, no null character is written at the end of the sequence of multibyte characters.

wcstombs returns -1 cast to **size_t** if it encounters an invalid wide character before it has converted *number* characters. Otherwise, it returns the number of characters converted, excluding the null character that ends the sequence.

Cross-reference
Standard, §4.10.7.4

See Also
mbstowcs, multibyte characters

Notes
The operation of this function is affected by the program's locale, as set by the function **setlocale**. See **localization** for more information.

wctomb() — Library function
(Library/general utilities/multibyte characters)
Convert a wide character to a multibyte character
#include < stdlib.h >
int wctomb(char *string, wchar_t widecharacter);

wctomb converts *widecharacter* to its corresponding multibyte character and stores the result in the area pointed to by *string*.

If *string* is set to NULL, then **wctomb** merely checks to see if the current set of multibyte characters include state-dependent encodings. It returns zero if the set does not include state-dependent codings, and a number other than zero if it does.

If *string* is set to a value other than NULL, then **wctomb** does the following:

1. It returns zero if *widecharacter* is zero.

2. It returns -1 if the value of *widecharacter* does not correspond to a legitimate multibyte character for the present locale.

3. If the value of *widecharacter* does correspond to a legitimate multibyte character, then it returns the number of bytes that comprise that character.

wctomb never returns a value greater than that of the macro **MB_CUR_MAX**.

Cross-reference
Standard, §4.10.7.5

See Also
MB_CUR_MAX, mblen, mbtowc, multibyte characters, wchar_t

Notes
The operation of this function is affected by the program's locale, as set by the function **setlocale**. See **localization** for more information.

The address pointed to by *string* should have **MB_CUR_MAX** bytes of storage allocated to it. If not, you may overwrite memory currently in use.

while — C keyword
(Language/statements/iteration statements)
Loop construct
while(*condition*) *statement*

while introduces a conditional loop. Unlike a **do** loop, a **while** loop tests *condition* before execution of *statement*. The loop ends when *condition* is no longer satisfied. Hence, the loop may not execute at all, if *condition* is initially false.

For example,

```
while (variable < 10)
```

introduces a loop whose statements will continue to execute until **variable** is equivalent to ten or greater. The statement

```
while (1)
```

will loop until interrupted by **break, goto,** or **return**.

Example
For an example of this statement, see **sscanf**.

Cross-references
Standard, §3.6.5.1
The C Programming Language, ed. 2, pp. 60*ff*

See Also
C keywords, do, for, iteration statements, while

Section 3:
Appendix A

The following lists all of the entries in the Lexicon in their logical order. The Lexicon is tree structured, with the root entry being the one entitled **Standard**. The logical structure of the Lexicon closely follows that of the Standard itself; articles on related topics are grouped together for easy access. In instances where an article describes an entity that has more than one use (e.g., the operator "*"), the article's position in the logic tree is based on a judgement of how that entity is used most frequently by C programmers.

Each Lexicon entry has a "path name" that gives its position in the logic tree. It is possible to read your way from any one entry in the Lexicon to any other simply by following the path names of the articles.

```
Standard
        Definitions
                address
                alias
                alignment
                argument
                ASCII
                behavior
                bit
                block
                byte
                compile
                compliance
                constraints
                diagnostic message
                false
```

```
        bitwise operators
              |
              ^

            < <
            > >
        cast operators
        equality operators
              = =
              ! =
        function prototypes
        logical operators
              & &
              | |
        multiplicative operators
              *

              /
              %
        primary expressions
        postfix operators
              .
              ->
              [ ]
              function call
        relational operators
              <
              < =
              >
              > =
        unary operators
              &
              + +
              - -

              ~
              !
              sizeof
external definitions
        function definition
        object definition
lexical elements
        token
        comment
              */
              /*
        constants
              character constant
```

ERANGE
HUGE_VAL
range error
exponent-log functions
      exp()
      frexp()
      ldexp()
      log()
      log10()
      modf()
hyperbolic functions
      cosh()
      sinh()
      tanh()
integer-value-remainder
      ceil()
      fabs()
      floor()
      fmod()
power functions
      pow()
      sqrt()
trigonometric functions
      acos()
      asin()
      atan()
      atan2()
      cos()
      sin()
      tan()
non-local jumps
      setjmp.h
      jmp_buf
      longjmp()
      setjmp()
signal handling
      signal.h
      raise()
      sig_atomic_t
      SIG_DFL
      SIG_ERR
      SIG_IGN
      SIGABRT
      SIGFPE
      SIGILL

Index

! to ~

C/UNIX Order Form

Prentice Hall Publishers will continue to make available the First Edition of The C Programming Language by Kernighan and Ritchie for programmers using compilers developed prior to the Draft Proposed ANSI Standard. To order copies of this title as well as the other books in our C/UNIX list, kindly complete this form.

QUANTITY	TITLE/AUTHOR (abbreviated)	ISBN	PRICE	TOTAL
	The C Programming Language, 1/E, Kernighan/Ritchie	013-110163-3	$27.00 paper	
	The C Programming Language, 2/E, Kernighan/Ritchie	013-110362-8	$28.00 paper	
		013-110370-9	$40.00 cloth	
	The C Answer Book, 1/E, Tondo/Gimpel	013-109877-2	$21.00 paper	
	The C Answer Book, 2/E, Tondo/Gimpel	013-109653-2	$21.00 paper	
	ANSI C: A Lexical Guide, The Mark Williams Company	013-037814-3	$35.00 paper	
	UNIX Sys V Programmer's Guide, AT&T	013-940438-4	$36.95 paper	
	UNIX Sys V STREAMS Primer, AT&T	013-940529-1	$21.95 paper	
	UNIX Sys V STREAMS Prog's Guide, AT&T	013-940537-2	$24.95 paper	
	UNIX Sys V Network Prog's Guide, AT&T	013-940461-9	$24.95 paper	
	UNIX Sys V Prog's Ref Man, AT&T	013-940479-1	$36.95 paper	
	UNIX Sys V User's Ref Man, AT&T	013-940487-2	$34.95 paper	
	UNIX Sys V User's Guide, 2/E, AT&T	013-940545-3	$29.95 paper	
	UNIX Sys V Utilities Release Notes, AT&T	013-940552-6	$21.95 paper	
	AT&T Computer Software Catalog: UNIX System V Software	013-050154-9	$23.95 paper	
	AT&T Computer Software Catalog: Workstation Software	013-050162-X	$22.95 paper	
	UNIX Sys User's Handbook, Bolsky	013-937764-6	$18.95 paper	
	UNIX For People, Birns, et al.	013-937442-6	$28.00 paper	
	UNIX Primer, Lomuto, et al.	013-937731-X	$28.95 paper	
	UNIX Ref Guide, McNulty	013-938957-0	$27.95 paper	
	DOS: UNIX Systems, Seyer/Mills	013-218645-4	$27.95 paper	
	Design of UNIX O/S, Bach	013-201799-7	$42.00 paper	
	Operating System Des: XINU Approach, Comer	013-637539-1	$46.00 cloth	
	Oper Sys. Design: Internetworking, Comer	013-637414-X	$46.00 cloth	
	Oper Sys Des & Implementation, Tanenbaum	013-637406-9	$42.00 cloth	
	MINIX for the IBM PC/XT/AT:			
	1) 512K for the AT	013-584418-5	$110.00	
	2) 640K for the PC/ PC XT	013-584426-6	$110.00	
	3) MINIX for the IBM PC/XT/AT Reference Manual	013-584400-2	$34.50 paper	
	UNIX Prog Environment, Kernighan/Pike	013-937681-X	$24.95 paper	
	Advanced UNIX Prog, Rochkind	013-011800-1	$29.95 paper	
	Portable C & UNIX Sys Prog, Lapin	013-686494-5	$24.95 paper	
	MIP: R2000 RISC Architecture, Kane	013-584749-4	$24.95 paper	
	UNIX Relational Database Management, Manis	013-938622-X	$30.00 paper	
	UNIX Sys Software Readings	013-938358-1	$21.95 paper	
	UNIX Sys Readings & Applications, I, AT&T	013-938532-0	$19.00 paper	
	UNIX Sys Readings & Applications, II, AT&T	013-939845-7	$19.00 paper	
	vi User's Handbook, Bolsky	013-941733-8	$18.95 paper	
	Guide to vi, Sonnenschein	013-371311-3	$19.95 paper	
	Troff Typesetting, Emerson, et al.	013-930959-4	$27.95 paper	

(over, please)

QUANTITY	TITLE/AUTHOR (abbreviated)	ISBN	PRICE	TOTAL
_____	Intro to Compiler Construction, Schreiner, et al.	013-474396-2	$38.00 cloth	_____
_____	UNIX C Shell Field Gde., Anderson, et al.	013-937468-X	$27.95 paper	_____
_____	Preparing Documents w. UNIX, Brown, et al.	013-699976-X	$27.95 cloth	_____
_____	C Answer Book, Tondo, et al.	013-109877-2	$21.00 paper	_____
_____	Advanced C Programming, Rochkind	013-010240-7	$32.95 paper	_____
_____	C Trainer, Feuer	013-109745-8	$24.33 paper	_____
_____	C: A Reference Manual, 2/E, Harbison, et al.	013-109802-0	$25.95 paper	_____
_____	C Companion, Holub	013-109786-5	$22.67 paper	_____
_____	Programming in C w/Bit of UNIX, Moore	013-730094-8	$25.95 paper	_____
_____	Learning To Program in C, Plum	013-527847-3	$33.00 paper	_____
_____	C Notes, Zahn	013-109778-4	$17.95 paper	_____
_____	C Prog in Berkeley UNIX Envirmnt, Horspool	013-109977-9	$27.00 paper	_____
_____	C Programmer's Hndbk, Bolsky	013-110073-4	$22.95 paper	_____
_____	Crafting C Tools, Campbell	013-188418-2	$25.95 paper	_____
_____	C Puzzle Book, Feuer	013-109926-4	$25.00 cloth	_____
_____	Numerical Sftware Tools in C, Kempf	013-627274-6	$28.00 paper	_____
_____	C Programming Guidelines, Plum	013-109992-2	$34.00 paper	_____
_____	A Software Tools Sampler, Miller	013-822305-X	$26.67 paper	_____
_____	Systems Software Tools, Biggerstaff	013-881764-2	$19.95 paper	_____
_____	Clipper 32-Bit Microproc. Manual, Fairchild	013-138058-3	$23.95 paper	_____
			TOTAL	_____

SAVE!

If payment accompanies order, plus your state's sales tax where applicable, Prentice Hall pays postage and handling charges. Same return privilege refund guaranteed. Please do not mail in cash.

☐ **PAYMENT ENCLOSED**—shipping and handling to be paid by publisher (please include your state's tax where applicable).

☐ **SEND BOOKS ON 15-DAY TRIAL BASIS** & bill me (with small charge for shipping and handling).

Name _____

Address _____

City _____ State _____ Zip _____

I prefer to charge my   ☐ Visa   ☐ MasterCard

Card Number _____ Expiration Date _____

Signature _____

All prices listed are subject to change without notice.
OFFER NOT VALID OUTSIDE U.S.

MAIL YOUR ORDER TO: Prentice Hall, Book Distribution Center, Route 59 at
Brook Hill Drive, West Nyack, NY 10994

Attention Corporate Customers: For orders over 20 copies to be billed to a corporate address, call (201) 592-2498.

For individuals ordering fewer than 20 copies, call (201) 767-5937.

Prentice Hall C/UNIX Titles Are Available At Better Bookstores